A Bibliography of
Songsters Printed in America
Before 1821

Music the mighty Artist Man can rule
As long as it has numbers he his Soul

A Bibliography of
SONGSTERS
Printed in America
Before 1821

IRVING LOWENS

American Antiquarian Society · Worcester

1976

Publication of this book was made
possible by means of a grant from
The Scheide Fund of Community Funds, Inc.,
New York, N.Y.

TABLE OF CONTENTS

Introduction   vii

Key to Library Symbols and Census of Copies   xxi

Private Libraries   xxxiii

Foreign Libraries   xxxiii

Bibliographies Cited   xxxiv

A Bibliography of Songsters Printed
in America Before 1821   3

Geographical Directory of Printers,
Publishers, Booksellers, Engravers, &c.   193

An Index of Compilers, Authors, Proprietors,
and Editors   215

A Table Correlating Years and Item Numbers   219

Title Index   220

INTRODUCTION

For some peculiar reason, the familiar use of the word "songster" to designate an anthology of song lyrics is not recognized in any of the standard English or American dictionaries. According to the *Oxford English Dictionary,* the original meaning of the word was "a female singer, a songstress," but by the time it was mentioned in Aelfric's treatise on grammar (ca. 1000 A.D.), it no longer exclusively designated the feminine analogue of the masculine noun "singer." The suffix -*ster* (that dictionary tells us) at first was "freely used to form feminine agent-nouns. . . . The few instances in which it is used as a masculine are renderings of the Latin designations of men exercising functions which among the English were peculiar to women." This was the state of affairs throughout the Old English period, and "in the south the suffix continued to be predominantly feminine throughout the Middle English period." In the north, however, "it came very early to be used, indiscriminately with -*er,* as an agential ending irrespective of gender; from the sixteenth century onwards, the older words in -*ster,* so far as they have survived, have been regarded as masculines, in several instances giving rise to feminines in -*ess,* as . . . *songstress.*" Thus, the primary meaning of the word is given as "one who sings, a singer" in the *OED.*

Two other meanings of the word "songster" emerged later, according to the *OED:* "2. A poet; a writer of songs or verse" is traced back as far as James I's 1585 (*recte* 1584) *The Essayes of a Prentise in the Divine Art of Poesie;* and "3. A bird that sings; a song-bird" was apparently first used by Dryden in his "Flower and Leaf" (1700).

Some further etymological considerations

Plainly, these definitions do not describe the sort of item that is under consideration in this bibliography. Yet despite this (and the lack of any entry under "songster" in such reputable works of references as Oscar Thompson's *International Cyclopedia of Music and Musicians,* Grove's *Dictionary of Music and Musicians,* Percy A. Scholes's *Oxford Companion to Music,* and Willi Apel's *Harvard Dictionary of Music,* among others), it is a simple enough matter to document a connection between the word "songster" and the anthology of song lyrics as early as the first half of the eighteenth century.

The first usage of the word "songster" I have been able to trace in a compilation of song texts is as the alternate title of *The universal musician: or songster's delight* (London, 1737?), later editions of which were published in 1738 and 1750. Close on the heels of this collection there followed: *The merry companion: or universal songster* (London, 1739), with later editions in 1742, 1745, and 1750; *The ladies' delight: or the merry songster* (London, 1741); *The vocal medley, or universal songster* (York, 1749?); *Vocal melody or the songster's magazine* (London, 1751) in three volumes; *The goldfinch: or new modern songster* (Glasgow, 1753) with later editions in 1782 and 1783; *Melpomene: or the songster's merry companion* (Waltham, 1753?); and *The vocal companion: or the delightful and merry songster* (London, 1757?). The earliest use of the word "songster" as part of the regular title rather than the alternate title known to me occurs in *The polite songster* (London, 1758). It did not take long for the usage to cross the Atlantic. *The mock bird; or new American songster* (New York, 1761) marks its first appearance in the pages of this bibliography, but it was not until Chauncey Langdon adopted it for *The select songster or a collection of elegant songs* (New Haven, 1786) that it was used in a regular title in what is now the United States.

While it must be conceded that the precise meaning of the word "songster" as it was utilized in conjunction with song anthologies is not crystal clear, the primary *OED* definition ("one who sings; a singer") seems to fit the earlier collections reasonably well. However, as "songster" came to be adopted for regular titles with greater frequency, it began to take on a different connotation. Long before the end of the eighteenth century, the word had come to refer to the compilation itself rather than to the singer of the lyrics it contains.

Of birds and songsters

It is both curious and interesting to note that the *OED* tertiary definition of "songster" ("a bird that sings; a song-bird") is by no means irrelevant to this story. Indeed, the names of song-birds were greatly favored as titles in the eighteenth century, and between 1730 and 1744, no less than ten English song-birds were called upon to indicate that the little volume the prospective purchaser held in his hands was a collection of song lyrics and not an ornithological treatise, as the unwary might suspect. In order of appearance, the birds serving this musical purpose were: *The skylark* (London, 1730?); *The court parrot* (London, 1731) with a later edition in 1733; *The nightingale* (London, 1738) with later editions and other collections bearing the same title in 1742, 1760, 1770, 1776, 1785, and 1798; *The lark* (London 1740) with a later edition in 1742; *The canary bird* (London, 1745) with a later edition in 1760; *The bull-finch* (London, 1748?), perhaps the most popular of the English bird titles, with later editions and other collections bearing the same name in 1750, 1753, 1757, 1760, 1761, 1763, 1764, 1769, 1772, 1775, 1780, 1781, and 1788; *The goldfinch* (London, 1748), with other editions and collections bearing the same name in 1750, 1753, 1762, 1777, 1782, 1783, 1785, 1788, and 1800; *The linnet* (London, 1749); *The robin* (London, 1749); and *The thrush* (London, 1749). For good measure, there was also *The aviary* (London, 1744?), with later uses of the same title in 1750, 1756, and 1763.

The names of singing birds were also popular titles in the Colonies, but there were a few fascinating sea-changes. The songs in *The American mock bird* (New York, 1760) are unquestionably English in origin—the work appears to be a reprint by James Rivington of an as yet unidentified English songster—but at least its name is patriotic. The mock bird (better known today as the mockingbird) is indigenous to American soil and was not known in the British Isles in 1760. It is ironic that Rivington should have chosen just this title in the light of his later Loyalist reputation. Other American songsters named after birds include *The American cock robin* (New York, 1764) and *The wood-lark* (Philadelphia, 1765?), the latter of which seems to be a reprint by William Bradford, not of some English edition of a songster by the same name (as might be gathered from the title-page) but of *The bull-finch* (London, 1761). Since both the woodlark and the bullfinch are native to England, the reason for the change of title is a bit obscure—perhaps Bradford wanted to disguise the piracy.

The songster defined

For purposes of this bibliography, I define a songster as a collection of three or more secular poems intended to be sung. Since a songster is primarily a collection of *song lyrics,* under ordinary circumstances it would contain no musical notation. However, since it is a collection of poems *intended to be sung,* it may well contain frequent references to the names of the tunes the compiler had in mind when he chose the lyrics. More often than not, these tunes were those the average purchaser reasonably could be expected to recognize and sing from the mention of the title alone. Except for special-purpose songsters (such as those issued from time to time containing the texts of the current theatrical hit songs), to cite unfamiliar tunes by name would have defeated one of the main purposes of the songster genre, which was to enable the purchaser to sing the words of an unfamiliar text without actually supplying the music. In some instances, the metrical pattern of the lyric was so distinctive that the tune could be identified with no trouble at all and direct mention of the tune name was simply omitted. "To Anacreon in Heaven," "Yankee Doodle," and "Derry Down" are characteristic examples of tunes that were treated in this manner quite frequently.

The reason for defining a songster as a collection of *secular* song lyrics is a practical one: it is to exclude from consideration in this bibliography the hundreds (perhaps thousands) of hymn books published in this country before 1821. To include them would obscure the nature of the entire class of materials here under consideration. A collection of *religious* song lyrics must be defined as a hymn book, not as a songster, even though such a definition eliminates such compilations as Amos Pilsbury's *Sacred songster* (Charleston, S.C., 1809; frequently reprinted), a rather awkward circumstance. To do otherwise would be self-defeating.

Why must a songster contain "three or more" items? Since it is difficult to conceive of a "collection" containing only two exemplars, a collection of three was adjudged the absolute minimum. This qualification served to eliminate from the bibliography a fair number of chapbooks, otherwise indistinguishable from others herein listed, containing only two songs. The line has to be drawn someplace, however. A few other common-sense qualifications of the definition have also been observed: an item must have been published in book or pamphlet form and it must contain at least eight pages in order to be included. Thus, sheet music, four-page chapbooks, and broadsides have been omitted.

On the other hand, items containing materials in addition to a collection of three or more secular poems intended to be sung have not been excluded from this bibliography, even though the song anthology may constitute only a small fraction of the total contents. If an almanac, a dancing manual, a guide to the meaning of dreams, a fortune-telling manual, a joke book, a guide to Freemasonry, a pocket notebook, an oration, or a what-you-will happens to contain *a separate section of songs* which conforms to the general definition outlined here, I have considered it a songster and it will be found in this bibliography. The guiding principle, the reader should remember, is that of the *separate section*. If three or more secular poems intended to be sung are scattered throughout the text, the item has not been considered a songster and will not be found in this bibliography.

What about a collection of three or more secular poems intended to be sung which includes musical notation? There are, of course, dozens of song anthologies of this sort. Should they be considered songsters? If the texts and not the tunes are central, I have included such items in the bibliography. The twenty-six such atypical text-tune combinations found here serve a useful purpose in that they provide the user with a handy, authentic, early notated source of many of the favorite tunes merely referred to by name in more orthodox songsters.

Of course, there simply is no way to eliminate borderline cases no matter how one refines the definition of a class of objects. Whenever I ran across one of these problem children, it was my general practice to include it in the bibliography rather than to exclude it.

The genus songster described

The earliest book printed on this side of the Atlantic to qualify as a songster, in terms of the definition set down above, was *The constitutions of the Free-masons,* "London printed; Anno 5723. Re-printed in Philadelphia by special order, for the use of the brethren in North-America. In the year of Masonry 5734, Anno Domini 1734." Appropriately enough, the printer was Benjamin Franklin. *The constitutions* contains a separate section of five Masonic songs on pp. 83-94. By the end of 1820, no less than 649 other songsters had been published. Copies of 542 of the 650 songsters listed in this bibliography have been located. There is reasonably convincing evidence that the 108 other songsters, no exemplars of which have been found as of this writing, actually did see the light of day.

To those unfamiliar with early songsters, it may seem a little unusual that just about one title out of six seems to have disappeared. Actually, the rather high incidence of unlocated titles is hardly an unexpected state of affairs. By and large, songsters were not deluxe productions handed down from generation to generation, from father to son, from mother to daughter. They were utilitarian objects, generally cheap and shoddy goods. Many were chapbooks sold by itinerant peddlers for a few cents each—there are eighty-five such ephemeral creations in this bibliography. If songsters did not disintegrate with heavy use (there is considerable evidence of wear and tear in the relatively few copies that have survived), they eventually were discarded as useless. Many dealt with topical matters, soon forgotten as fashions in mores and politics changed. The social historian should view with skepticism those few early American songsters such as *The American musical miscellany* (Northampton, 1798) and the *Nightingale* (Portsmouth, 1804) which can be found in comparatively large numbers of pristine copies—they are not likely to have seen much use nor achieved much popularity in their time. The valuable songsters tend to be those which are known in a single, well-used copy: a description which holds true for 257 of the items listed in this bibliography.

What were the songs in the songsters about? As a reasonably objective indication of content, I tallied up the adjectives to be found on the title-pages of those actually located, combined them in compatible groupings, and arrived at the following table:

Adjectives on early American songster title-pages

105*	patriotic (75), national (15), political (6), republican (6), democratic (2), liberty (1)
83	sentimental (57), amatory (10), elegant (7), amorous (3), love (2), polite (2), passionate (1), refined (1)
79	comic (28), humorous (28), entertaining (7), witty (4), jovial (4), satirical (3), convivial (2), merry (2), facetious (1)
50	naval (24), sea (14), nautical (4), martial (6), military (2)
49	modern (40), fashionable (9)
33	American (31), Yankee (2)
26	Scotch (19), Scottish (6), Scots (1)
25	English (25)
22	Irish (22)
22	Masonic (21), Freemasons (1)
14	ancient (14)
10	Anacreontic (10)

A content analysis of the extant pre-1821 songsters shows that 65 percent, or 354 items, were intended to be used by both men and women. An additional 22 percent (117 items) were addressed to a primarily male audience. More songsters were designed for children (thirty-seven, or 7 percent) than for women (thirty-four, or 6 percent).

For men only

In the light of the mores of the period, the large number of songsters published "for men only" is not very surprising but the reader

*Number of times mentioned

should by no means assume that Americans favored bawdy songs. Indeed, the purity of our song collections is quite astounding, especially when compared with what was going on in merry old England. A particular market for sung bawdry developed there in the second half of the eighteenth century in conjunction with the growth of men's private drinking clubs, and the songs of these clubs formed one of the principal wellsprings of erotic literature in England at the time. Such titles as *The buck's delight,* the *Covent Garden repository* (Covent Garden being the fashionable prostitutes' quarter in London as well as a musical center), and *The frisky songster* included many ditties that would bring a blush to the cheek of well-bred ladies. Perhaps the best known "dirty" songster of all time is Robert Burns's *Merry muses of Caledonia* (Edinburgh, 1800?), the original of which has survived in but a single copy, now in the library of the Earl of Rosebery. (It is available in a scholarly edition published in Edinburgh in 1959 with notes by James Barke, Sidney Goodsir Smith, and J. DeLancey Ferguson.) Songsters to delight the most hardened rakes abounded in Great Britain.

On this side of the Atlantic, there was absolutely nothing comparable, although Americans were not averse to turning an honest penny by printing other kinds of salacious literature, to judge by the evidence. I have managed to find only a single American imprint which tries in any way to cater to the salacious. This is *The amorous songster* (New York, 1800), a 96-page collection "printed for the Sporting Club" which blows its own horn loudly. "Compared with this vigorous volume," boasts the title-page, "*The frisky songster* is a lifeless chap." No American edition of *The frisky songster* is known (although there are copies of a Scottish edition published around 1800 in the Kinsey Collection at Indiana University and in the Bodleian Library) and I doubt that one ever was issued, but *The amorous songster,* with its stereotyped Phyllidas and Corydons, is a pious fraud. It is as pure as *The enchanting humming-bird* or *Little robin red breast.* I am at a total loss to account for the failure of British sung bawdry to weather the sea trip before 1821.

The real reason for the considerable number of songsters prepared for male consumption exclusively was the rapid growth and strong influence of Freemasonry in the Colonies. While it is true that only fourteen songsters exclusively devoted to Masonic poems intended to be sung appear to have been published before 1821, there were sixty-one containing separate sections of Masonic songs similar to that in the 1734 *Constitutions*—but not infrequently far more comprehensive—that appeared during the same period. And even though women were excluded from the Masonic rituals, many of the general song-sters intended for their eyes included a section of favorite Masonic ditties. Even the most cursory examination of the songster literature reveals the astonishing ubiquity and the considerable importance of Freemasonry in the early history of vocal music in our country, a circumstance which has hitherto been completely overlooked by social historians.

Where songsters were published

New England was not the main source of supply for songsters—the center of publication was further south. Of the twenty-six pre-Revolutionary songsters located, only six originated in Massachusetts. Between them, New York and Pennsylvania were the source of eighteen. New York led in songster production only until 1790, how-ever. By 1792, Pennsylvania had forged ahead, and its leadership in the field was never seriously challenged again. Massachusetts main-tained third place, running neck and neck with New York throughout the first decade of the nineteenth century, and of the remaining states, only Maryland made a really significant contribution to the genre. Al-together, Pennsylvania, New York, Massachusetts, and Maryland ac-counted for more than three-fourths of all American songsters pub-lished before 1821. The following table shows the extent to which the middle states dominated songster production.

AMERICAN SONGSTER PRODUCTION THROUGH 1820 (BY STATES)

States	Through																
	1775	90	92	94	96	98	00	02	04	06	08	10	12	14	16	18	20
Pa.	7	19	25	33	45	49	57	65	91	113	119	122	130	143	152	183	188
N.Y.	11	22	22	24	28	40	48	55	59	67	69	76	93	103	112	129	157
Mass.	6	11	13	18	26	37	49	54	59	65	70	75	83	89	99	108	108
Md.	—	—	—	1	4	12	18	21	24	30	31	35	47	52	60	66	66
All others	2	5	9	12	15	28	38	44	51	57	65	71	82	94	109	125	131
Totals	26	57	69	88	118	166	210	239	284	332	354	379	435	481	532	611	650

The figures for songster production by states do not give an accurate picture of the situation, at least so far as Massachusetts is concerned, however. There, the publishing of songsters was quite decentralized.

A breakdown by cities reveals that Boston was more comparable to Baltimore than to New York as a point of origin.

AMERICAN SONGSTER PRODUCTION THROUGH 1820 (BY CITIES)

Cities	Through																
	1775	*90*	*92*	*94*	*96*	*98*	*00*	*02*	*04*	*06*	*08*	*10*	*12*	*14*	*16*	*18*	*20*
Phila.	6	19	26	34	46	49	57	65	90	110	115	118	124	137	146	172	177
N.Y.	12	22	22	25	29	37	45	51	54	59	60	61	75	83	87	102	128
Boston	6	6	7	10	15	21	24	28	32	34	39	43	48	53	58	63	63
Balto.	—	—	—	1	4	12	19	22	25	31	32	36	48	51	59	63	63

In addition to Boston, songsters were issued in eleven other Massachusetts towns: Worcester (thirteen), Dedham (seven), Newburyport (five), Northampton (five), Brookfield (four), Charlestown (four), Salem (three), Andover (one), Greenfield (one), Haverhill (one), and Wrentham (one).

Where songsters are now located

This bibliography locates 1,939 exemplars (not counting duplicate copies) of 650 different American songsters published before 1821. They are to be found in 183 university, college, public, and private libraries and collections in thirty-one states, the District of Columbia, England, Scotland, and Germany. I have tried to examine at least one exemplar of every extant songster listed and in most instances, many more. Within its self-defined boundaries, the bibliography is as complete as more than fifteen years of assiduous sleuthing can make it. This does not mean, of course, that thirty-five unique songsters completely unknown to me will not turn up as soon as the bibliography is published—indeed, that is exactly what happened when I once before decided that my labors were ended. A single volume containing more than thirty chapbooks, none of which I had seen before, surfaced in the Library Company of Philadelphia, and most of them were unique eight-page songsters printed in the City of Brotherly Love shortly after the turn of the nineteenth century, apparently by a printer newly arrived from Ireland. This discovery left me with a trauma that set back the official completion of the bibliography by some years.

Actually, the holdings of songsters are not so widely dispersed as it might seem. Three institutions, the American Antiquarian Society,

Brown University, and the Library of Congress, have made something of a specialty of songsters—among them, they hold just about half of the 257 unique exemplars uncovered and more than a quarter of all known exemplars. The following table illustrates the comparative strength of the collections in those institutions holding exemplars of more than fifty copies:

INSTITUTIONAL HOLDINGS OF PRE-1821 AMERICAN SONGSTERS

Institution	Number of exemplars	Number of unique exemplars
American Antiquarian Society	239	55
Brown University	163	40
Library of Congress	153	31
Harvard University	78	8
Library Company of Philadelphia	76	35
New York Public Library	74	9
Boston Public Library	70	7
New-York Historical Society	63	6
Massachusetts Grand Lodge, Free and Accepted Masons	56	1
Yale University	51	3

All of these institutions have been personally canvassed by me, in addition to the Henry E. Huntington Library (San Marino), the Watkinson Library of Trinity College (Hartford), the Connecticut Historical Society, the U.S. Department of the Navy Library (Washington), the Scottish Rite Supreme Council Library (Washington), the Newberry Library (Chicago), the Boston Athenaeum, the Massachusetts Historical Society, the Enoch Pratt Free Library (Baltimore), the Johns Hopkins University, the Peabody Institute (Baltimore), the Maryland Historical Society, the William L. Clements Library of the University of Michigan (Ann Arbor), Columbia University, Princeton University, the Historical Society of Pennsylvania, the Free Library of Philadelphia, the American Philosophical Society (Philadelphia), the Grand Lodge Library, Free and Accepted Masons of Pennsylvania, the Carnegie Library (Pittsburgh), the University of Pennsylvania, the Rhode Island Historical Society, the Providence Public Library, the John Carter Brown Library (Providence), the University of Virginia, and the private libraries of Lester Levy (Pikesville, Md.) and the late W. N. H. Harding (Chicago; now in the Bodleian Library, Oxford).

Unique copies in other institutions have been examined by me either at the Library of Congress (through the courtesy of the Interlibrary Loan System) or in microfilm. The census of copies herein indicates the specific exemplar which is described in each numbered entry of the bibliography.

Explanation of the entries

Items are listed chronologically by title, alphabetically within each year, and are numbered seriatim. The large majority of songsters was compiled anonymously; an index of authors, compilers, proprietors, and editors (where known) is appended. It was a custom of the time to give most songsters alternate titles; these are listed, with reference to the main title, in an appended alphabetical title index. Other aids for the user include a table correlating years and item numbers, a key to library sigla and a census of known copies, and a geographical directory of printers, publishers, booksellers, and engravers.

Where a copy of a songster with a title-page is extant, a full transcription with original punctuation and spelling is given with an indication of line endings. Capitals are utilized to indicate the short title of the songster; capitalization is otherwise modernized and is used only for words beginning sentences and for proper names. No attempt has been made to imitate typography. Where no copy of the songster is known, or where no title-page is known, a title and imprint based on the best available source is given in brackets.

Since songsters are not essentially complex bibliographical entities, no signatures or measurements are included. A statement of pagination is given, followed by an enumeration of contents. Where a songster has been described in an earlier published bibliography, that fact is mentioned and a citation of the previous entry is listed. Full titles of the bibliographies to which reference is made may be found in the list of bibliographies cited.

The location of all copies known to the author is indicated with the sigla developed for the National Union Catalog by the Library of Congress, now generally accepted as standard. Where no copy has been found, that is so stated, followed by some indication of the reasons why I believe the songster was, in fact, actually published.

A count of the actual number of songs in each extant songster, with an indication of whether or not that count conforms to that of the index (where the songster has an index) is included since a disagreement as to number may well indicate the existence of a different edition. Reference is also made to earlier and later editions of a particular songster where such are known to exist, as well as to songsters related in content although not necessarily in name.

Acknowledgments

In a certain sense, every bibliography represents the work of many individuals even though it may bear the name of a single author, and because of its unusually long period of gestation, this bibliography must acknowledge its indebtedness to a particularly lengthy list of institutions and people. I have already cited those institutions where I was privileged to work; in all of them, I was courteously and helpfully received and made to feel very much at home. People there made my task as easy as possible.

As I scan my notes, I am amazed at the number of years that have slipped by since the late Richard S. Hill, formerly the head of the Reference Section in the Music Division of the Library of Congress, first introduced me to the world of songsters and set me to chasing after them, at first in connection with his intensive researches on the origins of the text and tune of our national anthem, but not long after that, on directions all my own. To him and to my former colleagues in the Library of Congress, William Lichtenwanger and Carroll D. Wade (both now retired from the Music Division), I owe more than I can tell. It is also a bit embarrassing to have to acknowledge the assistance of not one but three directors of the American Antiquarian Society, the late Clarence S. Brigham, the late Clifford K. Shipton, and the current incumbent, Marcus A. McCorison. Without their unfailing interest in my work (and their persistent prodding), there would be no bibliography of American songsters published before 1821. Other fellow members and staff of the AAS to whom I owe a debt of gratitude include James E. Mooney, formerly assistant director (now director of the Historical Society of Pennsylvania), who answered many inquiries, John B. Hench, editor of publications, who saw the bibliography through the press with astonishing speed and accuracy, and most especially William H. Scheide, whose generous contribution to the Society made the publication of this bibliography possible. In addition, a research grant from the American Council of Learned Societies allowed me to make extensive visits to many libraries and to break the back of the location problem.

Introduction

To mention the names of all those who helped me with my work, either in person or in correspondence, would be quite literally impossible. The following individuals, however, all contributed to the completeness and accuracy of the bibliography in smaller or larger degree, and my acknowledgement of that fact here is but a small token of my appreciation:

Laura P. Abbott (Vermont Historical Society), Thomas R. Adams (John Carter Brown Library, Brown University), Otto E. Albrecht (University of Pennsylvania), John Alden (Rare Books Department, Boston Public Library), Julius P. Barclay (Special Collections, Stanford University Libraries), Julia Barrow (Essex Institute), Geraldine Beard (New-York Historical Society), Marion E. Brown (John Hay Library, Brown University), the late Barney Chesnick (Library Company of Philadelphia), Robert O. Dougan (Henry E. Huntington Library), P. William Filby (Maryland Historical Society), Robert S. Fraser (Princeton University Library), Gillet Griffin (Princeton University Library), Thompson R. Harlow (Connecticut Historical Society), Christine D. Hathaway (John Hay Library, Brown University), Georgia Haugh (William L. Clements Library, University of Michigan), Gertrude D. Hess (American Philosophical Society Library), Allen D. Hill (Bennington Historical Museum Library), the late Edward G. Howard (Maryland Historical Society), Carolyn E. Jakeman (Houghton Library, Harvard University), Clara M. Kennedy (Windsor Library Association), John D. Kilbourne (Maryland Historical Society), the late Ernst C. Krohn, Thomas Lange (Pierpont Morgan Library), Mildred M. Ledden (New York State Library), Violet E. Lowens (D.C. Public Library), Annette Mullen (Teachers College, Columbia University), Charles H. Ness (Pennsylvania State Library), Howard H. Peckham (William L. Clements Library, University of Michigan), Dorothy M. Potter (Essex Institute), Richard H. Shryock (American Philosophical Society Library), Donald A. Sinclair (Special Collections, Rutgers University Library), Lewis M. Stark (Rare Book Division, New York Public Library), Roger E. Stoddard (Houghton Library, Harvard University; formerly John Hay Library, Brown University), Gretchen Tobey (New Hampshire Historical Society Library), Mason Tolman (New York State Library), Lillian Tonkin (Library Company of Philadelphia), Evelyn A. Tucker (Vermont Historical Society), Lawrence J. Turgeon (Vermont State Library), R. N. Williams II (Historical Society of Pennsylvania), Lyle H. Wright (Henry E. Huntington Library), and the late John Cook Wyllie (Alderman Library, University of Virginia).

And finally, obeisance to my long-suffering wife Margery, who not only helped in every way possible, but saw me through.

Irving Lowens

Reston, Virginia
9 June 1975

KEY TO LIBRARY SYMBOLS

AND

CENSUS OF COPIES

Note: A number in *italics* indicates the only copy known; an asterisk (*) indicates the exemplar from which the title-page was transcribed in the bibliographical entry.

California

C   California State Library, Sacramento: 511

CL   Los Angeles Public Library: 139

CLU   University of California, Los Angeles: 43, 279 (variant), 478

CSmH Henry E. Huntington Library, San Marino: 1, 43, 60, 65, 87, 117, 139 (imperfect), 182, 272, 279 (variant), 285, 348, 403, 404, 433, 434 (2 copies, 1 imperfect), 436, 439, 441, 455, 460, 475, 507*, 510 (imperfect), 521, 526, 541, *542**, 543, *546**, 552, 580, 615, 631, 649

CSt   Stanford University, Palo Alto: 272, 287, 306, 347, 367, 433, 471, 556*

CU   University of California, Berkeley: 433

Connecticut

Ct   Connecticut State Library, Hartford: 12, 203, 433, 491, 631

CtHC Hartford Seminary Foundation, Hartford: 323

CtHT Trinity College, Hartford: 239, 433, 526

CtHT-W Watkinson Library, Trinity College, Hartford: 70, 117, 139, 163, 203, 236, 276, 279, 339, 383, 399, 423, 443, 535, 569, 573, 636

CtHi Connecticut Historical Society, Hartford: 47, *111**, 198* (imperfect), 426, 451, 474, 525*, 649

CtW   Wesleyan University, Middletown: 515, 649

CtY   Yale University, New Haven: 23, 43 (2 copies), 44, 58*, 72, 96, 102, 108, 117, 125, 136, 139, *142** (imperfect), 170, 173 (imperfect), 203, 205* (2 copies, 1 imperfect), 239, 273, 276, 279 (variant), 287 (imperfect), 295, 307, 325*, 347, 348, 362, 399, 403, 409, 426*, 429*, 460, 464, 468, 471, 475, 477, 487, 499, 511, 518 (imperfect), 555 (imperfect), 572, 577, 579*, 580, 586, 631, 643

DLC U.S. Library of Congress: 23*, 34*, 37*, 43, 57*, 60* (2 copies), 65*, 68* (2 incomplete copies), 72*, 83 (imperfect), 94*, 101*, 105 (imperfect), 112*, 115* (imperfect), 117* (5 copies), 118*, 124*, 126 (2 imperfect copies), 128*, 131 (imperfect), 136*, 139* (2 copies), 145*, 146*, 148*, 156*, 170* (2 copies), 171*, 172 (imperfect), 177*, 182, 183*, 185 (imperfect), 192*, 193 (imperfect), 200 (imperfect), 206, 207 (imperfect), 213, 220*, 231*, 234*, 236*, 239 (2 imperfect copies), 242*, 254* (2 copies), 261*, 267*, 272, 273 (imperfect), 279*, 279 (variant), 285*, 286*, 289*, 306*, 308, 312*, 313 (imperfect), 314 (imperfect), 336*, 341* (2 copies, 1 imperfect), 344*, 347*, 349*, 352*, 357*, 360*, 362 (imperfect), 364*, 367, 379* (imperfect), 383*, 388*, 389*, 390*, 394*, 397*, 399*, 403*, 406*, 413, 414, 420*, 421*, 422 (imperfect), 423*, 427*, 431*, 432*, 433*, 434*, 436, 439*, 441* (2 copies), 442*, 443, 446, 448*, 449*, 452*, 455*, 473*, 475* (2 copies), 477*, 478, 480*, 482*, 484*, 485*, 486*, 491*, 496*, 499* (2 copies), 502*, 504 (imperfect), 505*, 508*, 509 (imperfect), 510*, 513*, 517, 518 (imperfect), 524*, 526, 528*, 530*, 531*, 535* (2 copies), 541 (imperfect), 554*, 558*, 564 (imperfect), 567*, 572*, 573*, 577*, 578*, 580*, 583*, 585*, 586*, 612*, 615, 629*, 636*, 639, 640*, 642 (imperfect), 647* (imperfect), 648*, 649

DN U.S. Department of the Navy: 476*

DSC Scottish Rite Supreme Council: 1, 23 (imperfect), 36*, 60 (imperfect), 71*, 84*, 112, 125*, 131 (imperfect), 145, 148, 150*, 163*, 231, 232*, 239 (imperfect), 254, 263*, 272*, 273*, 294*, 295*, 312 (variant, lacks frontispiece), 336, 347, 348*, 391*, 392*, 420, 468 (imperfect), 471* (2 copies), 491, 510, 511*, 512*, 517*, 518, 526, 541 (imperfect), 544*, 559*, 567, 568*, 577, 618 (imperfect), 631*, 649 (2 copies)

Delaware

DeHi Historical Society of Delaware, Wilmington: 558

DeWI Wilmington Institute Free Library and the New Castle County Free Library: 124, 132, 433, 558, 570

DeWint Henry Francis DuPont Winterthur Museum, Winterthur: 139, 426 (imperfect), 557

Florida

FTaSU   Florida State University, Tallahassee: 497

Illinois

IC   Chicago Public Library: 357

ICHi   Chicago Historical Society: 239, 295, 436, 518 (imperfect), 573

ICN   Newberry Library, Chicago: 132 (imperfect), 139, 200*, 209*, 239 (imperfect), 261, 279 (variant), 350*, 375 (imperfect), 399, 409, 439, 460, 477, 518 (imperfect), 554, 561*, 562*, 585, 638*

ICU   University of Chicago: 43, 108, 139, 170, 279 (variant), 415, 416, 419, 526 (imperfect), 552, 572

IEN   Northwestern University, Evanston: 139

IU   University of Illinois, Urbana: 72, 139, 183, 279 (variant), 295 (imperfect), 326 (imperfect), 347, 433, 439 (imperfect), 499, 573

Iowa

IaAS   Iowa State University of Science and Technology, Ames: 485, 486

IaCrM   Iowa Masonic Library, Cedar Rapids: 1, 23, 60, 124, 126, 136, 239, 272, 285, 294, 336, 349, 420, 471, 510, 511, 517, 518, 526, 541, 572, 577, 631, 649

IaU   University of Iowa, Iowa City: 307, 535 (imperfect)

Indiana

InU   Indiana University, Bloomington: 120

InU-Li Indiana University, Lilly Library, Bloomington: 279 (variant), 458, 475, 535

Kansas

KWiU   Wichita State University, Wichita: 433

Kentucky

KyBgW   Western Kentucky State University, Bowling Green: 349

KyLo   Louisville Free Public Library: 349

KyLoF   Filson Club, Louisville: 572

Louisiana

LNHT	Tulane University, New Orleans: 501
LNSM	St. Mary's Dominican College, New Orleans: 295
LU	Louisiana State University, Baton Rouge: 433

Massachusetts

MA   Amherst College, Amherst: 433

MB   Boston Public Library: *21**, 23, 43, 47, *56**, 60, 72, 101, 117, 122 (imperfect), 124, 130 (imperfect), 139, *155** (imperfect), 170 (imperfect), 182, 189, 193* (imperfect), 199*, 203*, 227, 231, 233*, 239 (imperfect), 242, 254, 261, 272, 273, 295, 307, 313, 334 (imperfect), 343 (imperfect), 352, 353*, 383, 413, 414, 415, 416, 419, 432, 433, 434 (2 copies), 436, 439, 443, *444**, 446, 450, 457, 458*, 477, 485, 486, 499 (imperfect), 502, 509, 511, 518 (imperfect), 535, 552, 567, 573 (2 copies), *576**, 580, *584**, 618, *621**

MBAt   Boston Athenaeum: 44, 65, 72, 124, 126, 139, 182, 279 (imperfect), *281**, 353, 403, 443, 485, 486, 573

MBC   American Congregational Association, Boston: 321, 512

MBFM   Massachusetts Grand Lodge, F. & A.M., Boston: 1, 23, 29 (2 copies, 1 imperfect), 60, 65, 71 (imperfect), 112, 124, 125 (imperfect), 136, 145, 146, 148, 150, 164, 206, *230**, 231, 232 (imperfect), 239 (2 imperfect copies), 254, 263, 272, 273, 294 (2 copies), 295, 312 (imperfect), 312 (variant), 336* (2 copies, 1 imperfect), 347, 348, 391, 392 (imperfect), 409, 420, 468, 471 (3 copies), 491, 510, 511, 512, 517 (2 copies), 518 (3 copies), 526, 537, 544, 559, 567, 570, 572, 573 (2 copies), 577 (imperfect), 618 (imperfect), 631, 649

MBr   Public Library of Brookline: 433

MBtS   St. John's Seminary, Brighton: 411

MH   Harvard University, Cambridge: 28, 43, 60, 71, 83*, *86** (imperfect), 92 (imperfect), 112, 117, 124, 133*, *135**, 139, 149*, 170, *172**, 189*, *191**, 198 (imperfect), 200, 212, *214** (imperfect), 236, 261, 263, 273, 275 (imperfect), *276**, 279 (imperfect variant), 286 (imperfect), 294, 306, *311** (imperfect), 334 (imperfect), 339, 341, 347 (imperfect), 357, 367, *373**, *375**, 383, 388, 415, 416, 419, 423 (imperfect), 432 (imperfect), 433, 434, 439, 443, 454, 455, *459**, 464, *470**, 477, 485, 486, 499 (2 copies), 502 (imperfect), *503**, 504 (imperfect), 510, 518, 535 (imperfect), 567, 573, 580, 584, 585, *617**, 618, 631, 636, 639, 643 (imperfect)

MHi   Massachusetts Historical Society, Boston: 23, 29*, 65, 139, 150, 171, 182, 227 (imperfect), 261, 276, 286 (imperfect), 347, 367, 375, 383, 433, 443, 455, 486, 555 (imperfect)

MLy   Lynn Public Library: 433, 649

MMeT   Tufts University, Medford: 117, 295, 423

MNF   Forbes Library, Northampton: 139

MS   City Library, Springfield: 227

MSa   Salem Public Library: 433, 518, 640

MSaE   Essex Institute, Salem: 170, *342**, 347, 420, 427, 434, 443, 504* (imperfect), 568, 582, 640

MTa   Taunton Public Library: 433

MU   University of Massachusetts, Amherst: 139

MW   Worcester Public Library and Central Massachusetts Regional Library Headquarters: 394

MWA   American Antiquarian Society, Worcester: 12, 23, *30** (imperfect), 34, *38** (imperfect), *40**, *41**, *43** (2 copies), *44**, *45** (imperfect), 47 (imperfect), *48** (2 copies), *55** (imperfect), 57 (imperfect), 58 (imperfect), *59**, 60 (imperfect), 65 (2 copies, 1 imperfect), 72, 84, *85**, *87**, *88**, *92**, *98**, 101, *102**, *105**, 108, 112, 117, 118 (imperfect), 120 (imperfect), *122**, 124, 125, *126**, *127** (imperfect), *130**, 133 (imperfect), 136, 139, 145, 146, *147**, 148 (imperfect), *152**, *153**, *160** (imperfect), *161** (imperfect), *164**, *167**, 168 (imperfect), *169**, 170, 171, 172 (imperfect), *173**, *175** (imperfect), 177 (imperfect), *178**, *179**, *182**, 183 (imperfect), 188, *190**, 192 (2 copies), *195** (imperfect), *196**, 199, 203, 205, *206**, *210**, 212, 223, 227 (imperfect), *229**, 231, 232, *235**, 236 (imperfect), *237** (imperfect), *239**, 261, 263, 267, *270**, 272, 273, *275**, 276, *277**, 279, 279 (variant), 286, *287**, *288**, 289, 294, 295, 302 (imperfect), *304**, *305**, 306, 307, 314 (imperfect), *321**, *323**, *326**, *328**, *330** (imperfect), *334**, *335**, *339**, 341, *343**, 344, *346**, 347, 348, 349, 350, 352, *359**, 361 (imperfect), *363**, *365**, *367**, *369**, *374**, 375, *376** (imperfect), *381**, 383, *384**, *385**, *386**, *393**, *394**, *398**, 399, 403, *411**, 419 (imperfect), 420, 423, *425**, *425** (variant), 426, 427, *428**, 429 (imperfect), *430* (imperfect), 433, 434, 439, 441, *445**, 446, *447**, 451, *453**, 460, 464, 467 (imperfect), *468**, *469**, 473, 475, 477, *478**, 482, 485, 486, 490, 491, *493**, *494**, *495**, *497** (2 copies), *498**, 499, *500** (imperfect), 505, *506**, *509**, 510, 511, *514**, *516**, 517, 518, *519**, 520, *521**, 526, 529 (imperfect), 535, 536, *537**, 538, 539, *541**, *543**, 544, *545**, 547, *552**, 554, *557**, *560** (imperfect), 561, 564,

565 (imperfect), 566*, 568, 569*, 571 (imperfect), 572, 573, 574, 577, 580, *581**, 582, 584 (imperfect), 585, 593, 616*, 617, 618, *634**, 635*, 639*, 642*, 643*, 649 (2 copies, 1 imperfect)

MWH   College of the Holy Cross, Worcester: 139

MWHi   Worcester Historical Society, Worcester: 43, 568, 649

MWiW   Williams College, Williamstown: 367, 433

MWiW-C   Chapin Library, Williams College, Williamstown: 475

Maryland

MdBE   Enoch Pratt Free Library, Baltimore: 126, 413, 414, 423, 433, 519, 541

MdBFM   Free and Accepted Masons of Maryland, Grand Lodge Library, Baltimore: 126, 526, 541, 573

MdBG   Goucher College, Baltimore: 108

MdBJ   Johns Hopkins University, Baltimore: 334 (imperfect), 413, 414, 415*, 416*, 422*

MdBL   Loyola College, Baltimore: 570

MdBP   Peabody Institute, Baltimore: 360, 413, 414, 415, 416, 417, 418, 433, 569

MdHi   Maryland Historical Society, Baltimore: *100**, *166**, 170, 265 (2 copies), 279 (variant), 289 (2 copies), 347 (imperfect), 360, 370*, *407**, 415 (2 copies, 1 imperfect), 416 (2 copies, 1 imperfect), 419, 422 (imperfect), 423, 433, 475, 476, 499, 529, 540 (imperfect), 558, *609**

MdW   Woodstock College, Woodstock: 411

Maine

MeB   Bowdoin College, Brunswick: 455

MeBa   Bangor Public Library: 394

MeHi   Maine Historical Society, Portland: 394, 433, 455

Michigan

MiD   Detroit Public Library: 433

MiD-B   Burton Historical Collection, Detroit Public Library: 272, 443, 631, 649

MiU   University of Michigan, Ann Arbor: 170, 279 (variant), 433, 567

MiU-C   William L. Clements Library, University of Michigan, Ann Arbor: *31**, 72, 92 (imperfect), 122 (imperfect), 124,

139, 232, 236, 258*, 272, 274*, 279 (2 variants), 306, 344, 383, 434, *463**, 499, 518, 557, 649

Minnesota

MnHi Minnesota Historical Society, St. Paul: 433
MnU University of Minnesota, Minneapolis: *240**, 467, 580

Missouri

MoSW Washington University, St. Louis: *424**
MoSpD Drury College, Springfield: 433

New York

N New York State Library, Albany: 4*, 23, 72, 124, 139, 171 (imperfect), 182, 286, 341, 391, 434, 443, *462**, 468, *551**, 639

NBLiHi Long Island Historical Society, Brooklyn: 419, 433, 526

NBu Buffalo and Erie County Public Library, Buffalo: 433

NBuDD DeLancey Divinity School, Buffalo (No longer in existence): 295

NBuG Grosvenor Reference Division, Buffalo and Erie County Public Library, Buffalo: 57, 101 (imperfect), 117, 139, 170, 171, *186**, 212, 236, 239, 261, 279 (variant), 313, 334 (imperfect), 335, 347, 350 (imperfect), 367, 383, 394, 399, 419, 423, 439, 477, 499, 501, 520, 535, 540, 558

NCH Hamilton College, Clinton: *372**, 433

NCooHi New York State Historical Association, Cooperstown: 419

NGH Hobart and William Smith Colleges, Geneva: 420, 433

NHi New-York Historical Society, New York: 28*, 34, 57, 72, 97*, 117, 122 (imperfect), 139, 149 (imperfect), 170, *176**, 178 (imperfect), 182, 185*, *213**, *228**, 231, 236, 239 (2 imperfect copies), 246*, 279 (variant), 306, 307*, 312 (imperfect variant), 335 (imperfect), 336, 341, *358** (imperfect), 360, 399, 419, 423, 433, *436**, 439, 441, *443**, 448, 454*, *460**, 475, 478, 479 (imperfect), *501**, 512, 517, 518 (imperfect), 520, *529**, *536**, 539, 552 (imperfect), 558, 561, 562 (imperfect), 573, 577, 593, *613**, *614**, *618**, 635, *637**

NHpR Franklin D. Roosevelt Library, Hyde Park: 139

NIC Cornell University, Ithaca: 125, 239, 294, 295, 336, 434, 443, 468, 491, 518, 540, 541, 558, 577, 618, 631, 649

NN New York Public Library: 23, 43 (2 copies), 44 (imperfect), 47, *50**, *53**, 72, *77**, 98, *108**, 117, 139 (2 copies),

150, 167, 170, 171 (imperfect), 172, 182, 185, 188*, 196, 202*, 207*, 223*, 239, 246, 254, 272 (2 copies), 273, 276 (imperfect), 279 (variant), *301**, 307, 321, 347, 348, 367, *371**, *383*, 394, 399, *401**, 403, 404*, 409, *410**, 423 (imperfect), 432, 433, 434, 439, 443, 460, *465**, 471, 477, 488, *489**, 499, 502, 510, 526, 535, 537, 541, 547*, 552, 568, 572, 573, 585, 615, 629, 649

NNC Columbia University, New York: 139, 279 (variant), *320** (imperfect), 367, 433, 468, 497 (variant), *620**

NNC-T Teachers College, Columbia University, New York: *549**

NNF Fordham University, New York: 543

NNFM Grand Lodge of New York, F. & A.M. Library and Museum, New York: 1, 23, 112, 125, 136, 231, 239 (imperfect), 294, 295, 336, 347, 391, 420, 443, 468, 510, 511, 512, 517, 518 (imperfect), 526, 541, 567, 573, 618, 631, 649

NNMer Mercantile Library Association, New York: 509

NNPM Pierpont Morgan Library, New York: *424**

NNS New York Society Library, New York: 577

NNUT Union Theological Seminary, New York: 139, 433, 499, 573

NPV Vassar College, Poughkeepsie: *158**

NRHi Rochester Historical Society: 295

NRU University of Rochester: 419, 518

NRU-Mus Sibley Music Library, Eastman School of Music, University of Rochester: 139 (2 copies), 171, 239, 585

NSchU Union College, Schenectady: 136

NT Troy Public Library: 433

NUtHi Oneida Historical Society, Utica: 537

North Carolina

NcA-S Sondley Reference Library, Pack Memorial Public Library, Asheville: 285, 336, 615

NcD Duke University, Durham: 60, 239, 248* (imperfect), 273, 279 (imperfect variant), 433, 477, 535 (imperfect)

NcU University of North Carolina, Chapel Hill: 357, 433

North Dakota

NdFM Masonic Grand Lodge, Fargo: 572, 631, 649

Key to Symbols
New Hampshire

Nh	New Hampshire State Library, Concord: 443
NhD	Dartmouth College, Hanover: 279 (variant)
NhHi	New Hampshire Historical Society, Concord: 239, 279 (variant)

New Jersey

NjHi	New Jersey Historical Society, Newark: 121* (2 copies, 1 imperfect)
NjMD	Drew University, Madison: 464
NjN	Newark Public Library: 121
NjP	Princeton University, Princeton: 16* (imperfect), 20*, 43, 72, 87 (imperfect), 139, 434, 457, 475, 490
NjPT	Princeton Theological Seminary, Princeton: 139
NjR	Rutgers—The State University, New Brunswick: 117, 366* (title-page only), 433, 446 (imperfect), 526, 541, 559, 580, 620

Ohio

OC	Public Library of Cincinnati and Hamilton County, Cincinnati: 139, 276, 433, 642
OCM	Cincinnati Masonic Temple, Cincinnati: 60, 347, 420, 517, 541, 573, 618, 631, 649
OCl	Cleveland Public Library: 139, 295, 335, 433
OClW	Case Western Reserve University, Cleveland: 403
OClWHi	Western Reserve Historical Society, Cleveland: 279 (imperfect variant), 295, 348, 526, 573
OFH	Rutherford B. Hayes Library, Fremont: 139
OGraD	Denison University, Granville: 433
OU	Ohio State University, Columbus: 423, 433, 434, 543

Pennsylvania

P	Pennsylvania State Library, Harrisburg: 433, 596*
PBL	Lehigh University, Bethlehem: 117, 170, 475, 638
PBm	Bryn Mawr College, Bryn Mawr: 433
PCC	Crozer Theological Seminary, Chester: 557

PHi   Historical Society of Pennsylvania, Philadelphia: 1*, 28, 34, 55, 117, 118, 120 (imperfect), 170, 219, 220 (imperfect), 223, 227*, *244*, 249*, 251** (imperfect), 252 (imperfect), 255* (imperfect), 256*, 257 (imperfect), 259* (imperfect), 262 (imperfect), 273, 279* (variant), 294, 306, 329 (imperfect), 336 (2 copies, 1 imperfect), 356* (imperfect), 360, *368*, 399, 409, 437, 438*, 460 (imperfect), 467*, 475, 477, *481** (2 copies), 490*, 503, 515*, 538*, 539*, 541, 563* (imperfect), 611*, 640

PMA   Allegheny College, Meadville: 367, 510

PP   Free Library of Philadelphia: 34, 43, *66** (imperfect), 87, 139, 170, 179, 196, 279 (variant), 350 (imperfect), *354*, 382*, 405*, 413, 414, 415 (2 copies), 416 (2 copies), 417*, 418*, 423, 451*, 474*, 478, 497, 532 (imperfect), 541, 579, 640

PPAmP   American Philosophical Society, Philadelphia: 1 (imperfect), 120*, *408*, 435*, 456*

PPB   Philadelphia Bar Association: 265, 289

PPL   Library Company of Philadelphia: *14** (imperfect), *19*, 48 (imperfect), 57, 71, 96*, 101, *110*, 117, *123*, 124 (imperfect), 146, 172, *194*, 204*, 212*, 231, *241** (imperfect), 245*, 247*, 250*, 252*, 253*, 257*, 260*, 261, 262*, *264*, 268* (imperfect), *269* (variant), 271*, 273, 278* (imperfect), 279, *282*, 284*, 290*, 291** (imperfect), *293*, 296*, 297* (imperfect), *299*, 300*, 303*, 306, 308*, 310*, 313*, *315*, 317*, 324*, 329*, 332*, 338*, 361 (imperfect), 383, *395** (imperfect), 399, 403, 433, 443, 446*, 477, 478, 490, 491 (imperfect), 509, 518*, 564*, 574, 582*, 615*, 616, 632*, *633*, 649

PPPFM   Free and Accepted Masons of Pennsylvania, Grand Lodge Library, Philadelphia: 34 (7 copies), 60, 84, *113*, 124 (3 copies), 125, 131*, 206, *216*, 217*, 231, 232, 239 (2 copies, 1 imperfect), 272, 285, 294, 295, 312 (imperfect; 2 imperfect variants), 336 (4 copies), 337, 347 (3 copies), 391, 420, 471 (imperfect), 491, 511 (2 copies), 512, 517, 518 (4 copies, 1 imperfect), 526, 537, 541, 567, 568 (2 copies), 570*, 573 (2 copies), 577 (3 copies), 618 (3 copies), 649 (3 copies)

PPRF   Rosenbach Foundation, Philadelphia: 475

PPi   Carnegie Library of Pittsburgh: 433

PPiU   University of Pittsburgh: 122 (imperfect), 566, 640

PSt   Pennsylvania State University, University Park: *331*, 537, 574*

PU   University of Pennsylvania, Philadelphia: 1, 34, *91*, 139, 172, 182, 272, 294, 367, 433, 434, 477, 499, 512, 541, 580

Rhode Island

RHi   Rhode Island Historical Society, Providence: 29, 64*, 172, 295, 347, 510, 511, 573

RP   Providence Public Library: 272, 295, 334 (imperfect)

RPB   Brown University, Providence: 29 (imperfect), 41, 44, *46**, 55 (imperfect), 58 (imperfect), 64 (imperfect), 72 (2 copies, 1 imperfect), *81**, 84, 97, *107** (imperfect), 108, 117, 118, 122 (2 imperfect copies), 124, 130, *134** (imperfect), 139, 145, 147 (imperfect), 148 (imperfect), *154**, *165** (imperfect), *168**, 171, 172, *180**, *197**, 202 (imperfect), 206, 207 (imperfect), *208**, 212, 219*, *222**, 223, *226**, 233, 239 (imperfect), 242, *243**, 248 (imperfect), 261, *265**, 267, 276, 279 (imperfect variant), *283**, 286, 289, 292*, 294, 295, *298**, 302*, 304, 306, 307, 313, *314**, *327**, *333**, 334, 336, *337**, 341, 343, 344 (imperfect), *361**, *362**, 370, *377** (imperfect), 383, 393, 394, 399, *400**, *411** (imperfect), *412**, 419, 422, 423, 426 (imperfect), 427, 429 (imperfect), 432, 433, 434, 436, *437**, 439, 441, 443, 446, 448, *450**, 455, 457 (imperfect), 458, 460, *461**, 464, 471 (imperfect), *472**, 477, *479** (imperfect), 482, 485, 486, *487**, *488**, 495, 499, 502, 510, 512, 517, 518 (2 copies), *522**, 523 (imperfect), 525 (imperfect), *527**, *532**, *533**, 535, *540**, 547, *548** (imperfect), *550**, 552 (2 copies), 554, *555**, 556 (imperfect), 558, 564, *565**, *571** (imperfect), 573 (2 copies), 580, 583, 585, 586, *587**, *588**, *589**, *590**, *591**, 593, *594**, *610**, 611, 615, *622**, *623**, *624**, *625**, *626**, 629, 635, 642, 649

RPJCB   John Carter Brown Library, Providence: *13** (title-page only), 23, 34, 43, 47*, 65, *70**, 72, 101, 105, 117, 124 (imperfect), 125, 136, 139, 164, 170 (imperfect), 172 (2 copies, 1 imperfect), 182, 206, 314

RPMa   Masonic Temple Library, Providence: 295, 347

South Carolina

ScC   Charleston Library Society: 433, 464

ScU   University of South Carolina, Columbia: 341, 360

Tennessee

THi   Tennessee Historical Society, Nashville: 568

TNJ   Joint University Libraries, Nashville: 640

Texas

TxU   University of Texas, Austin: 172, 307, 519, 572, 632, 633

Virginia

Vi   Virginia State Library, Richmond: 223, 272, 405, 433, 535
ViRVal   Valentine Museum, Richmond: 422
ViU   University of Virginia, Charlottesville: 60 (2 copies, 1 imperfect), *78** (imperfect), 206, *225** (imperfect), 295, 415, 416, 423, 460, 475, 512, *523**, *534**, 535, 552

Vermont

Vt   Vermont State Library, Montpelier: *309** (imperfect), 387, 510, 526
VtBFM   Vermont Grand Lodge Library, F. & A. M., Burlington: 510
VtBennM   Bennington Museum, Bennington: *221*, 321
VtBrt   Brattleboro Public Library: 499
VtHi   Vermont Historical Society, Montpelier: 164, 321, *387**, *402** (imperfect), *483**, 499 (2 copies), 510, 522, 526 (imperfect)
VtMiM   Middlebury College, Middlebury: 139, 499, 510 (2 copies)
VtMiS   Sheldon Art Museum, Middlebury: 510, 526
VtU   University of Vermont and State Agricultural College, Burlington: 499, 510, 526
VtWinds   Windsor Library Association, Windsor: 374

Wisconsin

WHi   State Historical Society of Wisconsin, Madison: 272, 443, 572, 573
WM   Milwaukee Public Library: 573
WMFM   Free and Accepted Masons of Wisconsin, Grand Lodge Library, Milwaukee: 272, 295, 420, 649
WU   University of Wisconsin, Madison: 139

Washington

WaU   University of Washington, Seattle: 139

PRIVATE LIBRARIES

Only unique or exemplar copies are listed

Levy	Lester S. Levy, Pikesville, Maryland: 413*, 414*, 419*
Lowens	Irving Lowens, Reston, Virginia: 279* (variant), 608*

FOREIGN LIBRARIES

Berlin	Gross National-Mutterloge: 518
Glasgow	Euing Collection, University Library: 139
Glasgow	Mitchell (Public) Library: 139
London	British Library: 44, 48, 72, 139, 239, 295, 439, 482, 519, 535, 558, 631
Oxford	Bodleian Library: 4 (imperfect), 53, *114*, 139, 170, 239 (imperfect), 279, 279 (variant), 394, 423 (imperfect), 458 (imperfect), 475, 499, 518, 535 (imperfect), 564, 573

BIBLIOGRAPHIES CITED

Adams   Adams, Sister Regina Mary. 'A Check-List of Connecticut Imprints from 1801 Through 1805.' Unpubl. Master's thesis, Department of Library Science, Catholic University, 1954.

Alagia   Alagia, Damian P. 'A Check-List of Maryland Imprints from 1815 Through 1818.' Unpubl. Master's thesis, Department of Library Science, Catholic University, 1951.

Ault   Ault, Norman. 'Poetical Miscellanies, Song Books, and Verse Collections of Multiple Authorship,' in *The Cambridge Bibliography of English Literature,* ed. F. W. Bateson (New York, 1941), II, 173-260.

Backus   Backus, Edythe N. *Catalogue of Music in the Huntington Library Printed Before 1801.* (Huntington Library Lists, No. 6.) San Marino, 1949.

BAL   Blanck, Jacob, ed. *Bibliography of American Literature.* New Haven, 1955–.

Barthelmess   Barthelmess, Richard. *Bibliographie der Freimaurerei in Amerika.* New York, 1856.

Bieber   Bieber, Albert A. *The Albert A. Bieber Collection of Plays, Poetry and Songsters.* New York, 1923; reprinted New York, 1963.

Bissainthe   Bissainthe, Max. *Dictionnaire de Bibliographie Haitienne.* Washington, 1951.

Brinley   *Catalogue of the American Library of the Late George Brinley.* 5 vols. Hartford, 1878-1897.

Bristol   Bristol, Roger Pattrell. *Maryland Imprints, 1801-1810.* Charlottesville, 1953.

Bristol-Evans   Bristol, Roger P. *Supplement to Charles Evans' American Bibliography.* Charlottesville, 1970.

Bristol Notes   Bristol, Roger P. 'American Bibliographical Notes,' in American Antiquarian Society, *Proceedings,* LXXXIII, 2 (1973).

BUCEM   Schnapper, Edith B., ed. *The British Union-Catalogue of Early Music Printed Before the Year 1801.* 2 vols. London, 1957.

CBEL   Bateson, F. W., ed. *The Cambridge Bibliography of English Literature.* 3 vols. New York, 1941.

Davis Davis, Katharine Norman. 'A Check-List of Richmond, Virginia Imprints from 1781 to 1805.' Unpubl. Master's thesis, Department of Library Science, Catholic University, 1956.

Devine Devine, George John. 'American Songsters 1806-1815.' Unpubl. Master's thesis, Department of English, Brown University, 1940.

Drake Drake, Milton. *Almanacs of the United States.* 2 vols. New York, 1962.

Evans Evans, Charles. *American Bibliography.* 14 vols. Chicago, 1903-34; Worcester, 1956-59.

Filby Filby, P. W., and Edward G. Howard. *Star-Spangled Books.* Maryland, 1972.

Frank Frank, John C. *Early American Poetry, 1610-1810; A List of Works in the New York Public Library.* New York, 1917.

Gibbons Gibbons, Mother Rosaria, O.S.U. 'A Check-List of Delaware Imprints from 1801 Through 1815.' Unpubl. Master's thesis, Department of Library Science, Catholic University, 1956.

Gilman Gilman, M. D. *The Bibliography of Vermont.* Burlington, 1897.

Gilmore Gilmore, Barbara. *A Puritan Town and Its Imprints; Northampton, 1786-1845.* Northampton, 1942.

Hamilton Hamilton, Sinclair. *Early American Book Illustrators and Wood Engravers, 1670-1870.* Princeton, 1958.

Hildeburn Hildeburn, Charles R. *A Century of Printing; The Issues of the Press in Pennsylvania, 1685-1784.* 2 vols. Philadelphia, 1885-86.

Johnson Johnson, H. Earle. *Musical Interludes in Boston, 1795-1830.* New York, 1943.

Kloss Kloss, Georg. *Bibliographie der Freimaurerei und der mit ihr in Verbindung gesetzten geheimen Gesellschaften.* Frankfurt, 1844.

Langhorne Langhorne, Mary Lou. 'A Check List of Richmond, Virginia Imprints from 1806 to 1820.' Unpubl. Master's thesis, Department of Library Science, Catholic University, 1958.

Lewis Lewis, Arthur Ansel. 'American Songsters 1800-1805.' Unpubl. Master's thesis, Department of English, Brown University, 1937.

Loughran Loughran, Clayton D. 'A Checklist of Delaware Imprints from 1816 Through 1835.' Unpubl. Master's thesis, Department of Library Science, Catholic University, 1956.

Lowens Lowens, Irving. 'The American Songster Before 1821: A List of Incomplete and Unlocated Titles,' *Papers of the Bibliographical Society of America,* LIV (1960), 61-69.

McCorison McCorison, Marcus A. *Vermont Imprints 1778-1820.* Worcester, 1963.

McCorison Addenda McCorison, Marcus A. *Additions and Corrections to Vermont. Imprints 1778-1820.* Worcester, 1968.

McMurtrie McMurtrie, Douglas C. *A Check List of Eighteenth Century Albany Imprints.* (New York State Library Bibliography Bulletin, No. 80.) Albany, 1939.

Meacham Meacham, Miriam D. 'A Check List of South Carolina Imprints for the Years 1811-1818.' Unpubl. Master's thesis, Department of Library Science, Catholic University, 1962.

Milnar Milnar, Virginia B. 'A Checklist of Philadelphia Imprints for 1801 and 1802.' Unpubl. Master's thesis, Department of Library Science, Catholic University, 1951.

Minick Minick, Amanda Rachel. *A History of Printing in Maryland, 1791-1800.* Baltimore, 1949.

Molnar Molnar, John W. 'Art Music in Colonial Virginia,' in *Art and Music in the South,* ed. F. B. Simkins (Farmville, Va., 1961).

Morris Morris, Robert. *The History of Freemasonry in Kentucky . . . to which are added . . . an American Masonic Bibliography.* Louisville, 1859.

Neeser Neeser, Robert W. *American Naval Songs and Ballads.* New Haven, 1938.

Nichols Nichols, Charles Lemuel. *Bibliography of Worcester.* 2nd ed. Worcester, 1918.

Noyes Noyes, R. Webb. *A Bibliography of Maine Imprints to 1820.* Stonington, Me., 1930.

Quenzel Quenzel, Carrol H. *Preliminary Checklist for Fredericksburg, 1778-1876.* (Virginia Imprint Series, No. 4.) Richmond, 1947.

Rosenbach	Rosenbach, A. S. W. *Early American Children's Books*. Portland, Me., 1933.
Sabin	Sabin, Joseph. *Bibliotheca Americana*. 29 vols. New York, 1868-1936.
St. Denis	St. Denis, Gaston Pierre. 'Checklist of Providence, Rhode Island Imprints from 1801 Through 1805.' Unpubl. Master's thesis, Department of Library Science, Catholic University, 1952.
Shaw	Shaw, Ralph R., and Richard H. Shoemaker. *American Bibliography, 1801-1819*. 19 vols. New York, 1958-63.
Shipton-Mooney	Shipton, Clifford K., and James E. Mooney. *National Index of American Imprints Through 1800; The Short-Title Evans*. 2 vols. Worcester, 1969.
Shoemaker	Shoemaker, Richard H. *A Checklist of American Imprints for 1820*. New York, 1964.
Sonneck	Sonneck, Oscar G. T. *Bibliography of Early Secular American Music*. Washington, 1905.
Sonneck Copyright	Sonneck, Oscar G. T. 'Copyright Entries to June 1825.' A card file, in Sonneck's hand, in the Music Division, Library of Congress.
Sonneck-Upton	Sonneck, Oscar G. T. *Bibliography of Early Secular American Music (18th Century)*. Rev. and enl. by William Treat Upton. Washington, 1945; reprinted New York, 1964.
Spargo	Spargo, John. *Anthony Haswell; Printer, Patriot, Balladeer*. Rutland, Vt., 1925.
Stark	Stark, Lewis M., and Maud D. Cole. *Checklist of Additions to Evans' American Bibliography in the Rare Book Division of the New York Public Library*. New York, 1960.
Stoddard	Stoddard, Roger E. *A Catalogue of Books and Pamphlets Unrecorded in Oscar Wegelin's Early American Poetry, 1650-1820*. Providence, 1969.
Swem	Swem, Earl G. *A Bibliography of Virginia*. Richmond, 1916.
Thorpe	Thorpe, Alice Louise. 'American Songsters of the 18th Century.' Unpubl. Master's thesis, Department of English, Brown University, 1935.

Turnbull   Turnbull, Robert J. *Bibliography of South Carolina, 1563-1950.* 6 vols. Charlottesville, 1956.

Webb   Webb, Erna Mae. 'A Check-List of Maryland Imprints from 1811 Through 1814.' Unpubl. Master's thesis, Department of Library Science, Catholic University, 1954.

Weiss   Weiss, Harry B. *A Catalogue of the Chapbooks in the New York Public Library.* New York, 1936.

Welch   Welch, d'Alté A. *A Bibliography of American Children's Books Printed Prior to 1821.* Worcester, 1972.

Whitty   Whitty, J. H. *A Record of Virginia Copyright Entries (1790-1844).* Richmond, 1911.

Wolfe   Wolfe, Richard J. *Secular Music in America, 1801-1825: A Bibliography.* 3 vols. New York, 1964.

Wolfstieg   Wolfstieg, August. *Bibliographie der Freimaurerischen Literatur.* 2 vols. 2nd ed. Leipzig, 1923.

Woodall   Woodall, Nancy Carboy. 'A Check List of New Haven, Connecticut Imprints for the Years 1817-1819.' Unpubl. Master's thesis, Department of Library Science, Catholic University, 1960.

A Bibliography of
Songsters Printed in America
Before 1821

1 THE | CONSTITUTIONS | OF THE | FREE-MASONS. | Containing the | history, charges, regulations, &c. | of that most ancient and right | worshipful fraternity. | For the use of the Lodges. | London printed; Anno 5723. | Re-printed in Philadelphia by special order, for the use | of the brethren in North-America. | In the year of Masonry 5734, Anno Domini 1734.

94 p. [1:] title-page; [2:] blank; [3]-[6:] dedication; 7-82: text; 83-94: songs.

Barthelmess p. 5-6, Evans 3744, Morris p. 5 ¶ CSmH, DSC, IaCrM, MBFM, NNFM, PHi*, PPAmP (imperfect), PU ¶ The printer was Benjamin Franklin. Contains 5 Masonic songs. Facsimile editions were published in 1855 by W. Leonard & Co., New York, in 1906 by the Grand Lodge of Pennsylvania, and in 1924 by the Masonic Service Association of Washington, D.C. The PU copy includes 27 pages of manuscript tunes for the Masonic songs.

2 [THE CONSTITUTIONS OF THE FREE-MASONS. Boston, Fleet, 1750.]

Evans 6454 ¶ No copy located ¶ Advertised 5 Feb. 1750 in the *Boston Evening-Post* "to be sold by the publisher of this paper." According to Evans, the book contains 94 p.

3 [THE SONGS OF ROBIN HOOD. New York: printed by James Parker. 1750.]

Evans 6613, Lowens U1 ¶ No copy located ¶ Advertised 5 Nov. 1750 in the New York *Gazette* as "just reprinted, and to be sold by the printer hereof, 10d. or cheaper by the dozen; all the 24 songs of the famous English archer, bold Robin Hood." *Later editions:* 66, 190, 196, 405.

4 THE | AMERICAN MOCK BIRD: | containing a new | collection | of the most | favourite songs | now in vogue. | New-York: | printed for James Rivington, and sold at his | warehouse in Philadelphia. MDCCLX.

[xii], 276 p. [i:] title-page; [ii:] blank; [iii]-[xii:] index; 1-276: songs.

Evans 8528, Sabin 1150, Sonneck-Upton p. 16 ¶ N*; Oxford (Bodleian Library) (imperfect) ¶ Contains 336 songs, all indexed. This is apparently a reprint of some unidentified English songster with a new title-page. The press work is so excellent that it makes one suspect that

the sheets may have been printed for Rivington in England. See 6 for
what may perhaps be a later edition, as well as 5 and 7 for related titles.
Despite the similarity in name, 12 is a different, unrelated songster.

1761

5 [THE MOCK BIRD; or new American songster: being a collection
    of all the newest and most approved songs. Designed for the enter-
tainment of the ladies and gentlemen of New-York, and other parts of
North-America. New York: sold by A. Thorne, next door to the Green-
Dragon, near the Moravian Meeting-House, 1761.]
    Lowens U2 ¶ No copy located ¶ Advertised 19 Mar. 1761 in the New
York *Gazette* as "just published, neatly printed on fine paper, and to
be sold by A. Thorne, next door to the Green-Dragon, near the Moravian Meeting-House, in New York." Possibly related to 4, 6, 7, or 12.

6 [THE NEW AMERICAN MOCK-BIRD. A collection of the best
    songs on different subjects. New-York: printed by Hugh Gaine,
1761.]
    Evans 8940, Ford I, 107, Lowens U3, Sabin 1150, Sonneck-Upton
p. 16 ¶ No copy located ¶ According to Ford, advertised 1762 in the
New York *Mercury,* No. 450, as "a collection of the most favorite songs
now in vogue." Sabin dates this imprint 1760. Possibly related to 4, 5,
7, or 12.

7 [A SONG BOOK which contains all the new songs that have been
    published in England to this time. New York: James Rivington,
1761.]
    Lowens U4, Sonneck-Upton p. 397 ¶ No copy located ¶ Advertised
16 Mar. 1761 in the New York *Mercury* as "this day published" by
James Rivington. Possibly identical with 4; possibly related to 5, 6,
or 12.

1762

8 [JEMMY CARSON'S COLLECTION. Philadelphia: printed by
    Andrew Steuart, 1762.]
    Evans 9083, Lowens U5, Sonneck-Upton p. 76, 216 ¶ No copy located
¶ Advertised 2 Dec. 1762 in the Philadelphia *Pennsylvania Gazette.*
A Dublin, 1744 edition is described on the title-page as "being a revival
of his own labours and lucubrations for thirty years past; with pieces
upon different subjects by several hands." Cf. Ault p. 240 for a Dublin,
1787 edition.

9 [A LITTLE PRETTY POCKET-BOOK, intended for the instruc-
    tion and amusement of little Master Tommy, and pretty Miss Polly.

With two letters from Jack the Giant-Killer. New-York: printed by Hugh Gaine, 1762.]

Evans 9159, Welch 778.1 ¶ No copy located ¶ Advertised 1762 in the New York *Mercury*. *Later editions:* 39, 43.

1763

10 [CLIO AND EUTERPE, a collection of celebrated songs and cantatas, set to musick by the most approved masters. With thorough bass for the harpsichord, and transposition for the German flute; containing near 600 airs. New York: J. Rivington, 1763.]

Sonneck p. 26 ¶ No copy located ¶ Advertised Oct. 1763 in *Rivington's New-York Gazette*. Probably refers to *Clio and Euterpe, or British harmony*, "a collection of celebrated songs and cantatas by the most approved masters, with the thorough bass for the harpsichord and transposition for the German flute," published 1758-62 in three volumes by Roberts in London. An American reprint is doubtful.

1764

11 [THE AMERICAN COCK ROBIN: or, a choice collection of English songs, both old and new, being such as are generally esteemed, and agreeable to the North-American taste. New-York: printed and sold by John Holt, at the Exchange. 1764.]

Evans 9569, Lowens U6, Sonneck-Upton p. 15 ¶ No copy located ¶ According to the annotated Evans at MWA, this entry was constructed from an advertisement. I have been unable to trace any pertinent advertisement in the New York newspapers for the year 1764.

12 THE | AMERICAN | MOCK-BIRD, | or | songster's delight: | being | a choice collection of entire new songs, as they are | now sung by the best singers at all the publick places | of diversion in England. | New-York: | printed by S. Brown, and sold by Garrat Noel, book- | seller, next door to the Merchant's Coffee-House, 1764.

216, viii p. [1:] title-page; [2:] blank; 3-216: songs; [i]-viii: index. Bristol-Evans B2453, Shipton-Mooney 41428 ¶ Ct, MWA* ¶ Contains 270 songs (266 indexed). A songster unrelated to 4 despite the similar title, but possibly related to 5, 6, and 7. Probably also a reprint of an unidentified English songster.

13 THE | WANDERING YOUNG GENTLEWOMAN: | or | Catskin's | garland, | in five parts. | To which is addded [sic], | Nancy Dawson. | Printed by Andrew Steuart, in Second- | Street, 1764.

Bristol-Evans B2536, Shipton-Mooney 40505 ¶ RPJCB* (photostat of title-page only) ¶ Thomas R. Adams, librarian of the John Carter Brown Library, advises that the location of the original from which their photostat of the title-page was taken is unknown. It would appear to be an 8-page chapbook; it is doubtful that it contained more than 2 songs.

1765

14 [THE WOOD-LARK:] | A choice collection | of the | newest and
   most favourite | English songs, | which have been | set to musick and sung at | the public theatres and gardens. | London, printed, | Philadelphia: | re-printed by William Bradford, at the London | Coffee-House.

1 p.l., ii, xiv, 190, 194 p. [i:] title-page; [ii:] blank; i-ii: dedication; [i]-xiv: index; [1]-190: The wood-lark, Part I; [1]-194: The wood-lark, Part II.

Bristol-Evans B2635, Lowens U7, Shipton-Mooney 41600, Sonneck-Upton p. 476 ¶ PPL* (imperfect) ¶ Contains 373 songs (all indexed), 189 in Part I and 184 in Part II. The only known copy lacks (in Part I) pp. 7-10, 95-96, 157-158, 161-180, 185-186, and (in Part II) pp. 145-146, 151-152, 163-166; the title-page and (in Part I) pp. 155-156 are mutilated, with the actual title missing and supplied from the caption-titles to Parts I and II. The item was advertised 13 July 1769 in the Philadelphia *Pennsylvania Gazette* by "William Woodhouse, bookbinder and stationer in Front-Street near Chesnut-Street and partly opposite Mr. John Bayly, goldsmith, Philadelphia, where merchants, shopkeepers and others may be furnished with . . . Wood lark and Black bird song books." No English songster by this title is known. However, *The wood-lark* does follow, almost exactly, the undated, ca. 1761 edition of *The bull-finch* "printed for R. Baldwin and J. Wilkie, in Paternoster Row." PPL dates this copy 1765, which is undoubtedly closer to the actual date of issue than the Woodhouse advertisement. There is a possibility that the songster may have been brought out by Bradford as early as 1762, but this does not seem likely.

1767

15 [THE MASQUE, a new song book. New-York: sold by Garrat
   Noel, 1767.]
   Evans 10674, Lowens U8, Sonneck p. 87, Sonneck-Upton p. 254 ¶ No copy located ¶ Advertised 30 July 1767 in the New York *Journal* as "this day published;" also advertised 15 June 1767 in the Boston *Gazette* as "just imported and to be sold by John Mein, at the London Bookstore" in a list of books which includes the following English songsters: *The warbler's delight* (cf. Ault p. 225), *The buck's delight* (cf. Ault p. 222), *The Brent* (cf. Ault p. 223), and *Frank Hammond's*

songs, or every buck and choice spirit's companion (not in Ault); also advertised 25 Sept. 1767 in the New London *Gazette* by Mein as above. A copy of the 1767 English edition is in Oxford (Bodleian Library); the 2nd edition (dated 1768) is in the British Library; later English editions were issued in 1769, 1770, 1777, and 1780 (cf. Ault pp. 224, 225, 226, 227, 232, and 244). This may well be a ghost-title—it is quite possible that no American edition was published.

1768

16 THE FAMOUS | TOMMY THUMB'S | LITTLE STORY-BOOK: | containing | his life and surprising adventures; | to which are added, | Tommy Thumb's fables, with morals | and, at the end, pretty stories, that | may be sung or told. | (Adorned with many curious pictures.) | Boston: printed and sold by W. | M'Alpine in Marlborough-Street, 1768.

  32 p. [1:] blank; [2:] frontispiece; [3:] title-page; 4-32: text.
  Bristol-Evans B2872, Shipton-Mooney 41890, Welch 1320.1 ¶ NjP* (imperfect) ¶ The only known copy lacks pp. 23-26, 31-32. Contains at least 4 juvenile songs. *Later editions:* 17, 21.

17 [THE FAMOUS TOMMY THUMB'S LITTLE STORY-BOOK: containing his life and surprising adventures; to which are added his fables, morals, pretty stories, and songs. Adorned with very curious plates. Price two coppers. Boston: Mein & Fleeming, 1768.]

  Welch 1320.2 ¶ No copy located ¶ Advertised 29 Aug. 1768 in the *Boston Chronicle* by John Mein; also advertised "to be had of John Mein at the London Book-Store" in *The renowned history of Giles Gingerbread* (Shipton-Mooney 41870). See 16 for a list of editions.

1769

18 [BLACK BIRD SONGBOOK. Philadelphia: sold by William Woodhouse, book-binder and stationer in Front-Street, near Chesnut-Street, 1769.]

  Bristol-Evans B2976, Lowens U9, Shipton-Mooney 41914, Sonneck-Upton p. 43 ¶ No copy located ¶ Advertised 13 July 1769 in the Philadelphia *Pennsylvania Gazette* by "William Woodhouse, book-binder and stationer in Front-Street, near Chesnut-Street . . . where merchants, shopkeepers and others may be furnished with . . . Wood lark and Black bird song books. Oxford (Bodleian Library) owns a copy of an Edinburgh, 1764 edition and there is a copy of the 3rd (1771) edition in London (British Library). Cf. Ault p. 222. Existence doubtful.

19 SECHS NEUE | POLITISCHE LIEDER, | Des erste: | Trau, schau, wem du thust ver- | trauen &c. | Das zweyte: | Ach wo soll

ich mich hin wenden, | Das dritte: | Es war ein junger Knab, | Das vierte: | Ach Gott, wem soll ichs klagen, | Das fünfte: | So gehts jetzt in der Welt, | Das sechste: | Es sterben zwey Brüder in einem | tag, | Gedruckt 1769.

[8] p. [1:] title-page; [2]-[8:] songs.

Bristol-Evans B3078, Shipton-Mooney 42003 ¶ PPL* ¶ Contains 6 songs in German, all listed on the title-page.

20 WILLIAM CROTTY. | To which are added, | Five other new songs, | viz. | I. The longing maid. | II. The lillies [sic] of France. | III. Kitty Fell. | IV. The genius of Britain, [sic] | V. The distressed soul. | Printed and sold by Andrew Steuart | in Second-Street.

8 p. [1:] title-page; 2-8: songs.

Bristol-Evans B2105, Hamilton 51a, Shipton-Mooney 41106 ¶ NjP* ¶ Contains 6 songs, all named on the title-page. Published no later than 1769, when Steuart's name disappears from the Philadelphia directories; may perhaps be earlier. According to Hamilton, Steuart imported chapbooks from Ireland and apparently reprinted those which sold out rapidly. This one gives every evidence that it is an American production, however, and it is of unusual interest because it contains two examples of what might be considered songs with clear sexual implications, something rarely found on this side of the Atlantic.

1771

21 THE FAMOUS | TOMMY THUMB'S | LITTLE STORY-BOOK: | containing | his life and surprising adventures. | To which are added, | Tommy Thumb's fables, with morals: | and, at the end, pretty stories, that | may be sung or told. | Adorned with many curious pictures. | Printed and sold at the printing-office.

32 p. [1:] blank; [2:] frontispiece; [3:] title-page; 4-32: text.

Evans 12040, Welch 1320.3 ¶ MB (copy not seen) ¶ Contains 9 juvenile songs. See 16 for a list of editions. According to Welch, the book was printed in Boston by John Boyle in Marlborough Street in 1771.

22 [THE NEW SONG BOOK being Miss Ashmore's favourite collection of songs, as sung in the theatres and public gardens in London and Dublin. To which are prefix'd the songs of The padlock, Lionel and Clarissa, and many other opera songs, never before published. Containing in the whole, near three hundred: in which are many originals, and a variety of other songs, by different composers, which upon comparing, will be justly allowed (by every person) to be the best of the kind yet published, and may well be termed "the beauties

of all the songs selected." Boston: reprinted and sold by William M'Alpine, in Marlborough-Street, 1771.]

Evans 11969, Lowens U10, Sonneck p. 101-02, Sonneck-Upton p. 263 ¶ No copy located ¶ Evans remarks that the item is a 24mo and contains a portrait. Advertised 25 Nov. 1771 in the Boston *Evening Post* as "just published and to be sold by William M'Alpine, in Marlborough-Street." Also advertised 5 Dec. 1771 in the Boston *Massachusetts Gazette,* with the statement that "the above mentioned book makes a neat small pocket volume, adorn'd with an elegant frontispiece of Miss Ashmore, and will be sold by the publisher at the same price they are sold for in Britain or Ireland." The title of the songster is given as "The new song book: being Miss Ashmore's favourite collection of songs, as sung . . ." A sketch of Miss Ashmore, who was better known as Mrs. Sparks, appears in Robert Hitchcock, *An Historical View of the Irish Stage,* 2 vols. (Dublin, 1788-94), II, 144-145, 168, 207-208. Miss Ashmore became Mrs. Sparks in the spring of 1772. No English or Irish editions of this work are known. *Later edition:* 26.

1772

23 A | CANDID DISQUISITION | of the | principles and practices | of the most | antient and honourable society of | Free and Accepted Masons; | together with | some strictures on the origin, | nature, and design of that in- | stitution. | Dedicated, by permission, | to the most noble and worshipful | Henry Duke of Beaufort, &c. &c. | Grand Master. | By Wellins Calcott, P. M. | —Ab ipso | ducit opes animumque ferro. Hor. Od. | London; printed: | reprinted and sold by Brother William | M'Alpine, in Marlborough-Street, | Boston. | A. L. 5772. A. D. 1772.

2 p.l., xiv, [2], 256 p. [i:] title-page; [ii:] blank; [iii]-[iv:] dedication; [i]-xiii: list of subscribers; [xiv:] additional subscribers; [xv]-[xvi:] Lodges held in the town of Boston; [1]-13: introduction; [14:] blank; [15]-219: text; [220]-227: Solomon's temple: an oratorio; [228]-255: some of the usual Free-Masons songs; 256: a translation of the Latin.

Barthelmess p. 12, Brinley 6709, Evans 12345, Morris p. 11 ¶ CtY, DLC*, DSC (imperfect), IaCrM, MB, MBFM, MHi, MWA, N, NN, NNFM, RPJCB ¶ Contains 19 Masonic songs. The MB copy is especially interesting, as it is dated 1772 by Epes Sargent, Jr. and includes two additional Masonic songs in his handwriting.

24 [THE STORER, or the American syren: being a collection of the newest and most approved songs. Williamsburg: printed by William Rind, and sold by Edward Cumins, at the new printing-office. 1772.]

No copy located ¶ Advertised 3 Dec. 1772 as "just published" by William Rind in the Williamsburg *Virginia Gazette.* Evans 13032,

Sabin 92226, and Sonneck-Upton p. 410 all cite the title incorrectly as
The storm and give 1773 as the year of publication. According to John
W. Molnar, "Art Music in Colonial Virginia" in *Art and Music in
the South* (Farmville, Va., 1961), pp. 89-90, "unquestionably the volume
must have been named in honor of Maria Storer of the Hallam-
Douglass Company . . . and patterned after a similar collection titled
The Brent, or English Syren. . . . The Brent was offered for sale in
Williamsburg in 1768."

1773

The storm, or the American syren: being a collection of the newest
and most approved songs. Williamsburg: printed by William Rind,
and sold by Edward Cumins, at the new printing-office, 1773.
    Evans 13032, Lowens U11, Sabin 92226, Sonneck-Upton p. 410. Ap-
parently a ghost-title for 24, based on a misread Williamsburg *Virginia
Gazette* advertisement dated 11 Feb. 1773.

1774

25 [AMERICAN ROBIN. A collection of new songs. New-York:
    Hodge and Shober, at the newest printing-office, in Maiden-Lane,
near the head of the Fly-Market, 1774.]
    Evans 13111, Lowens U12, Sonneck p. 10, Sonneck-Upton p. 20 ¶
No copy located ¶ Advertised 30 Dec. 1773 in the New York *Gazette*
as "just published and to be sold by Hodge and Shober, at the newest
printing-office, in Maiden-Lane, near the head of the Fly-Market, The
American robin, a collection of new songs. 1774." Note the 1774 imprint despite the 1773 newspaper date.

26 [MISS ASHMORE'S CHOICE COLLECTION of songs, such as
    are sung at the theatres and public gardens in London and Dublin.
To which are prefix'd the songs of The padlock, Lionel and Clarissa,
and many other opera songs, never before published. Containing in
the whole, near three hundred: in which are many originals, and a
variety of other songs, by different composers, which upon comparing,
will be justly allowed (by every person) to be the best of the kind yet
published, and may well be termed "the beauties of all the songs
selected." New-York: published and sold at Mr. William Bailey's store,
in Beaver-Street. 1774.]
    Evans 13124; Lowens U13, Sonneck p. 102, Sonneck-Upton p. 253
¶ No copy located ¶ Advertised 22 Aug. 1774 in the New York *Mercury*
as "just published and to be sold at Mr. William Bailey's store, in
Beaver-Street." This may be perhaps merely a bookseller's advertisement for 22, but the lapse of three years is somewhat long for a "just

published" notice, even for those days. As late as 20 Aug. 1784, the Baltimore *Maryland Journal* carried an advertisement for various books "to be had at William Murphy's book store and circulating library, Market-Street" which included this songster among others. See 22 for an earlier edition.

1777

27 [SONGS, COMIC, satyrical, and sentimental. By George Alexander
 Stevens. Philadelphia: printed and sold by Robert Bell, next door
to St. Paul's Church in Third-Street. M,DCC,LXXVII.]
 Evans 15603, Lowens U14, Sabin 91502, Sonneck-Upton p. 339 ¶ No copy located ¶ Advertised 26 Nov. 1777 in the Philadelphia *Pennsylvania Ledger;* also 11 Dec. 1777 in the Philadelphia *Pennsylvania Evening Post* as "just published, and now selling at Bell's book store next door to St. Paul's Church in Third-Street, Philadelphia, (the fine paper price two dollars and the common paper one dollar and a half): Songs, comic, satyrical, and sentimental. By George Alexander Stevens. For neither pedant nor for prude, these sonnets took their birth, But are dish'd up, as pleasant food, For sons of social mirth—prologue to the songs. This author being acknowledged to be the greatest master of the sing-song art in Europe, must be very acceptable to all who delight in this kind of sentimental entertainment." For English and Irish editions beginning in 1772, see CBEL II, 328. This edition is perhaps identical to 28, q.v. *Later editions:* 28, 238.

1778

28 SONGS, | COMIC, | satyrical, | and | sentimental. | By | George Al-
 exander Stevens. | I love fun!—Keep it up! | Lecture upon heads. |
Philadelphia: | printed by R. Bell, Third-Street. | M.DCC.LXXVIII.
 12, 252 p. [1:] title-page; [2:] blank; [3:] advertisement; [4]-5: the history of choice spirits and ballad-singing; [6]-9: description and inscription for poculum poculorum; [10:] blank; [11]-12: prologue to Steven's [sic] songs; [1]-247: songs; 248-252: index.
 Sabin 91503, Sonneck-Upton p. 399 ¶ MH, NHi*, PHi ¶ Contains 135 songs (133 indexed) by Stevens. See 27 for a possible earlier edition.

1779

A choice collection of Free Masons songs. To which is added Solomon's temple, an oratorio. Providence, printed by John Carter, at the printing office at Shakespear's Head. 1779.
 Evans 16222, Sonneck-Upton p. 76. Apparently a ghost-title for 29, based on a 5 June 1779 advertisement in the Providence *Gazette*.

29 A CHOICE | COLLECTION | of | Masons [sic] songs. | To which
is added, | Solomon's temple, | an | oratorio, | as performed at the |
Philharmonic-Room, in Dublin, | for the benefit of sick and distressed |
Free-Masons. | Providence: | printed and sold by Brother John Carter.
| A. L. 5779. A. D. 1779.

40, [1] p. [1:] title-page; [2:] blank; [3]-33: songs; [34]-40:
Solomon's temple; [41:] index.

Evans 16222, Morris p. 103 ¶ MBFM (2 copies, both imperfect),
MHi*, RHi, RPB (imperfect) ¶ Contains 24 Masonic songs. May also
have been issued without the index; the RPB and both MBFM copies
are deficient in this leaf.

30 [LOYAL AND HUMOROUS SONGS. New York: H. Gaine,
1779.]

76+ p. [1]-[16:] lacking; 17-52: songs; 53-55; loyal constitutional
toasts and sentiments; [56:] blank; 57-59: copy of a letter from E———
H——d, of London, in the year 1770, to the Reverend Doctor Rogers,
of New-York; 60-76: new and old compositions, by favour of respectable subscribers.

Evans 16326, Lowens U15, Sonneck p. 83, Sonneck-Upton p. 240 ¶
MWA* (imperfect) ¶ Contains at least 43 songs. Unfortunately, the
only known copy of this Loyalist songster is merely a fragment, lacking all before p. 17 and all after p. 76. It was advertised 11 Oct. 1779
in the New York *Gazette and Weekly Mercury* as "this day, will be
published, variety of loyal and humorous songs, on recent occasions:
birth and coronation odes, poems, serious and sarcastical, martial airs
and choruses, constitutional toasts and sentiments, calculated to pro-
mote loyalty and unanimity, by a Briton in New-York; with a copy
of a letter from E——— H—— in London to Dr. Rogers in New-York
1770, declaring them the mischief brewing, how some divines con-
template ruin. To which is added, several favourite old songs, with
some new ones, by respectable subscribers, concluding with a cantata,
called *The procession,* with *The standard of faction,* containing reci-ta-
tives, airs, and songs, characterizing the most violent persecutors of
the New-York loyalists. The copies already subscribed for will be
delivered as soon after publication as possible."

31 SONGS, | NAVAL | and | military. | But when our country's cause
provokes to arms, | How martial music every bosom warms. | Pope.
| New-York: printed by James Rivington. | M,DCC,LXXIX.

1 p.l., xi, [1], 128 p. [i:] title-page; [ii:] blank; [i]-xi: preface; [xii:]
blank; [1]-128: songs.

Evans 16530, Sabin 86929, Sonneck p. 142, Sonneck-Upton p. 400 ¶
MiU-C* ¶ Contains 105 songs, all in praise of British arms. Advertised
6 Mar. 1779 in *Rivington's Royal Gazette* (New York) as "in a few

days will be published, in a pocket volume;" advertised 21 April 1779 as "published."

1780

32 [A NEW AND SELECT COLLECTION of the best English, Scots and Irish songs, catches, duets, and cantatas, in the true spirit and taste of the three different nations—being an attempt to improve upon others in the true spirit of social mirth and good fellowship—with a collection of the various sentiments and hob-nobs in vogue. New-York: printed and sold by James Rivington, 1780.]

Evans 16874, Lowens U16, Sonneck p. 99, Sonneck-Upton pp. 76-77 ¶ No copy located ¶ Advertised 17 June 1780 in *Rivington's Royal Gazette* (New York), as "this day published. . . . Price of these 354 songs, neatly bound in red, only one dollar. To be had of the printer." The complete advertisement (taken from the 24 June 1780 issue of the newspaper) is transcribed as item No. 1242 in Gottesman.

1782

Fratrimonium excelsum. A new Ahiman Rezon: or, a help to a brother. With an elegant copper-plate frontispiece. Shewing, the excellency of secrecy; and the first cause of the institution of Free-Masonry; the principles of the craft, and the benefits arising from a strict observance thereof; the sort of men that ought to be initiated into the mystery, and the kind of Masons that are fit to govern Lodges, with their proper behaviour in and out of the Lodge. The ancient manner of constituting new Lodges, with all the charges, &c. Likewise, the prayers used in Jewish and Christian Lodges. Also, the old and new regulations, the manner of choosing and installing Grand-Master and Officers, &c. To which is added, a large collection of new Masons songs, entertaining prologues and epilogues, and Solomon's temple: an oratorio. With a list of all the Masters and Wardens of the different Lodges in Dublin. By a worthy brother. Dublin: printed for all the Lodges in England, Ireland and America, and sold by Thomas Wilkinson, bookseller, No. 40, Winetavern-Street.

1 p.l., xxiv, 203, [1] p.

PPPFM* (lacks frontispiece) ¶ Although 1770 is given as the publication date in the only located copy, it is clear that this particular edition cannot have been published before 1782 since a note appended to a song on p. 187 reads: "N.B. The music published in Walker's Magazine for February, 1782." This Masonic songster, containing 81 songs and naming many tunes, appears to have been used in America even though it was not published here.

13

33 [THE FREE MASONS POCKET BOOK, being a curious col-
    lection of original Masonic songs, never before published, calculated
for all the degrees of Masonry. To which is added a toast applicable
to each song. Humbly dedicated to the brethren in general. Sit lux,
et lux fuit. New-York: printed and sold by Lewis and Horner, No. 17,
Hanover-Square. 1782.]

Evans 17537, Lowens U17, Sonneck p. 54, Sonneck-Upton p. 147 ¶
No copy located ¶ Advertised 11 May 1782 through 3 July 1782 in
Rivington's Royal Gazette (New York) as "just published by Lewis
and Horner. . . . This collection is by far the greatest masterpiece of
anything of this kind hitherto attempted. The songs adopted to the
different offices, are inimitably and truly sublime. To be had of the
printer."

1783

34 AHIMAN REZON | abridged and digested: | as a | help to all that
    are, or would be | Free and Accepted Masons. | To which is added, |
a sermon, | preached in Christ-Church, Philadelphia, | at a general com-
munication, | celebrated, agreeable to the constitutions, on | Monday,
December 28, 1778, as the anniver- | sary of St. John the Evangelist. |
Published by order of | the Grand Lodge of Pennsylvania, | by William
Smith, D. D. | Philadelphia: | printed by Hall and Sellers. | M,DCC,
LXXXIII.

1 p.l., xvi, 166 p. [i:] blank; [ii:] frontispiece; [i:] title-page; [ii:]
endorsement, dated 22 Nov. 1781; [iii:] dedication to George Washington, dated 24 June 1782; [iv]-v: contents; [vi]-xvi: preface; [1]-11: a
letter of the celebrated philosopher John Locke; 12: glossary; [13]-
114: text; [115]-144: a collection of Masons songs; [145:] second title-
page: A | sermon | preached in Christ-Church, Philadelphia, | [for the
benefit of the poor] | by appointment of and before | the general com-
munication | of | Free and Accepted Masons | of the | state of Pennsyl-
vania, | on Monday, December 28, 1778. | Celebrated, agreeable to their
constitution, | as the anniversary of | St. John the Evangelist. | By Wil-
liam Smith, D. D. | provost of the College and Academy of Philadel-
phia. | Philadelphia: re-printed by Hall and Sellers. | MDCCLXXXIII;
[146:] endorsement, dated Philadelphia 29 Dec. 1778; [147:] dedication,
to George Washington; [148:] blank; [149]-166: text.

Barthelmess p. 6, Brinley 6697, Evans 17915, Hildeburn 4267, Morris
p. 15 ¶ DLC*, MWA, NHi, PHi, PP, PPPFM (7), PU, RPJCB ¶ Contains 15 Masonic songs. The RPJCB copy, formerly the property of
George Washington, appears to be extra-illustrated with plates added
between pp. 144-[145] and [148]-[149]. "Bro. Sellers informed that
2,000 books were printed, 1,000 of which were ordered to be neatly
bound." *Minutes,* Grand Lodge, 24 June 1783, I, 62.

35 [THE VOCAL MAGAZINE of new songs, containing English, Scotch and Irish songs, catches, glees, cantatas, airs and ballads, as are deemed most worthy of preservation, 2 vols. One dollar. For sale at Bell's book store, near St. Paul's Church, Third-Street, Philadelphia. 1783.]

Bristol-Evans B5842, Lowens U18, Shipton-Mooney 44490, Sonneck-Upton p. 445 ¶ No copy located ¶ Advertised 1 Oct. 1783 in the Philadelphia *Pennsylvania Gazette* as item 11 in a list of "New publications, now for sale, at Bell's book store, near St. Paul's Church, in Third-Street." This is probably *The vocal magazine, or compleat British songster*, Nos. 1-9 of which were published in London in 1781; an American edition is doubtful. Cf. Ault pp. 233, 234, 235.

La vraie maçonnerie d'adoption; précédée de quelques réflexions sur les loges irrégulières & sur la société civile, avec des notes critiques & philosophiques: et suivie de cantiques maçonniques. Dédiée aux dames. Par un chevalier de tous les ordres maçonniques. A Philadelphie, chez Philarethe, rue de l'Equerre, à l'A-Plomb. M.DCC.LXXXIII.

142, [2] p.

DLC, MWA* ¶ Contains 24 songs written by Guillemain de St. Victor. A fictitious imprint, probably printed in Paris.

1785

36 THE | FREE-MASON'S | POCKET COMPANION, | or | elements | of | Free-Masonry | delineated. | Friendship, on wings etherial, flying round, | Here stretch'd her arm, to bless the hallow'd ground; | Humanity, well pleas'd, here takes her stand, | Holding her daughter Pity in her hand: | Here Charity, which sooths [sic] the widow's sigh, | And wipes the dew-drop from the orphan's eye: | Here stands Benevolence, whose large embrace, | Uncircumscrib'd, takes in the human race; | She sees each narrow tie—each private end, | Indignant, Virtue's universal friend: | Scorning each frantic zealot, bigot, fool, | She stamps on Masons [sic] breasts her golden rule. | New-York: | printed by S. Loudon, printer to the State. | (Under the direction of a Brother.) | M,DCC,LXXXV.

1 p.l., [ix]-xii, 96 p. [i:] title-page; [ii:] blank; [ix]-xii: general objections against Free-Masonry, answered; [1]-65: text; 65-71: anthems and odes; 72-80: songs; 81-95: preludes, prologues, and epilogues; 95-96: contents.

DSC* ¶ Contains 17 Masonic songs. *Later edition:* 84.

37 [caption-title:] LIBERTY SONGS. | I. Liberty tree. | II. The battle of the kegs. | III. Burgoyne's defeat. | IV. On General Wayne's taking | Stony Point. | To which is added the noted song | called Roslin Castle.

8 p. [1:] caption-title; [1]-8: songs.

Sonneck-Upton p. 228 ¶ DLC* ¶ Contains 5 songs, all named in the caption-title.

38 [MOTHER GOOSE'S MELODY; or sonnets for the cradle. In two parts. Part 1st. contains the most celebrated songs and lullabies of the old British nurses, calculated to amuse children and to excite them to sleep. Part 2d, those of that sweet songster and nurse of wit and humour, Master William Shakespeare. Embellished with cuts, and illustrated with notes and maxims, historical, philosophical, and critical. The first Worcester edition. Worcester (Massachusetts) printed by Isaiah Thomas, and sold at his bookstore. MDCCLXXXV.]

94, [2] p. [i:] blank; [ii:] frontispiece; [iii:] title-page; [iv:] blank; [v]-x: preface; [11]-73: Mother Goose's melody; [74:] blank; [75:] half-title: Mother Goose's | melody. | Part II. | Containing the | lullabies of Shakespear [sic]; 76-94: Shakespeare's songs; [95]-[96:] advertisement for Thomas.

Evans 19105, Lowens U19, Sonneck-Upton 269, Welch 905.1 ¶ MWA* (imperfect) ¶ The only copy known is badly mutilated, lacking all before p. 13 and after p. 86; all leaves from pp. 13-86 partly lacking. The title-page is a reconstruction by Welch based on 87 and a 1786 advertisement in *The Wisdom of Crop the Conjuror* (Evans 20153). Contains 68 songs, all juvenile except for 16 by Shakespeare. *Later editions:* 87, 175, 198, 277, 424, 445.

1786

A collection of songs, designed for entertainment and edification. Boston: printed and sold by E. Russell, next Dr. Haskins, near Liberty-Pole. M,DCC,LXXXVI.

32 p.

MB* ¶ Not a songster. Contains 11 sacred songs.

39 [A LITTLE PRETTY POCKET-BOOK, intended for the instruction and amusement of little Master Tommy and pretty Miss Polly; with two letters from Jack the giant killer. As also a ball and pincushion; the use of which will infallibly make Tommy a good boy and Polly a good girl. To which is added a little song book, being a new attempt to teach children the use of the English alphabet by way of diversion. Philadelphia: printed and sold by W. Spotswood, Front-Street, between Market and Chesnut-Street. 1786.]

Evans 19759, Lowens U20 ¶ No copy located ¶ Advertised 12 July 1786 in the Philadelphia *Pennsylvania Herald* in a list of "books for the instruction and amusement of children, sold by W. Spotswood, printer and bookseller, Front-Street, between Market and Chesnut-

Street . . . price 9 pence." Perhaps an importation of the John Newbery imprint, which reached its 9th edition in 1760. Cf. CBEL II, 561. See 9 for a complete list of editions.

40 LITTLE | ROBIN RED BREAST; | a | collection | of pretty | songs, | for the instruction and | amusement of | children : | entirely new. | The first Worcester edition. | Worcester, (Massachusetts) | printed by Isaiah Thomas, | and sold at his book-store. | MDCCLXXXVI.
    1 p.l., 120 p. [i:] title-page; [ii:] blank; [1]-109: songs; [110]-120: directions for all good boys and girls to follow.
    Welch 782 ¶ MWA* ¶ Contains 35 juvenile songs. *Later edition:* 174.

41 THE | SELECT SONGSTER | or a | collection | of | elegant songs | with music prefixed to each | compiled by Philo. Musico. | "Music can soften pain to ease" | "And make despair & madness please" | Amos Doolittle sculpt. at N. Haven | New-Haven: printed by Daniel Bowen, in Chapel Street | 1786
    66 p. [1:] title-page; [2:] blank; [3]-4: preface; 5-65: songs; 66: index and eratum [sic].
    Evans 19750, Sonneck p. 132, Sonneck-Upton pp. 373-375 ¶ MWA*, RPB ¶ Contains 40 songs (all indexed), all with musical notation. The compiler was Chauncey Langdon.

42 [T. THUMB'S SONG BOOK. New-York: Hugh Gaine, 1786.]
    Welch 802.1 ¶ No copy located ¶ Advertised 1786 by Gaine in his printing of Mathurin Cordier's *Corderii colloquiorum,* 25th ed. (Evans 19588). Perhaps an English edition. *Later editions:* 48, 88, 104.

1787

43 A LITTLE PRETTY | POCKET-BOOK, | intended for the | instruction and amusement | of | little master Tommy, | and pretty Miss Polly. | With two letters from | Jack the giant-killer; | as also | a ball and pincushion; | the use of which will infallibly make Tommy | a good boy, and Polly a good girl. | To which is added, | a little song-book, | being | a new attempt to teach children | the use of the English alphabet, by way | of diversion. | The first Worcester edition. | Printed at Worcester, Massachusetts. | By Isaiah Thomas, | and sold, wholesale and retail, at his book- | store. MDCCLXXXVII.
    122, [4] p. [1:] blank; [2:] frontispiece; [3:] title-page; [4:] blank; [5:] dedication; [6:] blank; [7]-23: text; 24-65: songs; 66-122: text continued; [123]-[124:] advertisement for Isaiah Thomas.
    Evans 20459, Hamilton 115, Nichols 113, Rosenbach 120, Welch 778.2 ¶ CLU, CSmH, CtY (2), DLC, ICU, MB, MH, MWA* (2), MWHi, NjP, NN (2), PP, RPJCB ¶ Contains 42 juvenile songs. See 9 for a complete list of editions.

Little robin red breast; a collection of pretty songs, for children, entirely new. Printed at Worcester, Massachusetts, by Isaiah Thomas, MDCCLXXXVII.

Evans 20461, Sonneck-Upton p. 233; see also Welch 782 ¶ A ghost-title for 40, q.v., based on an unlocated 1787 newspaper advertisement.

1788

44 THE | AMERICAN SONGSTER: | being a | select collection | of the most celebrated | American, English, Scotch and Irish | songs. | "Music has charms to soothe a savage breast, | "To soften rocks, and bend the knotted oak." | Vir. | New-York: | printed for Samuel Campbell, No. 44, | Hanover-Square, and Thomas Allen, | No. 16, Queen-Street. | M,DCC,LXXXVIII.

xii, 204 p. [i:] title-page; [ii:] blank; [iii]-iv: dedication, to the lovers of music, in the United States of America; v-xii: index; 1-204: songs.

Evans 20930, Sabin 1220, Sonneck pp. 10-11, Sonneck-Upton p. 21. Indexed in Thorpe ¶ CtY, MBAt, MWA*, NN (imperfect), RPB; London (British Library) ¶ Contains 231 songs (227 indexed). Advertised 29 Mar. 1788 in the New York *Daily Advertiser* as "this day ... published by S. & R. Campbell ... and T. Allen." The advertisement is reprinted in Gottesman from the issue of 17 Apr. 1788. Eight of the songs are claimed as having "never before appeared in print." *Later editions:* 52, 89, 243.

45 THE | CHARMS OF MELODY: | or, a | choice collection | of the | most approved songs, | catches, duets, &c. | Philadelphia: | printed by M. Carey, | for Thomas Seddon, Market-Street. | M.DCC.LXXX-VIII.

96 p. [i:] title-page; [ii]-iv: index; [5]-96: songs.

Evans 20996, Lowens U21, Sonneck-Upton p. 58 ¶ MWA* (imperfect) ¶ Contains 114 songs (116 indexed). The only known copy is mutilated, portions of pp. 39-42, 73-74 being destroyed. The undated Irish editions owned by Oxford (Bodleian Library) (cf. Ault p. 231) are apparently not related to 45. For a related edition, see 82.

46 FOUR EXCELLENT | NEW SONGS, | called, | Yankee Doodle. | Death of General Wolfe. | Nancy Dawson. | Guardian angels. | New-York: | printed and sold by John Reid, at his | book and stationary [sic] store, | No. 17, Water Street, 1788.

8 p. [1:] title-page; 2-8: songs.

Bristol-Evans B6704, Shipton-Mooney 45260, Sonneck-Upton p. 403, Stark 890, Wegelin 594 ¶ RPB* ¶ Contains 4 songs (all named on the title-page). The Wegelin copy, reported in Sonneck-Upton, is now at RPB.

47 A | POETICAL DESCRIPTION | of | song birds: | interspersed with entertaining | songs, fables, and tales, | adapted to each subject: | for the | amusement of children. | Attention on each tune bestow, | For as they sing you'll wiser grow. | The first Worcester edition. | Printed at Worcester, Massachusetts, | by Isaiah Thomas, | sold at his bookstore in Worcester, and by | him and Company in Boston. | MDCCLXXXVIII.

88 p. [1:] blank; [2:] frontispiece; [3:] title-page; [4:] blank; 5-6: index; 7-9: introduction; [10:] blank; [11]-88: text and songs.

Evans 21399, Frank p. 41, Welch 1037 ¶ CtHi, MB, MWA (imperfect), NN, RPJCB* ¶ Contains 22 juvenile songs (all indexed).

48 TOMMY THUMB'S | SONG BOOK, | for all little | masters and misses, | to be sung to them by their nurses, | until they can sing themselves. | By Nurse Lovechild. | To which is added, | a letter from a lady on nursing. | The first Worcester edition. | Printed at Worcester, Massachusetts, | by Isaiah Thomas. | Sold at his bookstore. MDCCL-XXXVIII.

59, [4] p. [1:] blank; [2:] frontispiece; [3:] title-page; [4]-6: to Nurse Lovechild; 7: [half-title:] Artificial memory | for | infants; | whereby | they may acquire | the | knowledge of animals, | and | some of their sounds, | before | they can go or speak. | [catchword:] although; 8-19: text; 20-59: songs; [60]-[63:] advertisement for Isaiah Thomas.

Evans 21089, Sabin 96146, Sonneck-Upton p. 436, Welch 802.2 ¶ MWA* (2), PPL (imperfect); London (British Library) ¶ Contains 33 juvenile songs. Musical directions at foot of many pages: Affetuoso (21); Encore (22); Encore ventesimo (23); Acuto (24); Allegro (25); Pronto (31); Recitative (32); Timoroso (40); Giga (41); Lamentatione (42); Encore (43); Languido (45); Almain (46); Vivace (54); Adagio (57); Alto, Concertante (59). See 42 for a list of editions.

1789

49 [THE APOLLO; being a collection of such English songs as are most eminent for poetical merit. To which is added, a table of first lines, with the authors' names annexed. Philadelphia: printed by William Spotswood, Front-Street, between Market and Chesnut-Streets, and to be sold by Spotswood and Clarke, at their book-store in Market-Street, corner of Grant's-Lane. 1789.]

Evans 21660, Lowens U22, Sonneck-Upton p. 28 ¶ No copy located ¶ According to the annotated Evans at MWA, advertised 9 Apr. 1789 in the Philadelphia *Federal Gazette* as "American edition, just published." Also advertised 8 May 1789 in the *Maryland Journal & Baltimore Advertiser* as the fourth in a list of "American editions just published and to be sold by Spotswood and Clarke, at their book-store in Market-Street, corner of Grant's-Lane." The 1791 and 1794 Bath,

England editions (cf. Ault pp. 245, 249) of a songster with this title owned by Oxford (Bodleian Library) apparently are not related to the American imprints. *Later editions:* 58, 70, 71.

50 THE | PHILADELPHIA SONGSTER. | Part I. | Being a | collection of choice songs; | such as are | calculated to please the ear, | while they | improve the mind, and make the heart better. | By Absalom Aimwell, Esquire. | Music the fiercest grief can charm, | And fate's severest rage disarm: | Music can soften pain to ease, | And make despair and madness please. | Philadelphia, | printed and to be sold by John M'Culloch, in | Third-Street, near the Market.—Jan. 1789.

16 p. [1:] title-page; [2:] blank; 3-16: songs.

Evans 21628, Sonneck p. 116, Sonneck-Upton p. 331 ¶ NN* ¶ Contains 11 songs, all with musical notation. "Absalom Aimwell, Esquire" is a pseudonym for Andrew Adgate, better known as a tune-book compiler and as the president of the Uranian Academy in Philadelphia.

51 [THE YOUNG MASON'S MONITOR, and vocal companion. An American production. (Entirely new.) By Brother William M. Stewart. New-York: printed by Harrisson and Purdy, 1789.]

Evans 22164, Lowens U23, Sabin 91712, Sonneck-Upton p. 484 ¶ No copy located ¶ Advertised 15 Aug. 1789 through 31 Oct. 1789 in the New York *Weekly Museum,* as "just published." For a related edition see 64. *Later edition:* 69.

1790

52 [THE AMERICAN SONGSTER, being a collection of the most celebrated ancient and modern songs. Portsmouth: printed by John Melcher, 1790.]

Evans 22311, Lowens U24, Sonneck-Upton p. 20 ¶ No copy located ¶ Advertised 23 Aug. 1792 in the Portsmouth *New Hampshire Gazette;* see also a 19 Jan. 1793 advertisement in *Dunlap's American Daily Advertiser* (Philadelphia) for "The American songster, price bound two thirds of a dollar" listed under "new books, American editions for sale by William Spotswood." These advertisements may perhaps refer to 44, q.v., although this does not seem too likely. The Evans entry was probably constructed from an advertisement.

53 THE | CHARMER; | being a | select collection | of | English, Scots' and American songs, | including the modern: | with a | selection of favourite toasts and sentiments. | Philadelphia: | printed for W. Spotswood, Front-Street; T. Seddon, | and Rice & Co. Market-Street. | M DCC XC.

1 p.l., viii, 136 p. [i:] blank; [ii:] frontispiece; [i:] title-page; [ii:]

blank; [iii]-vi: index; [vii:] toasts and sentiments; viii: Masonic toasts; London, 1785; [1]-136: songs.

Ault p. 243, Evans 22400, Sonneck-Upton p. 58 ¶ NN*; Oxford (Bodleian Library) ¶ Contains 188 songs (187 indexed). Advertised 19 Jan. 1793 in *Dunlap's American Daily Advertiser* (Philadelphia). This was the apparent source for the 1793 ghost-title, *The vocal charmer* (Evans 26410, Sabin 100648, Sonneck-Upton p. 445).

54 [THE JOLLY HIBERNIAN in full glee; or, complete Irish jester, and wits vade-mecum. Containing a more humorous variety of original stories, comical bulls, witty repartees, entertaining anecdotes, jests, &c. than ever appeared in the Irish or any other language. To which are added, the facetious history of John Gilpin, and a new song in praise of St. Patrick. Philadelphia: printed by Henry Taylor, for Robert Campbell. 1790.]

Evans 22591, Lowens U25, Sonneck-Upton p. 218 ¶ No copy located ¶ Evans notes that 300 copies in sheets were offered at the sale of Henry Taylor's estate in 1791. Probably not a songster.

55 THE NEW | ENTERTAINING PHILADELPHIA | JEST-BOOK, | and | chearful [sic] witty companion: | being a choice collection | of the most humorous and diverting | jests, stories, anecdotes, | bon-mots, repartees, | new songs, poetical tales, &c. &c. | To which is added, a curious variety | of toasts, sentiments, & hob-nobs. | I love fun —Keep it up! G. A. Stevens. | Philadelphia: | printed for W. Woodhouse, Front, | near Market-Street. | M.DCC.XC.

1 p.l., 100 p. [i:] blank; [ii:] frontispiece; [1:] half-title: The new | entertaining Philadelphia | jest-book; [2:] blank; [3:] title-page; [4:] blank; [5]-88: text; 89-91: toasts, sentiments, hobnobs, &c.; 92-100: songs.

Lowens U26 ¶ MWA* (lacks frontispiece), PHi (imperfect), RPB (imperfect) ¶ Contains 12 songs. Undoubtedly this is Evans 22799, where the title is given as the "Philadelphia jest book, and cheerful witty companion." *Related edition:* 61.

Philadelphia jest book, and cheerful witty companion. Being a choice collection of the most humorous and diverting jests, stories, anecdotes, bon-mots, repartees, new songs, and a curious variety of toasts, sentiments and hob-nobs. Philadelphia: printed and sold by William Woodhouse, 1790.

Evans 22799, Sonneck-Upton p. 330 ¶ Apparently a ghost-title for 55, q.v., based on an unlocated newspaper advertisement.

56 SONGS, | for the amusement | of children. | Middletown: printed | by M. H. Woodward. | M,D,CC,XC.

31 p. [1:] title-page; [2:] blank; [3]-31: songs.

Evans 22894, Sabin 86911, Sonneck-Upton p. 400, Welch 1237 ¶ MB* ¶ Contains 10 songs. These are not juvenile in character despite the title.

57 THE | VOCAL REMEMBRANCER; | being a | choice selection | of the | most admired songs, | including the modern. | To which are added | favourite toasts and sentiments. | Philadelphia: | printed by William Spotswood. | M DCC XC.

1 p.l., viii, 184 p. [i:] blank; [ii:] frontispiece; [i:] title-page; [ii]-viii: index; viii: toasts and sentiments; [1]-184: songs.

Evans 23028, Sabin 100654; Sonneck p. 159, Sonneck-Upton p. 445. Indexed in Thorpe ¶ DLC*, MWA (lacks frontispiece), NBuG, NHi, PPL ¶ Contains 295 songs (300 indexed). *Later edition:* 79.

1791

58 THE | APOLLO: | being a | collection | of | English songs; | includ-ing a selection of | Masonic songs, anthems, odes, preludes, pro- | logues, epilogues, toasts, &c. | Philadelphia: | printed by William Spots-wood. | M.DCC.XCI.

[vi], 164 p. [i:] blank; [ii:] frontispiece; [iii:] title-page; [iv]-[vi:] index; [vi:] Masonic toasts—London, 1785; [1]-164: songs.

Evans 23128, Sonneck-Upton p. 28. Indexed in Thorpe ¶ CtY*, MWA (lacks frontispiece), RPB (lacks frontispiece) ¶ Contains 214 songs (203 indexed). Apparently a reprint of an English songster of ca. 1785 (see p. [vi]) which I have been unable to identify. The discrepancy between the number of songs indexed and the actual num-ber of songs in the collection indicates that the index may well pertain to 49, q.v. for a list of editions.

59 THE ENCHANTING | HUMMING-BIRD; | one of the most pleasing and delight- | ful collection [sic] of | songs | now extant—as sung with universal | applause at the Theatres-Royal | Vauxhall, Drury-Lane, Mary- | bone, Ranelagh, &c. | Including also the most admired | musical productions of | America, Ireland, and Scotland; | catches and glees: | together with a curious selection of | toasts, sentiments, and hob- | nobs. | Philadelphia: | printed and sold by Henry Taylor.

100 p. [1:] title-page; [2:] blank; [3:] caption-title, used as running-title: The humming-bird; [3]-99: songs; 100: toasts and sentiments.

MWA* ¶ Contains 106 songs. This would appear to be Evans 23456, despite the difference in title. According to Sonneck-Upton p. 194, it was advertised in the sale of Henry Taylor's estate as "one-half finished."

The humming-bird. Philadelphia, 1791.
Caption-title used as running-title in 59, q.v.

Humming bird, or collection of fashionable songs. Philadelphia: printed by Henry Taylor. 1791.
See under 59.
Evans 23456, Sonneck-Upton p. 194 ¶ Apparently a ghost-title for 59, q.v., based on the caption-title. According to Sonneck-Upton p. 194, this was advertised in the sale of Henry Taylor's estate as "one-half finished."

60 THE | NEW | AHIMAN REZON. | Containing the laws and con-
   stitutions of the | Grand Lodge of Virginia. To which is added, | the history of Masonry, from the crea- | tion, to the death of Queen Eliza-beth. | Also illustrations of the royal | art; and a variety of other mat- | ter relative to that insti- | tution. Carefully colla- | ted, from the most ap- | proved authors, an- | cient as well as | modern. | By John K. Read, | present Deputy Grand Master of Virginia, | and member of the Sub-lime Lodge of | Perfection, of Charleston, | South-Carolina. | Causa latet vis est notissima. | "Ovid Met." | 1.4. ver. 207. | Richmond: printed by John Dixon. | M,DCC,XCI.

   1 p.l., xvi, [4], 9, [1], 241, [1] p. [i:] blank; [ii:] sanction, dated 1 May 5792; [i:] title-page; [ii:] blank; [iii:] dedication to George Washington; [iv:] blank; [v]-vii: editor's preface, dated Richmond, 1 Sept. 5791; [viii:] blank; [ix]-xvi: preface; [xvii]-[xx:] contents; 1-9: history of the Grand Lodge of Virginia; [10:] blank; [1]-222: the new Ahiman Rezon; 223-228: rules and regulations for the Georgia Grand Lodge; [229]-241: a collection of Masonic songs; [242:] cor-rigenda.

   Barthelmess p. 6, Brinley 6699, Davis 53, Evans 23727, Morris p. 20 ¶ CSmH, DLC* (2), DSC (imperfect), IaCrM, MB, MBFM, MH, MWA (imperfect), NcD, OCM, PPPFM, ViU (2 copies, 1 imperfect) ¶ Contains 14 Masonic songs.

61 [THE NEW ENTERTAINING PHILADELPHIA JEST-
   BOOK, and chearful witty companion, &c. I love fun—keep it up! G. A. Stevens. Philadelphia: published, printed and sold by W. Wood-house, at the Bible, No. 6, South Front-Street. 1791.]

   Evans 23598, Lowens U27, Sonneck-Upton p. 330 ¶ No copy located ¶ The item appears to have been taken from an advertisement for "books published by W. Woodhouse" in James Hervey, *Meditations and Contemplations* (Philadelphia: W. Woodhouse, 1791), Evans 23440, as is also 62. It is likely that 61 and 55, q.v., are identical.

The nightingale: being a collection of the best Scots, English, and

Irish songs: to which is added, toasts, sentiments, and hob-nobs. Sold by the booksellers in Great-Britain, Ireland and America. 1791.

7, [1], 100 p.

MH* ¶ Apparently an English imprint.

62 [THE NIGHTINGALE; or, songster's companion. Consisting of an elegant and polite selection of the most approved ancient and modern songs. [Two lines of verse.] Philadelphia: published, printed and sold by W. Woodhouse, at the Bible, No. 6, South Front-Street. 1791.]

Evans 23634, Lowens U28, Sonneck-Upton p. 297 ¶ No copy located ¶ The item appears to have been taken from an advertisement for "books published by W. Woodhouse" in James Hervey, *Meditations and Contemplations* (Philadelphia: W. Woodhouse, 1791), Evans 23440, as is also 61.

63 [THE VOCAL ENCHANTRESS, or town and country songster. A collection of the most celebrated new songs. Published and sold by Rice & Co., No. 50 Market-Street, Philadelphia. 1791.]

Sonneck-Upton p. 445 ¶ No copy located ¶ Advertised 9 Apr. 1791 in *Dunlap's American Daily Advertiser* (Philadelphia), as the 11th in a list of "new books, just arrived by the ship Dublin Packet, from Dublin, and for sale by Rice & Co. No. 50 Market-Street, two doors from Second-Street." Cf. Ault p. 237. Existence doubtful.

64 THE | YOUNG MASON'S MONITOR; | containing | some nec-essary hints to | young brethren— | yet not beneath the attention of any. | To which is annexed, | a collection of | Masonic songs, odes, &c. | many of them new and excellent. | Compiled by B. Wheeler, secretary | of St. John's Lodge, No. 1, Providence. | Printed at Providence, | for the editor, in the Year of Light | 5791.

46, [1] p. [1:] title-page; [2:] blank; [3:] dedication; [4:] lines written by Brother Stewart, N. Y.; [5]-12: text; [13]-46: songs; 46: Masonic toasts; [47:] index.

Evans 23996, Sabin 103176 ¶ RHi*, RPB (imperfect) ¶ Contains 27 Masonic songs (22 indexed). Perhaps related to 51, 69, qq.v.

1792

65 THE | CONSTITUTIONS | of the | ancient and honourable frater-nity | of | Free and Accepted Masons: | containing their | history, charges, addresses, &c. | collected and digested from their | old records, faithful traditions, and Lodge books. | For the use of Masons. | To which are added, | the history of Masonry in the Common- | wealth of Massachusetts, | and the | constitution, laws, and regulations | of their

Grand Lodge. | Together with a | large collection of songs, epilogues, &c. | "Pectora jungit amor pietasque ligavit amantes." | "I beseech you, brethren, that ye submit yourselves unto such, and to every one that help- | eth with us and laboureth."——St. Paul. | Printed at Worcester, Massachusetts, | by Brother Isaiah Thomas. | In the Christian era MDCCXCII; in the Year of Light VMDCCXCII.

1 p.l., 288 p. [i:] blank; [ii:] frontispiece; [i:] title-page; [ii:] blank; [iii:] endorsement, signed John Warren, chairman, and dated Boston, 1 May 5792; [iv:] blank; [v]-vi: sanction; [vii:] dedication to George Washington; [viii:] blank; ix-x: preface; xi-xvi: contents; [17]-19: preliminary illustrations and remarks; [20:] blank; [21]-215: text; [216]-286: oratorio, odes, anthems, prologues and songs; 286-288: toasts.

Barthelmess p. 6, Brinley 6713, Evans 24052, Sabin 25798 ¶ CSmH, DLC*, MBAt, MBFM, MHi, MWA (2 copies, 1 imperfect), RPJCB ¶ Contains 47 Masonic songs (all indexed). See 148 for a related song-ster. *Later edition:* 146.

Gesänge für Freimaurer. Der Loge Eugenia gehoerig. Philadelphia 5792.

xii, 131 p.

DLC*, MWA, NNFM ¶ Contains 100 Masonic songs in German. According to Emil O. Weller, *Die falschen und fingirte Druckorte* (Leipzig, 1864), p. 151, this is not an American publication. It is a spurious imprint brought out by Cnobloch at Leipzig in 1792.

66 THE | LIFE AND DEATH | OF | ROBIN HOOD, | complete in | twenty-four | songs. | Philadelphia: | printed and sold by Stewart & Cochran, No. 34, | South Second-Street.

107, [1] p. [1:] title-page; [2:] introductory poem and preface; [3]-107: songs; [108:] index.

Bristol-Evans B8045, Lowens U29, Rosenbach 160, Shipton-Mooney 46563 ¶ PP* (imperfect) ¶ Contains 24 songs (all indexed). The only known copy lacks pp. 83-86. For other collections of Robin Hood songs, see 3, 190, 196, and 405. Running-title: Robin Hood's garland.

67 [MONSTROUS GOOD SONGS for 1792. Boston: 1792.]

Evans 24551, Lowens U30, Sonneck-Upton p. 267 ¶ No copy located ¶ The Evans entry was constructed from a bookseller's catalog, accord-ing to the annotated copy of Evans at MWA. The title was in common use in England; see Ault pp. 248, 249, 250, 251, 253, 254 for yearly issues, all in Oxford (Bodleian Library).

Robin Hood's garland. Philadelphia, 1792.

Running-title in 66.

68 THE | VOCAL MUSE; | or | ladies [sic] songster. | Containing | a
  collection of elegant | songs: | selected from British and American |
authors. | Around th'enchanting music rings, | And every vocal grove
responsive sings. | Livingston. | Philadelphia: | printed for the propri-
etors. | M,DCC,CXII [i.e., M,DCC,XCII].
  [xii], 168 p. [i:] title-page; [ii:] blank; [iii]-[xii:] index; [1]-168:
songs.
  Evans 24978, Lowens U31, Sabin 100653, Sonneck p. 159, Sonneck-
Upton p. 445 ¶ DLC* (2 copies, both incomplete) ¶ Contains 242 songs
(240 indexed). Copy 1 at DLC lacks pp. [i]-[ii], 3-10, 47-48, 77-80,
89-92; copy 2 lacks pp. 41-44, 95-96, 99-106, 111-118, 121-132. Advertised
5 Oct. 1792 in *Dunlap's American Daily Advertiser* (Philadelphia) as
"just published." The misprint in the date has given rise to a ghost
edition of 1812. For a later, related imprint, see 97.

69 [THE YOUNG MASON'S MONITOR. By William M. Stewart.
  To which is annexed a collection of Masonic songs, odes, etc. Portsmouth: printed and for sale by John Melcher. 5792.]
  Evans 24819, Lowens U32, Sabin 91713. ¶ No copy located ¶ Evans
notes that the item is a 16mo. Advertised 27 Sept. 1792 in the Portsmouth *New Hampshire Gazette* as "just published and for sale by"
Melcher. See 51 for an earlier edition; see 64 for a related edition.

1793

70 THE | APOLLO: | being a | collection | of | English songs | includ-
  ing a selection of | Masonic songs, anthems, odes, preludes, pro- |
logues, epilogues, toasts, &c. | A new edition, with additions. | Philadel-
phia: | printed by William Spotswood. | 1793.
  [xii], 108 p. [i:] title-page; [ii]-[iv:] blank; [v]-[viii:] index; [ix:]
Masonic toasts; [x:] blank; [xi]-[xii:] index continued; [1]-108: songs.
  CtHT-W, RPJCB* ¶ Contains 172 songs (238 indexed). A truncated
edition of 71, lacking pp. 109-164. Apparently the work was sold in
both forms. The 21 Jan. 1793 advertisement in *Dunlap's American
Daily Advertiser* (Philadelphia) may pertain to either 58 or 70. 70 is
printed from the same plates as 71 through p. 108. It is, of course, possible that this edition is merely an imperfect copy of 71, but the
existence of two identically imperfect copies in seemingly tight contemporary bindings makes this unlikely, despite the index which
clearly pertains to 71. See 49 for a list of editions.

71 THE | APOLLO: | being a | collection | of | English songs | includ-
  ing a selection of | Masonic songs, anthems, odes, preludes, pro- |
logues, epilogues, toasts, &c. | A new edition, with additions. | Phila-
delphia: | printed by William Spotswood. | 1793.

1 p.l., [xii], 164 p. [i:] blank; [ii:] frontispiece; [i:] title-page; [ii]-[iv:] blank; [v]-[viii:] index; [ix:] Masonic toasts; [x:] blank; [xi]-[xii:] index continued; [1]-164: songs.

Evans 25115, Sonneck p. 13, Sonneck-Upton pp. 28-29 ¶ DSC*, MBFM (imperfect), MH, PPL ¶ Contains 238 songs (all indexed). An expanded edition of 58, q.v. Cf. 70; see 49 for a list of editions.

72 THE | DECLARATION | OF | INDEPENDENCE; | a | poem: | accompanied by | odes, songs, &c. | adapted to the day. | A firm, unshaken, uncorrupted soul, | A steady spirit, regularly free.—Thomson. | By a citizen of Boston. | Printed at Boston, | Faust's Statue, No. 45, Newbury Street. | MDCCXCIII.

24 p. [1:] title-page; [2:] blank; [3:] dedication to His Excellency John Hancock, Esq.; [4:] preface, signed Boston, 1 July 1793; [5]-19: text; [20:] anthem composed for Thursday morning, 4 July 1793; [21]-24: odes and songs.

Evans 26084, Frank p. 43, Sonneck-Upton p. 104 ¶ CtY, DLC*, IU, MB, MBAt, MWA, MiU-C, N, NHi, NN, NjP, RPB (2 copies, 1 imperfect), RPJCB; London (British Library) ¶ Contains 5 songs. The "citizen of Boston" was George Richards; the printers were Thomas and Andrews. This was reprinted in 1870 (in New York) in an edition of 50 copies. See 182 for another work by Richards.

73 [JACHIN AND BOAZ. New York: Berry, Rogers & Berry, 1793.] vi, 50, 12 p.

Barthelmess p. 30, Kloss 1887 ¶ No copy located ¶ Kloss reports this an 8vo edition and locates a copy in the library of the Grand Lodge of Rhode Island which I have been unable to locate. Editions without songs were issued in 1799, 1801, 1808, 1817, 1822 (in Spanish), and 1825. See 409 for a related item. *Later editions:* 86, 112, 113, 125, 150, 232, 254, 348, 391, 392, 409, 468, 491, 544, 570.

74 [THE JOVIAL SONGSTER. Philadelphia: printed and sold by H. Kammerer. 1793.]

Evans 25675, Lowens U33, Sonneck-Upton p. 218 ¶ No copy located ¶ Advertised 25 June 1793 in the Philadelphia *Federal Gazette* as the 10th in a list of "American editions lately published, for sale at H. Kammerer's." Many English editions are known—cf. Ault p. 237 (1784), 239 (1785?), 242 (4th ed., 1789); an undated, ca. 1790 edition is in London (British Library). *Later editions:* 95, 151, 152.

75 [MERMAID, or nautical songster. New York: for sale at the printing office of John Harrisson, Yorick's Head, No. 3 Peck-Slip, 1793.]

Bristol-Evans B8413, Lowens U34, Shipton-Mooney 46822, Sonneck-Upton p. 258 ¶ No copy located ¶ Advertised 20 Apr. 1793 in the New

York *Weekly Museum* as "for sale at the printing office of John Harrisson, Yorick's Head, No. 3 Peck-Slip." *Later editions:* 114, 154, 545.

76 [THE MOCKING-BIRD: a collection of songs, a number of which are set to music. Philadelphia: printed and sold by John M'Culloch, No. 1, North Third-Street. 1793.]

Evans 25830, Lowens U35, Sonneck-Upton p. 265 ¶ No copy located ¶ Advertised 30 Mar. 1793 in the Philadelphia *National Gazette* as "for sale" by M'Culloch.

77 MRS. POWNALL'S | ADDRESS, | in behalf of the | French musicians, | delivered on her benefit concert night, | at Oeller's Hotel, Chesnut-Street, Philadelphia. | To which are added, | pastoral songs, | written by herself at an early period of life. | Also the songs performed at the concerts.—New Theatre. | Philadelphia. | Printed and sold at Story's Office, (No. 36) Fourth- | Street nearly opposite the Indian Queen Tavern.

4, 28 p. [1:] title-page; [2:] blank; [3]-4: to the reader; [1]-4: Mrs. Pownall's address; [5:] second title-page: Pastoral songs, | composed | at an early period of the author's life. | By Mary A. Pownall. | Philadelphia. | M.DCC.XIII [sic]; [6:] blank; [7]-15: songs; [16:] note to song the Vth; [17]-28: new songs, sung at the concerts—New Theatre, Philadelphia.

Evans 26032, Frank p. 42, Sonneck p. 92, Sonneck-Upton p. 272 ¶ NN* ¶ Contains 14 songs. Advertised 26 Mar. 1793 in *Dunlap's American Daily Advertiser* (Philadelphia) as "this day . . . published." The imprint on the cover-title differs as follows: Printed and sold by | Enoch Story, | Fourth-Street, nearly opposite the Indian- | Queen, (No. 36.) Philadelphia. | Printing, | in general, executed in the neatest | manner, and at reasonable | prices.

Pastoral songs, | composed | at an early period of the author's life. | By Mary A. Pownall. | Philadelphia. | M.DCC.XIII [sic].
See 77.

78 THE | SYREN | or | musical bouquet | being | a new selection | of favourite songs sung at the various places of | amusement | in | Great Britain Ireland and | America. | New York | printed by Iohn Harrisson | for Berry & Rogers & Iohn Reid

2 p.l., 194+ p. [i:] blank; [ii:] frontispiece; [iii:] title-page; [iv:] blank; [1]-194+: songs.

Evans 24839, Lowens U36, Sabin 94131 ¶ ViU* (imperfect) ¶ Contains 171 songs. The only copy extant lacks all after p. 194. Apparently an American reprint of *The Edinburgh syren, or musical bouquet* (cf. Ault p. 247) of 1792. Advertised 26 Jan. 1793 in the New York

Weekly Museum as "Thursday [i.e., 31 Jan.] will be published" and on 2 Feb. 1793 as "just published."

Vauxhall songs for 1793.
See under The new ladies [sic] memorandum-book of 1794.

The vocal charmer. Philadelphia: printed and sold by William Spotswood. 1793.
Evans 26410, Sabin 100648, Sonneck p. 159, Sonneck-Upton p. 445 ¶ A ghost-title based on a misreading of a 19 Jan. 1793 advertisement in *Dunlap's American Daily Advertiser* (Philadelphia), apparently pertaining to 53, q.v.

79 [THE VOCAL REMEMBRANCER; being a choice selection of the most admired songs, including the modern. Philadelphia: printed and sold by William Spotswood. 1793.]
Evans 26411, Lowens U37, Sabin 100654, Sonneck p. 169, Sonneck-Upton p. 446 ¶ No copy located ¶ Advertised 19 Jan. 1793 in *Dunlap's American Daily Advertiser* (Philadelphia) among "new books. American editions. For sale by William Spotswood . . . song books . . . price sewed, 4s. 2," with the additional comment that "the above are embellished with engraved frontispieces, and will be found to contain the beauties of English poetry in that line." Perhaps a late advertisement for 57, q.v.

1794

80 [AMERICAN ACADEMY OF COMPLIMENTS. Philadelphia: from the press of Mathew Carey. 1794.]
Evans 26551, Lowens U38 ¶ No copy located ¶ Follows a long English tradition of including songs in letter-writing manuals. For an early example, see *The delightful new academy of complements* [sic] (York, 1744?), "whereunto are added, fifteen of the newest songs sung at court and city," an imperfect copy of which is at CSmH. Cf. Backus 529. For related American imprints, see 98, 176, and 235. *Later editions:* 108, 119, 265, 287, 407.

The Baltimore songster. Baltimore: sold by J. Keatinge, 1794.
Evans 26607, Sonneck-Upton p. 194 ¶ Apparently a ghost-title for 90, q.v., based on a 26 Mar. 1795 advertisement in the Baltimore *Telegraphe*.

81 THE | BRISTOL | BRIDEGROOM. | To which is added | A mother's farewell, | and | Happiness in death. | New-Haven—printed. 12 p. [1:] title-page; [2:] blank; [3]-12: songs.
RPB* ¶ Contains 3 songs, as named on the title-page.

82 [CHARMS OF MELODY; a choice collection of the most approved
    songs, catches, duets, &c. Philadelphia: printed for Mathew Carey,
118, Market-Street, 1794.]

Evans 26760, Lowens U39, Sonneck-Upton p. 58 ¶ No copy located
¶ Advertised 28 Nov. 1794 in the Philadelphia *Aurora and General
Advertiser* as 30th in a list of "books, printed for and published by
Mathew Carey, 118, Market-Street, price 25 cents." Probably 45, q.v.

83 THE | DEMOCRATIC SONGSTER: | being a collection of the
    newest | and most admired | republican songs, | interspersed with
many originals. | To which is added, | some of the most admired | French
airs. | Baltimore: | printed for | Keatinge's book store, | Market-Stret
[sic] | [To be continued monthly.] | M,DCC,XCIV.

36 p. [i:] title-page; [ii:] blank; [3]-36: songs.

Minick 165 ¶ DLC (imperfect), MH* ¶ Contains 20 songs. Song
IX is misnumbered Song X; two songs are numbered Song XVIII.
Apparently no further numbers were published. See 214 for a related
edition.

The democratic songster, being a collection of the newest and most
admired songs, interspersed with many originals. To which will be
added, some of the most admired French airs. Baltimore: printed by
James Angell, for George Keatinge, Market-Street, 1794.

Evans 26871, Sonneck-Upton p. 105 ¶ Apparently a ghost-title for
83, q.v., based on an unlocated newspaper advertisement.

84 THE | FREE-MASON'S | POCKET COMPANION; | or | ele-
    ments | of | Free-Masonry | delineated. | Friendship, on wings ethe-
rial, flying round, | Here stretch'd her arm to bless the hallow'd ground; |
Humanity, well pleas'd, here takes her stand, | Holding her daughter
Pity in her hand: | Here Charity which sooths [sic] the widow's sigh,
| And wipes the dew-drop from the orphan's eye: | Here stands
Benevolence, whose large embrace, | Uncircumscrib'd, takes in the hu-
man race; | She sees each narrow tie—each private end, | Indignant,
Virtue's universal friend: | Scorning each frantic zealot, bigot, fool,
| She stamps on Masons' breasts her golden rule. | New-London: |
printed by Brother Samuel Green. | In the Christian era MDCCXCIV;
in | the Year of Light VMDCCXCIV.

95 p. [1:] title-page; [2:] blank; [3]-71: text; 71-77: anthems and
odes; 78-87: songs; 88-89: prologue; 90-93: constitution of the Grand
Lodge of Conn.; 94-95: contents.

Evans 27014 ¶ DSC*, MWA, PPPFM, RPB ¶ Contains 18 Masonic
songs. See 36 for an earlier edition.

The Free-Mason's pocket companion; or elements of Free-Masonry
delineated. Norwich: sold by John Trumbull. 1794.

Evans 27014 ¶ Undoubtedly a ghost-title for 84, q.v., based on a 14 Aug. 1794 advertisement in the Norwich *Packet,* as follows: "Just received, and for sale at this [John Trumbull's] office, (price two shillings) The Free-Mason's pocket companion; or elements of Free-Masonry delineated."

85 THE | HISTORY | of a | little child, | found under a haycock. | To
    which is added, | little stories for children. | Boston: | printed and
sold by N. Coverly. | 1794 | Price three-pence.
    16 p. [1:] title-page; [2]-12: text; 13-16: songs.
    Evans 47085, Welch 676 ¶ MWA* ¶ Contains 6 juvenile songs. *Related item:* 111.

86 JACHIN AND BOAZ; | or, an | authentic key | to the door of |
    Free-Masonry, | both ancient and modern. | Calculated not only for the instruction of every new-made | Mason; but also for the information of all | who intend to become Brethren. | Containing, | I. A circumstantial account | of all the proceedings in making | a Mason, with the several obli- | gations of an Entered Appren- | tice, Fellow-Craft, and Master; | the prayers, and also the sign, | grip and pass-word of each | degree. | II. The manner of open- | ing a Lodge, and setting the | Craft to work. | III. The Entered Appren- | tice, Fellow-Craft, and Master's | lectures, verbatim, as delivered | in all Lodges; with the song at | the conclusion of each part. | IV. The origin of Mason- | ry; description of Solomon's | temple; history of the murder | of the Grand Master Hiram, by | the three Fellow-Crafts; their | discovery and punishment; | the burial of Hiram by King | Solomon's order; with the five | points of fellowship, &c. | V. The ceremony of the | installment of the Master of dif- | ferent Lodges on St. John's day. | Description of the regalia, &c. | VI. Ceremony observed | at the funeral of a Mason. | VII. A safe and easy me- | thod proposed, by which a man | may gain admittance into any | Lodge, without passing through | the form required, and thereby | save a guinea or two in his | pocket. | VIII. Toasts, songs, &c. | Illustrated with | a beautiful frontispiece of the regalia, jewels, | and emblematical ornaments belonging to Masonry: | and | an accurate plan of the drawing on the floor of a Lodge. | Interspersed with a variety of notes and remarks, sufficient to render | the whole clear to the meanest capacity. | To which are added, | a select collection of songs, and a list of toasts and | sentiments, proper for the Society of Free Masons. | With a list of all the regular Lodges in Scotland. | Boston: | printed by J. Bumstead, for E. Larkin, Cornhill. | 1794.
    1 p.l., 62+ p. [i:] blank; [ii:] frontispiece; [i:] title-page; [2:] blank; [3]-[4:] preface; [4:] advertisement; [5]-[6:] description of the frontispiece; [7]-43: text; 43-60: odes, anthems, and songs; 60-62+: toasts and sentiments.

MH* (imperfect) ¶ Bristol-Evans B8704, Lowens U40, Shipton-Mooney 47088 ¶ Contains 23 Masonic songs. The only located copy of the earliest American edition known lacks the frontispiece and all after p. 62. It would appear that the imprint should contain 64 p. as 150, q.v. See 73 for a complete list of editions.

The ladies [sic] new memorandum-book for 1794. Containing oeconomical tables, country dances for 1794, new and full moons, perpetual diary, a collection of choice new songs, chronological notes for 1794, and a variety of other useful and pleasing matter. Providence: printed by Carter and Wilkinson, and sold at their book and stationery store, opposite the Market. 1794.

Drake 12931, Evans 27191 ¶ Undoubtedly a ghost-title for the 1794 *New ladies* [sic] *memorandum-book,* q.v., based on an unlocated Providence newspaper advertisement.

87 MOTHER GOOSE'S | MELODY: | or | sonnets for the cradle. |

In two parts. | Part I. Contains the most celebrated songs | and lullabies of the good old nurses, | calculated to amuse children and to excite | them to sleep. | Part II. Those of that sweet songster and | nurse of wit and humour, Master William | Shakespeare. | Embellished with cuts, | and illustrated with notes and maxims, | historical, philosophical, and critical. | The second Worcester edition. | Worcester, (Massachusetts) | printed by Isaiah Thomas, | and sold at his bookstore. | MDCC-XCIV.

94, [2] p. [i:] blank; [ii:] frontispiece; [iii:] title-page; [iv:] blank; [v]-x: preface, including one page of typeset music on p. vi; [11]-73: Mother Goose's melody; [74:] blank; [75:] half-title: Mother Goose's | melody. | Part II. | Containing the | lullabies of Shakespear [sic]; 76-94: Shakespeare's songs; [95]-[96]: advertisement for Isaiah Thomas.

Backus 1298, Evans 29122, Rosenbach 179, Sonneck-Upton p. 269, Welch 905.2 ¶ CSmH, MWA*, NjP (imperfect), PP ¶ Contains 68 songs, all juvenile except for 16 by Shakespeare. See 38 for a list of editions.

The new ladies [sic] memorandum-book, for the year M.DCC.XCIV. Containing, Extract from "Paul & Mary" Economical tables for marketing, servants [sic] wages, expences [sic], &c. Country dances for 1794 New and full moons Perpetual diary Vauxhall songs for 1793 Songs by Dibdin Miscellaneous songs Select poetry Watermen's and coach fares Chronological notes for 1794 Birth-days of the royal family Ditto of the sovereigns of Europe Holidays in 1794 And much other pleasing and useful information London: printed for James Evans. North America: Boston, sold by Messrs. Thomas and Andrews, Ebenezer Larkin, Jun. and David West; in Worcester, by

Mr. Isaiah Thomas; and in Providence, Rhode Island, by Messrs. Carter and Wilkinson.

2 p.l., 156 p.

DLC* (2), MWA (imperfect) ¶ Contains 24 songs. An English imprint; probably the prototype for the series which began with 120, q.v.

Rosanna, or The cruel lover. To which is added A toast. Danbury, Nathan Douglas, 1794.

8 p.

Bristol-Evans B8855, Shipton-Mooney 47205, Trumbull Supplement 2578 ¶ RPB* ¶ Contains only 2 songs. See 376 for a 3-song edition of this chapbook.

Tom Paine's jests; being an entirely new and select collection of patriotic bon mots, repartees, anecdotes, epigrams, observations, &c. on political subjects. By Thomas Paine, and other supporters of the rights of man. Speak truth and shame the devil. Seria mixta jocis. Philadelphia: printed for Mathew Carey, No. 118, Market-Street. M.DCC.XCIV.

65, [7] p.

Evans 27469 ¶ MWA* ¶ This edition contains no songs; see 117 for a discussion of this item.

88 TOMMY THUMB'S | SONG BOOK, | for all little | masters and
    misses, | to be sung to them by their nurses, | until they can sing themselves. | By Nurse Lovechild. | To which is added, | a letter from a lady on nursing. | The second Worcester edition. | Printed at Worcester, Massachusetts, | by Isaiah Thomas, | sold wholesale and retail at his bookstore. | MDCCXCIV.

59, [4] p. [1:] blank; [2:] frontispiece; [3:] title-page; [4]-6: to Nurse Lovechild; 7: [half-title:] Artificial memory | for | infants; | whereby | they may acquire | the | knowledge of animals, | and | some of their sounds, | before | they can go or speak. | [catchword:] although; 8-19: text; 20-59: songs; [60]-[63:] advertisement for Isaiah Thomas.

Bristol-Evans B8897, Sabin 96146, Shipton-Mooney 47241, Welch 802.3 ¶ MWA* ¶ Contains 33 juvenile songs as 48, q.v. See also 42 for a list of related editions.

A tribute to the swinish multitude: being a choice collection of patriotic songs. Collected by the celebrated R. Thomson. London: printed. New-York: reprinted by Samuel Loudon & Son, No. 82 Water-Street. M,DCC,XCIV.

Evans 27795, Sonneck-Upton p. 437 ¶ A ghost-title for 105, q.v., based on a New York copyright of 19 July 1794 granted to John Goodeve, proprietor.

1795

89 [AMERICAN SONGSTER; being a select collection of the most
   celebrated American, English, Scotch, and Irish songs. Boston: sold
by William Spotswood, No. 55, Marlborough-Street. 1795.]
     Evans 28182, Lowens U41, Sonneck-Upton p. 21 ¶ No copy located
¶ Perhaps based on a 1795 advertisement in a Boston newspaper for
44 or 52, q.v. I have been unable to locate such an advertisement,
however.

90 [THE BALTIMORE SONGSTER; being a complete collection
   of new songs, including the newest ones sung at the theatres, Philadelphia and Baltimore, and many originals. Baltimore: printed for
Keatinge's book-store, 1795.]
     Lowens U42, Minick 149 ¶ No copy located ¶ Advertised 26 Mar.
1795 in the Baltimore *Telegraphe* under "new publications, printed in
Baltimore for Keatinge's book-store." See also the same title under
1794. *Later editions:* 140, 169.

91 LE | CHANSONNIER | RÉPUBLICAIN, | dédié | aux patriotes. |
   Par différens auteurs. | A Philadelphie, | de l'imprimerie de la Société
| Typographique. | L'an III de la république.
     132 p. [1:] title-page; [2:] blank; [3:] avis; [4:] blank; [5]-129:
songs; [130]-132: index; 132: [in colophon:] Imprimé par la Société
Typographique des | réfugiés du Cap-Français, à Philadelphie, | chez
Parent.
     PU* ¶ Contains 68 songs in French (all indexed). Dated from the
song on p. 24 "chanté à la section des Tuileries, le décadi 20 Pluviose,"
8 Feb. 1795 in the French revolutionary calendar.

A choice collection of above one hundred and twenty love songs, merry
catches and jovial healths being the newest now extant. Worcester,
1795.
     See 98.

92 THE | COLUMBIAN SONGSTER: | being a | select collection | of
   genuine | songs. | From the press of | Thomas and Waldo, | Brook-
field, Massachusetts. | 1795.
     36 p. [1:] title-page; [2:] blank; [3]-36: songs.
     Evans 28457, Sonneck-Upton p. 79. Indexed in Thorpe ¶ MH (im-
perfect), MWA*, MiU-C ¶ Contains 35 songs.

93 [THE COLUMBIAN SONGSTER, containing a great variety of
   melodious and entertaining songs. Boston: printed by E. Russell, and
sold near Liberty-Pole. 1795.]

Evans 28457, Lowens U43, Sonneck-Upton p. 79 ¶ No copy located ¶ Evans apparently took his information from a broadside at MSaE, *The virtuous, faithful and loving wife's garland* (Evans 29819), which contains the following in colophon: "[Boston: printed by E. Russell, and] sold near Liberty-Pole; 1795.—(Price four cents.)—Where shop-keepers, travelling traders, &c. may be supplied with The Columbian songster, (pr. 16 cents single) containing a great variety of melodious and entertaining songs, and several other new pieces; very cheaply by the grose [sic] or dozen." It is possible that the songster here referred to may be 92, but this does not appear too likely.

94 FEAST OF MERRIMENT. | A new American jester. | Being a
  most curious collection of | witty jests—merry stories—smart repartees
— | droll   adventures—funny   jokes—wise | sayings—anecdotes—wag-
geries— | whims—puns—bon mots— | and laughable tricks, | many of
which were never before published. | To which are added | a clever
collection of | curious epitaphs, | humorous epigrams—amorous and
facetious | songs—conundrums—toasts—sen- | timents, &c. &c. | Com-
piled principally for the amusement of long | winter evenings—to expel
care—drown grief— | create mirth—and give the reader a light heart |
and chearful [sic] countenance. | By Well-Fed Domine Double-Chin,
Esq. | Burlington, printed by I. Neale, for | Neale and Kammerer, Jun.
| No. 24, North Third Street, Philadelphia. | 1795.
  132 p. [i:] title-page; [ii:] blank; [iii]-v: preface, dated Philadelphia,
Oct. 1795; [vi:] blank; [7]-109: text; [110]-120: facetious epigrams,
epitaphs, &c.; 121-132: songs.
  Evans 28656, Sonneck-Upton p. 138 ¶ DLC* ¶ Contains 9 songs.

95 [THE JOVIAL SONGSTER; containing a selection of humorous,
  droll, and hunting-songs. Baltimore: printed for Keatinge's book-
store, 1795.]
  Bristol-Evans 9156, Lowens U44, Minick 237, Shipton-Mooney 47472
¶ No copy located ¶ Advertised 26 Mar. 1795 in the Baltimore *Telegraphe* under "New publications, printed in Baltimore for Keatinge's
book-store." See 74 for a list of editions.

96 THE | LITTLE SCHOLAR'S | PRETTY | POCKET COMPAN-
  ION, | or youth's | first step | on the | ladder of learn[ing,] | in |
rhyme and prose. | To lead the tottering step to nature's breeze, | Pluck
out the weed, and cultivate the seeds. | By a friend to the youth of
Columbia. | Bennington, | printed by Anthony Haswell.
  [36] p. [1:] title-page; [2]-[36:] text.
  Evans 28810, McCorison 345, Welch 783 ¶ CtY, PPL* ¶ Contains
3 juvenile songs.

97 THE | MEDLEY; | or, | new Philadelphia songster. | Containing, | a collection of the most approved | songs. | Among which are | many of the most celebrated ballads, | songs, duets, &c. which were sung | at the New Theatre. | Philadelphia: | printed by Neale & Kammerer, Jun. | 1795.

    1 p.l., 222 p. [i:] title-page; [ii:] blank; [1]-222: songs.

    Sonneck-Upton p. 257 ¶ NHi*, RPB ¶ Contains 300 songs. The first 162 pages are apparently copied from the same pages in 68, q.v.

Mirth and music; or, a collection of the newest and choicest songs, sung at all seasons. Containing love songs, merry catches and jovial healths. Worcester, 1795.

    See 98.

98 A NEW | ACADEMY of | compliments: | or, the | lover's secretary: | being wit and mirth improved, by the | most elegant expressions used in the | art of courtship, | in divers examples of writing or indit- | ing letters, relating either to love or | business. | Also, | the silent language; or, a compleat [sic] rule | for discoursing by motion of the hands, without | being understood by the company. | Together with | instructions for writing figure hand, bills | of exchange, receipts, casting accompts [sic], &c. | The significations of moles, and the interpretations | of dreams. A never failing method for women to | get good husbands. | To which is added, | a choice collection of above one hundred | and twenty love songs, merry catches and jovial | healths being the newest now extant; with plain in- | structions for dancing. | Printed at Worcester. | 1795.

    144 p. [1:] blank; [2:] frontispiece; [3:] title-page; [4:] blank; [5]-[6:] preface; [7]-[8:] contents; [9]-93: Wit's improvement, or, a new academy of compliments; [94]-139: Mirth and music; or, a collection of the newest and choicest songs, sung at all seasons. Containing love songs, merry catches and jovial healths; [140]-[144:] The modish dancing master. Or brief and plain instructions for dancing country dances.

    Evans 29145 ¶ MWA*, NN ¶ Contains 51 songs, despite the claim on the title page of "above 120 . . . songs." See 80 for a list of related imprints. *Later edition:* 235.

99 [THE PLEASING SONGSTER: or festive companion: containing a . . . collection of songs . . . calculated for the entertainment of the social mind. . . . Philadelphia: 1795.]

    Evans 29328, Lowens U45, Sonneck-Upton p. 333 ¶ No copy located ¶ The British Library contains a copy with identical title but with a London, 1787 imprint. Cf. Ault p. 240.

100 REILY'S COURTSHIP | to | Cooleen Bawn, | to which are added, | Reily's trial for running a- | way with Cooleen Bawn | Reily's re-

leasement and mar- | riage with Cooleen Bawn. | The hum, a hum. |
Entered according to order.

8 p. [1:] title-page; 2-8: songs.

MdHi* ¶ Contains 4 songs, all named on the title-page. The chap-book probably was printed in Baltimore around 1795. *Later editions:*
166, 209, 297, 371, 531, 609. *Editions after 1820:* (a) 1826, Hanover, Pa.:
Daniel Philip Lange (MH); (b) 1826, n.p. (MdBP). *Related editions:*
442, 508.

101 THE | SKY LARK: | or | gentlemen and ladies' | complete song-
    ster. | Being a collection of the most | modern and celebrated |
American, English and Scotch | songs. | "Music has charms to soothe a
savage breast, | To soften rocks, and bend the knotted oak." | Worcester:
| from the press of | Isaiah Thomas, Jun. | Sold at his bookstore and by
the book- | sellers in Boston.—1795.

228 p. [i:] title-page; [ii:] blank; [iii]-x: index; [11]-228: songs.

Evans 29517, Sabin 81667, Sonneck p. 137, Sonneck-Upton p. 386.
Indexed in Thorpe ¶ DLC*, MB, MWA, NBuG (imperfect), PPL,
RPJCB ¶ Contains 174 songs (171 indexed). *Later edition:* 130.

102 SOCIAL HARMONY; | or, the | cheerful songster's compa- | nion.
    | The vocal muse has pow'r | To sooth [sic] the troubled breast, | To
cheer the darkest hour, | And lull each grief to rest; | To banish sorrow,
care and strife, | And give a double zest to life. | New-York: | printed
by Samuel Campbell, | No. 124, Pearl-Street. | M,DCC,XCV.

108 p. [1:] title-page; [2:] blank; [3]-108: songs.

Evans 29541, Sabin 85691, Sonneck-Upton p. 388. Indexed in Thorpe
¶ CtY, MWA* ¶ Contains 96 songs.

103 [THE SONGSTER'S MAGAZINE. Containing a choice collec-
    tion of the most approved songs in the English language. Philadel-
phia: 1795.]

Evans 29542, Lowens U46, Sabin 86952, Sonneck-Upton p. 405 ¶
No copy located.

104 [TOM THUMB'S SONG BOOK, for all little masters and misses,
    to be sung to them by their nurses. By Nurse Lovechild. To which
is added a letter from a lady, on nursing. Boston: printed and sold by
Samuel Hall, No. 53, Cornhill. 1795.]

Evans 28987, Lowens U47, Sonneck-Upton p. 436, Welch 802.4 ¶
No copy located ¶ Evans reports that the item is a 48mo. Welch
reports advertisements for a Hall edition in 1791, 1792, 1793, 1794, and
1796. See 42 for a list of editions.

105 A | TRIBUTE | to the | swinish multitude: | being | a choice col-
    lection | of | patriotic songs. | Collected by the celebrated | R. Thom-

son. | London: printed. | New-York: re-printed by Samuel Loudon & Son, | No. 82, Water-Street. | M,DCC,XCV.

96 p. [i:] half-title: A | tribute | to the | swinish multitude; [ii:] blank; [iii:] title-page; [iv:] blank; [v]-x: to the public, alias the "swinish multitude," signed R. Thomson; [11]-96: songs.

Evans 29629, Sonneck-Upton p. 437 ¶ DLC (lacks half-title), MWA*, RPJCB ¶ Contains 42 songs. See 117 for a related edition.

106 [THE WARBLING SONGSTER, or cure for dulness [sic].
    Philadelphia, 1795.]
    Evans 29827, Lowens U48, Sonneck-Upton p. 448 ¶ No copy located.

107 [THE] | WINTER EVENINGS [sic] AMUSEMENT, | or, | jo-
    vial companion. | Containing | a choice collection | of | songs, | much admired. | And sung at most genteel places of | amusement. | Boston. | Printed and sold by J. White, near Charles- | River Bridge, and by W. T. Clap, in | Fish-Street. 1795.
    24 p. [1:] title-page; [2:] index; [3]-24: songs.
    Bristol-Evans B9432, Lowens U49, Shipton-Mooney 47690, Sonneck-Upton p. 473 ¶ RPB* (imperfect) ¶ Contains 18 songs (all indexed). The only copy extant lacks pp. 11-12 and the title-page is mutilated. *Later edition:* 215.

1796

108 THE AMERICAN | ACADEMY | OF | COMPLIMENTS; | or,
    the complete American secretary: | containing | the true art of in-diting letters suitable to the capaci- | ties of youth and age; relating to familiar conversa- | tion between friends and acquaintance [sic], hus-band and | wife, children and parents, masters and apprentices, | brothers and sisters, and kindred in general; also, | love letters on all occasions, with others relating to | trade and business of all kinds, in an apt, easy, and | plain style. | Likewise, rules for directing, superscribing, and sub- | scribing of letters; also, the titles of persons of quali- | ty, and all other degrees. | With dialogues very witty and pleasing, relating to love, | familiar discourse, and other matters for the improv- | ing the ele-gance of the English speech, and accom- | plishment in discourse. | To which are added, | I. The art of good breeding, and behaviour, with in- | structions for carving fish, flesh, and fowl, after the | new manner. II. The English fortune-teller, as to | what relates to good and bad fortune in maids, wi- | dows, widowers, and bachelors. III. Joyful tidings | to the female sex. IV. Treatises of moles. V. Inter- | pretation of dreams. | With a collection of the newest songs. | Philadelphia: | printed by Godfrey Deshong, and | Richard Folwell. | M,DCC,XCVI.
    106 p. [1:] title-page; [2:] preface; [3]-93: text; 93-106: songs.

Bristol-Evans B9447, Shaw 5696, Shipton-Mooney 47698, Stark 1170 ¶ CtY, ICU, MdBG, MWA, NN*, RPB ¶ Contains 9 songs. For a list of other editions and related imprints, see 80.

109 [AMERICAN SONGS, with a variety of small matters for pedlars, etc. Fairhaven, Vt.: J. P. Spooner, 1796.]
Bristol-Evans B9451, McCorison 376A, Shipton-Mooney 47700 ¶ No copy located ¶ According to McCorison, advertised in D. Defoe, *Wonderful life . . . Robinson Crusoe* (Fairhaven, 1796).

The disobedient son, and cruel husband. Being a full and true account of one Mr. John Jones, a gentleman's son in Wiltshire, whose father left him an estate of twenty hundred pounds a year, and married a lady of great fortune in the same place; but being reduced to poverty and want with riotous living, he killed his wife and children, and afterwards hanged his mother on a tree in the orchard, with the last dying words of this wretch, who was hanged before his mother's door. To which are added, The wild rover. And The humours of whiskey. Dublin: printed by W. Jones, Thomas-Strt.[?] January, 1796.
8 p.
Bristol-Evans B9528, Shipton-Mooney 47767 ¶ PPL* ¶ Apparently included in Bristol-Evans on the mistaken assumption that the imprint is fictitious. The imprint gives every evidence of authenticity, however. Jones emigrated from Ireland, and set up shop as a printer in Philadelphia in 1796. See 110, which appears to be his earliest known American chapbook.

110 FOUR NEW SONGS, viz.| The | shipwreck'd sailors | on the | rocks of Scylla. | To which are added | The | French fleet June 1st. | Also The sorrowful goal [sic] groans, of | Sarah Delany; | with The sweet little girl that I love; | and The | American independance [sic]. | Philadelphia: | printed by William Jones, 1796.
8 p. [1:] title-page; 2-8: songs.
Bristol-Evans 9546, Shipton-Mooney 47783 ¶ PPL* ¶ Contains 4 songs although 5 are named on the title-page; "The French fleet June 1st" is omitted.

Green upon the cape. To which are added, Erin go bragh. The birth of Paddy O'Rafferty. Alone by the light of the moon. Dublin. Printed for the purchasers.
8 p. [1:] title-page; 2-8: songs.
Shaw 50545 ¶ PPL* ¶ Shaw probably considers the Dublin imprint fictitious. There is a strong likelihood, however, that the songster was, in fact, printed in Dublin by William Jones just before he emigrated from Ireland to the United States in 1796.

111 THE | HISTORY | OF A | LITTLE BOY | found under a hay-
cock. | To which is added, | The royal alphabet. | Likewise, | Little
stories for little | children. | Boston: | printed by J. White and C. | Cam-
bridge, near Charles' | River Bridge.

30 p. [1:] blank; [2:] frontispiece; [3:] title-page; [4:] blank; [5]-
26: text; [27]-30: songs.

Evans 21889, Welch 675.3 ¶ CtHi* ¶ Contains 5 juvenile songs.
According to Welch, White and Cambridge "were together through
1743 only." *Related item:* 85.

112 JACHIN AND BOAZ; | or, an | authentic key | to the door of |
Free-Masonry, | both ancient and modern. | Calculated not only for
the instruction of every new | made Mason; but also for the informa-
tion | of all who intend to become Brethren. | Containing, | I. A cir-
cumstantial account of all the | proceedings in making a Mason, | with
the several obligations of an | Entered Apprentice, Fellow- | Craft, and
Master; the prayers, | and also the sign, grip, and pass- | word of each
degree, with the ce- | remony of the mop and pail. | II. The manner
of opening a Lodge, | and setting the Craft to work. | III. The Entered
Apprentice, Fellow- | Craft, and Master's lectures, verbatim, | as de-
livered in all Lodges; with the | song at the conclusion of each part.
| IV. The origin of Masonry; de- | scription of Solomon's temple; his- |
tory of the murder of the Grand | Master Hiram by the three Fellow-
| Crafts; their discovery and pu- | nishment; the burial of Hiram by |
King Solomon's order; with the | five points of fellowship, &c. | V. The
ceremony of the instalment [sic] | of the Masters of different Lodges | on
St. John's day—description | of the regalia, &c. | VI. Ceremonies used
at the funeral | of a Mason. | VII. A safe and easy method pro- | posed,
by which a man may obtain | admittance into any Lodge, with- | out
passing through the form re- | quired, and thereby save a guinea | or
two in his pocket. | VIII. Anthems, odes, songs, toasts, | &c. | Illustrated
with | a beautiful frontispiece of the regalia, jewels, and | emblematical
ornaments belonging to Masonry. | And | an accurate plan of the draw-
ing on the floor of a Lodge, | interspersed with a variety of | notes and
remarks, | necessary to explain and render the whole clear to the mean-
est capacity. | By a gentleman belonging to the Jerusalem Lodge; a
frequent visitor | at the Queen's Arms, St. Paul's Church-Yard; the
Horn, in Fleet-Street; | Crown and Anchor, Strand; and the Saluta-
tion, Newgate-Street. | Try me—prove me. | A new edition, greatly
enlarged and improved. | New-York: | printed by Tiebout & O'Brien,
for Evert Duyckinck & Co. | booksellers and stationers, No. 110, Pearl-
Street. | M,DCC,XCVI.

1 p.l., vi, 58 p. [i:] blank; [ii:] frontispiece; [i:] title-page; [ii:]
blank; [iii]-iv: preface to the first edition; [v]-vi: advertisement; [1]-
40: text; 40-54: odes, anthems, and songs; [55]-58: toasts and sentiments.

Evans 31147 ¶ DLC*, DSC, MBFM, MH, MWA, NNFM ¶ Contains 16 Masonic songs. See 73 for a list of editions.

113 JACHIN AND BOAZ; | or, an authentic key to the door of | Free-Masonry, | both ancient and modern. | Calculated not only for the instruction of every new made Mason, but | also for the information of all who intend to become Brethren. | Containing, | I. A circumstantial account of | all the proceedings in making | a Mason, with the several obli- | gations of an Entered Apprentice, | Fellow-Craft, and Master; the | prayers, and also the sign, | grip, and pass-word of each | degree, with the ceremony | of the mop and pail. | II. The manner of opening a | Lodge, and setting the Craft | to work. | III. The Entered Apprentice, | Fellow-Craft, & Master's lec- | tures, verbatim, as delivered | in all Lodges; with the song | at the conclusion of each part. | IV. The origin of Masonry; | description of Solomon's Tem- | ple; history of the murder of | the Grand Master Hiram by | the three Fellow-Crafts; their | discovery and punishment; | the burial of Hiram by King | Solomon's order; with the | five points of fellowship, &c. | V. The ceremony of the instal- | ment [sic] of the Masters of dif- | ferent Lodges on St. John's | day.—Description of the re- | galia, &c. | VI. Ceremonies used at the fu- | neral of a Mason. | VII. A safe and easy method | proposed, by which a man | may obtain admittance into | any Lodge, without passing | through the form, required, | and thereby save a guinea or | two in his pocket. | VIII. Anthems, odes, songs, toasts, &c. | Illustrated with | a beautiful frontispiece of the regalia, jewels and emblematical | ornaments belonging to Masonry, and an accurate plan of the | drawing on the floor of a Lodge, interspersed with a variety | of notes and remarks, necessary to explain and render the | whole clear to the meanest capacity. | By a gentleman belonging to the Jerusalem Lodge, a frequent | visitor at the Queen's Arms, St. Paul's Church-Yard; the Horn, in | Fleet-Street; Crown and Anchor, Strand; and the Salutation, New- | gate-Street. | Try me—prove me. | A new edition, greatly enlarged and improved. | Philadelphia: | printed for H. & P. Rice, | No. 50, Market, and No. 16, South Second-Street, | by Snowden & M'Corkle. | 1796.

1 p.l., vi, 58 p. [i:] blank; [ii:] frontispiece; [i:] title-page; [ii:] blank; [iii]-iv: preface; [v]-vi: advertisement; [1]-40: text; 40-54: odes, anthems, and songs; [55]-58: toasts and sentiments.

PPPFM* ¶ Contains 16 Masonic songs as 112. See 73 for a list of editions.

114 THE | MERMAID: | or, | nautical songster, | being | a new collection | of | favourite sea-songs. | Here social mirth serenely smiles, | And joyful songs inspire the breast; | Music the weight of care beguiles, | And lulls each gloomy thought to rest. | The fifth edition, with great

additions. | New-York: | printed and sold by John Harrisson, at his | book-store and printing-office, Yorick's | Head, No. 3, Peck-Slip. | M,DCC,XCVI. | [Price twelve cents.]

1 p.l., 78, [4] p. [i:] blank; [ii:] frontispiece; [i:] title-page; [2:] advertisement; [3]-77: songs; 78: the sailor's description of a hunting; [79:] toasts and sentiments; [80]-[82:] index.

Oxford (Bodleian Library)* ¶ Contains 60 songs (61 indexed). No earlier edition, either American or English, has come to light. Cf. Ault p. 251. For a list of other editions, see 75.

115 PADDY'S RESOURCE: | being | a select collection | of | original and modern | patriotic | songs, | toasts and sentiments, | compiled for the use | of | all firm patriots. | First American edition. | Philadelphia: | printed for, and sold by T. Stephens. | M,DCC,XCVI.

1 p.l., 72 p. [i:] blank; [ii:] frontispiece; [1:] title-page; [2:] blank; [3:] preface; [4:] index; [5]-69: songs; 70-72: toasts and sentiments.

Evans 30937, Lowens U50, Sonneck-Upton p. 324 ¶ DLC* (imperfect) ¶ Contains 59 songs (all indexed). The only known copy lacks pp. 9-12, 33-36, 67-70. The English or Irish edition from which this imprint was evidently borrowed is unknown, but for a Dublin edition of 1798 in Oxford (Bodleian Library), see Ault p. 254. The American 1798 edition differs considerably from this one in content. *Later edition:* 160.

116 [SONGS FROM THE ROCK to hail the approaching day; sacred to truth, liberty, and peace. Inscribed to the sovereign people. By the author of Flowers from Sharon [i.e. Richard Lee]. [Two lines from] Isaiah. Philadelphia: printed for Richard Lee. 1796.]

Evans 32368, Lowens U51 ¶ No copy located ¶ A London, 1794 edition is located at NNUT.

117 TOM PAINE'S JESTS; | being an entirely | new and select collection | of | patriotic bon mots, repartees, anecdotes, | epigrams, observations, &c. | on | political subjects, | by Thomas Paine, | and other | supporters of the rights of man. | To which is added, | A tribute to the swinish multitude, | being a choice collection of | patriotic songs | Speak truth and shame the devil. | Seria mixta jocis. | Philadelphia: | printed for Mathew Carey, No. 118, | Market-Street. | M.DCC.XCVI.

72 p. [1:] title-page; [2:] blank; [3]-4: dedication to the swinish multitude, dated London, 2 Sept. 1794; [5]-30: jests, &c.; 31: 2nd title-page: A | tribute | to the | swinish multitude: | being | a choice collection | of | patriotic songs. | Collected by the celebrated | R. Thomson; [32:] blank; [33]-37: to the public, alias the swinish multitude, signed R. Thomson; [38:] blank; [39]-72: songs.

BAL 6446, Evans 30952, Sabin 58242, Sonneck-Upton p. 435. Indexed in Thorpe ¶ CSmH, CtHT-W, CtY, DLC* (5), MB, MH, MMeT,

MWA, NBuG, NHi, NN, NjR, PBL, PHi, PPL, RPB, RPJCB ¶ Contains 19 songs. A 1794 edition of *Tom Paine's jests* (Evans 27469) at MWA omits the collection of songs. See 105 for a completely different collection of songs issued under the *Tribute to the swinish multitude* title.

A | tribute | to the | swinish multitude: | being | a choice collection | of | patriotic songs. | Collected by the celebrated | R. Thomson. [Philadelphia, 1796.]
　　See 117.

118 THE | VOCAL COMPANION. | Being a | choice collection | of the | most approved songs, | catches, duets, &c. | Philadelphia: | printed for Mathew Carey, | No. 118, Market-Street. | 1796.
　　1 p.l., 196 p. [i:] blank; [ii:] frontispiece; [i:] title-page; [ii:] blank; [iii]-viii: index; [9]-196: songs.
　　Evans 31515, Sabin 100649, Sonneck-Upton p. 445. Indexed in Thorpe ¶ DLC*, MWA (lacks frontispiece), PHi, RPB ¶ Contains 217 songs (213 indexed).

1797

119 [AMERICAN ACADEMY OF COMPLIMENTS: or the complete American secretary. With a collection of the newest songs. Wilmington: printed by Peter Brynberg. 1797.]
　　Evans 31717, Lowens U52, Sonneck-Upton p. 15 ¶ No copy located ¶ Apparently constructed by Evans from an advertisement. I have not succeeded in tracing any advertisement for the work in the extant Wilmington newspapers of the year 1797. See 80 for a list of editions.

120 THE | AMERICAN | LADIES [sic] POCKET BOOK | for | MDCCXCVII | Philadelphia published by W. Y. Birch | No. 17 South Second Street.
　　1 p.l., 155 p. [i:] title-page; [ii:] blank; [i:] address, dated Philadelphia, 26 Nov. 1796; [ii:] explanation of the calendar; [iii]-iv: contents; [5]-[129:] text; [130]-133: poems; 134-138: songs; 139-140: epigrams; 141-143: enigmas; 144: charades; [145]-146: country dances for the year 1797; 147-150: a new marketing table; 151-155: miscellany; 155: [in colophon:] printed by J. Thompson.
　　Drake 10417, Evans 29972, Lowens U53 ¶ InU, MWA (imperfect), PHi (imperfect), PPAmP* ¶ Contains 9 songs. The first in a long series, apparently all containing songs, which ended in 1827. These pocket books usually were issued in the previous November of the year given on the title-page, but for convenience of reference, they are keyed in this bibliography by date of use rather than actual year of

issue. Possibly related to 225 and 241, q.v. *Later editions:* 138, 167, 184, 211, 229, 240, 266, 288, 316, 333, 345, 356, 368, 380, 408, 435, 456, 481, 503, 534, 563, 611, 635. *Editions after 1820:* (a) 1821, Philadelphia: A. Small (PHi); (b) 1822, Philadelphia: A. Small (PHi); (c) 1823, Philadelphia: A. Small (PHi, RPB); (d) 1824, [Philadelphia: A. Small] (no copy located); (e) 1825, Philadelphia: A. Small (MHi, MdBP); (f) 1826, Philadelphia: R. H. Small (PHi); (g) 1827, Philadelphia: R. H. Small (PHi).

121 A | COLLECTION | OF | ESSAYS, | on a variety of subjects. | In | prose and verse. | Newark | Printed by John Woods. | 1797.
  84, [5]-58, [iii]-28, [3]-24, 8 p. [1:] title-page; [2:] blank; [3]-84: text; [5:] caption-title: The | prompter; [5]-58: text; [iii]-[iv:] blank; [v]-vi: preface; [7:] caption-title: The Morris-town ghost | delineated; [7]-28: text; [3:] caption-title: Court of King's Bench, | Westminster. | Sitting of June twenty-four, | before Lord Kenyon and a special jury. | The King v. Williams, | for publishing Paine's Age of reason. | Mr. Erskine's speech on the part of the prosecution; [3]-24: text; [5:] resolution by the Republican Society of Newark, dated 14 July 1794 and signed Aaron Pennington, secretary; [6:] blank; [7:] caption-title: An | oration | delivered | on the | fourth July, 1794; [7]-22: text; [1:] caption-title: Patriotic songs, | selected for celebrating the | anniversary of | American independence. | [1]-8: songs.
  Evans 34482 ¶ NjHi* (2 copies, 1 imperfect), NjN ¶ Contains 5 songs. This curious production apparently consists of a number of unrelated items bound together. As the second copy of NjHi (part of the Ely Collection) contains only the 1st, 3rd, 4th, and 6th groupings, perhaps the whole collection was haphazardly put together. However, no separate copy of the *Patriotic songs* has come to light, although some of the other sections do appear to have been sold individually.

122 THE | COLUMBIAN SONGSTER, | or | jovial companion: | being a collection of two hundred and twenty | choice songs, | selected from various volumes and de- | tached parcels—of which | near fifty are American productions. | Mirth, love, and sentiment, are here happily blended. | The chastest ear unoffended. | From Greenleaf's Press— New-York, 1797.
  1 p.l., viii, [1]-96, [2], 97-232 p. [i:] blank; [ii:] frontispiece; [i:] title-page; ii-viii: index; [1]-96: songs; [96a:] blank; [96b:] illustration; 97-232: songs.
  Evans 31961, Sabin 14879, Sonneck p. 27, Sonneck-Upton p. 79. Indexed in Thorpe ¶ MB (lacks frontispiece and plate), MWA*, MiU-C (lacks plate), N, NHi (imperfect), PPiU (imperfect), RPB (2 copies, one lacking frontispiece and plate, the other imperfect) ¶ Contains 227 songs (221 indexed). See 306 and 320 for related imprints.

123 DIBDIN'S | MUSEUM, | being | a collection | of the newest and most admired | songs. | Philadelphia: | printed by R. Aitken, No. 22 Market-Street. | For Joseph Charless. | M.DCC.XCVII.

72 p. [1:] title-page; [2:] blank; [3]-72: songs.

Evans 32039, Sonneck p. 39, Sonneck-Upton p. 107 ¶ PPL* ¶ Contains 71 songs. The title is misleading—many of the songs are not by Dibdin.

Free-Masonry. Unparalleled sufferings of John Coustos. New York, 1797.

See 136.

124 THE | FREEMASON'S | MONITOR; | or, | illustrations | of | Masonry: | in two parts. | By a Royal Arch Mason, | K. T.—K. of M.— &c. &c. | Part I. | Printed at Albany, | for Spencer and Webb, Market-Street. | 1797.

284 p. [i:] title-page; [ii:] blank; [iii:] copyright notice, N. Y., 12 Sept. 1797, Spencer and Webb, proprietors; [iv:] blank; [v]-vi: preface, dated 26 Sept. 1797; [vii]-[xii:] contents; [13]-216: illustrations of Masonry, book 1; [217:] second title-page: The | Freemason's | monitor; | or, | illustrations | of | Masonry: | in two parts. | Part II. | Containing, | an account of the ineffable | degrees of Masonry. | Printed at Albany, | for Spencer and Webb, Market-Street. | 1797; [218:] blank; [219]-[220:] preface, dated Sept. 1797; [221]-269: illustrations of Masonry; [270:] blank; [271]-284: Masonic songs.

Barthelmess p. 30, Brinley 6759, Evans 33173, McMurtrie 161, Morris p. 23, Sabin 25810, Sonneck-Upton p. 147 ¶ DLC*, DeWI, IaCrM, MB, MBAt, MBFM, MH, MWA, MiU-C, N, NNFM, PPPFM (3), PBL (imperfect), RPB, RPJCB (imperfect) ¶ Contains 9 Masonic songs. Reprinted in 1899 as No. 1 of the publications of the Masonic Historical Society of New York. The compiler of this extremely popular guide to Freemasonry was Thomas Smith Webb. *Later editions:* 231, 295, 347, 420, 510, 511, 512, 567, 568. *Editions after 1820:* (a) 1821, Salem (DSC, MB, MWA, NNFM, PHi, PPPFM); (b) 1822, Philadelphia [in Spanish, with songs omitted] (DLC, PPL, PU).

125 JACHIN AND BOAZ; | or, an | authentic key | to the door of | Free Masonry, | both ancient and modern, | calculated not only for the instruction | of every new made Mason; but | also for the information of all who | intend to become Brethren. | Illustrated with | a beautiful frontispiece of the regalia, jewels, | and emblematical ornaments belonging to Masonry. | And | an accurate plan of the drawing on the floor of a | Lodge, interspersed with a variety of | notes and remarks, | necessary to explain and render the whole clear to | the meanest capacity. | By a gentleman belonging to the Jerusalem | Lodge; a frequent visitor at the Queen's Arms. St. | Paul's Church-Yard; the Horn,

in Fleet-Street; | Crown and Anchor, Strand; and the Salutation, | Newgate-Street. | Try me—prove me. | A new edition, greatly enlarged and improved. | Albany: | printed by Charles R. & George Webster, | at their bookstore, in the White-House, corner | of State and Pearl-Streets. | M.DCC.XCVII.

1 p.l., 75, [1] p. [i:] blank; [ii:] frontispiece; [i:] title-page; [ii:] contents; [iii]-iv: preface; [v:] advertisement; [vi]-[vii:] description of the frontispiece; [8]-55: text; 55-71: odes, anthems, and songs; 71-75: toasts and sentiments; [76:] advertisement for Webster's bookstore.

Bristol-Evans B10092, Shipton-Mooney 48158 ¶ CtY, DSC*, MBFM (imperfect), MWA, NIC, NNFM, PPPFM, RPJCB ¶ Contains 16 Masonic songs. As 112, q.v. See also 73 for a list of editions.

126 THE | MARYLAND | AHIMAN REZON, | of | Free & Accepted Masons: | containing | the history of Masonry, | from the establishment of the Grand Lodge | to the present time; with their | ancient charges, addresses, | prayers, lectures, prologues, | epilogues, songs, &c. | Collected from their | old records, faithful traditions, & Lodge-books. | Compiled | by order of the Grand Lodge of Maryland, | by Brother G. Keatinge, W. M. B. L. | "May all our lessons through the world extend, | "Then man will be of man the certain friend; | "No different faith or party disunite, | "And doing good be every man's delight." | Baltimore: | printed by W. Pechin—for George Keatinge's | wholesale & retail book-store. | 1797.

[iv], [9]-86, [2], [87]-94, [105]-272 p. [i:] title-page; [ii:] blank; [iii:] sanction, dated 7 May 5797; [iv:] blank; [9]-86: proceedings of the grand conventions of Free-Masons on the Eastern shore of the State of Maryland; [86a]-[86b:] contents; [87]-94: constitution and rules; [105]-216: the Ahiman Rezon; [217]-232: prologues, epilogues, &c.; [233]-272: Masonic songs.

Barthelmess p. 6 (given as a 1799 imprint in error), Evans 32330, Minick 359, Morris p. 22 ¶ DLC (2, both imperfect), IaCrM, MBAt, MWA*, MdBE, MdBFM ¶ Contains 50 Masonic songs.

Masonic. Songs, oratorio, odes, anthems, prologues, epilogues, and toasts. Waterford, 1797.

See 131.

The Morris-Town ghost delineated, and patriotic revolutionary songs. By Ransford Rogers. Morris-Town: printed by E. Cooper & Co. 1797.

Evans 34482. Apparently a ghost-title for 121, q.v., based on groupings 3 and 6 in that olla podrida. Evans locates a copy of this imprint at NjHi, but a search by the librarian of that institution, Mr. William H. Gaines, failed to turn it up.

127 THE | NIGHTINGALE. | A | collection | of the | most elegant | songs, | now in vogue. | "The charms of sweet music no pencil can paint." | Samuel Preston, Amherst. | 1797.

40 p. [1:] title-page; [2:] blank; [3]-40: songs.

Bristol-Evans B10041, Lowens U54, Shipton-Mooney 48207 ¶ MWA* (imperfect) ¶ Contains 34+ songs. The only copy extant lacks pp. 9-16.

128 THE | NIGHTINGALE | of | liberty: | or | delights of harmony. | A choice collection | of | patriotic, Masonic, & entertaining | songs. | To which are added | toasts and sentiments, | moral, humorous, and re-publican. | Thou sweetest songster of the feather'd tribe, | Carol, with notes harmonious, songs to liberty. | New-York: | printed by John Harrisson, | and sold at his book-store, No. 3 Peck-Slip. | 1797.

1 p.l., 83 p. [i:] blank; [ii:] frontispiece; [1:] title-page; [2:] advertisement for John Harrisson; [3]-80: songs; 81: toasts and sentiments; 82-83: index.

Evans 32584, Sonneck-Upton p. 297 ¶ DLC* ¶ Contains 59 songs (all indexed).

Patriotic songs, | selected for celebrating the | anniversary of | American independence. [Newark, 1797.]

See 121.

129 [EINE SCHÖNE SAMMLUNG der neuesten Lieder zum gesell-schaftlichen Vergnügen. Reading: gedruckt bey Jungmann und Comp. 1797.]

Evans 32809, Lowens U55 ¶ No copy located ¶ Copyright, Pa., 17 Jan. 1797, Gottlob Jungmann, proprietor.

130 THE | SKY LARK: | or | gentlemen & ladies' | complete songster. | Being the largest collection of the most | modern and celebrated | American, English & Scotch | songs | ever yet published. | Second edition. | 1797. | Worcester: | from the press of and for | Isaiah Thomas, Jun. | Sold wholesale and retail at his bookstore.

310, [2] p. [i:] title-page; [ii:] blank; [iii:] preface, signed Isaiah Thomas, Jun., and dated Worcester, Oct. 1797; [iv:] blank; [v]-xii: index; 13-282: songs; [283]-300: appendix containing a number of celebrated Masonic songs; [301]-310: a collection of the newest cotillions and country dances; [311]-[312:] advertisement for books available at Isaiah Thomas, Jun., Worcester.

Evans 32839, Sabin 81667, Sonneck p. 137, Sonneck-Upton p. 386 ¶ MB (imperfect), MWA*, RPB ¶ Contains 290 songs (293 indexed). In the preface, Thomas "dedicates the tribute of gratitude to Mr. Williamson, late of the Haymarket Theatre, Boston, for the friendly and interested part he has taken, in order to render the work of the greatest merit of any extant." See 101 for an earlier edition.

131 [descriptive tag:] MASONIC. | [title:] SONGS, oratorio, odes, | anthems, prologues, | epilogues, and toasts: | adapted to | the different degrees of | Masonry. | Waterford: | compiled, printed, & published, | by Brother James Lyon. | In the Year of Light, | VMDCCXCVII.

vii, [1], [5]-140 p. [i:] title-page; [ii:] endorsement, dated Waterford, 14 Mar. 5797; [iii]-vii: index; [viii:] blank; [5]-15: oratorio; [16:] blank; [17]-137: songs; [138]-140: toasts.

Barthelmess p. 28 (incorrectly dated 1789), Evans 32439, Sonneck-Upton p. 254 ¶ DLC (imperfect), DSC (imperfect), PPPFM* ¶ Contains 74 Masonic songs (71 indexed).

132 THE | SYREN, | or | vocal enchantress: | being a collection of the new- | est and most admired | miscellaneous,—pathetic, and passionate,—Anacre- | ontic and jovial,—comic, ingenious, and | witty,—sea, hunting, and Masonic | songs. | Selected from the most approved sentimental, | humorous, and ingenious publications; | including all the best songs of Dibdin Edwin [sic], &c. | Wilmington; | printed for and sold by James Wilson, book-seller | and stationer, No. 5, High Street, opposite | the Upper Market-House. | 1797.

1 p.l., 38, 36, 24, 48, 28, [5] p. [i:] title-page; [ii]-[1:] blank; [2:] advertisement for James Wilson's book stock; [3:] [additional title-page:] The syren: | part I. | Miscellaneous songs. | Wilmington: | printed for Bonsal & Niles, and James Wilson; [4:] blank; [5]-38: songs; [1:] [additional title-page:] The syren: | Part II. | Pathetic & passionate songs. | Wilmington: | printed for Bonsal & Niles, and James Wilson. | D; [2:] blank; [3]-36: songs; [1:] [additional title-page:] The syren: | part II [*recte*, III]. | Anacreontic & jovial songs. | Wilmington: | printed for Bonsal & Niles, and James Wilson. | G; [2:] blank; [3]-24: songs; [1:] [additional title-page:] The syren: | part IV. | Comic, ingenious & witty | songs. | Wilmington: | printed for Bonsal & Niles, and James Wilson. | I; [2:] blank; [3]-48: songs; [1:] [additional title-page:] The syren: | part V. | Sea, hunting & Masonic | songs. | Wilmington: | printed for Bonsal & Niles, and James Wilson. | N; [2:] blank; [3]-28: songs; [29]-[33:] index.

Evans 32901, Sabin 94132, Sonneck-Upton p. 420. Indexed in Thorpe ¶ DeWI, ICN (imperfect), RPB* ¶ Contains 171 songs (all indexed). The DeWI and ICN copies have a different index extending over 6 pages and listing 176 items, but are otherwise identical. *Later edition:* 133.

133 THE | SYREN, | or | vocal enchantress: | being a collection of the new- | est and most admired | miscellaneous,—pathetic, and passionate,—Anacre- | ontic and jovial,—comic, ingenious, and | witty,—sea,

hunting, and Masonic | songs. | Selected from the most approved senti-
mental, | humorous, and ingenious publications; | including all the best
songs of | Dibdin Edwin [sic], &c. | Wilmington: | printed by Bonsal
and Niles, in Market-Street | 1797.

   1 p.l., 38, 36, 24, 48, 28, [5] p. [i:] title-page; [ii]-[1:] blank; [2:]
advertisement for James Wilson's book stock; [3:] [additional title-
page:] The syren: | part 1. | Miscellaneous songs. | Wilmington: |
printed for Bonsal & Niles, and James Wilson; [4:] blank; [5]-38:
songs; [1:] [additional title-page:] The syren: | part II. | Pathetic &
passionate songs. | Wilmington: | printed for Bonsal & Niles, and
James Wilson. | D; [2:] blank; [3]-36: songs; [1:] [additional title-
page:] The syren: | part II [*recte,* III]. | Anacreontic & jovial songs. |
Wilmington: | printed for Bonsal & Niles, and James Wilson. | G;
[2:] blank; [3]-24: songs; [1:] [additional title-page:] The syren: |
part IV. | Comic, ingenious & witty | songs. | Wilmington: | printed for
Bonsal & Niles, and James Wilson. | I; [2:] blank; [3]-48: songs; [1:]
[additional title-page:] The syren: | part V. | Sea, hunting & Masonic |
songs. | Wilmington: | printed for Bonsal & Niles, and James Wilson. |
N; [2:] blank; [3]-28: songs; [29]-[33:] index.

   MH*, MWA (imperfect) ¶ Contains 171 songs (all indexed). As
132, q.v., except for variant title-page.

134 THE | TEA-DRINKING WIFE. | To which are added, | The
    tempest. | And | Pretty Nancy. | New-York: | printed for the hawk-
    ers.—1797.

   8 p. [1:] title-page; [2]-8: songs.

   Bristol-Evans B10122, Shipton-Mooney 48265 ¶ RPB* (imperfect)
¶ Apparently contains 3 songs, all named on the title-page. The only
known copy lacks the two inner leaves (pp. 3-6).

135 THE | THEATRICAL SONGSTER: | or | amusing companion.
    | Containing | a choice collection | of much admired | songs. | Sung
at the theatres in Boston, and | other genteel places of amusement. | Bos-
ton. | Printed and sold by J. White, near Charles'- [sic] | River Bridge,
and by the booksellers. 1797.

   24 p. [1:] title-page; [2:] index; [3]-24: songs.

   Sabin 95293, Sonneck-Upton p. 426 ¶ MH* ¶ Contains 15 songs
(all indexed). The report in Sabin that this copy is "missing" is
erroneous.

136 [descriptive tag:] FREE-MASONRY. | [title:] Unparalleled suf-
    ferings | of | John Coustos, | who nine times underwent | the most
cruel tortures ever invented by man, | and | sentenced to the galley four
years, | by command of the inquisitors at Lisbon, | in order to extort
from him | the secrets of Free-Masonry; | from whence | he was released
by the gracious interposition of his late | majesty, King George II. | To

this edition is added, | a selection of Masonic songs, | and | a complete list of Lodges, | foreign and domestic. | New-York: | printed by Jacob S. Mott, for Charles | Smith, No. 51, Maiden-Lane. | 1797.

2 p.l., ii, iv, 282 p. [i:] title-page; [ii:] blank; [iii:] dedication; [iv:] blank; [i]-ii: preface; [i]-iv: introduction; [1]-200: text; [201]-254: songs; [255]-282: list of foreign Lodges.

Evans 31999 ¶ CtY, DLC*, IaCrM, MBFM, MWA, NNFM, NSchU, RPJCB ¶ Contains 44 Masonic songs. *Later editions:* 137, 163, 164, 208, 263, 559.

137 [THE UNPARALLELED SUFFERINGS of John Coustos, who nine times underwent the most cruel tortures invented by man, and was sentenced to the galley four years, by command of the inquisitors at Lisbon, in order to extort from him the secrets of Freemasonry; from whence he was released by the interposition of the King of Great Britain. With an account of the inquisition, a collection of Masonic songs, and a list of Lodges. New-London: printed and sold by Charles Holt. 1797.]

Evans 31998, Lowens U56 ¶ No copy located ¶ Evans reports that the item is an 8vo with 280 p. Advertised 13 Dec. 1797 in the New London *Bee* as "just received, and for sale at this office." Existence doubtful. For a list of editions, see 136.

1798

An account of the unparalleled sufferings of John Coustos. Norwich, 1798.
See 163.

138 [THE AMERICAN LADIES POCKET BOOK, with an almanac, for the year 1798. Philadelphia: published by William Y. Birch, No. 17, South Second Street. 1797.]

Drake 10446, Evans 31722, Lowens U57, Sonneck-Upton p. 16 ¶ No copy located ¶ Evans reports that the title-page and frontispiece are engraved but gives no collation; according to Sonneck-Upton, this item was advertised 17 Jan. 1799 as "just published by William Y. Birch, 17 South Second St.," Philadelphia, and contains "new country dances, songs, &c." The advertisement referred to, however, was published earlier—on 24 Nov. 1798 in *Dunlap's American Daily Advertiser* (Philadelphia)—and clearly pertains to the 1799 almanac. I have been unable to locate an advertisement in the Philadelphia newspapers for the 1798 almanac. See 120 for a list of editions.

139 THE | AMERICAN MUSICAL MISCELLANY: | a | collection | of the newest and most appoved [sic] | songs, | set to music. | 'Tis

thine, sweet power, to raise the thought sublime, | Quell each rude passion, and the heart refine. | Soft are thy strains as Gabriel's gentlest string, | Mild as the breathing zephyrs of the spring. | Thy pleasing influence. thrilling thro' the breast, | Can lull e'en raging anguish into rest. | And oft thy wildly sweet enchanting lay, | To fancy's magick heaven steals the rapt thought away. | Printed at Northampton, Massachusetts. | By Andrew Wright, | for Daniel Wright and Company. | Sold by them, and by S. Butler, in Northampton; by I. Thomas, | Jun. in Worcester; by F. Barker, in Greenfield: and by | the principal booksellers in Boston.—1798.

300 p. [i:] title-page; [ii:] blank; [iii:] dedication, to all true lovers of song, in the United States of Columbia; [iv:] blank; [v]-vi: preface; [vii]-xii: index; [13]-300: songs.

Backus 40a, Bieber 164, Brinley 6935, Evans 33294, Filby B8, Gilmore 41, Sabin 1163, Sonneck pp. 7-10, Sonneck-Upton pp. 16-20. Indexed in Thorpe ¶ CL, CSmH (imperfect), CtHT-W, CtY, DeWint, DLC* (2), ICN, ICU, IEN, IU, MB, MBAt, MH, MHi, MNF, MU, MWA, MWH, MiU-C, N, NBuG, NHi, NHpR, NN (2), NNC, NNUT, NRU-Mus (2), NjP, NjPT, OC, OCl, OFH, PP, PU, RPB, RPJCB, VtMiM (Flanders), WU, WaU; Glasgow (Euing Collection, University Library), Glasgow (Mitchell Public Library), London (British Library), Oxford (Bodleian Library) ¶ Contains 111 songs with musical notation or reference to musical notation (all indexed). Reprinted in facsimile (Earlier American Music 9) in 1972 by Da Capo Press, New York, with a new introduction by H. Wiley Hitchcock.

140 [THE BALTIMORE SONGSTER; or festive companion. A choice and approved collection of songs, interspersed with many originals, and the patriotic song of Hail Columbia! Second edition. Baltimore: printed for Henry S. Keatinge, No. 148 Balt. Street, 1798.]

Evans 33367, Lowens U58, Minick 411, Sonneck-Upton p. 36 ¶ No copy located ¶ Advertised 15 Aug. 1798 in the Baltimore *Telegraphe* among "new publications, Henry S. Keatinge's book and stationery store No. 148 Balt. Street." See 90 for a list of editions.

141 [THE BLACKBIRD. Being a collection of favourite Scots, English, and Irish songs. To which is added, The adventure of John Gilpin, from London to Edmonton: . . . New-York: printed for Benjamin Gomez, bookseller and stationer, No. 97 Maiden-Lane. 1798?]

70 p.

Bristol-Evans B10241, Shipton-Mooney 48371 ¶ No copy located ¶ According to Lewis M. Stark, Chief of the Rare Book Division, New York Public Library, the Bristol-Evans entry "is no doubt based on a card typed for our Imprint Catalog in 1932," where it is stated that NN "has photostat of title-page of Pennypacker copy." Mr. Stark advises that the photostat title-page "has been missing for several years." Since the paging was given, he assumes that "probably a privately owned copy was brought into the library and a photostat made for our title-page collection." There is no Pennypacker collection at NN.

142 THE | BUCK'S | POCKET COMPANION; | or, | merry fellow: | a choice | collection | of | songs. | Selected with care from the | latest European and American | publications: | including the modern | toasts and sentiments. | "Hence, loathed melancholy, | "Mirth admit me of thy crew." | New-Haven: | printed by George Bunce. | M.DCC.XC-VIII.

71 p. [1:] title-page; [2:] blank; [3]-67: songs; 68: [toasts and sentiments]; [69]-71: index.

Bristol-Evans B10249, Lowens U59, Shipton-Mooney 48431 ¶ CtY* (imperfect) ¶ Contains 54 songs (all indexed). The only known copy lacks pp. 3-4, 39-40, 67-68. An English edition, tentatively dated 1797, is now in Oxford (Bodleian Library). *Later editions:* 246, 270.

A choice collection of Masonic songs. Norwich, 1798.
See 163.

143 [A CHOICE COLLECTION of songs (neatly bound) printed for the travelling book-seller. Suffield, Conn., 1798.]

Bristol-Evans B10261, Lowens U60, Shipton-Mooney 48392 ¶ No copy located ¶ Advertised 30 May 1798 in the Suffield *Impartial Herald* as "first published and for sale at this office."

144 [A COLLECTION OF MASONIC SONGS, extracted from the Freemason's Monitor. Albany, printed by Brother J. Fry, in State Street, 5798.]

28 p.

Morris p. 103, Wolfstieg °39845 ¶ Morris locates a copy of this imprint in the library of the Rhode Island Grand Lodge, and calls the item an 8vo. No copy has been found in that library or elsewhere, however.

145 THE | COLUMBIAN SONGSTER | and | Freemason's | pocket companion. | A collection | of the | newest and most celebrated | sentimental, | convivial, | humourous, | satirical, | pastoral, | hunting, | sea and | Masonic | songs, | being the largest and best collection | ever published in America. | Selected by S. Larkin. | Portsmouth: New-Hampshire, | printed by J. Melcher, for S. Larkin, | at the Portsmouth bookstore | 1798.

216 p. [i:] title-page; [ii:] blank; [iii:] preface, dated Portsmouth, 1798; [iv:] blank; [v]-x: index; 11-216: songs.

Evans 33983, Sabin 14878, Sonneck p. 27, Sonneck-Upton p. 79 ¶

DLC*, DSC, MBFM, MWA, RPB ¶ Contains 252 songs (all indexed). Usually bound up with 148, q.v., but apparently also issued separately, as per a 25 Apr. 1798 advertisement in the Boston *Columbian Centinel*.

146 CONSTITUTIONS | of the | ancient and honorable fraternity | of | Free and Accepted Masons; | collected and digested from their | old records, faithful traditions, and Lodge books; | for the use of Lodges. | Together with the | history and general regulations | of the | Grand Lodge of Massachusetts. | Compiled by the Rev. Thaddeus Mason Harris, A. M. | member of the Massachusetts Historical Society, and chaplain to the Grand | Lodge of Massachusetts. | Brethren, submit yourselves unto such, and to every one that helpeth | with us and laboreth.—St. Paul. | Second edition, revised and corrected; with large additions. | Published under the sanction of the Grand Lodge. | Printed at Worcester, Massachusetts, | by Brother Isaiah Thomas, | in the Christian era MDCCXCVIII; in the Year of Light IƆƆDCCXCVIII.

1 p.l., [viii], 288 p. [i:] blank; [ii:] frontispiece; [i:] title-page; [ii:] blank; [iii:] endorsement, dated Boston, 25 June 5798; [iv:] blank; [v]-[vi:] sanction; [vii]-[viii:] preface, signed T. M. Harris, dated Worcester, 7 July 5798; 1-6: contents; [7]-264: text; [265:] half-title: Part V. | Select anthems and songs | for | special occasions; [266:] blank; 267-284: anthems and songs; 285-288: toasts.

Brinley 6714, Evans 33303 ¶ DLC*, MBFM, MWA, PPL ¶ Contains 14 Masonic songs. For an earlier edition, see 65.

147 THE | ECHO: | or, | federal songster. | Being a | large collection | of the most celebrated, modern | poetical writings, | of different authors. | First editon [sic]. | Brookfield: (Massachusetts,) | from the press of E. Merriam & Co. | Sold by them in Brookfield, and | by G. Merriam in | Worcester.

248 p. [1:] title-page; [2:] blank; [3:] advertisement; [4:] blank; [5]-192: songs; [193]-230: appendix, containing a variety of Masonic songs; [231]-236: a collection of the most celebrated cotillions and country dances; [237]-243: index; [244:] blank; [245]-248: toasts and sentiments.

Evans 33663, Sabin 21779, Sonneck-Upton p. 118. Indexed in Thorpe ¶ MWA*, RPB (imperfect) ¶ Contains 170 songs (171 indexed). Advertised 5 Nov. 1798 in the Walpole, N.H. *Farmer's Weekly Museum* as "this day published"; also advertised 13 Nov. 1798 in the Brookfield *Political Repository. Later edition:* 189.

Fashionable songs for the year 1798.
See 172.

148 THE | FREE-MASON'S | POCKET COMPANION. | A collection | of | Masonic songs. | Selected by S. Larkin. | Portsmouth:—

New-Hampshire, | printed by J. Melcher, | for S. Larkin, | 1798.
    70, [2] p. [1:] title-page; [2:] blank; [3]-70: songs; [71]-[72:] index.
    Evans 33983, Sonneck-Upton pp. 79, 147 ¶ DLC*, DSC, MBFM, MWA (imperfect), RPB (imperfect) ¶ Contains 62 Masonic songs (all indexed). Usually bound with 145, q.v., but also issued separately, as per the RPB copy. Apparently based on the selection of Masonic songs in 65, q.v.

The Gosport tragedy or the perjured ship carpenter, to which is added, Bonny Wully, (a Scotch ballad. [sic] New-York: printed for the hawkers. 1798.
    8 p.
    Evans 33809, Hamilton 177a ¶ MWA*, NjP ¶ Contains only 2 songs. For a later edition with 3 songs and a complete list of 3-song editions, see 253.

Horrid tortures; or, the unparalleled sufferings of John Coustos, Putney, 1798.
    See 164.

149 THE | HUMMING BIRD; | or, | new American songster; | with
    modern | toasts and sentiments. | Boston: | printed and sold by | Spotswood and Etheridge. | 1798.
    1 p.l., 278, x p. [i:] blank; [ii:] frontispiece; [1:] title-page; [2:] blank; [3]-240: songs; [241]-266: appendix containing the most celebrated Masonic songs; [267]-276: toasts and sentiments; [277]-278: Masonic toasts; [i]-x: index.
    Evans 33913, Sonneck p. 70, Sonneck-Upton pp. 194-195 ¶ MH*, NHi (imperfect) ¶ Contains 236 songs (all indexed).

150 JACHIN AND BOAZ; | or, an | authentic key | to the door of |
    Free-Masonry, | both ancient and modern. | Calculated not only for the instruction of every new-made | Mason; but also for the information of all | who intend to become Brethren. | Containing, | I. A circumstantial account | of all the proceedings in making | a Mason, with the several obli- | gations of an Entered Appren- | tice, Fellow-Craft, and Master; | the prayers, and also the sign, | grip and pass-word of each | degree. | II. The manner of open- | ing a Lodge, and setting the | Craft to work. | III. The Entered Appren- | tice, Fellow-Craft, and Master's | lectures, verbatim, as delivered | in all Lodges; with the song at | the conclusion of each part. | IV. The origin of Mason- | ry.; [sic] description of Solomon's | temple; history of the murder | of the Grand Master Hiram, by | the three Fellow-Crafts; their | discovery and punishment; the | burial of Hiram by King Solomon's | order; with the five points of | fellowship, &c. | V. The ceremony of the | installment of the Master of dif- | ferent lodges on St. John's day. | Description of

the regalia, &c. | VI. Ceremony observed | at the funeral of a Mason. | VII. A safe and easy me- | thod proposed, by which a man | may gain admittance into any | Lodge, without passing through | the form required, and thereby | save a guinea or two in his | pocket. | VIII. Toasts, songs, &c. | Illustrated with | a beautiful frontispiece of the regalia, jewels, and | emblematical ornaments belonging to Masonry : | and | an accurate plan of the drawing on the floor of a Lodge, | interspersed with a variety of notes and remarks, sufficient to render | the whole clear to the meanest capacity. | To which are added, | a select collection of songs, and a list of toasts and | sentiments, proper for the Society of Free Masons. | Boston : | printed by J. Bumstead, for E. Larkin, Cornhill. | 1798.

1 p.l., 64 p. [i:] blank; [ii:] frontispiece; [1:] title-page; [2:] blank; [3]-[4:] preface; [4:] advertisement; [5]-[6:] description of the frontispiece; [7]-43: text; 43-60: odes, anthems, and songs; 60-64: toasts and sentiments.

Evans 34506 ¶ DSC*, MBFM, MHi, NN ¶ Contains 23 Masonic songs. As 86, q.v. See 73 for a list of editions.

151 [JOVIAL SONGSTER. A collection of the most esteemed songs, sung at the American and English theatres. Fourth edition. Baltimore : printed for Henry S. Keatinge, No. 148 Balt. Street. 1798.]

Evans 33943, Lowens U61, Minick 435, Sonneck-Upton p. 218 ¶ No copy located ¶ Advertised 15 Aug. 1798 in the Baltimore *Telegraphe* among "new publications, Henry S. Keatinge's book and stationery store, No. 148 Balt. Street." Perhaps based on the 4th English edition of 1789 (see Ault p. 242) with alterations. See 74 for a list of editions.

152 THE | JOVIAL SONGSTER : | containing | a variety | of | patriotic and humorous | songs. | The fourth edition, with additions. | [Copy right secured.] | Music, purest, noblest pleasure, | That the gods on earth bestow; | Adding wealth to every treasure, | Taking pain from every woe. | —New-York— | printed and sold by | John Harrisson, No. 3 Peck-Slip. | 1798.

1 p.l., 82 p. [i:] blank; [ii:] frontispiece; [1:] title-page; [2:] advertisement; [3]-78: songs; 79: toasts and sentiments; 80-82: contents.

Bristol-Evans B10370, Lowens U62, Shipton-Mooney 48491 ¶ MWA* ¶ Contains 76 songs (all indexed). Probably based on the 4th English edition of 1789 (see Ault p. 242) with alterations and additions. See 74 for a list of editions.

153 THE | LARK : | a | small collection | of | much admired | songs. | Northampton.

24 p. [1:] title-page; [2:] blank; [3]-24: songs.

MWA* ¶ Contains 15 songs.

154 THE | MERMAID: | or | nautical songster. | Being | a new collec-
tion | of | favorite | sea songs. | The sixth edition, with additions. |
Here social mirth serenely smiles, | And joyful songs inspire the breast;
| Music the weight of care beguiles, | And lulls each gloomy tho't to
rest. | Copy right secured. | —— New-York —— | printed and sold by
J. Harrisson, | Yorick's Head, No. 3 Peck-Slip. | 1798.

 82 p. [1:] blank; [2:] frontispiece; [3:] title-page; [4:] advertisement; [5]-79: songs; 79: the sailor's description of a hunting; 80:
toasts and sentiments; 81-82: index.

 Sonneck-Upton pp. 258-259 ¶ RPB* ¶ Contains 59 songs (61 indexed).
See 75 for a list of other editions.

155 [descriptive tag:] THE WHIM of the day. | [title:] The | merry
companion. | Containing | twenty-six | of the | newest and most ap-
proved | songs. | Sung at the theatres in Boston, and | other genteel
places of amuse- | ment. | Boston: | printed and sold by J. White, near
| Charles-River Bridge, 1798.

 24 p. [1:] title-page; [2:] index; [3]-24: songs.

 Evans 34100, Lowens U63, Sonneck-Upton p. 259 ¶ MB* (imperfect) ¶ Contains 26 songs (all indexed). The only known copy lacks
pp. 9-12. See 195 for a related edition.

156 NAUTICAL SONGSTER | or | seamans [sic] companion. | To
encrease [sic] the joys of | Saturday night: | a collection of the new-
est | and most approved | songs | interspersed with many originals. |
Baltimore: | printed for Henry S. Keatinge | 1798.

 1 p.l., 64 p. [i:] blank; [ii:] frontispiece; [1:] title-page; [2:] blank;
3-4: index; [5]-64: songs.

 Evans 34167, Minick 444, Sabin 52068, Sonneck p. 97, Sonneck-Upton
p. 287 ¶ DLC* ¶ Contains 42 songs (all indexed).

157 [NEW FEDERAL SONGSTER. Boston: John W. Folsom, 1798.]
 Information from Welch 929 ¶ No copy located ¶ Advertised in
1798 by Folsom in *The foundling; or the history of Lucius Stanhope*
(Evans 33750), "price twenty-five cents."

158 THE NEW | HOLYDAY PRESENT; | or, the | child's plaything.
| Calculated | to allure and "teach the young ideas how | to shoot." |
Boston: | printed and sold by John W. Folsom, | No. 30, Union-Street.
| 1798.

 30 p. [1:] blank; [2:] frontispiece; [3:] title-page; 4-23: text; 24-30:
songs.

 Evans 34198, Welch 936.1 ¶ NPV* (imperfect) ¶ Contains 9 juvenile
songs. The only known copy lacks the frontispiece. *Later editions:*
218, 351.

159 [THE NIGHTINGALE; or charms of melody. Baltimore: printed
for Henry S. Keatinge, No. 148 Balt. Street, 1798.]
Evans 34237, Lowens U64, Minick 449, Sonneck-Upton p. 297 ¶
No copy located ¶ Advertised 15 Aug. 1798 in the Baltimore *Telegraphe*
among "new publications, Henry S. Keatinge's book and stationery
store, No. 148 Balt. Street."

160 PADDY'S RESOURCE. | Being | a select collection | of | original
and modern | patriotic songs: | compiled for the use | of the | people
of Ireland. | To which is added, | Arthur O'Connor's address. | From
the latest edition—with corrections. | New-York: | printed by R. Wil-
son, 149, Pearl-Street; | at the request of a number of Hibernians in
this | country, who were desirous of having | copies of them. | 1798.
2 p.l., 48 p. [i:] title-page; [ii:] blank; [iii]-[iv:] index; [1]-37:
songs; 38-48: Arthur O'Connor's address.
Evans 34290, Lowens U65, Sonneck-Upton p. 324 ¶ MWA* (imperfect) ¶ Contains 30 songs (all indexed). The only known copy
lacks pp. 45-48. A copy reported at DLC is lost. For an earlier edition,
see 115.

161 [THE PATRIOTIC SONGSTER for July 4th, 1798. (Addressed
to the volunteers of Baltimore.) Containing all the late patriotic
songs that have been published. Baltimore: printed and sold at S. Sower's
printing office, No. 67, Market Street, at his book-store in Fayette-
Street, and at Thomas, Andrews and Butler's bookstore. (Price eleven-
pence). 1798.]
[3]-10+ p. [3]-10+: songs.
Evans 34314, Lowens U66, Minick 452, Sonneck p. 115, Sonneck-
Upton p. 327 ¶ MWA* (imperfect) ¶ Contains at least 4 songs. Title
from Evans 34314. The MWA fragment would seem to be part of
this otherwise unknown imprint, which was advertised 2 July 1798 in
the Baltimore *Federal Gazette* to be published "to-morrow at S. Sower's
printing office, No. 67, Market-Street, at his book-store in Fayette-
Street, and at Thomas, Andrews and Butler's bookstore (price eleven-
pence)."

Select anthems and songs for special occasions. Worcester, 1798.
See 146.

A song book. Containing upwards of forty of the most modern and
elegant songs now in vogue. Amherst, Newhampshire [sic], printed
by Samuel Preston. 1798.
Evans 34571, Sonneck-Upton p. 397 ¶ Apparently a ghost-title for
127, q.v., based on an unlocated newspaper advertisement.

162 [THE TEMPLE OF HARMONY, and songster's pocket companion. Baltimore: H. S. Keatinge, 1798.]

Lowens U67, Minick 411 ¶ No copy located ¶ Existence inferred from 222, which contains a frontispiece with the following imprint: "Baltimore publish'd by H. S. Keatinge. April 25th 1798." *Later edition:* 222.

163 AN ACCOUNT | of the | unparalleled sufferings | of | John Coustos, | who nine times underwent | the most cruel tortures ever invented by man. | And sentenced to the galleys four years, | by command of the | inquisitors at Lisbon, | in order to extort from him | the secrets of | Free-Masonry; | from whence | he was released by the interposition of his late majesty, | King George II. | To which is added, | a selection of Masonic songs. | Norwich:——published at the press of J. Trumbull; | 1798. | Sold at his printing office & book-shop, a few rods west | from the Court-House.

40 p. [1:] title-page; [2:] blank; [3:] preface to a late New York edition of this work; [4:] blank; [5]-34: text; [35]-40: a choice collection of Masonic songs.

Evans 33580 ¶ CtHT-W, DSC* ¶ Contains 7 Masonic songs. For a list of editions, see 136.

164 HORRID TORTURES; | or, the | unparalleled sufferings | of | John Coustos: | who nine times underwent the most cruel tortures | ever invented by man, and sentenced to the gallies [sic], four | years, by command of the inquisitors of Lisbon, | in order to extort from him the | secrets of Free-Masonry. | From whence he was released by the interposition of his | late majesty King George the II. To which is added, | a selection of | Masonic songs. | Putney: | printed by C. Sturtevant, for | Justin Hinds. | M,DCC,XCVIII.

76 p. [1:] title-page; [2:] blank; [3:] preface, to the late New York edition of this work; [4:] blank; [5]-71: text; 71-76: songs.

Evans 33581, McCorison 489 ¶ MBFM, MWA*, RPJCB, VtHi ¶ Contains 5 Masonic songs. For a list of editions, see 136.

165 [THE VOCAL MEDLEY; or, a new collection of fashionable modern songs. Alexandria: printed by Cottom and Stewart, for Robert and John Gray, 1798?]

96 p. [1:] title-page; [2:] blank; [3:] prefatory note; [4:] blank; [5]-96: songs.

RPB* (imperfect) ¶ Contains 91 songs. The only copy extant lacks the title-page; the words "the end" appear at the foot of p. 96. *Later edition:* 223.

The whim of the day. The merry companion. Boston, 1798.
See 155.

166 [caption-title:] WILLIAM REILY'S | COURTSHIP, trial, and marriage | [Baltimore, 1798.]

12 p. [1:] caption-title and beginning of "William Reily's courtship;" 2-12: songs.

Bristol-Evans B10675, Minick 464, Shipton-Mooney 48758 ¶ MdHi* ¶ Contains 4 songs. The chapbook was printed in Baltimore around 1798 by Michael Duffey, according to Minick; pp. 9-12 contain "The Baltimore volunteers," which is characterized as "a new song composed on the grand review of the Baltimore city & county volunteers, by Generals, Smith & Swan, on October 29, 1798." For a complete list of editions, see 100.

1799

167 THE | AMERICAN LADIES [sic] | POCKET BOOK, | for the year 1799: | containing | an almanack, | ruled pages for memorandums, | observations & engagements; | also for accounts of monies | received, paid or lent, for | every day in the year; | miscellaneous moral and enter- | taining pieces, in prose and | verse; | new and celebrated songs; | new country dances; | a marketing table; and | several other useful tables. | To be continued annually. | Philadelphia: | published by William Y. Birch, No. 17, South- | Second-Street, betwixt Market and | Chesnut-Streets, | where is also published, | "The gentleman's annual pocket remembrancer."

143, [1] p. [i:] title-page; [ii:] blank; iii: contents; 4: country dances; 5-127: text; 127-136: songs; 137-142: tables; 143: common notes, &c.; [144:] advertisement for Birch; colophon: printed by J. Gales.

Bristol-Evans B10203, Drake 10480, Shipton-Mooney 48338, Stark 1223 ¶ MWA*, NN ¶ Contains 10 songs. See 120 for a list of editions.

168 THE | AMERICAN SONGSTER; | or, | Federal museum of melody & wit. | In four parts. | Containing | a collection of much admired | songs, | selected from the writings of various English | and American authors. | Baltimore: | printed and sold by Warner & Hanna, | No. 2, North Gay-Street, 1799.

245, [7] p. [1:] title-page; [2:] blank; [3]-35: Part I. American patriotic songs; [36:] blank; [37]-72: Part II: Irish patriotic songs; [73]-180: Part III: Dibden's [sic] songs; [181]-245: Part IV: Favorite songs; [246]-[252:] index.

Evans 35108; Minick 467, Sonneck p. 11, Sonneck-Upton p. 21. Indexed in Thorpe ¶ MWA (imperfect), RPB* ¶ Contains 168 songs (all indexed). *Later edition:* 185.

169 THE | BALTIMORE SONGSTER, | being a | collection of the most esteemed | songs, | sung at the American and English | theatres. | A choice selection | for the | sons of Comus, | and such as wish to

be merry & happy. | Third edition. | In this book various songs you'll find, | Suited to each taste, each voice and mind. | Baltimore: | printed by Warner & Hanna, | for Thomas, Andrews & Butler | 1799.

48 p. [1:] title-page; [2:] blank; [3]-48: songs.

MWA* ¶ Contains 51 songs. No earlier editions have been located. See 90 for a list of editions.

170 A | COLLECTION | OF | SONGS, | selected from the works of | Mr. Dibdin. | To which are added, | the newest and most favourite | American patriotic songs. | Let there be music, let the master touch | The sprightly string, and softly breathing flute. | —Ev'n age itself is cheer'd with music; | It wakes a glad remembrance of our youth, | Calls back past joys, and warms us into transport! | Rowe. | If to be merry's to be wise, to be wise is to be merry. | Philadelphia: | printed by J. Bioren for H. & P. Rice, | and sold by J. Rice, Baltimore. | 1799.

1 p.l., 328, x p. [i:] title-page; [ii:] blank; [1]-328: songs; [i]-x: index.

Ault p. 254, Evans 35407, Filby B9, Sonneck p. 27, Sonneck-Upton pp. 74-75. Indexed in Thorpe ¶ CtY, DLC* (2), ICU, MB (imperfect), MH, MSaE, MWA, MdHi, MiU, NBuG, NHi, NN, PBL, PHi, PP, RPJCB (imperfect); Oxford (Bodleian Library) ¶ Contains 404 songs (403 indexed). A very extensive collection of Charles Dibdin's songs, perhaps based on the 1797 Irish edition (cf. Ault p. 252) called *Dibdin's charms of melody,* a copy of which was owned by W. N. H. Harding and was willed by him to the Bodleian Library. A reprint of pp. 313-328 designed by Lester Douglas was issued in 1945 under the title *The newest and most favourite American patriotic songs, 1799.* Copies of this handsome keepsake are at DLC, NjP, and Vi.

171 THE | COLUMBIAN | SONGSTER. | Being a large collection of | fashionable songs, | for | gentlemen & ladies. | In a series of numbers. | Printed by | Nathaniel Heaton, Jun. | M,DCC,XC,IX.

36, 36, 36, 36, 36, 36, 30, vi p. [1:] title page; [2:] blank; [3:] caption title: No. I; [3]-36: songs; [1:] caption title: No. II; [1]-36: songs; [1:] caption title: No. III; [1]-36: songs; [1:] caption title; No. IV; [1]-36: songs; [1:] caption title: No. V; [1]-36: songs; [1:] caption title: No. VI; [1]-36: songs; [1:] caption title: No. VII; [1]-24: songs; [25]-30: toasts and sentiments; [i]-vi: index.

Evans 35331, Sabin 14880, Sonneck p. 28, Sonneck-Upton p. 79. Indexed in Thorpe ¶ DLC*, MHi, MWA, N (imperfect), NBuG, NHi (imperfect), NN (imperfect), NRU-Mus, RPB ¶ Contains 177 songs (all indexed). Apparently printed in Wrentham, Mass.

172 THE | COMPANION: | being | a selection | of the | beauties | of the most | celebrated authors, | in the English language. | In prose and verse. | 'Thou, cheerfulness, by heav'n design'd | To rule the pulse,

that moves the mind.' | Akenside. | Printed by Nathaniel and Benjamin Heaton, | for Joseph J. Todd, Providence, | at the sign of the Bible and Anchor. | M,DCC,XCIX.

 1 p.l., 280 p. [i:] blank; [ii:] frontispiece; [i:] title-page; [ii:] blank; [iii]-viii: contents; [9]-252: text; [253]-280: fashionable songs for the year 1798.

 Evans 35333, Sabin 15024, Sonneck-Upton p. 83. Indexed in Thorpe ¶ DLC (lacks frontispiece), MH*, MWA (lacks frontispiece), NN, PPL, PU, RHi, RPB, RPJCB (lacks frontispiece) ¶ Contains 18 songs. Another issue (Bristol-Evans B10745), identical with the above except for the omission of the frontispiece and a slightly variant title-page, also appeared. The variant title-page reads: The | companion | being | a selection | of the beauties | of the most celebrated | authors, | in the English language. . . . Copies of the variant issue are at RPJCB* and TxU.

Jachin and Boaz; or, an authentic key to the door of Free-Masonry. Calculated not only for the instruction of every new-made Mason; but also for the information of all who intend to become Brethren. Illustrated with an accurate plan of the drawing on the floor of a Lodge. And interspersed with variety of notes and remarks, necessary to explain and render the whole clear to the meanest capacity. By a gentleman belonging to the Jerusalem Lodge; a frequent visitor at the Queen's Arms, St. Paul's Church-Yard; the Horn, in Fleet-Street; Crown and Anchor, Strand; and the Salutation, Newgate-Street. Try me; prove me. Suffield: printed by Edward Gray. M,DCC,XCIX.

 Brinley 6732, Evans 36263 ¶ DSC*, MWA ¶ This edition contains no separate section of songs. See 73 for a complete list of editions with songs.

173 JACKEY DANDY'S | DELIGHT, | or the | history | of birds and
 beasts, | in verse and prose. | Adorned with cuts. | Printed and sold by | Nathaniel Coverly. 1799. | Great allowance made | to those who purchase by | the gross, or dozen.

 1 p.l., 15 [i.e. 17] p. [i:] blank; [ii:] frontispiece; [1:] title-page; [2]-12: text; 13-15 [i.e. 17]: songs.

 Evans 35659, Welch 663.10 ¶ CtY (imperfect), MWA* ¶ Contains 8 juvenile songs.

174 [LITTLE ROBIN RED BREAST; a collection of pretty songs,
 for children, entirely new. Printed at Worcester, Massachusetts, by Isaiah Thomas, Jun. 1799.]

 Evans 35735, Lowens U68 ¶ No copy located ¶ See 40 for an earlier edition.

175 MOTHER GOOSE'S | MELODY: | or | sonnets for the cradle. |In
 two parts. | Part I. Contains the most celebrated songs | and lullabies

of the good old nurses | calculated to amuse children and to excite |
them to sleep. | Part II. Those of that sweet songster and | nurse of
wit and humor, Master William | Shakespeare. | Embellished with cuts,
| and illustrated with notes and maxims | historical, philosophical and
critical. | The third Worcester edition. | Printed at Worcester: Massa-
chusetts, | by Isaiah Thomas, Jun. | Sold wholesale and retail by him
—1799.

91, [1] p. [i:] blank; [ii:] frontispiece; [iii:] title-page; [iv:] blank;
[v]-ix: preface; [10]-72: Mother Goose's melody; [73:] half-title:
Mother Goose's | melody. | Part II. | Containing the | lullabies of Shake-
spear [sic]; 74-91: Shakespeare's songs; [92:] illustration.

Evans 35847, Lowens U69, Sonneck p. 91, Sonneck-Upton p. 269,
Welch 905.3 ¶ MWA* (imperfect) ¶ Contains 68 songs, all juvenile
except for 16 by Shakespeare. The only known copy (a reconstruction
from two imperfect ones), lacks pp. [i]-[ii], 81-82. See 38 for a list
of editions.

176 A | NEW | ACADEMY | OF | COMPLIMENTS: | or | com-
plete secretary. | Containing the true art of indicting | letters; with
dialogues very witty | and pleasant, relating to love, | &c. | To which is
added, instructions for | carving, &c. | With a collection of new songs. |
Printed for B. Gomez, Maiden Lane.

144 p. [i:] blank; [ii:] frontispiece; [iii:] title-page; [iv:] blank;
[5]-7: preface; [8]-108: Academy of compliments, &c.; [109]-144: A
collection of choice songs.

Bristol-Evans B10875, Shipton-Mooney 48941 ¶ NHi* ¶ Contains 22
songs. For related editions, see 80 and 98. *Later edition:* 235.

177 AN | ORATION, | delivered | at Bennington, Vermont, August |
16th, 1799. | In commemoration of | the battle of Bennington. | Pub-
lished at the request of the audience. | By Anthony Haswell. | O let us
draw our term of freedom out | In its full length, and spin it to the
last, | So shall we gain still one day's liberty. | A day, an hour of
virtuous liberty | Is worth a whole eternity of bondage. | Bennington;
| printed by Anthony Haswell, | 1799.

36 p. [1:] title-page; [2:] request for publication, dated Bennington,
22 Aug. 1799; [3]-26: oration; 27-35: odes, songs, &c. performed on the
occasion; 35-36: toasts, &c.

Evans 35599, McCorison 529, Spargo 104 ¶ DLC*, MWA (imperfect) ¶ Contains 7 songs.

178 THE | SOCIAL COMPANION, | and | songster's pocket book, |
a | choice collection | of | new songs. | Portsmouth, N. H. | Printed
for and sold by Samuel Larkin, | at the Portsmouth Bookstore, | 1799.

60 p. [1:] title-page; [2:] blank; [3]-58: songs; 59-60: index; 60:
colophon: printed at the Oracle Press, in | Portsmouth, September 1799.

Evans 36330, Sabin 85686 ¶ MWA*, NHi (imperfect) ¶ Contains 44 songs (all indexed).

179 SONGS AND LULLABIES | of the | good old nurses. | Calcu-
lated to amuse chil- | dren. | Embellished with cuts; | and illustrated
with notes and maxims, | historical, philosophical | and critical. | First
Worcester edition. | Printed at Worcester: Massachusetts, | by Isaiah
Thomas, Jun. | Sold wholesale and retail by him—1799.

29, [2] p. [1:] blank; [2:] frontispiece; [3:] title-page; [4:] illustration; [5]-29: songs and lullabies; [30]-[31:] illustrations.

Evans 36335, Rosenbach 249, Welch 1236 ¶ MWA*, PP (imperfect)
¶ Contains 20 juvenile songs. According to Welch, the text "is a reprint
from standing pages of type" used for 175, "with only the page numbers
and the running caption changed from *Mother Goose's Melody* to
Songs and Lullabies.

180 SPANKING JACK | to which is added, | The frigate Constitu-
tion. | The galley slave. | The way-worn traveller. | The sailor's jour-
nal. | The soger [sic] lassie. | 1799.

8 p. [1:] title-page; 2-8: songs.

RPB* ¶ Contains 6 songs, all named on the title-page. *Later edition:* 262.

181 [THE VOLUNTEER SONGSTER, or vocal remembrancer: for
1799. Containing the newest and most approved songs now extant,
together with those sung at the New Theatre. Baltimore: printed by
Thomas Dobbin and for sale at this office and at Samuel Sower's
(Fayette-Street), 1799.]

Evans 36662, Lowens U70, Minick 547 ¶ No copy located ¶ Advertised 29 Jan. 1799 in the Baltimore *Telegraphe and Daily Advertiser*
as "for sale at this office and at Samuel Sower's (Fayette-Street), (price
18 cents)."

1800

182 THE ACCEPTED | of | the multitude of his brethren: | an | his-
torical discourse, | in two parts; | gratefully commemorating, | the |
unparalleled services, | and | pre-eminent virtues, | of | General George
Washington. | By George Richards, | ministering to, the First Universal
Society, Portsmouth, New-Hampshire. | "Our father is in good health,
he is yet alive."—Sacred writ. | The hope of immortality. | Printed and
published, as the act of Congress directs, | by Charles Peirce, at the
United States' | Oracle-Office; March, M,DCCC.

83 p. [1:] half-title: Washington: | an historical discourse, | by
George Richards; | Portsmouth, New-Hampshire. | Printed by C. Peirce;

[2:] blank; [3:] title-page; [4:] blank; [5:] dedication to Mrs. Martha Washington; [6:] blank; [7]-77: text; [78]-83: songs.

Evans 38399 ¶ CSmH, DLC, MB, MBAt, MHi, MWA*, N, NHi, NN, PU, RPJCB ¶ Contains 6 songs commemorating Washington's death, all apparently written by Richards. The "Solemn Dirge" (p. 82) and "Masonic Hymn" (p. 83) were sung at St. John's Church, Portsmouth, on 31 Dec. 1799, the first for the "municipal solemnities" and the second for the "funeral obsequies" of the occasion. This is a Portsmouth imprint.

183 THE | AMERICAN | JEST BOOK: | containing | a choice selection | of | jests, anecdotes, bonmots, stories, | advertisements, songs, | epigrams, &c. | "Laugh and be fat." | A new edition, | enlarged and improved. | Wilmington, | printed and sold by Bonsal & Niles—also sold at their | bookstore, No. 173, Market-Street, Baltimore. | 1800.

120 p. [1:] title-page; [2:] blank; [3]-111: text; 111-117: songs; 117-120: text continued.

Evans 36815 ¶ DLC*, IU, MWA (imperfect) ¶ Contains 8 songs. Earlier editions, issued in 1789 (Evans 21642), 1796 (Evans 29970 and 29971), and 1798 (Shipton-Mooney 48337) contain no separate section of songs.

184 [THE AMERICAN LADIES [sic] POCKET BOOK, for the year 1800. Philadelphia: William Y. Birch.]

Bristol-Evans B10962, Lowens U71, Shipton-Mooney 49003 ¶ No copy located ¶ See 120 for a complete list of editions.

185 THE | AMERICAN   SONGSTER; | or, | Federal   museum   of melody & wit. | In four parts. | Containing | a collection of much admired | songs, | selected from the writings of various English | and American authors. | Baltimore: | printed and sold by Warner & Hanna, | No. 2, North Gay-Street, 1800.

245, [7] p. [1:] title-page; [2:] blank; [3]-35: Part I, American patriotic songs; [36:] blank; [37]-72: Part II, Irish patriotic songs; [73]-180: Part III, Dibden's [sic] songs; [181]-245: Part IV, Favorite songs; [246]-[252:] index.

Evans 36822, Sonneck-Upton p. 21 ¶ DLC (imperfect), NHi*, NN ¶ Contains 168 songs (all indexed). For an earlier edition, see 168.

186 THE | AMOROUS | SONGSTER. | Compared with this | vigorous volume, | the | frisky songster | is a lifeless chap. | New-York: | printed for the Sporting Club. | 1800.

96 p. [1:] title-page; [2:] blank; [3]-96: songs.

Evans 36834, Sonneck-Upton p. 23 ¶ NBuG* ¶ Contains 72 songs.

187 [BUCK'S DELIGHT; or a pill to purge melancholy:—a choice
collection of songs selected with care from the latest European and
American publications. New York, 1800.]

Bristol-Evans B11002, Lowens U72, Shipton-Mooney 49051 ¶ No
copy located ¶ Information from an unidentified bookseller's catalogue
formerly in the possession of W. N. H. Harding who also owned 1798
and 1799 English editions of *The buck's delight; or, pills to purge
melancholy,* now at Oxford (Bodleian Library); an 1801 English edition of the same work is at NN. Although I have been unable to locate
any advertisement for 187 in the New York newspapers for 1800, I
consider its existence quite probable. It is described in the bookseller's
catalogue as an 18mo containing a woodcut.

188 A | COLLECTION | of the | newest cotillions | and | country
dances. | To which is added, | a variety of | modern songs. | Also, |
rules for conversation | and | instances of ill manners: | to be carefully
avoided by both sexes. | Printed and sold at Worcester: (Massachusetts.)
| July—1800.

36 p. [1:] title-page; [2:] blank; [3]-19: a collection of cotillions and
country dances; [20]-28: songs; [29]-34: rules for conversation; 34-36:
instances of ill manners.

Evans 37202, Sonneck-Upton p. 76 ¶ MWA, NN* ¶ Contains 7
songs. The probable compiler of the collection was John Griffiths. The
1788 (Northampton, Mass.) and 1794 (Greenfield, Mass.) editions cited
in Sonneck-Upton p. 76 do not contain songs.

189 THE | ECHO: | or, | Columbian songster, | being a | large collec-
tion | of the most celebrated, modern | poetical writings, | of differ-
ent authors, | second edition. | Brookfield: (Massachusetts.) | From the
press of E. Merriam | sold by him in Brookfield, and by, | Dan Merriam
in | Worcester.

215 p. [1:] title-page; [2:] blank; [3:] advertisement; [4:] blank;
[5]-168: songs; [169]-202: appendix containing a variety of Masonic
songs; [203]-208: collection of the most celebrated cotillions and country
dances; [209]-215: index.

Evans 37344, Sonneck-Upton p. 118 ¶ MB, MH* ¶ Contains 188 songs
(all indexed). A drastically altered edition of 147, q.v.

190 THE ENGLISH ARCHER; | or | Robert Earl of Huntington: |
vulgarly called | Robin Hood. | Containing | thirty-two songs. | To
which is prefixed, | a preface. | Giving a more full and particular ac-
count of his | birth, &c. than any hitherto published. | I'll send this
arrow from my bow, | and in a wager will be bound, | To hit the the
[sic] mark aright, altho' | It were for forty hundred pounds. | Doubt
not I'll make the wager good, | Or ne'er believe bold Robin Hood. |
Baltimore, | printed and sold by Bonsal & Niles, No. 173, | Market-
Street. | 1800.

144 p. [i:] title-page; [ii:] blank; iii-[v:] preface; 6-118: songs; caption-title: Robin Hood's garland; 119: epitaph; 120-144: caption-title: The complete country-dancer.

Bristol Notes B11030a ¶ MWA* ¶ Contains 32 songs. Although not mentioned on the title-page, the collection of 101 country-dances is unusually comprehensive. For other collections of Robin Hood songs, see 3, 66, 196, and 405.

191 FABLES | FOR THE | FEMALE SEX. | By Edward Moore. | Virtue in every clime and age, | Spurns at the folly-soothing page, | While satire, that offends the ear | Of vice and passion, pleases her. | Premising this, your anger spare. | And claim the fable, ye who dare. | Printed in Bennington, | by Anthony Haswell, | for the booksellers in | Albany, New York, &c.

48 p. [1:] title-page; [2:] blank; [3]-29: Fables for the female sex; [30]-47: Pastorals, and beautiful sentimental songs; 48: index.

Bristol-Evans B11090, McCorison 575, Shipton-Mooney 49117 ¶ MH* ¶ Contains 14 songs, all indexed. Many other editions contain no section of songs.

192 THE | FEDERAL SONGSTER: | being a | collection of the most celebrated pa- | triotic songs, hitherto published. | With a variety of others, | sentimental | and | convivial. | The man who has not music in his soul, | Is fit for treasons, stratagems and spoils. | Entered according to act. | New-London: | printed by James Springer. | 1800.

109, [3] p. [1:] title-page; [2:] blank; [3]-109: songs; [110]-[112:] index .

Evans 37413 ¶ DLC*, MWA (2) ¶ Contains 73 songs (all indexed).

193 THE | FESTIVAL OF MIRTH, | and | American tar's delight: | a fund of the newest | humorous, patriotic, hunting, and | sea | songs. | With a variety of curious | jests, bon mots, entertaining | and witty anecdotes, &c. | New-York; | printed for Thomas B. Jansen & Co. | No. 248 Pearl-Street. | 1800.

81, [2] p. [1:] blank; [2:] frontispiece; [3:] title-page; [4:] advertisement for Thomas B. Jansen & Co.; [5]-72: songs; [73]-79: treasury of wit; [80]-81: toasts and sentiments; [82]-[83:] index.

Ault p. 255, Evans 37420, Lowens U73, Sonneck-Upton p. 141 ¶ DLC (imperfect), MB* (imperfect) ¶ Contains 69 songs. The DLC copy is a fragment lacking all except pp. [1]-[2], [5]-12; the MB copy lacks p. [83].

Horrid tortures; or the unparalleled sufferings of John Coustos. Brookfield, 1800.

See 208.

194 THE | JOLLY FISHERMAN. | To which is added, | The honest
fellow. | The request. | The frizure; or the jolly | barber. | Dermot
and Shelah. | The Carlow lass. | Printed for the flying stationers.—1800.
   8 p. [1:] title-page; 2-8: songs.
   Bristol-Evans B11068, Shipton-Mooncy 49098 ¶ PPL* ¶ Contains 6
songs, all named on the title-page. The chapbook probably was printed
in Philadelphia.

195 [descriptive tag:] NEWEST FASHION. | [title:] The | jovial
songster. | Containing | a good collection | of | songs. | Boston. | Printed
by J. White, near Charles-River | Bridge.—1800.
   34 p. [1:] blank; [2:] frontispiece; [3:] title-page; [4:] index; [5]-
34: songs.
   Evans 38110, Lowens U74, Sonneck-Upton p. 219, 296. Indexed in
Lewis ¶ MWA* (imperfect) ¶ Contains 26 songs (all indexed). The
only known copy is partly mutilated, lacking portions of pp. 27-30.
Differs considerably in content from 233. Essentially a new edition of
155, q.v. Unrelated to 298 despite the similar title. *Later editions:* 233,
393.

196 THE | LIFE AND DEATH | OF | ROBIN HOOD, | complete |
   in twenty-four | songs. | New-York: | printed in the year 1800. |
[Price twelve cents.]
   80 p. [1:] title-page; [2:] blank; [3]-80: songs.
   Evans 37827; Welch 1124 ¶ MWA*, NN, PP ¶ Contains only 23
songs despite the title-page claim of 24. For other collections of Robin
Hood songs, see 3, 66, 190, and 405.

197 MARY'S DREAM | to which is added, | The land of Fredon, |
   also, | Jolly Bacchus, | New-York: | printed for the hawkers, | and
sold at No. 64, Maiden-Lane.
   8 p. [1:] title-page; [2]-8: songs.
   RPB* ¶ Contains 3 songs, all named on the title-page. The chapbook probably was printed around 1800.

198 MOTHER GOOSE'S | MELODY; | or | sonnets for the cradle. |
   In two parts. | Part I. Contains the most celebrated | songs and
lullabies of the good old | nurses, calculated to amuse children, | and to
excite them to sleep. | Part II. Those of that sweet songster | and nurse
of wit and humour, Mas- | ter William Shakespeare. | Embellished with
cuts, | and illustrated with notes and maxims, | historical, philosophical,
and critical. | Printed by S. Hall, in Cornhill, Boston. | 1800.
   1 p.l., 95 p. [i:] blank; [ii:] frontispiece; [i:] title-page; [ii:] blank;
[iii]-10: preface; [11]-73: Mother Goose's melody, Part I; [74:] blank;
[75]-92: Mother Goose's melody, Part II; 93-95: introduction to spelling.
   Bristol-Evans B11091, Shipton-Mooney 49118, Welch 905.4 ¶ CtHi*

(imperfect), MH (imperfect) ¶ The CtHi copy lacks pp. iv-5 and 75-76; the MH copy lacks pp. [i]-16 and 81-95, with pp. 17-18 mutilated. Contains 68 songs, all juvenile except for 16 by Shakespeare. This edition is based on 87; see 38 for a complete list of editions.

Newest fashion. The jovial songster. Boston, 1800.
     See 195.

199 THE | NIGHTINGALE; | or | rural songster; | in two parts, |
     Part I.—Containing favorite, innocent, | entertaining and sentimental songs. | Part II.—Containing the most | approved patriotic songs. | [Many of which are original.] | Dedham: | printed by H. Mann. | 1800.
     125, [3] p. [1:] title-page; [2:] preface; [3]-125: songs; 125-[128]: index.
     Bristol-Evans B11095, Shipton-Mooney 49123 ¶ MB*, MWA ¶ Contains 94 songs (all indexed).

Pastorals, and beautiful sentimental songs. Bennington, [1800.]
     See 191.

200 PATRIOTIC MEDLEY, | being a choice | collection of patriotic, sentimental, | hunting and sea | songs, | interspersed | with Anacreontic songs & Cythe- | rian poems, | selected from the most approved authors. | New York: | printed for Jacob Johnkin, | Maiden Lane. | 1800.
     208, [7] p. [1:] title-page; [2:] blank; [3]-208: songs; [209]-[215:] index.
     Evans 38195, Sonneck-Upton p. 327 ¶ DLC (imperfect), ICN*, MH ¶ Contains 170 songs (172 indexed). *Later edition:* 280.

201 [THE REPUBLICAN HARMONIST; being a select collection of republican, patriotic and Masonic songs, odes, sonnets, &c. American and European. By D. E., a cosmopolite. Philadelphia: 1800.]
     Evans 37343, Lowens U75, Sonneck-Upton p. 352 ¶ No copy located ¶ Copyright Pa., 7 May 1800, Daniel Ebsworth, proprietor. For a related edition see 242. *Later edition:* 220.

Robert, Earl of Huntington
     See 190

Robin Hood's garland. Baltimore, 1800.
     See under 66, 190.

202 THE | SAILOR'S MEDLEY: | a collection | of the most admired | sea and other | songs. | Philadelphia: | printed for Mathew Carey, No. 118 | High-Street.—1800.

1 p.l., 72 [i:] blank; [ii:] frontispiece; [1:] title-page; [2:] blank; [3]-70: songs; [71]-72: index.

Evans 38447, Sonneck-Upton p. 368 ¶ NN*, RPB (lacks frontis-piece) ¶ Contains 76 songs (71 indexed).

203 THE | SONGSTER'S ASSISTANT. | Containing | a variety of the best songs, | set to music in two parts. | Most of the music | never before published. | By T. Swan. | [a circular canon for two voices in the form of a horn, with text beginning, "Now we are met, . . ."] | A. Ely sculpt. | Suffield. Printed by Swan and Ely.

36 p. [1:] title-page; [2:] index; 3-36: songs.

Sabin 94019, Shaw 50257, Sonneck p. 142, Sonneck-Upton pp. 404-405 ¶ Ct, CtHT-W, CtY, MB*, MWA ¶ Contains 22 songs (all indexed) with musical notation.

204 THE | SPENDTHRIFT | clapt into limbo. | To which are added, | Love in my pocket. | The modern beau. | One bottle more. | Printed in the year 1800.

8 p. [1:] title-page; 2-8: songs.

Bristol-Evans B11124, Shipton-Mooney 49149 ¶ PPL* ¶ Contains 4 songs, all named on the title-page. The chapbook probably was printed in Philadelphia.

205 SPICER'S | POCKET COMPANION; | or, the | young Mason's monitor. | Containing | some necessary hints, to | young brethren, | yet not beneath the attention of any. | To which is annexed, | a collec-tion of | Masonic songs, and others, | with notes. | Part second. | Printed at Northampton, | by Andrew Wright.—For the compiler.

31, [1] p. [1:] title-page; [2:] lines written by Brother Stewart, N.Y.; [3]-9: text; [10]-31: songs; [32:] tosts [sic] and sentiments.

Bristol-Evans B11125, Gilmore 65, Sabin 89428 ¶ CtY* (2 copies, 1 imperfect), MWA ¶ Contains 18 songs, all with musical notation or reference to musical notation. The compiler was probably Ishmael Spicer, who collaborated with Andrew Adgate in the compilation of the successful tune-book, *The Philadelphia harmony* (Philadelphia: J. M'Culloch, 1789; many later editions). No "Part first" is known.

206 THE | SPIRIT | OF | MASONRY. | In moral and elucidatory lec-tures. | By Wm. Hutchinson, Master of the Barnardcastle Lodge of | Concord. | New-York: | printed by Isaac Collins, No. 189, Pearl-Street, for | Cottom & Stewart, booksellers and stationers, | Alexandria. | 1800.

1 p.l., vi, [2], 174, 22 p. [i:] blank; [ii:] frontispiece; [i:] title-page; [ii:] blank; [iii:] sanction; [iv:] blank; v-vi: dedication; [vii:] con-tents; [viii:] blank; [1]-174: text; [1]-16: appendix; [17]-22: songs.

Barthelmess p. 12, Evans 37671 ¶ DLC, MBFM, MWA*, NNFM, PPPFM, RPB, RPJCB, ViU ¶ Contains 4 Masonic songs.

207 THE | SYREN; | a choice collection of | sea, hunting, and other |
     songs. | Philadelphia: | printed for Mathew Carey, No. 118, | High-
Street.

     1 p.l., 72 [i:] blank; [ii:] frontispiece; [1:] title-page; [2:] blank;
[3]-72: songs.

     Evans 38597, Sabin 94130, Sonneck-Upton p. 420 ¶ DLC (lacks
frontispiece), NN*, RPB (lacks frontispiece) ¶ Contains 79 songs.

208 HORRID TORTURES; | or, the | unparalleled sufferings | of |
     John Coustos: | who nine times underwent the most cruel | tortures
ever invented by man, and sen- | tenced to the gallies [sic], four years,
by com- | mand of the inquisitors of Lisbon, in | order to extort from
him the | secrets of Free Masonry. | From whence he was released by
the inter- | position of his late majesty King | George the II. | To which
is added, | a selection of | Masonic songs. | Brookfield, Massachusetts, |
printed by E. Merriam & Co. | April 1800.

     83 p. [i:] title-page; [ii:] blank; [iii]-iv: preface to a late New-York
edition of this work; [5]-73: text; [74:] blank; [75]-83: songs.

     RPB* ¶ Contains 7 Masonic songs. See 136 for a list of editions.

209 WILLIAM RILEY'S | COURTSHIP | to | Collian Band, | shew-
     ing | how he was persecuted by her father;—also how she was |
confined in her chamber until she was crazy; sent to | Bedlam, where
she was kept in close confinement un- | til Riley came with the Lord
Lt. of Ireland, &c | rescued her from out of the hands of his en- |.emies,
& made her perfectly happy by | marriage. | To which is added |
The shoemaker's favorite. | Together with | Contentment. | New-Haven,
printed: Suffield, re-printed, | 1800.

     8 p. [1:] title-page; [2:] blank; [3]-8: songs.

     Evans 39103 ¶ ICN* ¶ Contains 3 songs, all named on the title-page.
See 100 for a list of editions.

210 THE | YOUTHFUL JESTER, | or | repository of wit | and | iono-
     cent [sic] amusement. | Containing: | moral and humourous tales—
merry | jests—laughable anecdotes—and | smart repartees. | The whole
being as innocent as it is enter- | taining. | Baltimore: | printed by War-
ner & Hanna, corner of Market | and South Gay Streets—1800.

     108 p. [1:] title-page; [2:] blank; [3]-72: text; 73-108: songs.

     Evans 39160, Welch 689.1 ¶ MWA* ¶ Contains 27 songs. A later
edition containing no songs was published in 1806 (Welch 689.2).

1801

211 [THE AMERICAN LADIES [sic] POCKET BOOK, for the
     year 1801. Philadelphia: William Y. Birch.]

     Lowens U76 ¶ No copy located ¶ See 120 for a list of editions.

212 THE | AMERICAN MOCK-BIRD; | or, | cabinet of Anacreon. |
Being | a selection of the most elegant | and fashionable | songs; |
as sung in the Anacreontic and Philharmonic | Societies, and in most
genteel circles. | With | a number of choice Masonic | songs and senti-
ments. | New-York: | published by David Longworth, | at the Shak-
speare Gallery, | No. 11, Park. | 1801.

258, [6] p. [1:] title-page; [2:] blank; [3]-244: songs; [245]-258:
Masonic odes and songs; 258: advertisement for D. Longworth; [259]-
[264:] index.

Bieber 163, Shaw 53. Indexed in Lewis ¶ MH, MWA, NBuG, PPL*,
RPB ¶ Contains 284 songs (271 indexed).

213 THE | BEAUTIES | and | super-excellency | of | Free Masonry | at-
tempted. | By Francis Hoskins, | late a member of No. 19. Antient
York Masons, | Philadelphia. | Dedicated to His Excellency | Thomas
M'Kean, L. L. D. | Governor of the state of Pennsylvania. | Philadel-
phia: | printed for the author, | by Cochran & M'Laughlin, No. 108,
Race-Street. | November 20th, 1801.

71, [1] p. [1:] title-page; [2:] blank; [3:] dedication; [4:] blank;
[5:] preface; [6:] God the great architect; 7-29: text; 30-56: songs; 57:
the anthem; 58-64: Solomon's temple; an oratoria [sic]; 65: epilogue;
66: toats [sic]; 67: contents; [68]-71: subscribers' names; [72:] advertisement.

Milnar 139, Shaw 677 ¶ DLC, NHi* ¶ Contains 35 Masonic songs.

A collection of Mason songs. Philadelphia, 1801.
See 216.

214 THE | DEMOCRATIC | SONGSTER: | being a collection of new
| republican songs, | mostly originals [sic], | to which is added, a
number of toasts, | drank [sic] at the celebration of the complete | tri-
umph of republicanism in America. | "Resistance to tyrants obedience
to God" | Jefferson. | Baltimore | printed for Keatinge's book store. | 1801.

[2], 5-28 p. [1:] title-page; [2:] blank; [5]-28: songs.

Bristol 18, Lowens U77, Shaw 407 ¶ MH* (imperfect) ¶ Contains
12 songs. May be incomplete, as the toasts mentioned on the title-page
are lacking and the pagination is irregular. See 83 for a related title.

Evenings [sic] amusement. The jovial companion. Boston, 1801.
See 215.

Jachin and Boaz; or, an authentic key to the door of Free-Masonry
calculated not only for the instruction of every new-made Mason; but
also for the information of all who intend to become Brethren. Illustrated with an accurate plan of the drawing on the floor of a Lodge.
And interspersed with a variety of notes and remarks, necessary to

explain and render the whole clear to the meanest capacity. By a
gentleman belonging to the Jerusalem Lodge; a frequent visitor at
the Queen's Arms, St. Paul's Church Yard; the Horn, in Fleet Street;
Crown and Anchor, Strand; and the Salutation, Newgate Street. Try
me; prove me. London: printed: Re-printed in the United States. 1801.
59 p.

Shaw 50250 ¶ MWA* ¶ This edition contains no separate section of
songs. See 73 for a list of editions.

215 [descriptive tag:] EVENINGS [sic] AMUSEMENT. [title:] The
| jovial companion. | Containing | a good collection | of | songs. |
Boston: | printed and sold by J. White, near | Charles River Bridge.
| 1801.

24 p. [1:] title-page; [2:] index; [3]-24: songs.

Krohn* ¶ Contains 17 songs (all indexed). A later edition of 107,
q. v.

216 THE | MASONIC ALMANAC, | and | pocket companion. | From
July to the end of the | year 1801. | Containing: | a list of Lodges,
held under the | jurisdiction of the Right Wor- | shipful Grand Lodge
of Pennsyl- | vania, together with a variety | of songs, sentimnets [sic],
&c. &c. | Philadelphia: | printed by John Bioren, | No. 88 Chesnut
Street; | for John Rain. | 1801.

48 p. [1:] title-page; 2: prefatory note, signed John Rain, of Lodge
No. 2; [3]-8: almanac; 9-11: list of Lodges held under the jurisdiction
of the Right Worshipful Grand Lodge of Pennsylvania; 12-14: a list
of the officers of the Grand and Subordinate Lodges, held in the city of
Philadelphia; [15]-36: a collection of Mason songs; 36-46: miscellany;
47-48: toasts and sentiments; 48: errata.

Drake 10554, Milnar 170, Shaw 886 ¶ PPPFM* ¶ Contains 12
Masonic songs.

The Mason's pocket companion.
A caption-title in 217.

217 MUSE OF MASONRY; | comprising | a number of Masonic songs,
| (chiefly adapted to familiar tunes,) | with appropriate | toasts
and sentiments. | Together with a number of | prayers generally made
use of | at the opening of a Lodge, | and making of a Mason. | New-
York: | printed and sold by John Tiebout, | No. 246 Water-Street. |
1801.

1 p.l., 64 p. [i:] blank; [ii:] frontispiece; [1:] title-page; [2:] blank;
[3]-58: songs; [59]-61: a collection of Masonic toasts and sentiments;
[62]-64: prayers generally made use of in Lodges.

Shaw 522 ¶ PPPFM* ¶ Contains 48 Masonic songs. A caption-title
on p. [3] reads: The Mason's pocket companion.

218 [THE NEW HOLYDAY PRESENT; or, the child's plaything.
Exeter, N.H.: Henry Ranlet, 1801.]
Welch 936.2 ¶ No copy located ¶ Advertised by Ranlet in 1801 in
The history of little Goody Goosecap (Shaw 658). See 158 for a list of
editions.

219 RECUEIL | DE | CANTIQUES, | de la loge | française l'aménité, |
no. 73. | Séante à l'or ∴ de Philadelphie. | homo sum | Et humani a
me nihil alienum puto. | Ter. | Imprimé par ordre de la dite loge. | À
Philadelphie: | chez Thomas et William Bradford, | Premiere rue sud,
No. 8.
55 p. [1:] half-title: Recueil | de | cantiques maçoniques; [2:] blank;
[3:] title-page; [4:] blank; [5]-55: songs.
Milnar 121, Shaw 532 ¶ PHi, RPB* ¶ Contains 31 Masonic songs
with French texts. *Later edition:* 452.

220 THE | REPUBLICAN HARMONIST: | being a | select collection
| of republican, patriotic, and senti- | mental | songs, odes, sonnets,
&c. | American and European: | some of which are original, and most
of the others now | come for the first time from an American press. |
With a | collection of toasts and sentiments. | While hard oppression's
iron chain, | The sons of Europe dragg [sic] along, | We who its links
have snapt in twain, | Will chaunt to liberty a song. | By D. E. A citi-
zen of the world. | The second edition, with additions and alterations.
| Boston: | printed for the people. | 1801.
141, [3] p. [1:] title-page; [2:] blank; [3:] to the reader; [3]-140:
songs; 140-141: toasts and sentiments; [142]-144: index.
Shaw 1235 ¶ DLC*, PHi (imperfect) ¶ Contains 65 songs (all
indexed). A note to the reader on p. 3 states: "The contents of the
following pages as far as the song entitled Robin's lament—inclusive
—are the composition of the selector." For an earlier edition, see 201;
for a related songster, see 242.

221 [caption-title:] SONGS, for the 16th of August, 1801. Jefferson
and Liberty, a new song, by Anthony Haswell, Tune—Handel's
Clarinet. [Bennington: A. Haswell, 1801.]
12 p.
McCorison 603 ¶ VtBennM (Hall Park McCullough Collection) ¶
Contains 5 songs. Copy not examined.

222 THE | TEMPLE OF HARMONY, | and | songster's | pocket com-
panion: | being | a collection of approved | songs. | Baltimore: printed
by George Fryer. | 1801.
1 p.l., 147, [5] p. [i:] blank; [ii:] frontispiece bearing imprint:
Baltimore publish'd by H. S. Keatinge. April 25th 1798; [1:] title-page;
[2:] blank; [3]-147: songs; [148]-[152:] index.

Bristol 56, Shaw 1389. Indexed in Lewis ¶ RPB* ¶ Contains 164 songs (163 indexed). See 162 for an earlier edition.

223 THE | VOCAL MEDLEY; | or, a new | collection of fashionable, | modern songs. | "Inflam'd by music soldier's [sic] fight; | "Inspir'd by music poet's [sic] write; | "Music can heal the lover's wounds, | "And calm fierce rage by gentle sounds | "Philosophy attempts in vain, | "What music can with ease attain, | "So great is music's pow'r." | Alexandria: | printed by Cottom and Stewart, | for Robert and John Gray, booksellers and | stationers. | 1801.

196 p. [1:] title-page; [2:] blank; [3:] prefatory note; [4:] blank; [5]-186: songs; 187-191: Monsieur Tonson—a tale; [192]-196: index.

Sabin 100652, Shaw 1589. Indexed in Lewis ¶ MWA, NN*, PHi, RPB, Vi ¶ Contains 182 songs (all indexed). See 165 for an earlier edition.

1802

224 [THE AMERICAN LADIES [sic] POCKET BOOK, for the year 1802. Philadelphia: William Y. Birch.]
Lowens U78 ¶ No copy located ¶ See 120 for a list of editions.

225 THE AMERICAN | LADIES' POCKET-BOOK: | or, | an useful register | of | business and amusement, | and | a complete repository | of | fashion, literature, the drama, | painting, and music, | for the year 1802. | Embellished with thirteen beautiful engravings. | (To be continued annually.) | Philadelphia: | published by John Morgan. | H. Maxwell, printer.

1 p.l., [84], 36 p. [i:] blank; [ii:] frontispiece; [1:] title-page; [2:] blank; [3]-[4:] table of contents; [5]-[6:] explanation of the engravings; [7:] table; [8]-[19:] almanac; [20:] eclipses for the year 1802; [21]-[46:] memorandums; [47]-[48:] marketing and shopping table; [49]-[77:] text; [77]-[82:] new country dances; [82]-[84:] new charades; 1-36: songs.

ViU* (imperfect) ¶ The only copy located lacks pp. 9-10 in the section of songs as well as 12 of the 13 engravings called for on the title-page. Apparently an imitation of the series begun with 120, q.v. for a complete list of editions. *Later edition:* 241.

226 A | CHOICE COLLECTION | of | songs. | Selected from different authors. | To which is added, a | variety of humorous, pleasing, | and entertaining anecdotes. | New Haven: printed | for the amusement of every purchaser. | 1802.

11 p. [1:] title-page; [2:] blank; [3]-10: songs; 10-11: humorous anecdotes.

Adams 148, Shaw 2032. Indexed in Lewis ¶ RPB* ¶ Contains 7 songs.

227 THE | COMPLETE | POCKET SONG BOOK. | In two parts. | I. Containing an introduction to the grounds | of music. | II. A favourite collection of songs. | By Eliphalet Mason. | Printed at Northampton, Massachusetts. | By Andrew Wright.—For the compiler. | 1802.
    95, [1] p. [i:] title-page; [ii:] prefatory note, dated Simsbury, 1 Mar. 1802; [iii]-viii: a concise introduction to the grounds of music; [9]-95: A favourite collection of songs, part II; [96:] index.
    Brinley 6939, Shaw 2610, Wolfe 5633 ¶ MB, MHi (imperfect), MS, MWA (imperfect), PHi* ¶ Contains 33 songs (all indexed), all with musical notation. This might be considered a tune-book, but its exclusively secular content places it in the songster category.

228 CONCERT SONGS, | on the secret of | happiness. | Containing, | I. The rose of Sharon. | II. Rules of wisdom. | III. Concert cheer. | IV. A moral theme. | V. Virtue and vice no | companions. | New Haven: | printed for the author. | 1802.
    22, [1] p. [1:] title-page; [2:] blank; [3]-[23:] songs.
    NHi* ¶ Contains 5 songs.

229 THE | FAIR WARBLER, | and | ladies' | vocal remembrancer; | a collection | of the | most approved | songs. | Baltimore: | printed by G. Fryer. | 1802.
    1 p.l., 225 p. [i:] blank; [ii:] frontispiece; [1:] title-page; [2:] blank; [3]-217: songs; 218-225: index.
    Bristol 102, Shaw 2207 ¶ MWA* ¶ Contains 195 songs (194 indexed).

230 THE | FREE-MASON'S | COMPANION. | Being, a | choice collection | of the | newest and most celebrated | Masonic songs. | Assist, my muse, thy influence bring, | In praise of Masonry I sing: | In flowing notes my voice shall raise | To sing the worthy Mason's praise. | New-York: | printed for John Tiebout, | No. 246 Water-Street, | by L. Nichols. | 1802.
    40 p. [1:] blank; [2:] frontispiece; [3:] title-page; [4:] blank; [5]-28: Masonic songs; [29]-40: miscellaneous.
    Shaw 3165 ¶ MBFM* ¶ Contains 15 Masonic songs. See 283 and 298 for related editions.

231 THE | FREEMASON'S MONITOR; | or, | illustrations of Masonry: | in two parts. | By Thomas S. Webb, | Past Master of Temple Lodge, Albany, and H. P. of the | Providence Royal Arch Chapter. | Part I. | New-York: | printed by Southwick and Crooker, | No. 354, Water-Street. | 1802.

300 p. [i:] title-page; [ii:] blank; [iii:] copyright notice, N. Y., 12 Sept. 1797, Spencer & Webb, proprietors, with statements by Thomas Spencer dated Albany, Jan. 1798 advising that he has "sold and relinquished to Thomas S. Webb, his heirs, and assigns, all right, title, and interest as a proprietor in the copy right of The Freemason's monitor"; [iv:] sanction, dated Providence, 7 July 5802; [v]-vi: preface, dated 26 Sept. 1797; [vii]-xii: contents; xii: errata note; [13]-221: Freemason's monitor; [222:] blank; [223:] [second title-page:] The | Freemason's monitor; | or, | illustrations of Masonry: | in two parts. | By Thomas S. Webb, | Past Master of Temple Lodge, Albany, and H. P. of the | Providence Royal Arch Chapter. | Part II. | Containing, | an account of the ineffable degrees | of Masonry; | and the | history of Freemasonry | in America. | New-York | printed by Southwick and Crooker, | No. 354, Water-Street. | 1802; | [224:] blank; [225]-[226] preface, dated Sept. 1797; [227]-293: Freemason's monitor, part II; [294]-300: Masonic songs.

Barthelmess p. 30, Brinley 6760, Shaw 3509 ¶ DLC*, DSC, MB, MBFM, MWA, NHi, NNFM, PPPFM, PPL ¶ Contains 7 Masonic songs. The MWA and NHi copies have variant title-pages omitting "Part I" and the hyphen between "New" and "York" but are otherwise identical. The variant form is probably later. See 124 for a list of editions.

232 JACHIN AND BOAZ: | or, an | authentic key | to the door of | Free-Masonry, | ancient and modern. | Calculated, | not only for the instruction of every new made | Mason; but also, for the information of all | who intend to become Brethren. | Containing, | I. A circumstantial account of all the proceedings in making a Mason; | with the several obligations of an Entered Apprentice, Fellow-Craft, | and Master; the prayers, and also the sign, grip, and pass-word of | each degree, with the ceremony of the mop and pail. | II. The manner of opening a Lodge, and setting the Craft to work. | III. The Entered Apprentice, Fellow-Craft and Master's lectures, ver- | batim, as delivered in all Lodges; with the song at the conclusion of | each part. | IV. The origin of Masonry; description of Solomon's temple; his- | tory of the murder of the Grand Master Hiram by the three Fellow- | Crafts; their discovery and punishment; the burial of Hiram by King | Solomon's order; with the five points of fellowship, &c. | V. The ceremony of the instalment of the Masters of different Lodges | on St. John's day. Description of the regalia, &c. | VI. Ceremonies used at the funeral of a Mason. | VII. A safe and easy method proposed, by which a man may obtain ad- | mittance into any Lodge, without passing through the form required, | and thereby save a guinea or two in his pocket. | VIII. Anthems, odes, songs, toasts, &c. | Illustrated with | a beautiful frontispiece of the regalia, jewels, and emblem- | atical ornaments belonging to Masonry: and an accurate | plan of the drawing on the floor of a Lodge. | Interspersed with a variety of | notes and re-

marks. | Necessary to explain and render the whole clear to the meanest capacity. | By a gentleman, | belonging to the Jerusalem Lodge; a frequent visitor at the Queen's | Arms, St. Paul's Church-Yard; the Horn, in Fleet-Street; Crown and | Anchor, Strand; and the Salutation, Newgate-Street. | Try me—prove me. | New-York: | published by Evert Duyckinck. | L. Nichols—printer. | 1802.

1 p.l., vi, 58 p. [i:] blank; [ii:] frontispiece; [i:] title-page; [ii:] blank; [iii]-iv: preface; [v:] advertisement; [v]-iv [i.e., vi]: description of the frontispiece; [1]-40: text; 40-54: odes, anthems, and songs; [55]-58: toasts and sentiments.

Shaw 3036 ¶ DSC*, MBFM (lacks frontispiece), MWA, MiU-C, PPPFM ¶ Contains 16 Masonic songs, as 112. See 73 for a list of editions.

233 [descriptive tag:] NEWEST FASHION. | [title:] The | jovial songster. | Containing | a good collection | of | songs. | Sung at the most genteel places of | amusement. | Boston. | Printed by J. White, near Charles-River | Bridge.—1802.

20 p. [1:] title-page; [2:] index; [3]-20: songs.

Shaw 2474. Indexed in Lewis ¶ MB*, RPB ¶ Contains 15 songs (all indexed). See 195 for a list of editions.

Masonic songs. New York, 1802.

See 230.

234 THE | MEDLEY; | or, a | cure for the spleen. | Being a collection of chosen pieces in prose and verse, selected | from authors of merit, with a view to excite | mirth, and banish melancholy. | To which is added, The | vocal companion, | being a | choice collection | of the most approved | songs. | Whose even thoughts with so much plainness flow: | "Their sense—untutor'd infancy may know, | "Yet to such height in all their plainness wrought, | "Wit may admire, and letter'd pride be taught." | Franklin. | Philadelphia: | printed for the proprietor. | 1802.

1 p.l., viii, 152 p. [i:] blank; [ii:] frontispiece; [i:] title-page; [ii:] blank; [iii]-iv: advertisement; [v]-vii: index; [viii:] blank; [1:] An old man's experience, or poor Richard's maxims improved; [2:] blank; [3]-78: miscellany in prose; 79-152: songs.

Milnar 452, Shaw 2648 ¶ DLC* ¶ Contains 49 songs (all indexed). See 357 for a reprint from the identical plates under a different title.

235 A | NEW | ACADEMY | OF | COMPLIMENTS: | or, | complete secretary. | Containing | the true art of indicting [sic] letters; with dia- | logues very witty and pleasant, relating to | love, &c. | to which is added, | instructions for carving, &c. | With a collection of | new songs. | New-York: | Printed for Hugh M. Griffeth, No. 88, | Water-Street. | From the press of John Low. | 1802.

106 p. [1:] blank; [2:] frontispiece; [3:] title-page; [4:] blank; [5]-6: preface; [7]-70: text; [71]-106: songs.

Shaw 2739 ¶ MWA* ¶ Contains 31 songs. See 98 for an earlier edition; see 80 for a list of related editions.

236 THE | NEW-YORK | REMEMBRANCER, | or the | songster's magazine: | being a collection of the | newest and most admired | songs, | now extant. | Selected impartially. | Albany: | printed by John Barber, for Daniel Steele, | bookbinder and stationer, corner | of Court and Hudson Streets, | near the Court-House. | 1802.

234, [6] p. [1:] title-page; [2:] blank; [3]-234: songs; [235]-[240:] index.

Shaw 2794 ¶ CtHT-W, DLC*, MH, MWA (imperfect), MiU-C, NBuG, NHi ¶ Contains 203 songs (191 indexed).

Newest fashion. The jovial songster. Boston, 1802.
   See 233.

237 [AN ORATION delivered at Shaftsbury, on Sunday, January 10, 1802, at the interment of Capt. Aaron Cole in Masonic order. By Anthony Haswell. Published by particular request of the Lodges in the vicinity. Bennington: A. Haswell, printer, 1802.]

20 p. [1:] title-page; [2:] unknown; [3]-17: text; 17-20: songs.

Lowens U79, McCorison 644, Shaw 2384, Spargo 117 ¶ MWA* (imperfect) ¶ Contains 3 Masonic songs. The only known copy lacks the title-page, which is supplied from Spargo.

238 [SONGS, COMIC AND SATIRICAL. Written by George Alexander Stevens. with 24 wood cuts.]

No copy located ¶ Advertised as #83 in a list of "new books" in the *American ladies' pocket-book* (225) where it is described as a 12mo. See 27 for a complete list of editions.

The vocal companion. Philadelphia, 1802.
   See 234.

239 THE | VOCAL COMPANION, | and | Masonic register. | In two parts. | Part I. | Consisting of original and selected | Masonic songs, | anthems, dirges, prologues, epilogues, | toasts and sentiments, | charges, prayers, funeral procession, &c. | Part II. | A concise account of the | origin of Masonry in America; | with a list of the | Lodges in the six Northern states, | viz [sic] | Massachusetts, | New-Hampshire, | Rhode-Island, | Connecticut, | New-York, & | Vermont. | With the names of the officers, | and the number of members of which | each Lodge consists. | Boston: | printed by Brother John M. Dunham. | A.L. 5802—A.D. 1802.

1 p.l., 180, 103, v p. [i:] blank; [ii:] frontispiece; [i:] title-page; [ii:] published according to act of Congress; [iii]-iv: preface; [v]-viii: index to Part I; [9]-157: songs; [158]-164: an oratorio; [165]-170: Masonic toasts and sentiments; 170-180: prayers, charges, laws, and ceremonies; [i:] additional title-page: The | vocal companion, | and | Masonic register. | Part II. | Containing a list of all the Masonic | Lodges in the six Northern states, viz. | Massachusetts, | New-Hampshire, | Rhode-Island, | Connecticut, | New-York, and | Vermont. With the names of their respective officers, | and the number of members of which each | Lodge consists [sic]; | arranged according | to their senior-ity, under the | Grand Lodges to which | they severally belong. | Printed at Boston; | by Brother John Moseley Dunham. | (Copy right secured.) | Anno Lucis, | 5802; [ii:] blank; [iii]-v: history of Freemasonry, &c.; 6-103: list of Lodges; [i]-v: index to Part II.

Barthelmess p. 28, Brinley 6758, Morris p. 65, Sabin 100650, Shaw 2166, Sonneck Copyright (Mass., 3 Dec. 1802) ¶ CtHT, CtY, DLC (2 copies lacking frontispiece), DSC (lacks frontispiece), ICHi, ICN (lacks frontispiece), IaCrM, MB (lacks frontispiece), MBFM (2 copies lacking frontispiece), MH (lacks frontispiece), MHi (lacks frontis-piece), MWA*, NBuG, NHi (2 copies lacking frontispiece), NIC, NN, NNFM (lacks frontispiece), NRU-Mus, NcD, NhHi, PPPFM (2 copies, 1 lacking frontispiece), RPB (lacks frontispiece); London (British Library), Oxford (Bodleian Library) (lacks frontispiece) ¶ Contains 124 Masonic songs (all indexed).

1803

240 THE | AMERICAN LADIES [sic] | POCKET BOOK, | for the year 1803: | containing | an almanack, | ruled pages for memoran- | dams [sic], observations and en- | gagements; also for ac- | counts of monies received, | paid or lent, for every day | in the year. | Rural tales, &c. by Robert | Bloomfield, author of The | farmer's boy. | New and celebrated songs. | A marketing table, and se- | veral other useful tables. | To be continued annually. | Philadelphia: | printed by John Bioren, for William Young | Birch No. 17, South Second Street. | Where is published also | The gentleman's annual pocket remembrancer.

1 p.l., 153, [1] p. [i:] blank; [ii:] frontispiece; [1:] title-page; [2:] blank; [3:] contents; 4: eclipses and common notes; [5]-130: text; 131-144: songs; 145-[152:] tables; 153: currency rules; [154:] advertise-ment for William Y. Birch, stationer.

Drake 10601 ¶ MnU* ¶ Contains 10 songs. See 120 for a list of editions.

241 THE AMERICAN | LADIES' POCKET-BOOK; | or, | useful register | of | business and amusement: | for the year 1803. | Embel-lished with thirteen beautiful engravings. | To be continued annually. |

Philadelphia: | published by Samuel F. Bradford, and | John Conrad and Co. | R. Carr, printer.

72 p. [1:] title-page; [2:] blank; [3]-[4:] table of contents; [5]-[6:] explanation of the engravings; [7]-[8:] charades and rebuses; [9]-[11:] tables; [12:] eclipses in the year 1803; [13]-[24:] calendar; [25]-44: poems; 44-72: songs.

Shaw 50270 ¶ PPL* (imperfect) ¶ The only copy located lacks pp. [5]-[6] and the engravings called for on the title-page. Contains 29 songs (all indexed). See 225 for an earlier edition.

242 THE AMERICAN | REPUBLICAN HARMONIST; | or, | a col-
    lection | of | songs and odes: | written in America, | on American subjects and principles: | a great number of them never before | published. | Philadelphia: | printed by William Duane, No. 106, High- | Street. | 1803.

1 p.l., 130 p. [i:] title-page; [ii:] blank; [1]-130: songs.

Shaw 3675. Indexed in Lewis ¶ DLC*, MB, RPB ¶Contains 66 songs. Apparently derived from 220, q.v.

243 THE | AMERICAN SONGSTER: | being | a select collection | of
    the most celebrated | American, English, Scotch and Irish | songs. | "Music has charms to soothe the savage breast, | "To soften rocks, and bend the knotted oak." | Vir. | New-York: | printed for Samuel Camp-bell, No. 124, Pearl-Street. | 1803.

1 p.l., 204 p. [i:] title-page; [ii:] blank; [1]-204: songs.

Shaw 3676. Indexed in Lewis ¶ RPB* ¶ Contains 231 songs. Except that it lacks pp. [iii]-xii, this songster is identical with 44, q.v. for a list of editions.

244 THE | BATTLE OF FLODDEN. | To which is added, | Within
    a mile of Edinburgh. | The village wedding; or what a | fine thing to be married. | American independence; a new | patriotic song. | Contentment.

8 p. [1:] title-page; 2-8: songs.

PHi* ¶ Contains 5 songs, all named on the title-page. The chapbook probably was printed in Philadelphia around 1803.

245 THE | BATTLE OF THE KEGS. | Together with The | Boston
    launch. | To which is added, | The soldier tir'd. | July, 1803.

8 p. [1:] title-page; 2-8: songs.

PPL* ¶ Contains 3 songs, all named on the title-page. The chapbook probably was printed in Philadelphia. A New York edition of 1807 contains only the title song.

246 THE | BUCK'S | POCKET COMPANION; | or | merry fellow. |
    A choice | collection | of | songs. | Selected with care from the | latest

European and American | publications: | including the modern | toasts and sentiments | "Hence loathed melancholy, | "Mirth admit me of thy crew." | The fifth edition: | with additions. | New-York: | printed by Lazarus Beach, | for John Tiebout, No. 246, Water-Street. | 1803.

1 p.l., 70 p. [i:] blank; [ii:] frontispiece; [1:] title-page; [2:] entered according to law; [3]-64: songs; [65]-67: toasts and sentiments [68]-70: index.

Shaw 3900 ¶ NHi*, NN ¶ Contains 56 songs (53 indexed). As no earlier edition except 142 (q.v.) is known, this "fifth edition" is rather puzzling. Perhaps it is based on an English fourth edition, but I have been unable to locate any such songster. See also 270.

247 CAPTAIN GLEN'S | UNHAPPY VOYAGE to New-Barbary. | To which is added, | The | dreadful loss of the Hindostan. | Together with The | death of Frank Fid. | July, 1803.

8 p. [1:] title-page; 2-8: songs.

PPL* ¶ Contains 3 songs, all named on the title-page. The chap-book probably was printed in Philadelphia.

248 THE | CAROLINA HARMONIST; | containing | a choice collec-tion | of the | most popular songs. | To which is added, | a number of select | jests, bon-mots, toasts, &c. | calculated to kill care, and pro-mote | festivity. | Embellished with an elegant frontispiece. | "Music, the mighty artist, man, can rule, | "So long as it hath numbers—he a soul." | Charleston, | published by Crow & Query. | Printed by John J. Evans & Co. | 1803.

1 p.l., viii, 280 p. [i:] blank; [ii:] frontispiece; [i:] title-page; [ii:] blank; [iii]-viii: index; [1]-254: songs; [255]-280: jests, bon-mots, &c.

Lowens U80, Shaw 3934. Indexed in Lewis ¶ NcD* (imperfect), RPB (imperfect) ¶ Contains 232 songs (243 indexed). The NcD copy lacks the frontispiece and pp. 43-44, 53-54, 75-76, 93-94, 105-108, 145-146, 155-158, 165-166, 173-174, 207-210, 217-218, 225-252—pp. 79-80, 175-176, and 279-280 are mutilated. The RPB copy lacks pp. 11-14, 75-94, 227-230, 271-278.

249 CUPID'S | MISCELLANY. | Containing | the following favorite songs, viz. | North American death song,—page 2 | Content and a cot,—4 | Song on the death of a beautiful, but unfortunate | young girl, —5 | The widow, — 8 | Old Simon, — 11 | Death and a lady, — 12 | Henry's cottage maid, — 15 | Owen—a favorite song, — ib. | The maid with bosom cold, — 17 | All hands ahoy to the anchor, — 18 | Rebecca was the fairest maid, — 20 | Mad Mary—a new song, — 21 | The battle of the kegs,—23 | The modern beaux,—26 | The wounded hussar,— ib. | The Caledonian maid, — 27 | Old Toby Phillpot, — 28 | Philadel-phia: | printed for the purchaser. | 1803.

28 p. [1:] title-page; 2-28: songs.

Shaw 4034 ¶ PHi* ¶ Contains 17 songs, all named on the title-page. "Cupid's miscellany" was also used as the caption-title for the otherwise unrelated 438, q.v.

250 THE | DEATH OF WOLFE. | Together with | Poor Jack | and
    The | sequel. | To which are added, | The dying swan. | The wheelbarrow. | Seek the riddle in the skies. | June, 1803.
    8 p. [1:] title-page; 2-8: songs.
    PPL* ¶ Contains 6 songs, all named on the title-page. The chapbook probably was printed in Philadelphia. *Later edition:* 412. *Edition after 1820:* (a) 1825, n.p. (MdBP).

251 THE | EXILE OF ERIN, | Ellen O'Moore; | Erin go bragh. |
    Savorna delight [sic] | and | Pauvre Madelon.
    8 p. [1:] title-page; 2-8: songs.
    PHi* (imperfect) ¶ Probably contains the 5 songs named on the title-page. The only known copy lacks pp. 3-6. The chapbook was probably printed in Philadelphia around 1803.

Free-Masonry. Unparalleled sufferings of John Coustos. Boston, 1803.
    See 263.

252 THE GIRL | I LEFT BEHIND ME, | with The answer. | To
    which are added, | The female drummer. | The taylor's triumph. |
    Viva la .... A new song. | Printed for the purchasers, in the year |
    1803.
    8 p. [1:] title-page; 2-8: songs.
    PHi (imperfect), PPL* ¶ Contains 5 songs, all named on the title-page. The chapbook probably was printed in Philadelphia. *Later edition:* 385.

253 THE | GOSPORT TRAGEDY. | To which is added, | The | banks
    of the Shannon. | Together with The | valiant sailor. | July, 1803.
    8 p. [1:] title-page; 2-8: songs.
    PPL* ¶ Contains 3 songs, all named on the title-page. The chapbook probably was printed in Philadelphia. Editions of *The Gosport tragedy* containing less than 3 songs were printed in 1798 and 1805. *Later editions:* 421, 513. *Edition after 1820:* (a) 1825, n.p. (MdBP), identical in content to 513.

254 JACHIN AND BOAZ; | or, an | authentic key | to the door of |
    Free-Masonry, | both ancient and modern. | Calculated not only for
    the instruction of every | new-made Mason; but also for the informa-
    | tion of all who intend to become | Brethren. | Containing | I. A cir-
    cumstantial account of all the | proceedings in making a Mason, |
    with the several obligations of an | Entered Apprentice, Fellow-Craft,

| and Master; the prayers, and also | the sign, grip and pass-word of | each degree. | II. The manner of opening a Lodge, | and setting the Craft to work. | III. The Entered Apprentice, Fellow- | Craft, and Master's lectures, ver- | batim, as delivered in all Lodges: | with the song at the conclusion of | each part. | IV. The origin of Masonry; descrip- | tion of Solomon's temple; history | of the murder of the Grand Master | Hiram, by the three Fellow Crafts; | their discovery and punishment; | the burial of Hiram by King Solo- | mon's order; with the five points of | fellowship, &c. | V. The ceremony of the instalment | of the Master of different Lodges, | on St. John's day. Description of | the regalia, &c. | VI. Ceremony observed at the fune- | ral of a Mason. | VII. A safe and easy method propos- | ed, by which a man may gain ad- | mittance into any Lodge, without | passing through the form required, | and thereby save a guinea or two in | his pocket. | VIII. Toasts, songs, &c. | Illustrated with | a beautiful frontispiece of the regalia, | jewels, and emblematical ornaments be- | longing to Masonry:—and | an accurate plan of the drawing on the floor of a | Lodge. | Interspersed with a variety of notes and remarks, | sufficient to render the whole clear to the | meanest capacity—to which are added, | a select collection of songs, and a list of | toasts and sentiments, proper for the | Society of Free-Masons. | Boston: | printed by Gilbert and Dean, No. 56, State-Street. | 1803.

1 p.l., 63 p. [i:] blank; [ii:] frontispiece; [i:] title-page; [ii:] blank; [iii]-iv: preface; iv: advertisement; [5]-6: description of the frontispiece; [7]-43: text; 43-59: odes, anthems, and songs; 60-63: toasts and sentiments.

Shaw 5009 ¶ DLC* (2), DSC, MB, MBFM, NN ¶ Contains 23 Masonic songs. As 86, q.v. See 73 for a list of editions.

255 LADY WASHINGTON'S | LAMENTATION. | To which is added, | Wounded hussar. | Crazy Jane. | Death & a lady.

8 p. [1:] title-page; 2-8: songs.

PHi* (imperfect) ¶ Contains 4 songs, all named on the title-page. Pp. [1]-2 of the only copy located are mutilated; the imprint (if there was one originally) is lacking on the title-page. *Lady Washington's lamentation* was published several times in broadside form; see Sabin 101830, 101831, 101832. The chapbook appears to have been printed in Philadelphia around 1803. For a later, related chapbook, see 324.

256 MAD MARY. | A new song. | To which is added, | Rebecca was the fairest maid. | All hands ahoy to the anchor. | Owen, | a favorite song. | And | Old Simon. | Printed for the purchasers, in the year | 1803.

8 p. [1:] title-page; 2-8: songs.

PHi* ¶ Contains 5 songs, all named on the title-page. Probably printed in Philadelphia.

257 THE MAID | WITH | ELBOWS BARE, | a new song. | To
which are added, | Erin go bragh. | The flowers of Edinburgh. | Life
let us cherish. | The way-worn traveller. | The little sailor boy. | Love
and friendship. | Printed for the purchasers, in the year | 1803.
8 p. [1:] title-page; 2-8: songs.
PHi (imperfect), PPL* ¶ Contains 7 songs, all named on the title-
page. The chapbook probably was printed in Philadelphia.

258 THE | NIGHTINGALE: | or | ladies' vocal companion. | A new
selection | of the | most approved | songs. | 'Tis but a kindred sound
to move, | For music melts the mind to love. | New-York: | printed by
L. Nichols, | No. 308 Broadway, | 1803.
93, [3] p. [1:] title-page; [2:] blank; [3]-93: songs; [94]-[96:]
index.
MiU-C* ¶ Contains 89 songs (all indexed). *Later editions:* 341,
364, 522.

259 PATRICK O'NEAL. | To which are added, | For lack of gold. |
William. | Mary's dream. | The high mettled racer. | The female
drummer.
8 p. [1:] title-page; 2-8: songs.
PHi* (imperfect) ¶ Contains the 6 songs listed on the title-page.
The lower half of pp. [1]-2 in the only known copy is lacking; if there
once was an imprint, it is now lacking. The chapbook probably was
printed in Philadelphia around 1803.

260 SALLY AND THOMAS. | Together with The | banks of the
Dee, | with The | answer. | To which are added, | Queen Mary's
lamentation. | Since he's gone, farewel [sic] he. | The lovely nymph. |
June, 1803.
8 p. [1:] title-page; 2-8: songs.
PPL* ¶ Contains 6 songs, all named on the title-page. The chapbook probably was printed in Philadelphia.

Songster's magazine: being a collection of the newest and most prized
songs, now extant. Selected impartially. Bennington: A. Haswell &
Co., 1803.
McCorison 699 ¶ Advertised 29 Nov. 1803 in the Bennington *Vermont Gazette;* apparently a ghost-title for 236, q.v.

261 THE | SONGSTER'S MUSEUM; | or, a | trip to Elysium. | A | se-
lection | of the most approved | songs, duets, &c. | now in use, with
the notes, many of which were | never before published. | "Keep him
at least three paces distant who hates music." | Lavater. | "Hail music!
sweet enchantment hail! | "Like magic spells thy powers prevail: |
"On wings of rapture borne away, | "All nature owns thy universal

sway"——Garrick. | Printed at Northampton, Massachusetts. | By Andrew Wright. | For S. and E. Butler. Sold at their bookstore. | 1803.

204 p. [i:] title-page; [ii:] blank; [iii]-v: observations on song-singing; [vi:] blank; [vii]-xi: index; [xii:] blank; [13]-204: songs.

Gilmore 102, Sabin 94020, Shaw 5129, Wolfe 8451. Indexed in Lewis ¶ DLC*, ICN, MB, MH, MHi, MWA, NBuG, PPL, RPB ¶ Contains 113 songs (all indexed), all with musical notation or reference to musical notation. Frequently attributed to Timothy Swan.

262 SPANKING JACK, | to which are added, | Father and mother | and Suke, | Orphan Bess, | The wounded hussar, | The morn invites to love, | The way-worn traveler. | Philadelphia: | printed for the purchasers.

8 p. [1:] title-page; 2-8: songs.

Shaw 5085, Shaw 50614 ¶ PHi (imperfect), PPL* ¶ Contains 7 songs, those named on the title-page and one additional item on p. 8. PHi dates the chapbook 1803. See 180 for an earlier edition.

263 [descriptive tag:] FREE-MASONRY. | [title:] Unparalleled sufferings | of | John Coustos, | who nine times underwent | the most cruel tortures ever | invented by man, | and sentenced to the | galley four years, | by command of the inquisitors at | Lisbon, | in order to extort from him | the secrets of | Free-Masonry; | from whence he was released by the gracious | interposition of his late majesty, | King George II. | Boston: | printed and sold by Nathaniel Coverly. | 1803.

58 p. [1:] title-page; [2:] blank; [3:] preface; [4]-[5:] introduction; [6]-55: text; [56]-58: Masonic songs.

Brinley 6718, Shaw 4021, Shaw 5488 ¶ DSC*, MBFM, MH, MWA ¶ Contains 3 Masonic songs. For a list of editions, see 136.

264 WILLIAM & MARGARET. | Together with The | sailor's journal. | To which are added, | The miller. | Row dow dow. | The convent bell. | June, 1803.

8 p. [1:] title-page; 2-8: songs.

PPL* ¶ Contains 5 songs, all named on the title-page. The chapbook probably was printed in Philadelphia.

1804

265 THE | AMERICAN | ACADEMY OF COMPLIMENTS, | or, the | complete American secretary: | containing, | the true art of inditing letters suitable to the ca- | pacities of youth and age: relating a familiar | conversation between friends and acquaintance [sic], | husband and wife, children and parents, | masters and apprentices, brothers and sisters, | and kindred in general: also, love letters on | all occasions, with others relating to trade and | business of all kinds, in an apt, easy

and plain | style. | Likewise, rules for directing, superscribing, and | subscribing of letters; also the titles of persons | of quality, and all other degrees: | with dialogues very witty and pleasing, relating to | love, familiar discourse, and other matters, | for improving the elegance of the English speech, | and accomplishment in discourse. | To which are added, | I. The art of good breeding and behaviour, | with instructions for carving fish, flesh, and | fowl, after the new manner. II. The English | fortune teller, as to what relates to good and | bad fortune in maids, widows, widowers, and | bachelors. III. Joyful tidings to the female | sex. IV. Treatises on moles, V. Interpre- | tation of dreams. | With a collection of the newest songs. | Hudson, | printed and sold by Ashbel Stoddard. | 1804.

106, [1] p. [1:] title-page; [2:] blank; [3]-[4:] preface; [5]-82: text; 82-106: songs; [107:] advertisement for Ashbel Stoddard.

Shaw 5696 ¶ RPB* ¶ Contains 23 songs. See 80 for a list of other editions and related imprints.

266 [THE AMERICAN LADIES [sic] POCKET BOOK, for the year 1804. Philadelphia: printed by John Bioren for William Y. Birch.]

Lowens U81 ¶ No copy located ¶ See 120 for a list of editions.

267 THE | BALTIMORE MUSICAL MISCELLANY, | or | Colum- bian songster; | containing | a collection of approved | songs, | set to music. | To which is prefixed, | an essay on vocal music, with directions for | graceful singing, and the improve- | ment of the voice: | in two volumes. | Vol. I. | Copy-right secured. | Baltimore: | printed and sold by | Sower & Cole, and Samuel Butler. | 1804.

198, [6] p. [i:] title-page; [ii:] blank; [iii]-xii: an essay on vocal music; [xiii:] additional title-page: The Baltimore | musical miscellany, | containing | a choice collection | of the | most approved | songs; 14- 198: songs; [199]-[204:] index; [204:] colophon: Sower and Cole, printers.

Bristol 245, Filby B12, Shaw 5767, Wolfe 433. Indexed in Lewis ¶ DCL*, MdHi (2), MWA, PPB, RPB ¶ Contains 84 songs with musical notation or reference to musical notation. The index lists 142 items, referring to the songs both by first line and title (where given). See also 289.

268 THE | BLITHESOME BRIDAL, | being | a humorous description of a wedding. | To which are added, | Omnia vincet amor. | My Jo Janet. | And | The prisoner's welcome. | Printed in the year 1804.

8 p. [1:] title-page; 2-8: songs.

PPL* (imperfect) ¶ The only known copy lacks pp. 3-6; apparently contains the 4 songs named on the title-page. The chapbook probably was printed in Philadelphia.

269 BRYAN & PYREENE. | To which is added, | Barbara Allen: | and The | crafty farmer. | January, 1804.

    8 p. [1:] title-page; 2-8: songs.

    PPL* ¶ Contains 3 songs, all named on the title-page. The chap-book probably was printed in Philadelphia.

270 THE | BUCK'S | POCKET COMPANION; | a collection of | choice songs. | Selected with care from the newest | publications. | "Hence, loathed melancholy, | "Mirth admit me of thy crew." | Wilmington: | printed and sold by Bonsal & Niles— | also sold at their bookstore, No. 192, | Market-Street, Baltimore. | 1804.

    108 p. [1:] title-page; [2:] blank; [3]-108: songs.

    MWA* ¶ Contains 92 songs. See 142 for a list of editions.

271 THE | HAPPY SHEPHERD | with The answer. | To which are added, | Corporal Cas[e]y. | The tempest. | The bonny Scot. | Printed in the year 1804.

    8 p. [1:] title-page; 2-8: songs.

    PPL* ¶ Contains 6 songs, all named on the title-page. The chap-book probably was printed in Philadelphia.

Hunting songs. Philadelphia, 1804.

    See 283.

Idylles ou essais de poësie créole. New York, 1804.

    16 p.

    Shaw 6530 ¶ NHi* ¶ This edition contains no songs; see 389 for a related imprint which does contain songs.

272 ILLUSTRATIONS | OF | MASONRY. | By William Preston, | Past Master of the Lodge of Antiquity | acting by immemorial constitution. | The man, whose mind on virtue bent, | Pursues some greatly good intent | With undiverted aim; | Serene, beholds the angry crowd, | Nor can their clamors, fierce and loud, | His stubborn honor tame. | Blacklock. | The first American— | from the tenth London edition. | Alexandria: | printed by Cottom & Stewart, | and sold at their bookstores, in Alexandria | and Fredericksburg. | 1804.

    360 p. [i:] title-page; [ii:] blank; [iii:] dedication; [iv:] blank; [v]-vi: preface, dated Dean-Street, Fetter Lane, 1 June 1801; [vii]-x: introduction, dated 1 Jan. 1798; [11]-340: text; [341]-356: odes, anthems, and songs; [357]-360: contents, including index of songs.

    Barthelmess p. 12, Brinley 6746, Quenzel 38, Shaw 7115 ¶ CSmH, CSt, DLC, DSC*, IaCrM, MB, MBFM, MWA, MiD-B, MiU-C, NN (2), PPPFM, PU, RP, Vi, WHi, WMFM ¶ Contains 18 Masonic songs. See 273 for another edition.

273 ILLUSTRATIONS | OF | MASONRY. | By William Preston, |
Past Master of the Lodge of Antiquity, | acting by immemorial con-
stitution. | Hail! mystic art! ineffable! sublime! | The bond of charity,
mid every clime! | Whose silken cord, in love fraternal binds, | Ten
thousand thousand, varying forms and minds; | I bid thee, hail! blest,
magic power! 'tis thine, | Thou sun of life, and light, and peace, divine,
| One tide of bliss, far round a world to roll, | And human nature,
breathes one kindred soul; | A soul, that feels for joy; that melts, at
human woe, | And burns with kind philanthropy's celestial glow! | The
first American improved edition, | from Strahan's tenth London edi-
tion: | to which is annexed, | many valuable Masonic addenda; | and a
complete list of the | Lodges in the United States of America. | Edited
by | Brother George Richards, P.G.S.G.L.M. | Printed by W. & D.
Treadwell, Portsmouth. | 1804.

400 p. [i:] title-page; [ii:] blank; [iii:] dedication; [iv:] blank; [v]-
vi: American editor's preface, dated Portsmouth, N.H., 10 Dec. 5804;
[vii]-viii: Preston's introduction, dated 1 Jan. 1798; [ix]-xxi: contents;
xxi-xxiv: list of subscribing Lodges; [25]-268: text; [269:] half-title;
[270:] blank; [271]-379: appendixes 1-5; [380]-387: appendix 6: select
anthems, odes and hymns; [388]-400: appendix 7.

Barthelmess p. 12, Brinley 6747, Shaw 7116 ¶ CtY, DLC (imperfect),
DSC*, MB, MBFM, MH, MWA, NN, NcD, PHi, PPL ¶ Contains 9
Masonic songs. See 272 for another edition.

274 THE | LYING BALLAD, or the bare fac'd lies. | Wonders | of
the | world. | And The | answer. | To which is added | The won-
ders. | The | The [sic] birth of Washington. | And The | tars of Colum-
bia.

8 p. [1:] title-page; [2]-8: songs.

Sabin 105016, Shaw 6678 ¶ MiU-C* ¶ Contains 5 songs, all named
on the title-page.

275 THE | MERRY MEDLY [sic], | or, | pocket companion. | Being |
a collection of the best | sentimental, convivial, humourous, pa- |
triotic, pastoral, hunting, sea | and Masonic | songs, | among this collec-
tion is the celebrat- | ed new song called | Lady Washington's lamenta-
tion. | And a number of other new songs never | before published in
any collection. | Lansingburgh. | Printed by Francis Adancourt, | for
himself and Samuel Shaw. | 1804.

142, [2] p. [i:] title-page; [ii:] blank; [iii]-iv: preface; [v]-viii:
index; [ix:] blank; [10]-139: songs; 140-142: a collection of the newest
and most favorite country-dances, reels and cotillions; [143:] blank;
[144:] advertisement for Francis Adancourt.

Shaw 6772 ¶ MH (imperfect), MWA* ¶ Contains 93 songs (92
indexed). *Edition after 1820:* (a) 1829, Albany (RPB).

276 MIRTH AND SONG: | consisting of a | lecture on heads, | written
by | George Alexander Stevens, Esq. | and | The courtship, | with a
collection of | approved songs. | Boston: | printed by E. Lincoln, | for
John Whiting, of Lancaster. | 1804.

252 p. [1:] title-page; [2:] blank; [3]-58: lecture on heads; 59-61:
the courtship; 61-246: songs; [247]-252: index.

Shaw 7308. Indexed in Lewis ¶ CtHT-W, CtY, MH*, MHi, MWA,
NN (imperfect), OC, RPB ¶ Contains 155 songs (156 indexed).

277 MOTHER GOOSE'S | MELODY, | or, | sonnets for the cradle. |
Being the most celebrated | songs and lullabies of the | good old
nurses, calculated | to amuse children, and to | excite them to sleep. |
Embellished with cuts. | Printed in the year 1804.

15 p. [1:] blank; [2:] title-page; 3-15: songs.

Welch 905.5 ¶ MWA* ¶ Contains 12 juvenile songs. This edition
is not related to those printed by Isaiah Thomas. The title-page may
have been separated from the rest and reattached incorrectly, thus
making the blank page p. [2] and the title-page p. [1]. According to
Welch, "The printer could have been either J. White or N. Coverly."
See 38 for a list of editions.

278 THE | MOUNTAINS HIGH. | To which are added, | Savourna
delish shighan oh. | Peggy Bawn; | with | The answer. | And | Love
is the cause of my mourning. | Printed in the year 1804.

8 p. [1:] title-page; 2-8: songs.

PPL* (imperfect) ¶ The only known copy lacks pp. 5-8. Apparently
contains the 5 songs named on the title-page. The chapbook probably
was printed in Philadelphia.

279 NIGHTINGALE. | A | collection of the most | popular, ancient &
modern | songs; | set to music. | Selected by | Samuel Larkin. | Copy
right secured. | Published annually, by | William & Daniel Treadwell, |
printers & stationers. | Portsmouth, January, 1804.

[viii], [13]-288 p. [i:] title-page; [ii:] blank; [iii:] dedication; [iv:]
blank; [v]-[viii:] index; [13]-288: songs; 288: colophon: From the
music-press of H. Ranlet, Exeter.

Filby B11, Sabin 39040, Shaw 6617, Wolfe 6534. Indexed in Lewis ¶
CtHT-W, DLC*, MBAt (imperfect), MWA, NcD; Oxford (Bodleian Library) ¶ Contains 109 songs (all indexed), all with musical notation. There are three distinct 1804 issues of this songster, of which
the one described above is the earliest. Except for the title-pages, all
were apparently printed from identical plates.

The second issue title-page is as follows: The | nightingale. | A |
collection of the most | popular, ancient, and modern | songs: | set to
music. | Selected by | Samuel Larkin. | "Apollo struck the enchanting
lyre! | ——the muses sung | In strains alternate." | Copy right secured. |

Printed for | William and Daniel Treadwell, | booksellers, Portsmouth. 1804. Copies of this issue may be found at CLU, CSmH, CtY, DLC, ICN, ICU, IU, InU-Li, Lowens*, MH (imperfect), MiU, MiU-C, NBuG, NHi, NN, NNC, NcD (imperfect), NhD, NhHi, OClWHi (imperfect), PP, PPL, RPB (imperfect); Oxford (Bodleian Library).

The third issue title-page is as follows: The | nightingale. | A | collection of the most | popular, ancient, & modern | songs, | set to music. | Selected by | Samuel Larkin. | "Apollo struck the enchanting lyre! | ——the muses sung | In strains alternate." | Copy right secured. | Printed for | William and Daniel Treadwell, | booksellers, Portsmouth. | 1804. Copies of this issue may be found at MWA, MiU-C, PHi*.

280 [PATRIOTIC MEDLEY, a collection of songs. Baltimore, before 1804.]

Lowens U82 ¶ No copy located ¶ Information from *A Catalogue of All the Books, Printed in the United States* (Boston: for the booksellers, Jan. 1804), p. 58. The item is described as an 18mo, price 62½ cents, coarse, 50 cents. Perhaps a later edition of 200, q.v.

281 THE | REPUBLICAN SONGSTER. | Being a | collection of the most modern | and | patriotic songs, | now in vogue. | New-Hampshire: | printed for the purchaser. | 1804.

24 p. [1:] title-page; [2:] blank; [3]-24: songs.

Sabin 70041 ¶ MBAt* ¶ Contains 7 songs. See 398 for a related edition.

282 THE | SHEFFIELD 'PRENTICE. | To which are added, | The jovial cruising sailor. | American, commerce, & freedom. | The Indian chief. | Push about the jorum. | Ballynamony, Oro. | January, 1804.

8 p. [1:] title-page; 2-8: songs.

PPL* ¶ Contains 6 songs, all named on the title-page. The chapbook probably was printed in Philadelphia.

283 VARIETY; | or, the | songster's companion: | being | a collection of the most | celebrated | American, English, Irish and Scotch | songs. | Selected | from the latest editions. | "Music has charms——." | Philadelphia: | printed for the booksellers. | 1804.

[3]-40, [5]-40 p. [3:] title-page; [4:] blank; [5]-40: songs, with caption-title: The vocal syren; [5]-28: songs, with caption-title: Hunting songs; [29]-40: songs, with caption-title: Miscellaneous.

RPB* ¶ Contains 51 songs. Signed C on p. [5], D on p. 29, G on p. [5], G2 on p. 13, H on p. [29], H2 on p. 33, and thus apparently issued intentionally with this unorthodox pagination. The second pagination is identical with the first pagination in 298; 230 is also a related edition.

The vocal syren. Philadelphia, 1804.
   See 283.

284 THE | WANDERING SHEPHERDESS. | To which is added, |
   The highland laddie. | Banks of the Dee; | with | The answer. | To-
gether with | Bold mariners. | Printed in the year 1804.
   8 p. [1:] title-page; 2-8: songs.
   PPL* ¶ Contains 5 songs, all named on the title-page. The chapbook probably was printed in Philadelphia.

1805

285 THE | AHIMAN REZON | and | Masonic ritual. | Published by
   order of the | Grand Lodge | of | North-Carolina and Tennessee. |
Part I. | Newbern: | John C. Sims and Edward G. Moss. | 5805.
   [viii], 161, [3], [iv], 205, [3] p. [i:] half-title; [ii:] blank; [iii:]
title-page; [iv:] blank; [v:] dedication, dated Newbern, 4 Dec. 5805;
[vi:] blank; [vii]-[viii:] preface; [1]-161: Ahiman Rezon; [162]-[164:]
contents; [i]-[ii:] blank; [iii:] second title-page: The | Ahiman Rezon
| and | Masonic ritual. | Published by order of the | Grand Lodge | of |
North-Carolina and Tennessee. | Part II. | Newbern: | John C. Sims
and Edward G. Moss, | 5805; [iv:] blank; [1]-131: text; [132]-202:
Masonic songs, odes, and hymns; [203]-205: Masonic toasts and sentiments; [206]-[207:] contents; [208:] errata, part 1.
   Morris p. 87, Shaw 8472 ¶ CSmH, DLC*, IaCrM, NcA-S, PPPFM
¶ Contains 36 Masonic songs.

286 AN | ALMANACK; | for the year of our Lord, | 1806. | Being the
   second after bissextile, or leap year, and the | 30th of the indepen-
dence of America. | Calculated for the latitude and longitude of the
university | at Cambridge, in the Commonwealth of Massachusetts; but
| will serve the adjacent states, without any sensible error. | Containing
| every thing necessary for an almanack. | By Samuel Bullard. | To-
gether with a collection of pleasant and delightful | songs, | and many
other things useful and entertaining [sic]. | "Declare, ye sages, if ye find
| " 'Mongst animals of ev'ry kind, | "A creature that mistakes his plan,
| "And errs so constantly as man." Wilkie. | Dedham, (Mass.)—
printed by | Herman Mann. | 1805.
   36 p. [1:] title-page; [2]-[19:] text; [20:] blank; [21:] second title-
page: The | songster's | pocket companion; | containing | a number of |
favorite songs, | marches, &c. | From the music press of | Herman Mann,
| Dedham, (Mass.) | 1805; [22]-36: songs.
   Drake 3670, Shaw 8101, Shaw 9399, Wolfe 83. Indexed in Lewis
¶ DLC*, MH (imperfect), MHi (imperfect), MWA, N, RPB ¶ Contains 7 songs and 1 instrumental composition (*Baron Stuben's* [sic]
American march), all with music. There is no evidence that the
songster was ever issued except with the almanac.

287 THE | AMERICAN | ACADEMY OF COMPLIMENTS; | or, | the | complete American secretary: | containing, | the true art of inditing letters suitable to the ca- | pacities of youth and age: relating a familiar | conversation between friends and acquaintance [sic], | husband and wife, children and parents, | masters and apprentices, brothers and sisters, | and kindred in general; also, love letters on | all occasions, with others relating to trade and | business of all kinds, in an apt, easy and plain | style. | Likewise, rules for directing, superscribing, and | subscribing of letters: also the titles of persons | of quality, and all other degrees: | with dialogues very witty and pleasing, relating to | love, familiar discourse, and other matters | for improving the elegance of the English speech, | and accomplishment in discourse. | To which are added, | I. The art of good breeding and behaviour, | with instructions for carving fish, flesh and | fowl, after the new manner. II. The English | fortune teller, as to what relates to good and | bad fortune in maids, widows, widowers, and | bachelors. III. Joyful tidings to the female | sex. IV. Treatises on moles. V. Interpre- | tation of dreams. | With a collection of the newest songs. | Hudson: | printed and sold by Ashbel Stoddard. | 1805.

106, [1] p. [1:] title-page; [2:] blank; [3]-[4:] preface; [5]-82: text; 82-106: songs; [107:] advertisement for Ashbel Stoddard.

Shaw 7860 ¶ CSt, CtY (imperfect), MWA* ¶ Contains 24 songs. Very similar to 265, q.v.; see 80 for a list of other editions and related imprints.

288 THE | AMERICAN LADIES [sic] | POCKET BOOK, | for the year 1805: | containing | an almanack | ruled pages for memo- | randums, observations | and engagements; also | for accounts of monies | received, paid or lent, | for every day in the year. | Extract from Emeline, a | much admired novel, | selected poetry, | new and celebrated songs, | a marketing table, and | several other useful ta- | bles. | To be continued annually. | Philadelphia: | printed by John Bioren, for William Young | Birch, No. 37, South Second Street. | Where is published also | The gentlemans [sic] annual pocket remembrancer.

1 p.l., 141, [3] p. [i:] blank; [ii:] frontispiece; [1:] title-page; [2:] blank; [3:] contents; 4: common notes, &c.; [5]-124: text; [125]-135: songs; 136-[143:] tables; [144:] advertisement for William Y. Birch, stationer.

Drake 10660, Shaw 5700 ¶ MWA* ¶ Contains 12 songs. See 120 for a list of editions.

289 THE | BALTIMORE MUSICAL MISCELLANY, | or | Columbian songster; | containing | a collection of approved | songs, | set to music. | To which is prefixed, | an essay on vocal music, with directions for | graceful singing, and the improve- | ment of the voice, | in two

volumes. | Vol. II. | Copy-right secured. | Baltimore: printed by Cole and Hewes, | for S. Butler. | 1805.

192, [3] p. [1:] title-page; [2:] blank; [3:] editor's note; [4:] blank; [5]-192: songs; [193]-[194:] index; [195:] erratum.

Bristol 330, Filby B12, Shaw 5768, Shaw 7916, Wolfe 433. Indexed in Lewis ¶ DLC*, MdHi (2), MWA, PPB, RPB ¶ Contains 73 songs with musical notation or reference to musical notation (76 indexed). See also 267.

290 THE | BATTLE OF THE BOYNE. | To which added [sic], | The bold mariners. | The little sailor boy. | Sally in our alley. | Printed in the year 1805.

8 p. [1:] title-page; 2-8: songs.

Shaw 50499 ¶ PPL* ¶ Contains 4 songs, all named on the title-page. The chapbook probably was printed in Philadelphia.

291 CAPTAIN | BARNEY'S VICTORY | over | General Monk. | To which are added, | Crazy Jane: | Death, and a lady, [sic].

8 p. [1:] title-page; 2-8: songs.

PPL* (imperfect) ¶ The only known copy lacks pp. 5-6. Apparently contains the 3 songs named on the title-page. The chapbook probably was printed in Philadelphia around 1805.

292 A | CHOICE COLLECTION | of | admired songs, | selected from the | most approved operas; | interspersed with | comic songs, &c. | as sung at the Baltimore Theatre. | To which are added, | toasts & sentiments. | Baltimore: | printed by G. Dobbin & Murphy, Market-Street, | within one door of the bridge. | 1805.

60 p. [1:] title-page; [2:] blank; [3]-59: songs; 60: toasts and sentiments.

Bristol 341, Shaw 8184. Indexed in Lewis ¶ RPB* ¶ Contains 71 songs.

A collection of Masonic songs. Philadelphia, 1805.
See 294.

A | collection | of | Masonic songs, | with several ingenious | prologues and epilogues. | To which is added, | Solomon's temple, | an | oratorio, | as it was performed for the | benefit of sick and distressed | Free-Masons. | New-York. | Printed by Southwick & Hardcastle, | 2, Wall-Street. [1805]
See 312.

293 THE | FAIR THIEF. | Burn's [sic] farewel [sic]. | The | Dutch fisherman. | John Bull. | Hail, liberty; | Lullaby. | And The | Caladonian [sic] ladie [*recte* laddie].

8 p. [1:] title-page; 2-8: songs.

Shaw 50531 ¶ PPL* ¶ Contains 7 songs, those named on the title-page, and *Nong tong paw* on p. 6. The chapbook probably was printed in Philadelphia around 1805.

294 THE | FREE MASON'S COMPANION, | or | pocket preceptor. | Compiled for the | use of the craft. | By John Phillips, | Past Master of Lodge No. 2; | and Chief J. of the H. R. A. C. No. 52. | Philadelphia: | printed by Bartholomew Graves, | No. 40, N. Fourth-Street. | 1805.

xx, 211 p. [i:] title-page; [ii:] copyright notice, Pa., 19 Jan. 1805, John Phillips, proprietor; [iii:] dedication; [iv:] advertisement; [v]-ix: contents, including index of songs; [x]-xx: illustration of the principles of Free Masonry; [1]-162: text; [163]-205: a collection of Masonic songs; 205-206: toasts; 207: list of Grand Masters and their deputies; 208-211: list of Lodges.

Barthelmess p. 8, Morris p. 88, Shaw 9141, Wolfsteig 39900 ¶ DSC*, IaCrM, MBFM (2), MH, MWA, NIC, NNFM, PHi, PPPFM, PU, RPB ¶ Contains 32 Masonic songs (all indexed).

295 THE | FREEMASON'S MONITOR; | or, | illustrations of Masonry: | in two parts. | By Thomas Smith Webb, | Past Master of Temple Lodge, Albany, G. H. P. of the | Grand R. A. Chapter of Rhode-Island, and Grand Mas- | ter of the Providence Encampment of Knights Tem- | plars, &c. | A new and improved edition. | Printed for Henry Cushing, and Thomas S. Webb, | Providence. Sold also by Harrison & Hall, | Mill Bridge, Boston; Cushing & Apple- | ton, Salem; and Thomas & Whipple, | Newburyport. | 1805.

345 p. [i:] title-page; [ii:] blank; [iii:] copyright notice, R. I., 14 Nov. 1805, Thomas Smith Webb, proprietor; [iv:] sanction, dated Providence, 7 July 5802; [v]-vi: preface, dated 26 Sept. 1797; [vii]-xii: contents; [13]-249: Freemason's monitor, part I; [250:] blank; [251:] second title-page: The | Freemason's monitor; | or, | illustrations of Masonry; | in two parts. | By Thomas Smith Webb, | Past Master of Temple Lodge, Albany, and G. H. P. of | the Grand Royal Arch Chapter of Rhode-Island. | Part II. | Containing | an account of the ineffable | degrees of Masonry; | and the | history of Freemasonry | in America. | Salem: | printed for Henry Cushing, (the proprietor) | Providence. Sold also by J. S. Appleton, | Cushing & Appleton, Salem; and | Thomas & Whipple, New- | buryport. | 1805; [252:] blank; [253]-[254:] preface, dated Sept. 1797; [255]-318: Freemason's monitor, part II; [319]-324: Masonic songs; [325]-345: appendix, dated 9 Jan. 1806.

Barthelmess p. 30, St. Denis 150, 163, 164, 165, 166, Shaw 9700 ¶ CtY, DSC*, ICHi, IU (imperfect), LNSM, MB, MBFM, MMeT, MWA, NBuDD, NIC, NNFM, NRHi, OCl, OClWHi, PPPFM, RHi,

RP, RPB, RPMa, ViU, WMFM; London (British Library) ¶ Contains 5 Masonic songs. See 124 for a list of editions.

296 THE HARPER | to which are added, | Shannon's flowery banks, | The rambling boy, with The | answer. | Bung your eye, | Henry and Laury [*recte* Lawa]. | London | [*recte* Philadelphia], | printed for the purchasers.

8 p. [1:] title-page; 2-8: songs.

Shaw 50545 ¶ PPL* ¶ Contains 6 songs, all listed on the title-page. The imprint appears to be fictitious—the chapbook probably was printed in Philadelphia around 1805.

Hunting songs. New York, 1805.
See 298.

297 JAMIE REILY | and | Cooleen Bawn. | In three parts.

8 p. [1:] title-page; 2-8: songs.

PPL* (imperfect) ¶ The only copy known lacks pp. 3-8. Probably contains 3 songs. See 100 for a complete list of editions. The chapbook probably was printed in Philadelphia around 1805.

298 THE | JOVIAL | SONGSTER. | Containing | a collection of the best | humorous & entertaining | songs, | selected from those admired by the | most fashionable companies. | 'Tis music can their cares controul [sic], | And to Elysium charm the soul. | New-York: | printed by John Tiebout, | No. 238 Water-Street. | 1805.

40, [5]-40 p. [1:] blank; [2:] frontispiece; [3:] title-page; [4:] blank; [5]-28: hunting songs; [29]-40: miscellaneous; [5]-28: Masonic songs; [29]-40: miscellaneous.

Sabin 36772, Shaw 8714. Indexed in Lewis ¶ RPB* ¶ Contains 43 songs. The second pagination is identical with 230; the first pagination is identical with the second pagination in 283.

299 KATHARINE OGIE. | Guardian angels, | and The | answer: | Sally in our alley. | Jump at a crust. | Fare thee well.

8 p. [1:] title-page; 2-8: songs.

PPL* ¶ Contains 6 songs, all named on the title-page. The chapbook probably was printed in Philadelphia around 1805.

300 KING CRISPIN'S | GARLAND, | or, | the praise of the grand procession | of the shoe-makers in Falkirk, | October 25th, 1796. | To which is added, | The spinning wheel, | The tempest, | and | The jolly miller. Entered according to order.

8 p. [1:] title-page; 2-8: songs.

Shaw 50559 ¶ PPL* ¶ Contains 4 songs, all listed on the title-page. The chapbook probably was printed in Philadelphia around 1805.

Masonic songs. New York, 1805.
  See 298.

301 MOCK-BIRD: | consisting of | a complete collection of the most
    admired | American and English songs, | ballads, glees, &c. | which
have been sung with applause at the public theatres. | Also some of the
best and most favorite | Scotch, Irish, & Welch [sic] songs, | together
with a curious collection of | original toasts & sentiments, | used in the
most polite circles, | including a variety of scarce old songs, not to be
found in any | other collection. | Baltimore: | printed by Warner &
Hanna, corner of | South Gay & Market-Streets. | 1805.
    104, [4] p. [1:] title-page; [2:] blank; 3-100: songs; [101]-104: toasts
and sentiments; [105]-[108:] index.
    Bristol 379, Shaw 8916 ¶ NN* ¶ Contains 101 songs (98 indexed).

302 THE | MODERN SONGSTER; | or, | universal banquet of | vocal
    music. | Consisting of | a complete collection of the most admired |
American and English songs, | ballads, glees, &c. | which have been
sung with applause at the public theatres. | Also some of the best and
most favorite | Scotch, Irish, & Welch [sic] songs, | together with a
curious collection of | original toasts & sentiments, | used in the most
polite circles, | including a variety of scarce old songs, not to be found
in any | other collection, | with suitable observations on the art of sing-
ing, necessary to | be perused by all persons who wish to practice, with
pro- | priety, that agreeable pastime. | Listen to the voice of love. | First
Baltimore edition. | Baltimore: | printed by Warner & Hanna, corner
of | South Gay & Market-Streets. | 1805.
    1 p.l., 244, [8] p. [i:] blank; [ii:] frontispiece; [1:] title-page; [2:]
blank; [3:] directions for singing; [4:] blank; [5]-240: songs; [241]-
244: toasts and sentiments; [245]-[252:] index.
    Bristol 380, Shaw 8917. Indexed in Lewis ¶ MWA (imperfect),
RPB* ¶ Contains 237 songs (all indexed). *Later edition:* 519. *Edition
after 1820:* (a) 1825, Baltimore (MWA).

303 MOLLY MOG: | Looney Mactwolter, | and Judy O'Flanagan. |
    Gentle river. | Pauvre Madelon. | Barbado's [sic] bells: | and The |
post captain.
    8 p. [1:] title-page; 2-8: songs.
    Shaw 50573 ¶ PPL* ¶ Contains 6 songs, all named on the title-page.
The chapbook probably was printed in Philadelphia around 1805.

304 THE | MUSICAL SIREN; | being | esteemed | modern songs. | Se-
    lected | from the latest English and American | editions. | New-
York: | printed for the booksellers. | 1805.
    36 p. [1:] title-page; [2:] blank; [3]-36: songs.
    Shaw 8958. Indexed in Lewis ¶ MWA*, RPB ¶ Contains 33 songs.

305 THE NEW A B C; | being a | complete alphabet in verse, | to entice children to learn their letters. | To which is added, | a number of | Tom Thumb's songs. | Worcester: printed by I. Thomas, Jun. | Sold wholesale and retail at his book- | store—1805.

    31 p. [1:] blank; [2:] frontispiece; [3:] title-page; [4:] plate; [5:] alphabet; [6]-18: text; 19-31: songs.

    Shaw 8969, Welch 923.1 ¶ MWA* ¶ Contains 10 juvenile songs.

306 THE | PHILADELPHIA SONGSTER; | or a complete | vocal pocket companion: | being a collection | of | the most approved Anacreontic, political, | and sentimental | modern songs. | Selected from a variety of volumes. | "Mirth, love, and sentiment, are here happily blended, | "The chastest ear unoffended." | Philadelphia: | printed and published by B. Graves, | No. 40, N. Fourth-Street. | 1805.

    x, [2], 288 p. [i:] title-page; [ii:] blank; [iii]-x: index; [xi]-[xii:] blank; [1]-288: songs.

    Filby B13, Shaw 9140 ¶ CSt, DLC*, MH, MWA, MiU-C, NHi, PHi, PPL, RPB ¶ Contains 264 songs (248 indexed). See 122 and 320 for related editions. There were two printings, the earlier identifiable by a misprint in pagination (p. 134 misnumbered p. 104). The MH, NHi, and PHi copies are of a later printing in which p. 134 is correctly numbered; all other located copies are from the earlier printing.

307 POETRY | ON | DIFFERENT SUBJECTS, | written under the signature of | Timothy Spectacles. | By William C. Foster. | "Oft' from her careless hand the wand'ring muse | "Scatters luxuriant sweets, which well might form | "A living wreath to deck the brow of time." | Copy-right secured. | Salem, (N. Y.) | printed by John M. Looker, for the | author. | 1805.

    xii, 144 p. [i:] title-page; [ii:] blank; [iii]-v: index; v: errata; [vi:] blank; [vii]-xii: preface, dated Waterford, N. Y., 1804; [1]-107: poetry on different subjects; [108:] blank; [109]-128: patriotic songs; [129:] half-title: Appendix; [130:] blank; [131]-137: an oration, delivered at Waterford on the 4th of July, 1804, before an assemblage of mechanics; [138:] blank; [139:] half-title: List of subscribers; [140]-144: subscribers' names.

    Sabin 25269, Wegelin 964 ¶ CtY, DLC, IaU, MB, MWA, NHi*, NN, RPB, TxU ¶ Contains 10 patriotic songs by Foster. Pasted on the verso of the title-page (p. [ii]) in the NHi copy is a copyright notice, N. Y., 19 June 1805, William C. Foster, author.

308 THE | PRENTICE [sic] BOY. | To which are added, | The good ship Rover. | The crafty farmer. | Love and friendship. | Printed in the year 1805.

    8 p. [1:] title-page; 2-8: songs.

    Shaw 50600 ¶ PPL* (imperfect) ¶ The only known copy lacks pp.

3-8. Probably contains 4 songs, all named on the title-page. The chap-book probably was printed in Philadelphia.

309 THE | SENTIMENTAL | SONGSTER: | a collection of | useful
     & elegant | songs. | Bennington: Haswell & Smead, printers. | 1805.
     132 p. [1:] title-page; [2:] blank; [3]-132: songs.
     Lowens U83, McCorison 807, Spargo 150 ¶ Vt* (imperfect) ¶ The
only known copy is a fragment lacking pp. 25-93. It contains 38 songs.
Ship-carpenter or, the Gosport tragedy. To which is added, Capt.
Ward, and the Rainbow.
     8 p.
Shaw 50611 ¶ PPL* ¶ Contains only 2 songs. See under 1798 for an
earlier edition of *The Gosport tragedy* with two songs; see 253 for a
complete list of 3-song editions.

The | songster's | pocket companion; | containing | a number of | favor-
ite songs, | marches, &c. | From the music press of | Herman Mann, |
Dedham, (Mass.) | 1805.
     See 286.

310 TOM TUFF: | Decatur's victory. | James Irwin; | The | Rochester
     lass. | As sure as a gun.
     8 p. [1:] title-page; 2-8: songs.
     Shaw 50620 ¶ PPL* ¶ Contains 5 songs, all named on the title-page.
The chapbook probably was printed in Philadelphia around 1805.

311 THE | TOWN & COUNTRY | SONG-BOOK. | Consisting of | a
     complete collection of the most admired | American and English
songs, | ballads, glees, &c. | which have been sung with applause at the
public theatres. | Also some of the best and most favorite | Scotch, Irish,
& Welch [sic] songs, | together with a curious collection of | original
toasts & sentiments, | used in the most polite circles, | including a variety
of scarce old songs, not to be found in any | other collection, | with
suitable observations on the art of singing, necessary to | be perused by
all persons who wish to practice, with pro- | priety, that agreeable
pastime. | Listen to the voice of love. | First Baltimore edition. | Balti-
more: | printed by Warner & Hanna, corner of | South Gay & Market-
Streets. | 1805.
     105, [3] p. [1:] title-page; [2:] blank; [3:] directions for singing;
[4:] blank; [5]-105: songs; [106]-[108:] index.
     Lowens U84 ¶ MH* (imperfect) ¶ Contains 102+ songs. The only
extant copy lacks pp. 47-50, half of pp. 105-[106], and pp. [107]-[108].
Despite the identical title and pagination, 530 is an unrelated item.
Later edition: 454.

312 THE TRUE | AHIMAN REZON: | or a | help to all that are, or would be | Free and Accepted Masons. | With many additions. | The first American from the third London | edition, | by Lau. Dermott, D. G. M. | "As for his works in verse or prose, | "I own myself no judge of those; | "Nor can I tell what critics thought 'em, | "But this I know, all people bought 'em." | Swift. | New-York: | printed by Southwick & Harcdastle [sic], | 2, Wall-Street. | 1805.

1 p.l., 216, 60 p. [i:] blank; [ii:] frontispiece; [1:] title-page; [2:] blank; [3:] dedication, from the 3rd London edition; [4:] blank; [5:] explanation of the frontispiece; [6:] blank; [7]-12: contents; [13]-130: text; [131:] second title-page: A | collection | of | Masonic songs, | with several ingenious | prologues and epilogues. | To which is added, | Solomon's temple, | an | oratorio, | as it was performed for the | benefit of sick and distressed | Free-Masons. | New-York. | Printed by Southwick & Hardcastle, | 2, Wall-Street; [132:] blank; [133]-196: songs; 196-205: prologues and epilogues; [206]-211: Solomon's temple; [212]-216: list of subscribers; [1:] third title-page: The | constitutions | of the | ancient and honorable fraternity | of | Free and Accepted | Masons | in the | State of New-York; | collected and digested by order of the | Grand Lodge. | New-York: | published by Southwick & Hardcastle, | No. 2, Wall-Street. | Anno Lucis 5805; [2:] dedication to George Washington, dated A. L. 5785; [3]-4: list of Lodges in the state of New York; [5]-52: constitutions; [53]-59: appendix; 59-60: contents.

Barthelmess p. 6, Shaw 8318 ¶ DLC*, MBFM (lacks frontispiece) ¶ Contains 64 Masonic songs. There is a variant issue extant with the misprint in the spelling of Hardcastle's name on the title-page corrected. Copies of the variant are at DSC (lacks frontispiece), MBFM, NHi, and PPPFM (2 copies lacking frontispiece).

313 THE | UNION SONG BOOK; | or | American sky lark; | from the most approved modern songs, a great variety | of which have never before been printed in America. | Containing | sentimental, | humorous, | witty, | satyrical, | theatrical, | hunting, | sea and | Masonic songs. | Also | a number of toasts and sentiments. | Printed at Boston, | for William Tileston Clap, | No. 88, Fish Street. | 1805. | David Carlisle, printer, Cambridge Street.

xii, 312 p. [i:] title-page; [ii:] blank; [iii]-xii: index; [1]-310: songs; [311]-312: toasts and sentiments.

Bieber 255, Sabin 97818, Shaw 9509 ¶ DLC (imperfect), MB, NBuG, PPL* RPB ¶ Contains 294 songs (286 indexed).

314 WARBLER. | A | collection of the most popular | ancient and modern | songs: | in four numbers. | No. I. | Printed at Augusta by Peter Edes, | for | Ezekiel Goodale, bookseller, Hallowell. | 1805.

217, [7] p. [1:] title-page; [2:] blank; [3]-64: songs; [65]-112: Warbler, No. II; [113:] additional title-page: Warbler. | A | collection of the most popular | ancient and modern | songs: | in four numbers. | No. III. | Printed at Augusta by Peter Edes, | for | Ezekiel Goodale, bookseller, Hallowell. | 1805; 114-176: songs; [177]-217: Warbler, No. IV; [218]-[223:] index; [224:] advertisement for Ezekiel Goodale, dated Hallowell, 1805.

Noyes 316, Sabin 101272, Shaw 9685. Indexed in Lewis ¶ DLC (imperfect), MWA (imperfect), RPB*, RPJCB ¶ Contains 164 songs (all indexed).

315 THE | YORKSHIRE TRAGEDY, | To which are added, | Ellen O'Moore. | The American buck tail. | Donald & Flora.
    8 p. [1:] title-page; 2-8: songs.
Shaw 50633 ¶ PPL* ¶ Contains 4 songs, all listed on the title-page. The chapbook probably was printed in Philadelphia around 1805.

1806

An almanack; for the year of our Lord, 1806 . . . Dedham, (Mass.)—printed by Herman Mann. 1805.
    See 286.

316 [THE AMERICAN LADIES [sic] POCKET BOOK, for the year 1806. Philadelphia: printed by John Bioren for William Y. Birch.]
    Lowens U85 ¶ No copy located ¶ See 120 for a list of editions.

317 THE BEGGAR | GIRL, | To which is added, | Carmagnoles [sic], | Tom Bowling, | Tid re I. | Wounded hus- | sar. | Printed in the year 1806.
    8 p. [1:] title-page; 2-8: songs.
Shaw 50647 ¶ PPL* ¶ Contains 5 songs, all named on the title-page. The chapbook probably was printed in Philadelphia.

318 [THE BLACK BIRD. New York: Evert Duyckinck, 1806.]
    Existence inferred from 325, q.v. ¶ No copy located ¶ *Later editions:* 410, 506, 627. *Editions after 1820:* (a) 1825, New York: Christian Brown (DLC); (b) 1827, New York: Joseph M'Cleland (DLC, NHi, RPB).
    Edition (a) is something of a bibliographical curiosity. It contains two parts, the first of which is called *The black bird,* and the second of which is called *The dandy's companion.* The entire item is paginated 1 p.l., 72, [3]-70, [2] p., 2 l. *The dandy's companion* is identifiable from the half-title on p. 3 of the second grouping—apparently the title-page is missing in the only copy located. In this DLC copy, the additional 2 leaves tipped in after the index to *The dandy's companion* are an index to *The black bird.* The frontispiece on the preliminary

leaf is evidently designed for use with *The dandy's companion*. The content of Edition (a) is identical to that in the 140, [4] p. editions of *The black bird*—those of 410, 506, 627, and Edition (b) of 1827.

319 [THE COMIC SONGSTER, or a pill for care; a selection of the most approved comic songs sung at the Baltimore and Philadelphia theatres. Baltimore: G. Dobbin & Murphy, 1806.]

Bristol 435, Lowens U86, Shaw 10190 ¶ No copy located ¶ Advertised 1 Feb. 1806 in the Baltimore *Telegraphe* as "just published."

320 THE COMPLETE | MODERN SONGSTER, | or | vocal pocket companion: | containing upwards of 270 of the most ap- | proved English, American, Irish and Scotch, | Anacreontic, political, and senti-mental | modern songs, | selected | from a variety of volumes. | To which is annexed | a handsome collection of original | toasts and sentiments. | "Mirth, love and harmony are here happily blended, | "The chastest ear unoffended." | First American edition. | Philadelphia: | printed and published by B. Graves, No. 40, North Fourth-Street. | 1806.

xii, 276 p. [i:] title-page; [ii:] blank; [iii]-x: index; [xi]-[xii:] blank; [1]-274: songs; [275]-276: toasts and sentiments.

Lowens U87 ¶ NNC* (imperfect) ¶ Contains 223 songs (all indexed). Essentially an updated edition of 122, q.v. See also 306 for a related imprint. The only known copy lacks pp. 5-8.

321 A | DISCOURSE | delivered at the | dedication | of the new | Con-gregational | meetinghouse | in | Bennington. | On | the first of Janu-ary, A. D. 1806. | By Daniel Marsh, A. M. | (Published by request of the Society.) | From the press of Anthony Haswell, at his | book print-ing office, Bennington, 1806.

23, [1], 4 p. [1:] title-page; [2:] blank; [3]-23: text; [24:] blank; [1]-4: odes sung in the course of the celebration.

McCorison 861, Shaw 10790, Spargo 157 ¶ MBC, MWA*, NN, VtBennM, VtHi ¶ Contains 4 odes, probably written by Anthony Haswell, according to McCorison. See 328 for a related edition.

322 [THE JOVIAL SONGSTER, NO. I. By S. Jenks. Dedham, Mass., 1806 or before.]

Lowens U88 ¶ No copy located ¶ Existence inferred from 323, q.v.

323 THE | JOVIAL SONGSTER, | NO. II. | Being a selection | of some of the most favorite, and sentimental | songs; | some of which are original. | Set to music, chiefly in two parts. | By S. Jenks. | Printed at Dedham—Mass. | March—1806.

24 p. [1:] title-page; [2:] copyright notice, Mass., 4 Mar. 1806, Stephen Jenks, author; [3]-24: songs.

Johnson p. 345, Shaw 10634, Sonneck Copyright, Wolfe 4619 ¶ CtHC, MWA* ¶ Contains 14 songs, all with musical notation, and apparently most to music composed by Jenks. See also 322.

324 LADY WASHING- | TON'S ENQUIRY. | The hobbies. | The shepherd | boy. | To which is added | Hail Columbia. | Jockey to the fair. | A song. | Printed in the year 1806.

    8 p. [1:] title-page; 2-8: songs.

    Shaw 50692 ¶ PPL* ¶ Contains 6 songs, all named on the title-page. The chapbook probably was printed in Philadelphia. The first song was usually called *Lady Washington's lamentation*. See 255 for an earlier, related chapbook.

325 THE | LINNET; | or, | favorite companion. | A | collection | of the | newest and most admired | songs. | With a number of choice | toasts and sentiments. | New-York, | published by Evert Duyckinck, | No. 110 Pearl-Street. | M'Farlane & Long, print. | 1806.

    210, [6] p. [1:] title-page; [2:] blank; [3]-206: songs; [207]-210: toasts and sentiments; [211]-[216:] index.

    Sabin 41355, Shaw 10736 ¶ CtY* ¶ Contains 186 songs (all indexed). A caption-title on p. [3] reads "The black bird", the first 140 pp. were reprinted as 410, q.v. See also 318.

326 THE | NEPTUNE: | or a collection of the most entertaining | comic | and | sea songs: | being a selection from the newest and most | favourite publications, and may prove a | merry, jovial and sprightly companion | for the sons of hilarity and mirth. | Boston: | printed and sold by Thomas Fleet, | in Cornhill, 1806. | (Price nine pence.)

    36 p. [1:] blank; [2:] frontispiece; [3:] title-page; [4]-36: songs.

    Shaw 10945. Indexed in Devine ¶ IU (imperfect), MWA* ¶ Contains 24 songs. *Later edition:* 576.

327 THE | NIGHTINGALE: | containing | a collection | of | approved songs. | Albany: | printed and sold by E. & E. Hosford, | opposite the State Bank. | 1806.

    102, [3] p. [1:] title-page; [2:] blank; [3]-102: songs; [103]-[105:] index.

    RPB* ¶ Contains 75 songs (all indexed).

328 [caption-title:] ORIGINAL ODES, | designed to be sung at the | dedication of the meeting-house, | in Bennington, Vt. | Jan. 1, 1806. [Bennington: Anthony Haswell, 1806.]

    12 p. [1]-12: odes.

    McCorison 866, Shaw 11076 ¶ MWA* ¶ Contains 6 odes probably written by Anthony Haswell, according to McCorison. See 321 for a related edition.

329 THE RAMBLING | BOY. | With The answer. | To which is
  added, | Blue bells of | Scotland. | Good morrow to your | night cap.
| Capt. Stephen Decatur's | victory. | Green upon the cape. | Printed in
the year 1806.

  8 p. [1:] title-page; 2-8: songs.

  Shaw 50722 ¶ PHi (imperfect), PPL* ¶ Contains 6 songs, all named
on the title-page. P. 3 is misnumbered p. 6 in the PPL copy. The chapbook probably was printed in Philadelphia.

330 A | SELECTION | of | one hundred and forty | of | the most fa-
  vourite | English, Scotch, Irish, and | American | songs. | Carlisle; |
from the press of A. Loudon, | (Whitehall.) | 1806.

  [viii], 216 p. [i:] title-page; [ii:] blank; [iii]-[viii:] index; [1]-216:
songs.

  Shaw 11344 ¶ MWA* (imperfect) ¶ Contains 142 songs (all indexed). The only known copy lacks pp. 9-16. See 331 for a variant
edition.

331 A | SELECTION | of | one hundred and forty | o [sic] | the most
  favourite | English, Scotch, Irish, and | American | songs. | Carlisle:
| from the press of A. Loudon, | (Whitehall.)

  1 p.l., 216 p. [i:] title-page; [ii:] blank; [1]-216: songs.

  PSt* ¶ Contains 142 songs. Except for the variant title-page and the
lack of an index, this is identical to 330 and was printed from the same
plates.

332 TOM BOWLING, | to which is added, | The beggar girl. | Lady
  Wshington's [sic] la- | mentaion [sic] | Soldier's return. | The dis-
banded militia- | man. | Printed in the year 1806.

  8 p. [1:] title-page; 2-8: songs.

  Shaw 50736 ¶ PPL* ¶ Contains 5 songs, all named on the title-page.
The chapbook probably was printed in Philadelphia.

The youthful jester; or repository of wit and innocent amusement.
Containing moral and humorous tales—merry jests—laughable anecdotes, and smart repartees. The whole being as innocent as it is entertaining. Printed for the book-sellers. 1806.

  108 p.

  Shaw 11912, Shaw 11913, Welch 689.2 ¶ MWA* ¶ This edition
contains no songs. See 210 for an earlier edition with songs.

1807

333 THE | AMERICAN LADIES [sic] | POCKET BOOK, | for the
  year 1807: | containing | an almanac | ruled pages for memo- |
randums, observations | and engagements; also | for accounts of monies

| received, paid or lent, | for every day in the year. | Singular mode of travel- | ling in Lapland. | Selected poetry, | new and celebrated songs, | a marketing table, and | several other useful ta- | bles. | To be continued annually. | Philadelphia: | printed for William Y. Birch, No. 37, S. 2d. | and S. F. Bradford, No. 4, S. 3d. Street. | Where is published also, | The gentlemans' annual pocket remembrancer. | John Bioren, printer.

1 p.l., 134, 132-133 [i.e., 135-136] p. [i:] blank; [ii:] frontispiece; [1:] title-page; [2:] blank; [3:] contents; 4: common notes, &c.; [5]-120: text; [121]-130: songs; 131-133 [i.e., 136]: tables.

Shaw 11978 ¶ RPB* ¶ Contains 10 songs. See 120 for a list of editions.

334 THE | AMERICAN | SONGSTER. | Consisting of | a large col-
     lection | of the | newest and most fashionable | songs. | "Music the fiercest grief can charm, | "And fate's severest rage disarm; | "Our joys below it can improve, | "And antedate the bliss above." | Providence: | printed by David Heaton, Main-Street. | M,DCCC,VII.

282, [6] p. [1:] title-page; [2:] blank; [3]-72: The American song-ster, No. I; [73]-144: The American songster, No. II; [145]-216: The American songster, No. III; [217]-282: The American songster, No. IV; [283]-[288:] index.

Shaw 11981. Indexed in Devine ¶ MWA*, RPB. No. I only: MB. Nos. I and II only: MH, NBuG, RP, RPB. No. III only: MdBJ ¶ Con-tains 247 songs (172 indexed).

The battle of the kegs. Sold at No. 3, Pek-Slip [sic]. 1807.
4 p.
RPB* ¶ Contains only 1 song. For an earlier edition with 3 songs, see 245.

335 THE | BUDGET OF MIRTH, | being a | choice collection | of the
     | most approved and fashionable | songs. | By Thomas Wild. | —
Ev'n age itself is cheer'd with music; | It wakes a glad remembrance of our youth, | Calls back past joys, and warms us into transport! | Rowe. | Boston: | printed by Snellling [sic] and Simons, No. 5, Exchange | Buildings, Devonshire Street. | 1807.

1 p.l., 108 p. [1:] blank; [ii:] frontispiece; [1:] title-page; [2:] blank; [3:] preface, signed Thomas Wild, and dated Boston, 1 Dec. 1807; [4:] blank; [5]-104: songs; [105]-108: index.

Shaw 14219. Indexed in Devine ¶ MWA*, NBuG, NHi (lacks frontispiece), OCl ¶ Contains 64 songs (all indexed). The index in-cludes a column headed "Places to find music." Cited are: Blagrove (15), Etheridge & Bliss (8), Hewitt (13)—all publishers—and Musical Miscellany (1), Nightingale (3)—both songsters.

336 THE | FREE-MASON'S | VOCAL ASSISTANT, and | register |
     of the | Lodges of Masons | in | South-Carolina and Georgia. |

Charleston, (S. C.) | Printed by Brother J. J. Negrin, | No. 106, Queen-Street. | 1807.

4 p.l., [13]-120, [157]-255, [1] p. [i:] title-page; [ii:] preface; [iii:] dedication, signed J. J. Negrin; [iv:] "cantiuncula fratris Phil. Trajetta . . . cantata del fratello Phil. Trajetta"; [v]-[viii:] index; [13]-120: songs in English; [157]-208: songs in French; [209]-255: register of Lodges; [256:] index to register.

Barthelmess p. 28, Morris p. 108, Sabin 25812, Sabin 52255, Sabin 87840, Shaw 12620, Turnbull I, 434, Wolfe 2863 ¶ DLC, DSC, IaCrM, MBFM* (2 copies, 1 imperfect), NHi, NIC, NNFM, NcA-S, PHi (2 copies, 1 imperfect), PPPFM (4), RPB ¶ Contains 91 Masonic songs in English (88 indexed) and 48 Masonic songs in French (51 indexed). All but one of the 16 known copies lack pp. 121-156, which should contain tunes, according to the catchword on p. 120. The single variant copy is one of the two at MBFM, which contains 16 leaves of music embracing 17 tunes and one anthem, the whole engraved by J. L. Copp. Except for two leaves, which are bound in upside down between pp. 190-191, all leaves are found between pp. 120 and [157], but they are erratically paginated 157, 159, 162-163, 165, 168-169, 171, 174-175, 177, 190-191 (the misbound leaves), 193, 195, 198-199. There seems to be no correspondence between this pagination and that of the rest of the book, and I am at a loss to account for the eccentric numeration. That there are no leaves missing is indicated by the normal numbering of the songs found on the extant leaves; that these leaves are part of the book is indicated by the tune names "No. 16," "No. 18," and "No. 19" which plainly refer to the associated tunes on the leaves which are numbered and appear without title. It would seem that this imprint was constructed with a 36-page gap (3 12mo signatures) to take care of the music and with 12 pages (one 12mo signature) to take care of the preliminary matter, but that the printer miscalculated.

337 GENERAL | REGULATIONS | for the | government | of the | Grand Lodge | of New-Jersey. | Trenton: | [New-Jersey.] | Printed by George Sherman. | 1807.

44, [3] p. [1:] title-page; [2:] blank; [3]-24: general regulations; 25-26: list of warrants; 27-44: songs; [45]-[47:] contents.

Shaw 12612 ¶ PPPFM, RPB* ¶ Contains 11 Masonic songs.

338 THE KILMAINHAM MINUTE, | or the | execution of | Jamey O'Brian. | To which is added, | The bowl of egg-nog. | Printed in the year 1807.

8 p. [1:] title-page; 2-8: songs.

PPL* (imperfect) ¶ The only known copy lacks pp. 7-8. Apparently contains 4 songs. The chapbook probably was printed in Philadelphia.

339 THE | LADY'S CABINET | of | polite literature. | Containing | a
selection of the most delicate and refined | airs, songs, | poems, | and
various other | miscellaneous productions, | in verse and prose. | Vol. I.
The lute. Consisting of songs. | (Copy right secured.) | Boston: | pub-
lished by Russell & Cutler, | (proprietors of the work.) | Sold by Eth-
eridge & Bliss, | No. 12, Cornhill. | 1807.

202, vi p. [1:] title-page; [2:] blank; [3]-[4:] advertisement, dated
Boston, 4 Dec. 1807; [5]-202: songs; [i]-vi: index. A leaf containing
a copyright notice (Mass., 14 Dec. 1807, Russell & Cutler, proprietors)
is tipped in between pp. [4]-[5].

Shaw 12880 ¶ CtHT-W, MH, MWA* ¶ Contains 254 songs (all
indexed).

The lute. Boston: Russell & Cutler, 1807.

See 339.

340 [THE MILITARY SONGSTER, and soldier's camp companion;
being a collection of new and old patriotic songs; with many original
songs, composed to suit the present times. Baltimore, Fryer & Rider?
1807.]

Bristol 562, Lowens U89, Shaw 13081 ¶ No copy located ¶ Advertised 15 Aug. 1807 in the Baltimore *American* as "this day . . . published."

341 THE | NIGHTINGALE | or | ladies [sic] | vocal companion. |
While bleeding & low, on the heath she descried. | By the light of
the moon, her poor wounded hussar. | Albany | published by Packard &
Conant | No. 41 State Street | 1807.

2 p.l., 121, [6] p. [i:] blank; [ii:] frontispiece; [iii:] title-page; [iv:]
blank; [1]-121: songs; [122:] colophon: R. Packard, printer, Albany;
[123]-[127:] index.

Brinley 6942, Shaw 13254 ¶ DLC* (2 copies, 1 lacking frontispiece),
MH, MWA, N, NHi, RPB, ScU; Oxford (Bodleian Library) (imperfect) ¶ Contains 143 songs (all indexed). See 258 for a list of
editions.

342 [cover-title:] OLD | DAME MARGERY'S | HUSH-A-BYE: | em-
bellished with | fifteen elegant engravings | on copper-plates. | Phil-
adelphia: | published by Jacob Johnson, | No. 147 Market Street. |
Whitehall. . . . . . Printed by A. Dickinson, | 1807.

[32] p. [1:] cover-title; [2:] title-page; [3:] frontispiece; [4]-[5:]
blank; [6:] plate; [7]-[10:] text; [11]-[12:] plates; [13]-[16:] text;
[17:] blank; [18]-[19:] plates; [20:] blank; [21]-[24:] text; [25:] blank;
[26]-[27:] plates; [28:] blank; [29]-[30:] text; [31:] blank; [32:] advertisement.

Welch 959.1 ¶ MSaE* ¶ Contains 20 juvenile songs. *Later editions:*
478, 549, 579.

343 VICTORY; | or | British harmony. | Being | a collection of | new songs, | sung at the London theatres, | with unbounded applause. | To which is added, | a great variety of | toasts and sentiments. | Boston: | published by Ephraim C. Beals, | No. 10, State-Street. | 1807.

1 p.l., 72 p. [i:] blank; [ii:] frontispiece; [1:] title-page; [2:] blank; [3]-68: songs; 69-70: toasts and sentiments; 71-72: index.

Shaw 14123. Indexed in Devine ¶ MB (imperfect), MWA*, RPB ¶ Contains 73 songs (all indexed).

344 THE | VIRGINIA NIGHTINGALE, | containing | a choice collection | of | new songs. | Alexandria: | printed by Cottom and Stewart, | and sold at their bookstores in Alexandria and | Fredericksburg. | 1807.

180 p. [1:] title-page; [2:] blank; [3]-175: songs; [176]-180: index.

Quenzel 50, Sabin 100561, Shaw 14141 ¶ DLC*, MWA, MiU-C, RPB (imperfect) ¶ Contains 116 songs (112 indexed).

1808

345 [THE AMERICAN LADIES [sic] POCKET BOOK, for the year 1808. Philadelphia: printed by John Bioren for Wm. Y. Birch.]

Lowens U90 ¶ No copy located ¶ See 120 for a list of editions.

346 A | CHOICE COLLECTION | of | popular songs. | Viz. | Paddy's wedding, | The island, | Unfortunate Miss | Bailey, | Mary le More, | The rose, | My piggy dear. | "Copy right not secured"! ! ! | Printed to supply the most | urgent demands. | 1808.

20 p. [1:] title-page; [2:] blank; [3]-20: songs.

Shaw 14688 ¶ MWA* ¶ Contains 6 songs, all named on the title-page.

347 THE | FREEMASON'S MONITOR; | or, | illustrations of Masonry: | in two parts. | By Thomas Smith Webb, | Past Master of Temple Lodge, Albany, G. H. P. of | the Grand R. A. Chapter of Rhode-Island, and | Grand Master of the Providence Encampment | of Knights Templars, &c. | A new and improved edition. | Published by Cushing & Appleton, at the sign | of the Bible, Salem; and by Henry Cushing, | at the Bible & Anchor, Providence. | Joshua Cushing, printer, No. 79, State Street, Boston. | 1808.

336 p. [i:] title-page; [ii:] blank; [iii:] copyright notice, R. I., 14 Nov. 1805, Thomas Smith Webb, proprietor; [iv:] sanction, dated Providence, 7 July 5802; [v]-vi: preface, dated 26 Sept. 1797; [vii]-xii: contents; [13]-259: Freemason's monitor, part 1; [260:] blank; [261:] second title-page: The | Freemason's monitor; | or, | illustrations of Masonry: | in two parts. | By Thomas Smith Webb, | Past Master of Temple Lodge, Albany, and G. H. P. | of the Grand Royal Arch Chapter

of | Rhode-Island, &c. | Part second. | Containing | an account of the ineffable de- | grees of Masonry; | and the | history of Freemasonry | in America. | Published by Cushing & Appleton, at the sign | of the Bible, Salem; & by Henry Cushing, | at the Bible & Anchor, Providence. | Joshua Cushing, printer, No. 79, State Street, Boston. | 1808; [262:] blank; [263]-[264:] preface; [265]-328: Freemason's monitor, part 2; [329]-336: Masonic songs.

Brinley 6760, Shaw 16686 ¶ CSt, CtY, DLC*, DSC, IU, MBFM, MH (imperfect), MHi, MSaE, MWA, MdHi (imperfect), NBuG, NN, NNFM, OCM, PPPFM (3), RHi, RPMa ¶ Contains 7 Masonic songs. See 124 for a list of editions.

348 JACHIN AND BOAZ: | or, an | authentic key | to the door of | Free-Masonry, | ancient and modern. | Calculated, | not only for the instruction of every new | made Mason; but also, for the information | of all who intend to become Brethren. | Containing, | I. A circumstantial account of all the proceedings in making a Mason; | with the several obligations of an Entered Apprentice, Fellow-Craft, | and Master; the prayers, and also the sign, grip, and pass-word | of each degree, with the ceremony of the mop and pail. | II. The manner of opening a Lodge, and setting the Craft to work. | III. The Entered Apprentice, Fellow-Craft and Master's lectures, | verbatim, as delivered in all Lodges; with the song at the conclu- | sion of each part. | IV. The origin of Masonry; description of Solomon's temple; | history of the murder of the Grand Master Hiram by the three | Fellow-Crafts; their discovery and punishment; the burial of Hiram | by King Solomon's order, with the five points of fellowship, &c. | V. The ceremony of the instalment of the Masters of different Lodg- | es on St. John's day. Description of the regalia, &c. | VI. Ceremonies used at the funeral of a Mason. | VII. A safe and easy method proposed, by which a man may obtain | admittance into any Lodge, without passing through the form re- | quired, and thereby save a guinea or two in his pocket. | VIII. Anthems, odes, songs, toasts, &c. | Illustrated with | a beautiful frontispiece of the regalia, jewels, and emblematical | ornaments belonging to Masonry; and an accurate plan of the | drawing on the floor of a Lodge. | Interspersed with a variety of | notes and remarks, | necessary to explain and render the whole clear to the | meanest capacity. | By a gentleman, | belonging to the Jerusalem Lodge; a frequent visitor at the Queen's | Arms, St. Paul's Church-Yard; the Horn, in Fleet-Street; Crown | and Anchor, Strand; and the Salutation, Newgate-Street. | Try me—prove me. | New-York: | published by John Tiebout. | 1808. | Price 37 1-2 cents.

1 p.l., vi, 58 p. [i:] blank; [ii:] frontispiece; [i:] title-page; [ii:] blank; [iii]-iv: preface; [v:] advertisement; [v]-vi: description of the frontispiece; [1]-40: text; 40-54: odes, anthems, and songs; [55]-58: toasts and sentiments.

Shaw 16118 ¶ CSmH, CtY, DSC*, MBFM, MWA, NN, OClWHi ¶ Contains 16 Masonic songs. As 112, q.v. See also 73 for a list of editions.

Jachin and Boaz; or, an authentic key to the door of Fre-Masonry [sic], both ancient and modern. Calculated not only for the instruction of every new-made Mason; but also for the information of all who intend to become Brethren. Containing I. A circumstantial account of all the proceedings in making a Mason, with the several obligations of an Entered Apprentice, Fellow-Craft, & Master; the prayers, and also the sign, grip and password of each degree. II. The manner of opening a Lodge, and setting the Craft to work. III. The Entered Apprentice, Fellow-Craft, and Master's lectures, verbatim, as delivered in all Lodges; with the song at the conclusion of each part. IV. The origin of Masonry; description of Solomon's temple; history of the murder of the Grand Master Hiram, by the three Fellow Crafts; their discovery and punishment; the burial of Hiram by King Solomon's order; with the five points of fellowship, &c. V. The ceremony of the instalment of the Master of different Lodges, on St. John's day. Description of the regalia, &c. VI. Ceremony observed at the funeral of a Mason. VII. A safe and easy method proposed, by which a man may gain admittance into any Lodge, without passing thro' the form required, and thereby save a guinea or two in his pocket. Illustrated with an accurate plan of the drawing on the floor of a Lodge. Interspersed with a variety of notes and remarks, sufficient to render the whole clear to the meanest capacity. Windsor, Vt. Printed and sold by C. & W. S. Spear. 1808.

1 p.l., 48 p.

McCorison 1028, Shaw 16119 ¶ MWA* (lacks frontispiece) ¶ This edition contains no separate section of songs. See 73 for a complete list of editions.

349 MASONIC CONSTITUTIONS, | or | illustrations of Masonry; | compiled by the direction | of the | Grand Lodge of Kentucky, | and adopted by them for the | regulation and government | of the | subordinate Lodges under their jurisdiction, | with an appendix, | containing remarks on the degrees of | Master Mark Masons, | Super Excellent Master, and | Royal Arch Masons. | By James Moore and Cary L. Clarke, | members of the Grand Lodge of Kentucky. | Lexington: | printed by Daniel Bradford, at the office of the | Kentucky Gazette, on Main-Street. | 1808.

192 p. [i:] title-page; [ii:] blank; [iii:] copyright notice, Ky., 30 Mar. 1808, James Moore and Cary L. Clarke, proprietors; [iv:] blank; [v:] preface; [vi:] blank; [vii]-xxi: introduction; [xxii:] blank; [23]-163: text; [164]-188: odes, anthems, and songs; [189]-192: contents; 192: colophon: Daniel Bradford, printer.

Barthelmess p. 7, Morris p. 111, Shaw 15051, Shaw 15637 ¶ DLC*, IaCrM, KyBgW, KyLo, MWA ¶ Contains 22 Masonic songs. *Later edition:* 572.

Masonic songs. 1808.
See 350.

350 THE | NATIONAL SONGSTER. | Containing | a collection of the most | modern and admired, | patriotic, sentimental, Anacreontic, | comic, and Masonic, | songs, | original and selected. | To which is added | a number of select toasts and sentiments. | Embellished with a handsome engraving of the | genius of America. | Philadelphia: | published by Robert Desilver, | No. 110, Walnut-Street. | 1808.

1 p.l., [viii], 225, [1] p. [i:] blank; [ii:] frontispiece; [i:] title-page; [ii:] Town, printer, No. 113, North Second-Street; [iii]-[vii:] index; [viii:] index to the Masonic songs; [1]-188: songs; [189]-190: toasts and sentiments; [191]-225: Masonic songs; [226:] Masonic toasts and sentiments.

Shaw 15690. Indexed in Devine ¶ ICN*, MWA, NBuG (imperfect), PP (lacks frontispiece) ¶ Contains 192 songs (196 indexed).

351 [THE NEW HOLYDAY PRESENT; or, the child's plaything. Exeter, N. H.: Norris & Sawyer, 1808.]

Information from Welch 936.2 ¶ No copy located ¶ Advertised by Norris & Sawyer in *Gaffer Goose's golden plaything* (Shaw 15082). See 158 for a list of editions.

352 THE | NEW WHIM | of the | night, | or, the | vocal encyclopaedia. | Boston: | printed by Thomas Fleet, No. 5, Cornhill. | 1808. | Price —nine pence.

36 p. [1:] title-page; [2:] blank; [3]-36: songs; 36: index.
Shaw 15743 ¶ DLC*, MB, MWA ¶ Contains 26 songs (all indexed).

353 THE | NIGHTINGALE; | or, | polite | amatory songster. | A selection of | delicate, pathetic, and elegant | songs, | designed chiefly for the | ladies. | To which is added | an appendix, | containing some of the most popular | new songs. | Boston: | published and sold by | Wm. Blagrove, No. 61, Cornhill. | 1808. | E. C. Beals, printer.

1 p.l., 10, 144 p. [1:] blank; [ii:] frontispiece; [1:] title-page; [2:] blank; [3:] advertisement; [4:] blank; [5]-10: index; [1]-144: songs.
Shaw 15773 ¶ MB*, MBAt ¶ Contains 171 songs (all indexed).

354 PRETTY POEMS, songs, &c. | in easy language, | for the amusement of | little boys and girls. | By Tommy Lovechild. | Ornamented with cuts. | Litchfield: | printed by Hosmer & Goodwin. | 1808.

30, [1] p. [1:] blank; [2:] frontispiece; [3:] title-page; [4:] an ABC; [5]-30: pretty poems, &c.; [31:] advertisement of publisher's books.

Rosenbach 380 ¶ PP* ¶ Contains 26 juvenile songs. *Later editions:* 451, 497, 581.

1809

355 [ALEXANDRIA SONGSTER. Published before May, 1809.]

Lowens U91 ¶ No copy located ¶ Information from the back-advertisement on the DLC copy of *National martial music and songs* (Philadelphia: W. M'Culloch, 1809), which is dated May, 1809. Perhaps another title for *The Virginia nightingale* (Alexandria: Cottom and Stewart, 1807), 344, q.v.

356 THE | AMERICAN LADIES [sic] | POCKET BOOK, | for | the year 1809, | containing | an almanac | ruled pages for memo- | randums, observations | and engagements; also | for accounts of monies | received, paid or lent, | for every day in the year. | The natural bridge. | Select poetry, | new and celebrated songs, | a marketing table, and | several other useful ta- | bles. | To be continued annually. | Philadelphia: | printed for Wm. Y. Birch, No. 37, South Second St. | Where is published also, | The gentlemans' annual pocket remembrancer, | John Bioren printer.

144 p. [1:] title-page; [2:] blank; [3:] contents; [4]-120: text; [121]-139: songs; 140-144: tables.

Drake 10798, Shaw 50822 ¶ PHi* (imperfect) ¶ Contains 19 songs. According to Drake, lacks folded fashion-plate. See 120 for a list of editions.

357 THE | AMERICAN MEDLEY, | of | wit and entertainment; | or, | a selection of | humourous, | witty, | singular, | wonderful, | droll, and | interesting | narraitives [sic], stories, anecdotes, | &c. | Prose and verse. | To which are added, | a choice collection of approved | songs. | The whole calculated to promote mirth without licentiousness, | facetious amusement without injuring morals, and to eradi- | cate from the mind every symptom of spleen. | Sweet is the tale, however strange its air, | That bids the public eye, astonish'd stare! | Sweet is the tale howe'er uncouth its shape, | That bids the world's wide mouth with wonder gape. | Pindar. | Philadelphia: | printed for the booksellers. | 1809.

2 p.l., 152 p. [i:] blank; [ii:] frontispiece; [iii:] title-page; [iv:] blank; [1:] an old man's experience, or poor Richard's maxims improved; [2:] blank; [3]-78: text; 79-152: songs.

Shaw 16843a ¶ DLC*, IC, MH, NcU ¶ Contains 49 songs. A reprint of 234 from the original plates.

358 THE | AMERICAN | VOCAL COMPANION: | a collection of | choice songs. | Mirth, love, and sentiment, are here happily | blended, | The chastest ear unoffended. | Hudson: | printed for H. Steel. | 1809.
   66+ p. [1:] title-page; [2:] blank; [3]-[4:] unknown; [5]-66+: songs.
   Lowens U92 ¶ NHi* (imperfect) ¶ Contains 61+ songs. The only known copy lacks pp. 3-4 and all after p. 66. It would appear that the complete songster contained 72 p.

359 LE CHANSONNIER DES GRACES, | almanach | chantant | pour l'anne'e [sic] 1809, | dedie aux dames, | rédigé par Alexis Daudet. | A la Nouvelle-Orleans, | de l'imprimerie de Th. Lamberte. | M. DCCC. IX.
   48 p. [1:] title-page; [2:] blank; [3]-[8:] almanac; [9]-48: songs; 48: errata.
   Shaw 50836 ¶ MWA* ¶ Contains 29 songs in French.

360 [descriptive tag:] TRIBUT DE RECONNAISSANCE. [title:] Collection | des | différens discours et pièces de poésie | prononcés le jour de la fête donnée | à | Mr. Duncan M'Intosh, | par les | français réfugiés de St. Domingue, | aux quels ce sont joints | beaucoup d'Américains, | amis de la bienfaisance. | Baltimore, le 9 janvier, 1809. | Imprimé pour Coale et Thomas, | par Jean W. Butler. | 1809.
   1 p.l., 51 p. [i:] blank; [ii:] frontispiece; [1:] title-page; [2:] blank; [3]-27: French text; [28:] blank; [29:] additional title-page in English: [descriptive tag:] Tribute of public gratitude. [title:] Some account | of an | entertainment | given in honor of | Mr. Duncan M'Intosh, | in | Baltimore, | on the 9th January, 1809. | With a | collection of the pieces | delivered on that occasion. | Printed for Coale and Thomas, | by John W. Butler. | 1809.; [30:] blank; [31]-51: English text.
   Bissainthe 8184, Shaw 18782 ¶ DLC*, MdBP, MdHi, NHi, PHi, ScU ¶ Contains 6 songs in French, interspersed throughout the French text. The English translation does not include the songs; the following appears on p. 47: "The publishers regret that they could not procure translations of the different *couplets,* which were sung in the French language upon this occasion."

The | comic songster | for 1809.
   See 370.

361 THE | HUMMING BIRD. | A collection of | new favourite & national | songs. | Hither, love, they wild wing bend, | And see him die! | Baltimore | printed and sold by: | Warner & Hanna | 1809.
   107, [3] p. [1:] title-page; [2:] blank; [3]-105: songs; [106]-107: toasts and sentiments; [108]-[110:] index.
   Bristol 745, Shaw 17784. Indexed in Devine ¶ MWA (imperfect),

PPL (imperfect), RPB* ¶ Contains 108 songs (all indexed). Issued also, with altered pagination, as the second part of 363, q.v.

362 THE | MIDDLESEX | SONGSTER. | Containing | a collection of the most approv- | ed songs now in use. | By Daniel Belknap. | Dedham: | printed by H. Mann. | 1809.

47, [1] p. [i:] title-page; [ii:] copyright notice, Mass., 30 Sept. 1809, Daniel Belknap, author; [3]-47: songs; [48:] index and errata.

Shaw 16982, Sonneck Copyright, Wolfe 517. Indexed in Devine ¶ CtY, DLC (imperfect), RPB* ¶ Contains 22 songs (all indexed) with musical notation.

363 NEW | JOKE UPON JOKE, | containing | wit, humor, songs and the most approv- | ed songs now in use. | By Daniel Belknap. | printed and sold by Warner & Hanna. | 1809.

215, [3] p. [1:] title-page; [2:] blank; [3]-108: text; [109:] second title-page: The | humming bird. | A collection of | new favourite & national | songs. | Hither, love, thy wild wing bend, | And see him die! | Baltimore | printed and sold by: | Warner & Hanna | 1809.; [110:] blank; [111]-213: songs; [214]-215: toasts and sentiments; [216]-[218:] index.

Bristol 775, Shaw 18220 ¶ MWA* ¶ Contains 108 songs (all indexed). The songs were also issued separately with altered pagination as 361, q.v.

364 THE | NIGHTINGALE: | or, | ladies' | vocal companion. | Albany: | published by Benjamin D. Packard, No. 41 State-Street. | 1809.

1 p.l., 121, [6] p. [i:] title-page; [ii:] blank; [1]-121: songs; [122:] colophon: R. Packard, printer, Albany; [123]-[127:] index.

Shaw 18256 ¶ DLC* ¶ Contains 143 songs (all indexed). Identical in content to 341. See 258 for a list of editions.

365 [caption-title:] REPUBLICAN SONGS, | written for the celebration of the 16th of | August, 1809, in Bennington. | By A. Haswell.

[iv], 20 p. [i:] caption-title; [i]-20: songs.

McCorison 1080, Shaw 17722, Spargo 185 ¶ MWA* ¶ Contains 17 songs.

366 SONGS. | The battle of the Nile. | Tid re I. | The poor but honest soldier. | Honest Harry O. | The wounded hussar. | New-York: | printed for Christian Brown, No. 71, Water-Street. | 1809.

[8?] p. [1:] title-page; [2:] blank; [3-8: songs.]

Shaw 18658 ¶ NjR* (title-page only) ¶ Presumably an 8-page chapbook, containing 5 songs, all named on the title-page.

367 SPAIN. | An | account | of the | public festival | given by | the citizens of Boston, | at the Exchange Coffee House, | January 24, 1809, | in honor of | Spanish valour & patriotism. | With the | regular and volunteer toasts, | and all the | original songs and odes | sung on the occasion. | In which is also introduced | a brief sketch of Spain, | geographical, historical and political. | Spain is not a dead but sleeping lion. | Copy-rights of the "Sketch" and "National Ode," having been secured by the author, | agreeable to act of Congress; they are here published by permission of Mr. Paine. | Printed | by Russell and Cutler, | and for sale at their printing-office in Congress-Street, | Boston.

1 p.l., 36 p. [i:] title-page; [ii:] blank; [1:] a page of mottos; [2:] blank; [3]-19: text; [20]-36: songs.

Sabin 88852, Shaw 18667, Wegelin 1362 ¶ CSt, DLC, IU, MH, MHi, MWA*, MWiW, NBuG, NN, NNC, PMA, PU ¶ Contains 8 songs.

1810

368 THE | AMERICAN | LADIES' POCKET-BOOK | for | the year 1810. | Containing | an almanac. | Ruled pages for memo- | randums, observations | and engagements; also | for accounts of monies | received, paid or lent, | for every day in the year. | Falls of Niagara. | Select poetry, | new and celebrated songs, | a marketing table, and | several other useful ta- | bles. | To be continued annually. | Published | by W. Y. Birch, Bradford & Inskeep, Philadelphia; | and Inskeep & Bradford, New-York. | Where is published also, | The gentlemans' annual pocket remembrancer. | J. Bioren, printer.

1 p.l., 140 p [i:] blank; [ii:] frontispiece; [1:] title-page; [2]-3: contents; [4]-115: text; [116]-134: songs; 135-140: tables.

Drake 10838, Shaw 50907 ¶ PHi* ¶ Contains 21 songs. See 120 for a list of editions.

[The ancient and modern music of Ireland, with original songs. By John McCreery.]

According to Whitty, this item was copyrighted in 1810. It does not appear to have been issued, however, until 1824, when it was published in the following form: A selection, from the | ancient music of Ireland, | arranged for the | flute or violin, | some of the most | admired melodies, | adapted to | American poetry | chiefly composed by John M'Creery. | To which is prefixed, historical and critical obser- | vations on | ancient Irish music. | Petersburg: | printed by Yancey & Burton, Intelligencer Press, Bank Street. | 1824.

xxii, [7]-208 p. [i:] title-page; [ii:] blank; [iii]-xx: preface; [xxi]-xxii: index; [7]-208: songs.

Swem 3317 ¶ CtY, DLC*, NcD, NNUT, Vi, ViU ¶ On p. [iii] of the preface, M'Creery writes: "Nearly twenty years have elapsed since we first contemplated the publication of a selection of the finest Irish airs, accompanied by songs of American composition, breathing the free spirit of 'a muse unchecked by any slavish fear.'—Our friends were applied to, and promised their assistance.—Our proposals, published in this country, found their way into the British papers, and, we have reason to believe, stimulated Moore and Stevenson to undertake a similar work. The untimely death of our zealous and able coadjutor, Mr. John Burke [sic], co-operating with other circumstances equally beyond our controul [sic], compelled us to postpone the intended publication. Finally, a continuation of some of the same causes has obliged us, though with ample materials in our possession, to remodel our design on a scale greatly inferior to that originally laid down." M'Creery's "coadjutor" was John Daly Burk, some of whose songs are included in the 1824 volume along with many patriotic effusions from the pen of the Virginia poet.

369 THE | BACHELOR DECOYED, | or the | successful virgin, | to
   which is added | Tweed side, | and | Corridon and Phillida. | Pough-
keepsie—printed, | for the travelling booksellers.
   12 p. [1:] title-page; [2]-12: songs.
   MWA* ¶ Contains 3 songs, all named on the title-page. The chapbook was probably printed around 1810.

370 THE | COMIC SONGSTER; | being a collection of the most |
   admired songs, | sung at the theatres and concert rooms; | and a
number of | new national songs. | "I but ask a sprightly song, | To
speed the lazy flight of those dull hours." | Baltimore: | printed by Geo.
Dobbin and Murphy. | 10, Baltimore-Street. | 1810.
   72 p. [1:] title-page; [2:] blank; [3:] caption-title: The | comic
songster | for 1809; [3]-72: songs.
   Bristol 835, Shaw 19819. Indexed in Devine ¶ MdHi*, RPB ¶ Contains 76 songs.

371 JAMIE REILY'S COURTSHIP | to | Cooleen Bawn. | To which
   are added | Reily's trial for running away with Cool- | een Bawn. |
Reily's releasement and marriage with Cool- | een Bawn. | Hudson: |
printed for the hawkers.
   8 p. [1:] title-page; 2-8: songs.
   NN* ¶ Contains 3 songs. The chapbook was probably printed
around 1810. For a complete list of editions, see 100.

372 THE | LINNET, | being a | choice collection | of | modern songs.
   | Otsego, | printed by H. & E. Phinney, Jun. and sold | by them
wholesale and retail. | 1810.
   36 p. [1:] title-page; [2:] blank; [3]-36: songs.
   Shaw 20573 ¶ NCH* ¶ Contains 26 songs. The songster is signed
K-M₆.

373 THE | MERRY SONGSTER; | or, | jovial sailors' delight. | Being |
a collection of the most celebrated | songs. | Boston: | printed and
sold by J. White, near | Charles'-River Bridge—1810.
16 p. [1:] title-page; [2:] illustration; [3]-16: songs.
Shaw 20726 ¶ MH* ¶ Contains 9 songs.

374 NEW | MUSICAL BANQUET; | or, | choice | songs, | sentimen-
tal, lively, jovial, | and amorous. | Improved with the most popular
songs | lately published in London. | Apollo struck the lyre—the muses
sung | in strains melodious. | Windsor: | printed for J. Parks, Montpelier.
| 1810.
96 p. [1:] title-page; [2:] blank; [3]-96: songs.
McCorison 1198, Shaw 20879, Shaw 20880 ¶ MWA*, VtWinds
¶ Contains 82 songs. The VtWinds copy bears the following variant
imprint: Windsor: | printed by Farnsworth & Churchill. | 1810. Except
for this, it is identical to the MWA copy.

375 THE | PATRIOTICK | AND | AMATORY SONGSTER. | A se-
lection of approved | ancient and modern songs. | Boston: | printed
by Samuel Avery, | No. 10 State-Street. | 1810.
198 p. [1:] title-page; [2:] blank; [3]-192: songs; [193]-198: index;
198: colophon: Samuel Avery, printer.
Shaw 20999 ¶ ICN (imperfect), MH*, MHi, MWA ¶ Contains 167
songs (166 indexed).

376 ROSANNA, | or the | cruel lover. | To which is added | Few happy
matches. | Also The | happiness and misery | of | life. | Poughkeepsie
—printed. | For the travelling booksellers.
12 p. [1:] title page; [2:] blank; [3]-12: songs.
MWA* (imperfect) ¶ Contains 3 songs, all named on the title-page.
The only copy located lacks pp. 11-12. The chapbook was probably
printed around 1810. An edition containing only 2 songs was published
by Nathan Douglas of Danbury in 1794 (Bristol-Evans B8855; Evans
47205).

377 THE | SKY-LARK, | or | gentlemen & ladies' | vocal magazine: |
being a | choice collection | of | fashionable songs. | Otsego: | printed
and sold by H. & E. Phinney, Jun. | 1810.
144 p. [1:] title-page; [2:] blank; [3]-140: songs; [141]-144: index.
Lowens U93. Indexed in Devine ¶ RPB* (imperfect) ¶ Contains
109 songs (108 indexed). The only extant copy lacks pp. 119-120, which
are supplied in photostat from another imperfect copy, since disappeared, which was in the possession of L. B. Romaine in 1952.

378 SONGS, written for the celebration of the 16th of August, 1810, being the 33rd anniversary of Bennington battle. By Anthony Haswell. Bennington, Vt. Printed by Anthony Haswell.

11 p.

McCorison 1174, Shaw 20296 ¶ VtBennM (copy not seen).

379 THE | VOCAL COMPANION: | consisting of | songs, duets, glees, catches, canons, and canzonets, | selected from eminent European authors. | Boston: | printed and sold by Buckingham & Titcomb, Winter-Street. | 1810.

94+ p. [1:] title-page; [2:] blank; [3]-4: advertisement and directions for performing catches and canons; 5-94: songs.

Shaw 51042, Wolfe 9516 ¶ DLC* (imperfect) ¶ Contains 56 songs, all with musical notation. The only copy extant lacks all after p. 94. See 432 for a related edition. *Later edition:* 502.

1811

380 [THE AMERICAN LADIES' POCKET-BOOK for the year 1811. Philadelphia: printed by John Bioren for William Y. Birch.]

Lowens U94 ¶ No copy located ¶ See 120 for a list of editions.

381 AMUSEMENT, | or a | new collection | of pleasing | songs, | humorous jests, | and the | most approved | country dances; | selected from | various authors. | Montpelier Vt. | Printed and for sale at the Montpe- | lier book-store. | 1811.

[49]-72 p. [49:] title-page; [50:] blank; [51]-60: songs; [61]-67: humorous and interesting jests; [68]-72: country dances.

McCorison 1285, Shaw 22194 ¶ MWA* ¶ Contains 9 songs. Apparently issued separately and also as an integral part of 402, judging from the pagination. See 402 for a list of related editions.

382 THE BOLD MARINERS. | The rambling boy. | And | The answer. | Roslin Castle. | To which is added | The answer. | Flashy Tom. | January, 1811.

8 p. [1:] title-page; 2-8: songs.

Rosenbach 434, Shaw 22424 ¶ PP* ¶ Contains 6 songs, all named on the title-page.

383 THE | BOSTON MUSICAL MISCELLANY. | A selection of modern | songs, | sentimental, amatory, humorous, | Anacreontick. | Adapted for | the voice, violin, and German flute. | Boston: | printed by J. T. Buckingham. | 1811.

1 p.l., 192 p. [i:] title-page; [ii:] blank; [1]-189: songs; [190]-192: index.

Shaw 22438, Wolfe 993. Indexed in Devine ¶ CtHT-W, DLC*, MB, MH, MHi, MWA, MiU-C, NBuG, NN, PPL, RPB ¶ Contains 75 songs (74 indexed), all but two with musical notation. See 486 for a related imprint. *Later edition:* 485.

The British taxation, in North-America. A song, composed by an American, at the commencement of the late revolution, and sung with unbounded applause, by the patriots of '76. Damascus: printed by Daniel Willson, 1811.

12 p.

MWA* ¶ Contains only 2 songs. For a later edition with 3 songs, see 507.

384 A COLLECTION | OF | SONGS, | selected from the latest publi-
cations. | Printed for the purchaser. | Philadelphia, | September 1811.
18 p. [1:] title-page; [2:] blank; [3]-18: songs.
Shaw 22562 ¶ MWA* ¶ Contains 11 songs.

385 THE GIRL I LEFT BEHIND ME. | To which is added | The
answer. | Pretty Nancy. | Return, O Julia. | Yankee Doodle. | Janu-
ary, 1811.
8 p. [1:] title-page; 2-8: songs.
MWA* ¶ Contains 5 songs, all named on the title-page. The chapbook probably was printed in Philadelphia. See 252 for an earlier
edition.

386 THE | GOLD-FINCH: | a collection of choice | songs. | Albany: |
published by B. D. Packard. | R. Packard, printer. | 1811.
98, [2] p. [1:] title-page; [2:] blank; [3]-98: songs; [99]-[100:] index.
Shaw 22922 ¶ MWA* ¶ Contains 63 songs (all indexed).

387 THE | HARP: | a selection of | odes and songs, | ancient & modern,
| from the | Latin, | Greek, | Arabian, | Italian, | Sicilian, | French, |
German, | Spanish, | Scotch, | English, | Irish, and | American. | "O bards
of other times! Ye on whose souls the | blue hosts of your fathers rise!
strike the harp | in my hall, and let me hear the song." | Bennington,
Vt. | Printed by B. Smead, 1811.
180 p. [i:] title-page; [ii:] blank; [iii]-iv: advertisement; [v]-viii:
index; [9]-180: songs.
McCorison 1293, Shaw 22968 ¶ Vt, VtHi* ¶ Contains 140 songs (all
indexed).

388 THE | HUMOURIST; | a collection of | comic, patriotic, sentimen-
tal, | and Masonic | songs, | original and selected. | Embellished with

an engraving. | By W. Degrushe. | New-York: | printed for William Degrushe, by | Largin & Thompson, No. 189 | Water-Street. | 1811.

108 p. [1:] blank; [2:] frontispiece; [3:] title-page; [4:] blank; [5]-108: songs.

DLC*, MH ¶ Contains 88 songs.

389 IDYLLES | ET | CHANSONS, | ou | essais | de | poësie créole. | Par un habitant d'Hayti. | A Philadelphie: | de l'imprimerie de J. Edwards, Cinquième rue | sud, Nº 181. | 1811.

1 p.l., 22 p. [i:] blank; [ii:] frontispiece; [1:] title-page; [2:] blank; [3]-4: de la langue créole; [5]-22: idylles et chansons.

Shaw 23083 ¶ DLC* ¶ Contains 5 songs in Creole patois (1 of which is noted as a translation), preceded by 7 "idylles" probably not intended to be sung. A related imprint may be *Idylles ou Essais de poësie créole* (New York, 1804), a copy of which is at NHi. This contains only the 7 "idylles" and is complete in 16 pages.

390 THE | IRISH PEDLER [sic], | When my money was gone, | Rocks of Scilly, | Paddy O'Brian. | New-York: | printed and sold at No. 38, and 64, | Maiden-Lane. | 1811.

8 p. [1:] title-page; [2]-8: songs.

Shaw 23097 ¶ DLC* ¶ Contains 4 songs, all named on the title-page.

391 JACHIN AND BOAZ: | or an | authentic key | to the door of | Free-Masonry, | ancient and modern. | Calculated, | not only for the instruction of every new made Mason, | but also for the information of all who | intend to become Brethren. | Illustrated with | a beautiful frontispiece of the regalia, jewels and | emblematical ornaments belonging to Mason- | ry; and an accurate plan of the draw- | ing on the floor of a Lodge. | Interspersed with a variety of | notes and remarks, | necessary to explain and render the whole clear | to the meanest capacity. | By a gentleman, | belonging to the Jerusalem Lodge; a frequent visitor at | the Queen's Arms, St. Paul's Church-Yard; the Horn, in | Fleet-Street; Crown and Anchor, Strand; and the Salu- | tation, Newgate-Street. | Try me—prove me. | Poughkeepsie: | printed by C. C. Adams, | for Richard Scott, bookseller, | New-York. | 1811.

107 p. [1:] blank; [2:] frontispiece; [3:] title-page; [4:] blank; [5:] contents; [6:] advertisement; [7]-[8:] description of the frontispiece; [9]-10 preface; [11]-80: text; 81-100: odes, anthems, and songs; 101-107: toasts and sentiments.

Shaw 23855 ¶ DSC*, MBFM, N, NNFM, PPPFM ¶ Contains 16 Masonic songs. See 73 for a list of editions.

392 JACHIN AND BOAZ; | or, an | authentic key | to the door of | Free-Masonry, | both ancient and modern. | Calculated not only for

the instruction of every new- | made Mason; but also for the informa-
tion of all who | intend to become Brethren. | By a gentleman of Lon-
don. | Try me—prove me. | Printed in the year | 1811.

60 p. [1:] title-page; [2:] contents; [3]-[4:] preface to the first edition; [5]-55: text; 55-60: odes, anthems, and songs.

DSC*, MBFM (imperfect) ¶ Contains 9 Masonic songs. See 73 for
a list of editions.

393 THE | JOVIAL SONGSTER: | being a number | of | the most
celebrated—love—and sea | songs. | Printed & sold by J. White, Main-
Street, | Charlestown.—1811.

16 p. [1:] title-page; [2:] blank; [3]-16: songs.

Shaw 23134 ¶ MWA*, RPB ¶ Contains 13 songs. See 195 for a list
of editions.

The ministrel [sic]; a collection of celebrated songs, set to music.
Baltimore: published by F. Lucas, Jun. 138 Market St., G. Dobbin
and Murphy, printer, 1811.

Webb 31 ¶ Attributed by Webb to John Cole and located by her at
MdHi. Apparently a ghost-title for 423. MdHi is unable to locate any
1811 imprint of this nature.

The minstrel; a collection of ballads and legendary tales. Still the
legendary lay, O'er poets' bosom holds its sway, Still on the ancient
minstrel strain Time lays his palsied hand in vain. Walter Scott.
Boston, printed by J. Belcher. 1811.

2 p.l., 108 p.

Shaw 23401 ¶ MWA* ¶ Contains 24 "ballads and legendary tales"
in verse (all indexed). It is doubtful that these were intended to be
sung. This collection was apparently issued serially; there is a portion
of this imprint (pp. 19-36) at MB without title-page but with a printed
wrapper bearing the following imprint: "Boston, printed for the compilers, J. Belcher, printer. 1810" (Shaw 20749).

394 THE | MUSICAL REPERTORY. | A selection | of the most ap-
proved | ancient and modern | songs. | In four parts. | Published and
sold at the | Hallowell bookstore, | sign of the Bible. | By Ezekiel
Goodale. | Augusta: | printed by Peter Edes. | 1811.

209, [7] p. [1:] title-page; [2:] blank; [3]-209: songs; [210]-[216:]
index.

Noyes 562, Shaw 23478, Williamson 6698. Indexed in Devine ¶
DLC*, MW, MWA, MeBa, MeHi, NBuG, NN, RPB; Oxford (Bodleian Library) ¶ Contains 191 songs (all indexed). *Edition after 1820:*
(a) 1824, Boston: T. Bedlington (MH).

395 THE | NEW-YORK SONGSTER; | being | a collection | of the | most modern and approved | songs: | selected with care. | "Inflam'd by music soldiers fight; | Inspir'd by music poets write; | Music can heal the lover's wounds, | And calm fierce rage by gentle sounds: | Philosophy attempts in vain, | What music can with ease attain, | So great is music's pow'r." | New-York: | printed for Christian Brown, | 71 Water-Street. | George Forman, printer. | 1811.

228 p. [1:] title-page; [2:] blank; [3]-223: songs; 223-228: index.

Lowens U95 ¶ PPL* (imperfect) ¶ Contains 203 songs (all indexed). The only extant copy lacks pp. 51-58. A caption-title on p. [3] reads: The | nightingale. No songster issued under this title and related to 395 is known.

396 [THE NIGHTINGALE. New York, 1811.]

No copy located ¶ Existence inferred from the caption-title of 395, q.v.

397 PUSH THE GROG ABOUT, | The good ship Molly, | We conquer, dear girls, | The Dutch fisherman, | The echoing horn, | O'Whack. | New-York: | printed and sold at No. 38, and 64, | Maiden-Lane. | 1811.

8 p. [1:] title-page; [2]-8: songs.

DLC* ¶ Contains 6 songs, all named on the title-page.

398 THE | REPUBLICAN SONGSTER, | being | a collection | of the best | national songs, | suitable for commemorating our indepen- | dence, and for other occasions. | Sag-Harbor: | published by Alden Spooner. | 1811.

70, [2] p. [1:] title-page; [2:] preface; [3]-70: songs; [71]-[72:] index.

Shaw 23804 ¶ MWA* ¶ Contains 35 songs (all indexed). See 281 for a related edition.

399 THE SONGSTERS [sic] | REPOSITORY; | being a choice selec- | tion | of the most esteemed | songs | many of which have | not here- | tofore been | published. | W. Hopwood del. | Light dancing on the dasied [sic] ground, | Our wanton rings we trace around, | When the moon, with paly light, | Gems the modest brow of night. | New York published by Nathᶫ Dearborn Nᵒ 171 Willᵐ Sᵗ 1811.

168, 187-286 p. [1:] blank; [2:] frontispiece; [3:] title-page; [4:] blank; [5:] preface; [6:] dedication; [7]-12: index; [13]-168, 187-286: songs.

Brinley 6944, Sabin 86959, Shaw 23959. Indexed in Devine ¶ CtHT-W, CtY, DLC*, ICN, MWA, NBuG, NHi, NN, PHi, PPL, RPB ¶

Contains 264 songs (254 indexed). Apparently issued without pp. 169-186. The title-page of the MWA copy is printed in red.

400 TID RE I. | Also, | The disconsolate sailor, | to which is added, | Heaving of the lead. | New-York: | printed and sold at 64, & 38, Maiden-Lane.

8 p. [1:] title-page; [2:] blank; 3-8: songs.

RPB* ¶ Contains 3 songs, all named on the title-page.

401 THE TRUE AMERICAN, | Tom Tackle, | Fair Kate of Portsmouth, | Had Neptune, | Roger and Kate. | New-York: | printed and sold at No. 38, and 64, | Maiden-Lane. | 1811.

8 p. [1:] title-page; [2:] blank; 3-8: songs.

Frank p. 50 ¶ NN* ¶ Contains 5 songs, all named on the title-page.

402 THE | UNIVERSAL | FORTUNE-TELLER, | and | complete dream | dictionary, | with | charms and ceremonies | for knowing | future events. | By Margaret Finch, | queen of the gipsies. | Montpelier Vt. | Printed and for sale at the Montpe- | lier book-store. | 1811.

72 p. [1:] title-page; [2:] account of Margaret Finch; [3]-47: text; [48:] blank; [49:] second title-page: Amusement, | or a | new collection | of pleasing | songs, | humorous jests, | and the | most approved | country dances; | selected from | various authors. | Montpelier Vt. | Printed and for sale at the Montpe- | lier book-store. | 1811; [50:] blank; [51]-60: songs; [61]-67: humorous and interesting jests; [68]-72: country dances.

McCorison 1285, Shaw 22820 ¶ VtHi* (imperfect) ¶ Contains 9 songs. The only known copy lacks pp. [61]-72. This incorporates 381 (q.v.), and the collation is reconstructed from this item. The collection of songs is also included in 469 and 470. An English edition was printed in London by T. Maiden in 1816—a copy is located at MH.

403 VOCAL POETRY, | or | a select collection | of | English songs. | To which is prefixed, | an essay on song writing, | by John Aikin, M. D. | And ever, against eating cares, | Lap me in soft Lydian airs, | Married to immortal verse. | Milton. | Boston, | published by J. Belcher, Congress Street; | J. W. Burditt and Co. Court Street; | and Thomas and Whipple, | Newburyport. | 1811.

1 p.l., 261 p. [i:] blank; [ii:] frontispiece; [i:] title-page; [ii:] printed by J. Belcher; [iii]-v: advertisement, dated 20 July 1810, signed J. Aikin; [vi:] blank; [7]-41: an essay on song writing; [42:] blank; [43]-51: index; [52:] blank; [53]-261: songs.

Shaw 22162 ¶ CSmH, CtY, DLC*, MBAt, MWA, NN, OClW, PPL ¶ Contains 222 songs (all indexed). See CBEL, II, 23 for English editions.

404 WASHINGTON GARLAND; | two songs | on the | death and
character | of | Gen. G. Washington: | to which is added, | The |
death of Wolfe. | Philadelphia: | 1811.
8 p. [1:] title-page; [2:] death and character of Gen. G. Washington; [2]-8: songs.
Sabin 101894 ¶ CSmH, NN* ¶ Contains 3 songs.

1812

405 THE | ADVENTURES | OF | ROBERT EARL OF HUNTING-
TON, | commonly called | Robin Hood, | the | famous English
archer. | Being a complete history of all the merry adventures | and valiant battles, which he, Little John, and his | bold bow-men, performed
and fought at divers times | and on various occasions. | Baltimore: |
printed and sold by William Warner. | 1812.
110, [1] p. [1:] title-page; [2:] blank; [3]-[4:] preface; [5]-110:
songs; [111:] index.
Rosenbach 450, Shaw 26640, Welch 10 ¶ PP*, ViU ¶ Contains 31
songs (all indexed). For other collections of Robin Hood songs, see 3,
66, 190, and 196.

406 ALL'S WELL, | A post under government, | Ballinamona oro, |
Will you come to the bow'r, | Down by yon banks, | Ere around the
huge oak. | New-York: | printed for the book-sellers. | 1812.
8 p. [1:] title-page; [2]-8: songs.
Shaw 24594 ¶ DLC* ¶ Contains 6 songs, all named on the title-page.

407 THE AMERICAN | ACADEMY OF COMPLIMENTS; | or the
| complete American secretary: | containing | the true art of inditing
letters suitable to the capacities | of youth and age: relating to familiar
conversation be- | tween friends and acquaintance [sic], husband and
wife, | children and parents, masters and apprentices bro- | thers and
sisters, and kindred in general; also, love | letters on all occasions, with
others relating to trade | and business of all kinds, in an apt, easy and
plain | style. | Likewise, rules for directing, superscribing, and sub- |
scribing of letters; also, the titles of persons of qua- | lity, and all other
degrees: | with dialogues very witty and pleasing, relating to | love,
familiar discourse, and other matters for im- | proving the elegance of
the English speeches [sic] and ac- | complishment in discourse. | To
which are added, | I. The art of good breeding, and behaviour, with
instruc- | tions for carving fish, flesh and fowl, after the new | manner.
II. The English fortune teller, as to what re- | lates to good and bad
fortune in maids, widows, and | widowers, and batchelors [sic]. III.
Joyful tidings to the | female sex. IV. Treatises of moles. V. Interpreta-
| tion of dreams. | With a collection of the newest songs. | Baltimore:
printed and sold by William Warner.

106 p. [1:] title-page; [2:] preface; [3]-83: text; 84-106: songs.

MdHi* ¶ Contains 21 songs. The date of this edition is uncertain, but it could not have been earlier than 1812. The publisher, William Warner, was a partner in the firm of Warner & Hanna until 1812, when Hanna died. Warner continued the business under his own name from that year until his own death in 1824. The late Edward G. Howard, Consultant on Rare Books at the Maryland Historical Society (to whom I am indebted for this information), would assign the songster to the earliest part of the 1812-24 period on the basis of the paper and the type used. 407 is very similar in content to 266 and 287, qq.v.; see also 80 for a list of related imprints and other editions.

408 THE | AMERICAN | LADY'S POCKET-BOOK | for | the year 1812. | Containing | an almanac. | Ruled pages for me- | morandums, obser- | vations and engage- | ments; also for ac- | counts of monies re- | ceived, paid or lent, | for every day in the | year. | Account of the moun- | tains Vesuvius and | Etna. | Select poetry. | New and celebrated | songs. | A marketing table, and | several other useful | tables. | To be continued annually. | Published | by W. Y. Birch, No. 37, South Second | Street, Philadelphia: | where is published also, | The gentleman's annual pocket | remembrancer.

1 p.l., 144 p. [i:] blank; [ii:] frontispiece; [1:] title-page; [2:] blank; [3:] contents; [4:] common notes; [5]-128: text; [129]-138: songs; [139]-144: tables.

Drake 10912, Lowens U96, Shaw 51049 ¶ PPAmP* ¶ Contains 10 songs. See 120 for a list of editions.

409 THE | ANTICHRISTIAN AND ANTISOCIAL | CONSPIR-ACY. | An extract from the French of the | Abbé Barruel. | To which is prefixed, | Jachin and Boaz; | or, | an authentic key | to the door of | Free-Masonry, | ancient and modern. | Lancaster, | printed by Joseph Ehrenfried. | 1812.

[x], 438 p. [i:] title-page; [ii:] copy-right secured according to law; [iii]-vi: preface; [vii:] half-title: First part. | General secret, or lesser mysteries | of | Free-Masonry; [viii]-[ix:] blank; [x:] illustration; [1:] second title-page: Jachin and Boaz; | or, an | authentic key | to | the door of Free Masonry, | ancient and modern. Try me——prove me; [2:] blank; [3]-4: description of the regalia, and emblematical figures; [5]-6: preface; [7]-61: text; 62-78: odes, anthems, and songs; [79]-90: text continued; [91:] half-title: Second part. | Grand mysteries and secrets | of the | occult Lodges of Free Masonry; [92:] blank; [93]-174: text; [175:] half-title: Third part. | Antichristian philosophy; [176:] blank; [177]-298: text; [299:] half-title: Fourth part. | Antisocial conspiracy; [300:] blank; [301]-438: text.

Morris p. 158, Shaw 24756 ¶ CtY, ICN, MBFM, MBtS, MWA*,

MdW, NN, PHi ¶ Contains 13 Masonic songs. See 73 for a list of editions.

410 THE | BLACK-BIRD, | consisting of | a complete collection of the | most admired | modern songs. | New-York: | published by Evert Duyckinck, | No. 102, Pearl-Street. | G. Bunce print. | 1812.

140, [4] p. [1:] title-page; [2:] blank; [3]-140: songs; [141]-[144:] index.

Shaw 24882 ¶ NN* ¶ Contains 128 songs (all indexed). Identical with 325 through p. 140. See 318 for a list of editions.

411 THE | COLUMBIAN SONGSTER: | containing a collection | of the most admired | new, favourite, and patriotic | songs. | Baltimore: | printed and sold by William Warner; | at the Bible and Heart Office. | 1812.

105, [3] p. [1:] title-page; [2:] blank; [3]-105: songs; [106]-[108:] index.

Lowens U97, Shaw 25123, Webb 123. Indexed in Devine ¶ RPB* (imperfect) ¶ Contains 67 songs (all indexed). The only known copy lacks pp. 7-18.

412 DEATH OF GEN. WOLFE. | To which are added | The Indian chief, | Bright Phebus, | Anna's urn. | When the seas were roaring, | and | Within a mile of Edinburgh town. | New York: | printed for the hawkers.

8 p. [1:] title-page; 2-8: songs.

RPB* ¶ Contains 6 songs, all named on the title-page. See 250 for a list of editions.

413 THE | DIAMOND SONGSTER: | containing | the most approved | sentimental | English songs. | Baltimore: | published by F. Lucas, Jun'r. | B. W. Sower & Co. printers. | 1812.

70, [2] p. [1:] title-page; [2:] blank; [3]-70: songs; 70-[72:] index.

Rosenbach 459, Shaw 25267, Webb 131 ¶ DLC (imperfect), Levy*, MB, MdBE, MdBJ, MdBP, PP ¶ Contains 62 songs (63 indexed). One of a series of six miniature songsters issued by Lucas in 1812. The Levy copy contains an additional engraved title-page, and the binding is lettered "Songs, I." Apparently the intention was to bind up the six songsters in three volumes, with the first volume containing 413 and 414, the second 415 and 416, and the third 417 and 418. However, the PP copies vary in combination, with Rosenbach 457 containing 3 songsters (414-416-418), Rosenbach 458 containing 415-416, and Rosenbach 459 containing 413-417. In all other known copies, the indicated normal combinations were followed. For related editions, see 414, 415, 416, 417, 418. *Later editions:* 538, 539, 540.

414 THE | DIAMOND SONGSTER: | containing | the most approved | humourous | English songs. | Baltimore: | published by F. Lucas, Jun'r. | B. W. Sower, & Co. printers. | 1812.

   70, [2] p. [1:] title-page; [2:] blank; [3]-70: songs; [71]-[72:] index. Rosenbach 457 ¶ DLC, Levy*, MB, MdBE, MdBJ, MdBP, PP ¶ Contains 37 songs (all indexed). All copies except PP as issued with 413, q.v. for an explanation of this set and a list of related and later editions.

415 THE | DIAMOND SONGSTER: | containing | the most approved | sentimental | Scottish songs. | Baltimore: | published by F. Lucas, Jun'r. | B. W. Sower & Co. printers. | 1812.

   70, [2] p. [1:] title-page; [2:] blank; [3]-70: songs; [71]-[72:] index. Rosenbach 458, Rosenbach 459 ¶ ICU, MB, MH, MdBJ*, MdBP, MdHi (2 copies, 1 copy imperfect), PP (2), ViU ¶ Contains 50 songs (all indexed). The MdBJ copy has an additional engraved title-page, different from that of the Levy copy of 413-414, and the binding is lettered, "Songs, II." Apparently issued together with 416 in one volume, as all known copies except one of those at PP (Rosenbach 459) is found in this form. The imperfect copy at MdHi has a variant cover-title, for which see 416. See also 413 for a list of related and later editions.

416 THE | DIAMOND SONGSTER: | containing | the most approved | lively | Scottish songs. | Baltimore: | published by F. Lucas, Jun'r. | B. W. Sower & Co. printers. | 1812.

   70, [2] p. [1:] title-page; [2:] blank; [3]-70: songs; [71]-[72:] index. Rosenbach 457, Rosenbach 458 ¶ ICU, MB, MH, MdBJ*, MdBP, MdHi (2 copies, 1 imperfect), PP (2), ViU ¶ Contains 44 songs (45 indexed). All copies except PP (Rosenbach 457) as issued with 415, q.v. The imperfect copy at MdHi (bound with 415) has a different cover-title: The | Scottish songster: | being | a collection | of | the most approved Caledonian | songs, | sentimental and lively. | Baltimore: published by F. Lucas, Jun'r. | B. W. Sower, & Co. print. | 1812. See 413 for a list of related and later editions.

417 THE | DIAMOND SONGSTER: | containing | the most approved | sentimental | Irish songs. | Baltimore: | published by F. Lucas, Jun'r. | B. W. Sower & Co. printers. | 1812.

   70, [2] p. [1:] title-page; [2:] blank; [3]-70: songs; [71]-[72:] index. Rosenbach 459 ¶ MdBP, PP* ¶ Contains 50 songs (51 indexed). Issued with 413, q.v. for an explanation and a list of related and later editions. Apparently intended to be issued in one volume with 418, but no exemplar has been located.

418 THE | DIAMOND SONGSTER: | containing | the most approved | humorous | Irish songs. | Baltimore: | published by F. Lucas, Jun'r. | B. W. Sower & Co. printers. | 1812.

    70, [2] p. [1:] title-page; [2:] blank; [3]-70: songs; [71]-[72:] index. Rosenbach 457 ¶ MdBP, PP* ¶ Contains 32 songs (all indexed). Issued with 414. Apparently intended for issue in one volume with 417, but no exemplar has been located. See 413 for a list of related and later editions.

419 THE | EAGLE AND HARP; | a collection of | patriotic and humourous | songs and odes. | Baltimore: | published by J. and T. Vance, and J. Cole. | G. Dobbin & Murphy, print. | 1812.

    147 p. [1:] title-page; [2:] blank; [3]-144: songs; [145]-147: index. Filby B12, Sabin 21615, Shaw 25211. Indexed in Devine ¶ ICU, Levy*, MB, MH, MWA (imperfect), MdHi, NBLiHi, NBuG, NCooHi, NHi, NRU, RPB ¶ Contains 91 songs (all indexed). Apparently issued without pp. 121-124, as all known copies lack these pages and they are not cited in the index.

420 THE | FREEMASON'S MONITOR; | or | illustrations of Masonry: | in two parts. | By Thomas Smith Webb, | Past Master of Temple Lodge, Albany, G. H. P. of the | Grand R. A. Chapter of Rhode-Island, and Grand | Master of the Providence Encampment of Knights | Templars, &c. | A new and improved edition. | Salem: | published by Cushing and Appleton. | Joshua Cushing, printer. | 1812.

    300 p. [i:] title-page; [ii:] blank; [iii:] copyright notice, R. I., 14 Nov. 1805, Thomas Smith Webb, proprietor; [iv:] sanction, dated Providence, 7 July 5802; [v]-vi: preface; [vii]-xii: contents; [13]-226: Freemason's monitor, part first; [227:] second title-page: The | Freemason's monitor; | or, | illustrations of Masonry: | in two parts. | By Thomas Smith Webb, | Past Master of Temple Lodge, Albany, and G. H. P. | of the Grand Royal Arch Chapter of | Rhode Island, &c. | Part second. | Containing | an account of the ineffable degrees of | Masonry; | and the | history of Freemasonry in America. | Salem: | published by Cushing & Appleton. | Joshua Cushing printer. | 1812; [228:] blank; [229]-[230:] preface; [231]-291: Freemason's monitor, part second; [292:] blank; [293]-300: songs.

    Shaw 27491 ¶ DLC*, DSC, IaCrM, MBFM, MSaE, MWA, NGH, NNFM, OCM, PPPFM, WMFM ¶ Contains 7 Masonic songs. Contents identical with 347, q.v. See 124 for a list of editions.

421 THE | GOSPORT TRAGEDY, | or | the perjured ship-carpenter. | To which is added, | The rapids, | & | The done over tailor. | New-York: | printed for the book-sellers. | 1812.

    8 p. [1:] title-page; [2]-8: songs.

Shaw 25544 ¶ DLC* ¶ Contains 3 songs, all named on the title-page. An earlier edition printed in 1798 (Evans 33809) contains only 2 songs. An undated English edition of the "Gosport tragedy" ballad, ca. 1820, is in London (British Library). For a list of editions, see 253.

Hardcastle's annual Masonic register, for the year of Masonry, 5812. New York, Hardcastle and Van Pelt, 1812.

37 p.
Drake 6351, Shaw 22964 ¶ NHi, NNFM ¶ This edition contains no songs. See 613 for a list of editions with songs.

422 THE | HARP OF ERIN, | or the | Hibernian melody; | being a new | and the only entire | collection | of | Irish songs | ever published. | By Dennis O'Neil, Esq. | Also, a variety of | favourite and | patriotic songs, | such as are principally sung at the | different theatres. | Baltimore. | Printed and sold by Warner & Hanna. | And John & Thomas Vance—1812.

246, [6] p. [1:] title-page; [2:] blank; [3]-246: songs; [247]-[252:] index.
Shaw 26344, Webb 175 ¶ DLC (imperfect), MdBJ*, MdHi (imperfect), RPB, ViRVal ¶ Contains 163 songs (162 indexed).

The history of Robin Hood. Embellished with cuts. New York: T. Wilson, 1812.

30 p.
Shaw 26641 ¶ London (British Library) ¶ I have been unable to check the contents of this imprint; see 3 for a list of Robin Hood items known to contain songs.

Jachin and Boaz; | or, an | authentic key | to | the door of Free Masonry, | ancient and modern. [1812.]

See 409.

423 THE | MINSTREL; | a collection | of | celebrated songs, | set to music. | Copy right secured. | Baltimore: | published by F. Lucas, Jun. 136, Market-St. | G. Dobbin & Murphy . . . print. | 1812.

x, [2], [5]-316 p. [i:] title-page; [ii:] blank; [iii:] copyright notice, Md., 20 June 1812, John Cole, editor and proprietor; [iv:] blank; [v]-x: index; [xi:] index to the names of the Scotch and Irish airs; [xii:] blank; [5]-316: songs.
Shaw 25108, Webb 122, Wegelin 910, Wolfe 5865. Indexed in Devine ¶ CtHT-W, DLC*, MH (imperfect), MMeT, MWA, MdBE (imperfect), MdHi, NBuG, NHi, NN (imperfect), OU, PP, RPB, ViU; Oxford (Bodleian Library) (imperfect) ¶ Contains 144 songs (141 indexed), all with musical notation or reference to musical notation. 70 tunes are named and identified as either Scotch or Irish on p. [xi].

423a [MODERN APOLLO, containing 145 of the newest songs sung at the theatres and concerts throughout the United States— price 62 and a half cents. Washington, D. Rapine's Book Store, 1812.] No copy located ¶ Advertised 1 Feb. 1812 in the Washington (D.C.) *National Intelligencer* as "just published."

424 MOTHER GOOSE'S | MELODY, | or | sonnets for the | cradle. | Boston: | printed by N. Coverl[y] | Jun. Corner of Theatr[e] Alley. —1812.
[15] p. [1:] blank; [2:] frontispiece; [3:] title-page; [4:] alphabet; [5]-[15:] text.
Welch 905.6 ¶ NNPM* ¶ Contains 11 juvenile songs. For a complete list of editions, see 38.

425 THE | MOTHER'S GIFT, | or | Nurse Truelove's | lullaby. | Boston: | printed by N. Coverly, | Jun. Corner of Theatre | Alley.— 1812.
[15] p. [1:] blank; [2:] frontispiece; [3:] title-page; [4:] alphabet; [5]-[15:] songs.
Welch 907.1, Welch 907.2 ¶ MWA* (2; 1 variant) ¶ Contains 10 juvenile songs.

426 THE | MUSICAL MISCELLANY. | Being | a choice selection of favorite | patriotic, Yankee, Irish and Scotch | songs. | Why, soldier, why should we be melancholy, boys? | Sidney's Press. | For Increase Cooke & Co. book-sellers, | Church-Street, New-Haven. | 1812.
107, [1], 4 p. [1:] title-page; [2:] blank; [3]-107: songs; [108:] blank; [1]-4: index.
Shaw 26181 ¶ CtHi, DeWint (imperfect), CtY*, MWA, RPB (imperfect) ¶ Contains 67 songs (all indexed). Apparently issued together with 429, although otherwise unrelated to that songster. *Later edition:* 520.

427 THE | PATRIOTIC VOCALIST, | or | Fourth of July pocket companion. | A selection of | approved songs, | on national subjects, | for the use of | public assemblies, | celebrating the anniversaries of | American independence, | and | Washington's birth day. | Salem: | published by Cushing & Appleton, | July, 1812.
24 p. [1:] title-page; [2:] blank; [3]-24: songs.
Shaw 26390. Indexed in Devine ¶ DLC*, MSaE, MWA, RPB ¶ Contains 14 songs.

The | Scottish songster: | being | a collection | of | the most approved Caledonian | songs, | sentimental and lively. | Baltimore: published by F. Lucas, Jun'r. | B. W. Sower, & Co. print. | 1812.
Cover-title for a copy of 415-416 (bound together) at MdHi.

428 SONGS | FOR | THE NURSERY, | collected from the | works of
    the most renowned poets | and | adapted to | favorite melodies. |
Carlisle: | printed by Archibald Loudon. | 1812.

    72 p. [1:] title-page; [2:] blank; [3]-53: songs; [54:] blank; [55]-67:
Peter Puzzle's riddle-book; 68-72: A collection of moral and entertaining conundrums, never before made public.

    Sabin 86916, Welch 1238.1 ¶ MWA* ¶ Contains 114 juvenile songs.
Later editions: 551, 621.

429 THE | SONGSTER'S MUSEUM, | or, gentlemen and ladies' | vo-
    cal companion. | Being | a selection of the most | elegant and fashion-
able, modern | songs. | There is a time to be merry. | Sidney's Press. |
For Increase Cooke & Co. book-sellers, | Church-Street, New-Haven. |
1812.

    107, [1], 4 p. [1:] title-page; [2:] blank; [3]-107: songs; [108:]
blank; [1]-4: index.

    Shaw 26779 ¶ CtY*, MWA (imperfect), RPB (imperfect) ¶ Con-
tains 75 songs (all indexed). Apparently issued together with 426,
although otherwise unrelated to that songster.

430 THE | SYREN: | A collection | of the | most admired songs; | con-
    taining many which have not | before been published. | Washing-
ton: | published by W. Cooper. | 1812.

    134, [8] p. [1:] title-page; [2:] blank; [3]-134: songs; 134; colophon:
W. Cooper, printer; [135]-[140] index; [141:] advertisement for the
second edition of Thomas Jefferson's *A Manual of Parliamentary
Practice;* [142:] notice of removal by W. Cooper to Pennsylvania
Avenue, on the North side, between the theatre and Centre market.

    Lowens U98, Shaw 26841 ¶ MWA* (imperfect) ¶ Contains 141
songs (143 indexed). The only copy known lacks pp. 31-34, 39-40.
Later editions: 529, 594.

431 TO A WOODMAN'S HUT, | Life let us cherish, | Thimble's
    wife, | Immortal Washington, | To the freemen of Columbia, | Wis-
dom's favourite. | New-York: | printed for the book-sellers. | 1812.

    8 p. [1:] title-page; [2]-8: songs.

    Sabin 95880, Shaw 26886 ¶ DLC* ¶ Contains 6 songs, all named on
the title-page.

432 THE | VOCAL COMPANION: | consisting of | songs, duets,
    glees, catches, canons, and canzonets, | selected from eminent Euro-
pean authors. | Part second. | Boston: | printed and sold by J. T. Bucking-
ham, Winter-Street. | 1812.

    83, [1] p. [1:] title-page; [2:] blank; 3-83: songs; [84:] index.

    Shaw 27415, Wolfe 9516 ¶ DLC*, MB, MH (imperfect), NN, RPB

¶ Contains 30 songs (all indexed), all with musical notation. For related editions see 379 and 502. This item was usually issued with 502.

The vocal muse; or, ladies [sic] songster. Philadelphia: printed for the proprietors, 1812 [i.e., 1792].
A ghost-title for 68, q.v., based on a misprint in the date, i.e., M,DCC,CXII instead of M,DCC,XCII.

433 THE | WORKS, | in | verse and prose, | of the late | Robert Treat Paine, Jun. Esq. | with notes. | To which are prefixed, | sketches | of his | life, character and writings. | Diis....sacer est vates, divûmque sacerdos, | Spirat et occultum pectus et ora Jovem. | Milt: VI. Eleg. | Boston: | printed and published by J. Belcher. | 1812.
lxviii, [2], 464, [1] p. [i:] blank; [ii:] frontispiece; [iii:] title-page; [iv:] copyright notice, Mass., 28 Oct. 1812, Joshua Belcher, proprietor; [v]-viii: preface; [ix]-xii: contents; [xiii:] half-title: Sketches | of the | life, character and writings | of the late | Robert Treat Paine, Jun. Esq. | By Charles Prentiss. | "Nothing extenuate nor set down aught in malice"; [xiv:] blank; [xv]-lxxxiv: biography; [lxxxv:] half-title: Tributary lines, | to the memory of the late | Robert Treat Paine, Jun. Esq.; [lxxxvi:] blank; [lxxxvii]-[xc:] tributary lines; [1:] half-title: The | works | of | R. T. Paine, Jun. Esq.; [2:] blank; [3:] half-title: Part I. | Juvenile poems. | Consisting chiefly of | college exercises; [4:] editorial note; [5]-112: college exercises; [113:] half-title: Part II. | Miscellaneous poems; [114:] editorial note; [115]-239: miscellaneous poems; [240:] blank; [241:] half-title: Part III. | Odes and songs; [242:] blank; 243-296: odes and songs; [297:] half-title: Part IV. | Prose writings; [298:] blank; [299]-421: prose writings; [422:] blank; [423:] half-title: Notes; [424:] editorial note; [425]-464: notes; [465:] errata.
Shaw 26371, Wegelin 1077 ¶ CSmH, CSt, CU, Ct, CtHT, DLC*, DeWI, IU, KWiU, LU, MA, MB, MBr, MH, MHi, MLy, MSa, MTa, MWA, MWiW, MdBE, MdBP, MdHi, MeHi, MiD, MiU, MnHi, MoSpD, NBLiHi, NBu, NCH, NGH, NHi, NN, NNC, NNUT, NT, NcD, NcU, NjR, OC, OCl, OGraD, OU, P, PBm, PPi, PPL, PU, RPB, ScC, Vi ¶ Contains 20 odes and songs in the section so named, apparently all by Paine.

434 YANKEE CHRONOLOGY; | or, | Huzza for the Constitution! | A musical interlude, | in one act. | To which are added, | the patriotic songs of | The freedom of the seas, | and | Yankee tars. | By W. Dunlap, Esq. | New-York: | published by D. Longworth, | at the Dramatic Repository, | Shakspeare-Gallery [sic]. | Dec.—1812.
16 p. [1:] title-page; [2:] copyright notice, N. Y., 9 Dec. 1812, D. Longworth, proprietor; [3:] advertisement, dated New York, 28 Nov. 1812; [4:] dramatis personae; [5]-12: Yankee chronology; 13-16: songs.

Bieber 45, Shaw 25301 ¶ CSmH (2 copies, 1 lacking title-page), DLC*, MB (2), MH, MSaE, MWA, MiU-C, N, NIC, NN, NjP, OU, PU, RPB ¶ Contains 3 songs.

1813

435 THE | AMERICAN | LADY'S POCKET-BOOK | for | the year
1813. | Containing | an almanac. | Ruled pages for me- | morandums, obser- | vations and engage- | ments; also for ac- | counts of monies re- | ceived, paid or lent, | for every day in the | year. | Description of the cave | of elephants, &c. | Select poetry. | New and celebrated | songs. | A marketing table, and | several other useful | tables. | To be continued annually. | Published | by W. Y. Birch, No. 37, South Second | Street, Philadelphia: | where is published also, | The gentleman's annual pocket | remembrancer.

1 p.l., 144 p. [i:] blank; [ii:] frontispiece; [1:] title-page; [2:] blank; [3:] contents; [4:] common notes; [5]-130: text; [131]-138: songs; [139]-144: tables.

Drake 10952, Lowens U99, Shaw 51157 ¶ PPAmP* ¶ Contains 7 songs. See 120 for a list of editions.

436 THE | AMERICAN PATRIOTIC | SONG-BOOK, | a collection
of | political, descriptive, and | humourous songs, | of | national char- acter, | and | the production of American poets only. | Interspersed with | a number set to music. | To Hull, and such heroes, a garland we raise, | Their valour in battle exultingly praise. | Philadelphia: | printed and sold by W. M'Culloch, | No. 306, Market Street. | 1813.

1 p.l., 106, [cvii]-cviii p. [i:] blank; [ii:] frontispiece; [1:] title- page; [2:] blank; [3]-106: songs; [cvii]-cviii: index.

Shaw 27715, Wolfe 122 ¶ CSmH, DLC, ICHi, MB, NHi*, RPB ¶ Contains 51 songs (all indexed); musical notation for 18 songs. The CSmH copy is probably a later issue as it contains the 4 pages advertis- ing M'Culloch's books found in 437 as pp. [145]-[148]. *Later editions:* 437, 505.

437 THE | AMERICAN PATRIOTIC | SONG-BOOK, | a collection
of | political, descriptive, and | humourous songs, | of | national char- acter, | and | the production of American poets only. | Interspersed with | a number set to music. | To Hull, and such heroes, a garland we raise, | Their valour in battle exultingly praise. | Philadelphia: | printed and sold by W. M'Culloch, | No. 306, Market Street. | 1813.

142, [6] p. [1:] title-page; [2:] blank; [3]-106: songs; [cvii]-cviii: index; 109-142: songs; [143]-[144:] index; [145]-[148:] advertisement for W. M'Culloch.

Wolfe 122A. Indexed in Devine ¶ PHi, RPB* ¶ Contains 68 songs (67 indexed); musical notation for 20 songs. Except for the omission of the frontispiece, this songster is identical with 436 through p. cviii. The extensive advertisement for M'Culloch on pp. [145]-[148] includes mention of the following songsters he has for sale: (a) The merry songster (373); (b) Mocking bird (probably 301, although the possibility of either 472 or 473 cannot be ruled out despite the date); (c) Patriotic songster (probably 161); and (d) Philadelphia songster (306). Many tune-books are also mentioned. See also 436 and 505.

438 THE | AMERICAN SONGSTER, | or | gentleman's | vocal companion. | "Far, far from thee I sleep in death, | "So, Mary weep no more for me." | Philadelphia: | printed and published by John Bioren, | No. 88, Chesnut-Street. | 1813.

90 p. [1:] title-page; [2:] blank; [3]-4: toasts and sentiments; [5]-90: songs.

PHi* ¶ Contains 104 songs. A caption-title on p. [5] reads: Cupid's miscellany, &c. See 249 for an unrelated item using the same title.

439 THE | COLUMBIAN NAVAL MELODY; | a collection | of | songs and odes, | composed on the late naval victories and | other occasions. | Boston: | printed by Hans Lund. | 1813.

94, [2] p. [1:] title-page; [2:] blank; [3]-94; songs; [95]-[96:] index. Sabin 14875, Shaw 29191. Indexed in Devine ¶ CSmH, DLC*, ICN, IU (imperfect), MB, MH, MWA, NBuG, NHi, NN, RPB; London (British Library) ¶ Contains 45 songs (all indexed).

440 [THE COLUMBIAN NAVAL SONGSTER; being a collection of original songs, odes, &c. composed in honor of the four great naval victories. New York: Edward Gillespy, 1813.]

Lowens U100, Sonneck Copyright ¶ No copy located. *Later edition:* 441.

441 THE | COLUMBIAN NAVAL SONGSTER; | being a collection of original | songs, odes, etc. | composed in honour of the | five great naval victories, | obtained by | Hull, Jones, Decatur, Bainbridge and | Lawrence, | over the British ships | Gerriere [sic], Frolic, Macedonian, Java and | Peacock. | Compiled and arranged by | Edward Gillespy. | New-York: | printed and published by Edward Gillespy, No. 24 William- | Street, nearly opposite the Post Office. | 1813.

94, [2] p. [1:] title-page; [2:] copyright notice, N.Y., 6 Apr. 1813, Edward Gillespy, proprietor; [3]-7: preface; [8:] blank; [9]-94: songs; [95]-[96:] index.

Sabin 27396, Shaw 28638. Indexed in Devine ¶ CSmH, DLC* (2), MWA, NHi, RPB ¶ Contains 53 songs (all indexed). See also 440.

Cupid's miscellany. Philadelphia, 1813.
See 438.

442 THE FAVORITE SONG OF | GEORGE REILY, | to which are added | Patrick O'Neil. | Mary's dream. | And | Liberty tree. | Baltimore: | printed for the purchaser—1813.

8 p. [1:] title-page; 2-8: songs.

Shaw 28494 ¶ DLC* ¶ Contains 4 songs, all named on the title-page. *Later edition:* 508.

Free trade and sailors' rights. American glory. Philadelphia, 1813. See 455.

443 THE | GENTLEMAN'S POCKET REGISTER, | and | Free-Mason's | annual anthology | for the year of our Lord | 1813: | the first after bissextile or leap year. | Containing, | I. An almanack, with an unusual number | of astronomical tables. | II. A political and religious calendar. | III. List of the civil, naval and military | officers, and judiciary of the United States. | Governors, judiciary, &c. of New England. | An accurate court calendar, on a new plan. | IV. Catalogues of the grand and subordi- | nate Lodges, Chapters, &c. held in the New- | England states. | V. A moral and scientific miscellany. | VI. A copious chronological table. List | of roads, &c. | By John Lathrop, Jr. M.M.A.M. | "In faith and hope the world may disagree, | "But all mankind's concern is charity. | "On their own axes as the planets run, | "And make at once their journey round the sun. | "So, two consistent motions act the soul, | "And one regards itself, and one the whole." Pope. | Boston: | published by Charles Williams, and for | sale at his bookstore, No. 8, | State-Street. | E. G. House, printer, Court-Street.

252 p. [i:] title-page; [ii:] the planets, &c.; [iii]-v: preface; v: table of solar system; [vi]-[vii:] miscellany; [viii]-[31:] almanack; [32]-241: text; 241-248: songs; 248-249: toasts; 250-252: contents.

Drake 3750, Shaw 25505, Shaw 28913, Shaw 51198 ¶ CtHT-W, DLC, MB, MBAt, MH, MHi, MSaE, MiD-B, N, NHi*, NIC, NN, NNFM, Nh, PPL, RPB, WHi ¶ Contains 8 songs. See 444 for a related imprint.

444 THE | GENTLEMAN'S POCKET REGISTER, | and | Free-Mason's | annual anthology | for the year of our Lord | 1813: | the first after bissextile or leap year. | Containing, | I. An almanack, with an unusual number | of astronomical tables. | II. A political and religious calendar. | III. List of the civil, naval and military | officers, and judiciary of the United States. | Governors, judiciary, &c. of New England. | An accurate court calendar, on a new plan. | IV. Catalogues of the grand and subordi- | nate Lodges, Chapters, &c. held in the New- | England states. | V. A moral and scientific miscellany. | VI. A copious chronological table. List | of roads, &c. | By John Lathrop, Jr. M.M.A.M. | "In faith and hope the world may disagree, | "But all mankind's

concern is charity. | "On their own axes as the planets run, | "And make at once their journey round the sun. | "So, two consistent motions act the soul, | "And one regards itself, and one the whole." Pope. | Published | by Henry Whipple, Salem, and | C. Williams, Boston. | E. G. House, printer, Court-Street, Boston, [sic]

252 p. [i:] title-page; [ii]-36: text; [37]-241: text; 241-248: songs; 248-249: toasts; 250-252: contents.

Drake 3751 ¶ MB* ¶ This title-page represents a cancel leaf which has been pasted over an earlier title-leaf, not for 443, but for another almanac, *The gentleman's pocket almanack for the year of our Lord 1813* (Drake 3748), containing 36 pages; 443 is a revised issue of Drake 3748 with an altered title-page and the addition of pp. 37-252. Drake 3748 contains no songs. 444 contains 8 songs, as in 443, q.v.

445 MOTHER GOOSE'S | MELODY; | or, | sonnets for the cradle. |
Containing the most celebrated | songs and lullabies of the good | old nurses, calculated to amuse | children, and to excite them to | sleep. | Ornamented with cuts, | and illustrated with notes and | maxims, historical, philosophical, | and critical. | Windham: | printed by Samuel Webb. | 1813.

31 p. [1:] blank; [2:] frontispiece; [3:] title-page; [4:] alphabet and punctuation marks; [5]-31: songs.

Welch 905.7 ¶ MWA* (imperfect) ¶ The only known copy lacks all after p. 22. There are 19 juvenile songs in the torso. See 38 for a list of editions.

446 A | NATIONAL | SONG-BOOK, | being | a collection | of | patriotic, martial, and | naval | songs and odes, | principally of | American composition. | Compiled and published | by James J. Wilson, | Trenton. | 1813.

204 p. [i:] title-page; [ii:] blank; [iii:] dedication, signed James J. Wilson, and dated Trenton 1 May 1813; [iv:] blank; [v]-[xii:] index; [13]-204: songs; 204: errata.

Sabin 104642, Shaw 30551. Indexed in Devine ¶ DLC, MB, MWA, NjR (imperfect), PPL*, RPB ¶ Contains 182 songs (all indexed).

447 THE | NAVAL | SONGSTER, | or the | sailor's | pocket companion. | Boston: | N. Coverly, Jr. printer, Milk-Street, | 1813.

16 p. [1:] title-page; [2:] illustration; [3]-16: songs.

Shaw 29264 ¶ MWA* ¶ Contains 6 songs. Entirely different in content from Coverly's 521.

448 ODES, | NAVAL SONGS, | and other | occasional poems, | (never before published,) | by Edwin C. Holland, Esq. | Author of the several communications under | the signature of "Orlando." | I too, although around my humble name, | No laureate flow'r of minstrel

honor bloom, | With trembling hand, essay to raise the song, | That speaks of gallant deeds and heroes brave. | Charleston, S. C. | Printed for the author by J. Hoff, 117, Broad-St. | 1813. | (Copy-right secured.)

40 p. [i:] title-page; [ii:] blank; [iii:] dedication, to James Marshall, Esq. of Savannah; [iv:] blank; [v]-vi: preface, dated Charleston, S. C. Oct. 1813; [7:] half-title: Odes; [8:] blank; [9]-16: odes; [17:] half-title: Naval songs; [18:] blank; [19]-24: naval songs; [25:] half-title: Occasional poems; [26:] blank; [27]-40: poems.

Meacham 62, Shaw 28762, Turnbull I, 439, Wegelin 995 ¶ DLC*, NHi, RPB ¶ Contains 7 songs by Holland. The RPB copy cover-title bears the following legend: Note by the publisher. | There were up- | wards of four hun- | dred subscribers, who, within the short | space of one week, extended their pa- | tronage to the present undertaking.

449 THE POOR | BUT | HONEST SOLDIER. | To which is added, | the much admired songs | of | The American star. | Independence. | And | A sprig of shillelah. | Baltimore. | Printed for the purchaser—1813.

8 p. [1:] title-page; [2]-8: songs.

Shaw 29542, Webb 308 ¶ DLC* ¶ Contains 4 songs, all named on the title-page. *Later edition:* 524. *Edition after 1820:* (a) 1823, Balti-more (MdBP).

450 [cover-title:] POPULAR SONGS, | AND | BALLADS, | patriotic, sentimental, | and | miscellaneous. | Boston:—sold by Thomas Wells.

[24] p. [1]-[23:] songs (pp. [10], [12], [14], [16], [18], [20], [22], [24] blank).

Shaw 29549, Wolfe 7185 ¶ MB, RPB* ¶ Contains 12 songs, all with musical notation. A gathering of the songs which appeared in *Poly-anthos,* Ser. 3, I-II (1812-13), printed from the same plates.

451 PRETTY POEMS, | in easy language, | for the amusement of | little boys and girls. | By Tommy Lovechild. | Ornamented with cuts. | Hartford: | printed by Hale & Hosmer. | 1813.

30, [1] p. [1:] blank; [2:] frontispiece; [3:] title-page; [4:] capital letters, small letters, vowels, and points; [5]-30: pretty poems, &c. [31:] advertisement of publisher's books.

Rosenbach 478, Shaw 28988, Welch 804.1 ¶ CtHi, MWA, PP* ¶ Contains 22 juvenile songs. See 354 for a list of editions.

452 RECUEIL | DE | CANTIQUES & ODES | maçoniques, | dédié a la T.˙.R.˙.L.˙. Française, | L'Aménité, No. 73, | séante a l'or.˙.de Philadelphie. | Philadelphie, | chez le F.˙., A. J. Blocquerst, imprimeur, | Sixième rue sud, N°. 159. | 1813.

2 p.l., 156 p. [i:] title-page; [ii:] blank; [iii:] errata; [iv:] blank; [1]-156: songs.

DLC* ¶ Contains 67 Masonic songs in French. See 219 for an earlier edition.

453 SONGS, | DIVINE AND MORAL, | for the use of | children. | By
Isaac Watts. | Out of the mouths of babes and | sucklings thou hast
perfected | praise. Math xxi. 16. | Windham: | printed by Samuel Webb.
| 1813.

22, [2] p. [1:] front cover; [2:] frontispiece; [3:] title-page; [4:]
alphabets; [5]-22: text; [23:] alphabet and numbers; [24:] rear cover.

Welch 1418.5 ¶ MWA* ¶ Contains 10 juvenile songs. Other editions
do not contain secular songs.

454 THE | TOWN AND COUNTRY | SONG BOOK, | a collection |
of | new, favorite, and national | songs. | Philadelphia: | printed and
sold by John Bioren, No. 88, | Chesnut-Street. | 1813.

90 p. [1:] title-page; [2:] blank; [3]-4: toasts and sentiments; [5]-
90: songs.

Sabin 96368, Shaw 29963 ¶ MH, NHi* ¶ Contains 104 songs. See
311 for an earlier edition; 530 is unrelated despite the identical title.

455 [Descriptive tag:] FREE TRADE AND SAILORS' RIGHTS. |
American glory. | [title:] The victories | of | Hull, Jones, Decatur, |
Bainbridge; | as detailed in their official letters and | the letters of other
officers. | Together with | a collection of the public testimonials of re-
spect; | and | the songs and odes | written in celebration of those events.
| Illustrated with | engravings of the actions. | The designs by Wood-
side, the engravings by Mason. | Philadelphia; | published by the pro-
prietor. | Dennis Heartt, printer. | 1813.

58 p. [1:] title-page; [2:] copyright notice, Pa., 25 Feb. 1813, Thomas
Palmer, proprietor; [3:] blank; [4:] engraving; [5]-50: text; [51]-58:
songs and odes.

Sabin 25722, Shaw 28559 ¶ CSmH, DLC*, MH, MHi, MeB, MeHi,
RPB ¶ Contains 13 songs.

1814

456 THE | AMERICAN | LADY'S POCKET BOOK | for | the year
1814. | Containing | an almanac. | Ruled pages for memo- | randums
observations [sic] | and engagements; al- | so for accounts of | monies
received, paid | or lent, for every day | in the year. | Description of St.
Peters, | at Rome. | Select poetry. | New & celebrated songs. | A market-
ing table, and | several other useful | tables. | To be continued annually.
| Published | by W. Y. Birch, No. 37, South Second St. | Philadelphia. |
Where is published also, | The gentleman's annual pocket remem-
brancer.

1 p.l., 144 p. [i:] blank; [ii:] frontispiece; [1:] title-page; [2:] blank; [3:] contents; [4:] common notes; [5]-122: text; [123]-138: songs; [139]-144: tables.

Drake 10993, Lowens U101, Shaw 51265 ¶ PPAmP* ¶ Contains 14 songs. See 120 for a list of editions.

457 THE | AMERICAN MUSE: | or, | songster's companion. | New-York: | printed and sold by Smith & Forman, | at the Franklin Juvenile Bookstores, | 195 and 213 Greenwich-Street. | 1814.

211, [5] p. [1:] title-page; [2:] blank; [3]-211: songs; [212]-[216:] index.

Filby B15, Shaw 30674. Indexed in Devine ¶ MB*, NjP, RPB (imperfect) ¶ Contains 181 songs (all indexed). One in a series of 5 songsters printed from the same plates in this year by Smith & Forman with differing titles. The earliest was 477, which contains the first 72 pages of this imprint; another 72 pages was added in 473; a third 72 pages was added in this imprint and 463 (with which 457 is identical except for title-page); a fourth 72 pages was added in 464. Related imprints are 487 and 493, qq.v. What is essentially a revised and enlarged edition of these was published by Loomis in Albany in 1822 under two titles, *The songster's museum* (MH, MWA), and *The minstrel* (RPB).

458 AMERICAN | PATRIOTIC AND COMIC | MODERN SONGS. Commemorative of | naval victories, &c. | Newburyport, | printed and sold by W. & J. Gilman, | at their miscellaneous book-store, No. 2, Middle-Street. | Sold also by booksellers in the United States. | 1814.

48 p. [1:] title-page; [2:] illustration; [3]-48: songs.

Filby B16, Shaw 30678. Indexed in Devine ¶ InU-Li, MB*, RPB; Oxford (Bodleian Library) (imperfect) ¶ Contains 25 songs. The MB and Oxford (Bodleian Library) copies have the following cover-title: American | patriotic and comic | modern songs. | Newburyport, | published by W. & J. Gilman. | Sold at their book-store, No. 2, Middle-Street, | and by various booksellers. | 1814. The RPB copy cover-title differs in imprint as follows: Newburyport, | printed and sold by W. & J. Gilman, | at their miscellaneous book-store, No. 2, Middle-Street. | Sold also | by booksellers in the United States.

459 [caption-title:] THE | AMERICAN SONGSTER.

12 p. [1:] caption-title; [1]-12: songs.

MH* ¶ Contains 5 songs. Date of issue is uncertain, but 1814 is probably correct within a few years.

460 THE | AMERICAN STAR: | being a | choice collection | of the most approved | patriotic and other songs. | Together | with many original ones | never before published. | Richmond: | published by Peter

Cottom, | at his law and miscellaneous bookstore, second door above the Eagle Tavern. | 1814.

1 p.l., 180 p. [i:] blank; [ii:] frontispiece; [1:] title-page; [2:] copyright notice, N. Y., 29 Aug. 1814, Peter Cottom, proprietor; [3]-176: songs; [177]-180: index.

Filby B17, Langhorne 173, Shaw 30681, Sonneck Copyright. Indexed in Devine ¶ CSmH, CtY, ICN, MWA, NHi*, NN, PHi (lacks frontispiece), RPB, ViU ¶ Contains 148 songs (146 indexed). *Later edition:* 535.

Amusement, | or a | new collection | of pleasing | songs, | humorous jests, | and the | most approved | country dances | selected from | various authors. | Printed for travelling book-sellers. | 1814.

See 469 and 470.

461 THE | BIRTH-DAY OF FREEDOM. | The neglected fair. | The death of Wolfe: | Poor Jack. | Together with | the sequel. | The wounded hussar. | September, 1814.

8 p. [1:] title-page; 2-8: songs.

RPB* ¶ Contains 6 songs, all named on the title-page.

462 A | CHOICE COLLECTION | of | songs, duetts and catches: | compiled and partly set to music by R. Ellis. | "In air the trembling music floats, | "And, on the winds triumphant swell the notes." | Albany: | printed by Packard & Van Benthuysen. | 1814.

[25] p. [1:] title-page; [2-25:] songs.

Shaw 31407 ¶ N* ¶ Contains 24 songs, numbered I-XXIV, with musical notation in 1, 2, or 3 parts provided for all. Ellis composed "seconds" (as he terms an added vocal part) for 4 songs.

463 THE | COLUMBIAN HARMONIST, | or | songster's repository: | being a | selection | of | the most approved | sentimental, patriotic, | and other songs. | New-York: | printed and sold by Smith & Forman, | at the Franklin Juvenile Bookstores, | 195 and 213 Greenwich-Street. | 1814.

211, [5] p. [1:] title-page; [2:] blank; [3]-211: songs; [212]-[216:] index.

MiU-C* ¶ Contains 181 songs (all indexed). One of 5 related imprints. For an outline of the relationship see 457, with which this songster is identical except for title-page.

464 THE | COLUMBIAN HARMONIST, | or | songster's repository: | being a | selection | of | the most approved | sentimental, patriotic, | and other songs. | New-York: | printed and sold by Smith & Forman, | at the Franklin Juvenile Bookstores, | 195 and 213 Greenwich-Street. | 1814.

282, [6] p. [1:] title-page; [2:] blank; [3]-282: songs; [283]-[288:] index.

Filby B20, Sabin 14863, Shaw 31201 ¶ CtY, MH*, MWA, NjMD, RPB, ScU ¶ Contains 242 songs (239 indexed). One of 5 related imprints. See 457 for an outline of the relationships.

465 THE | COLUMBIAN | HARMONIST, | containing | the newest
    and much admired | naval and patriotic songs, | as well as a great
variety of | fashionable, sentimental and other | polite songs; | together
with most of those elegant odes, | occasioned by the recent successes |
of the American heroes, | Hull, Jones, Decatur, Bainbridge [sic] | Perry,
&c. | —Philadelphia— | Printed by Thomas Simpson. | —1814—
    90 p. [1:] title-page; [2:] blank; [3]-90: songs.
    NN* ¶ Contains 68 songs. Not related to 463 and 464 despite the
similar title.

466 [COLUMBIAN SONGSTER. Being a large collection of fashion-
    able songs, for gentlemen and ladies. Philadelphia, 1814.]
    32 p.
    Lowens U102, Sabin 14880 ¶ No copy located.

467 COMIC SONGS, | as sung at the theatres and principal | concerts.
    | To which is added, | an appendix, | containing | a number of the
most celebrated | popular songs. | Happy the man whose heart of such
a sort is, | As holds more butter-milk than aqua-fortis! | Pindar. | Phil-
adelphia: | printed by Peter A. Grotjan, No. 58, Walnut Street. | 1814.
    1 p.l., 146 p. [i:] title-page; [ii:] blank; [1]-[2:] index; [3]-146:
songs.
    Shaw 31203. Indexed in Devine ¶ MWA (imperfect), MnU, PHi*
¶ Contains 98 songs (97 indexed).

468 JACHIN AND BOAZ: | or an | authentic key | to the door of |
    Free-Masonry, | ancient and modern. | Calculated, | not only for the
instruction of every new made Ma- | son, but also, for the information
of all who | intend to become Brethren. | Illustrated with | a beautiful
frontispiece of the regalia, jewels and | emblematical ornaments belong-
ing to Mason- | ry; and an accurate plan of the draw- | ing on the floor
of a Lodge. | Interspersed with a variety of | notes and remarks, | nec-
essary to explain and render the whole clear to | the meanest capacity. |
By a gentleman, | belonging to the Jerusalem Lodge; a frequent visitor
| at the Queen's Arms, St. Paul's Church-Yard; the | Horn, in Fleet-
Street; Crown and Anchor, Strand; | and the Salutation, Newgate. |
Try me—prove me. | New-York: | published by E. Duyckinck, 102
Pearl-Street. | Nicholas Van Riper, print. | 1814.
    107 p. [1:] blank; [2:] frontispiece; [3:] title-page; [4:] blank; [5:]

contents; [6:] advertisement; [7]-[8:] description of the frontispiece; [9]-10: preface; [11]-80: text; 81-100: odes, anthems, and songs; 101-107: toasts and sentiments.

Barthelmess p. 30, Shaw 32697 ¶ CtY, DSC (imperfect), MBFM, MWA*, N, NIC, NNC, NNFM ¶ Contains 16 Masonic songs. As 112, q.v. See 73 for a list of editions.

469 THE LITTLE | GIPSY-GIRL, | or universal | fortune-teller, | with | charms and ceremonies | for knowing | future events. | By Margaret Finch, | queen of the gipsies. | Printed for travelling book-sellers. | 1814.

72 p. [1:] title-page; [2:] account of Margaret Finch; [3]-45: universal fortune-teller; [46]-47: song; [48:] blank; [49:] additional title-page: Amusement, | or a | new collection | of pleasing | songs, |humorous jests, | and the | most approved | country dances | selected from | various authors. | Printed for travelling book-sellers. | 1814; [50:] blank; [51]-60: songs; [61]-72: humorous and interesting jests and country dances.

MWA* ¶ Contains 10 songs. See 402 for a list of related imprints.

470 THE | LITTLE | GIPSY GIRL, | or universal | fortune-teller, | with | charms and ceremonies | for knowing | future events. | By Margaret Finch, | queen of the gipsies. | Tenth edition. | Windsor: | printed by Jesse Cochran, | and sold wholesale and retail at his | book-store.—1814.

70 p. [1:] title-page; [2:] account of Margaret Finch; [3]-48: universal fortune-teller; [49:] second title-page: Amusement, | or a | new collection | of pleasing | songs, | humorous jests, | and the | most approved country dances; | selected from | various authors. | Windsor: | printed by Jesse Cochran, and sold whole- | sale and retail at his book-store. | 1814; [50:] blank; [51]-58: songs; 59-70: humorous and interesting jests and country dances.

McCorison Addenda 1602A ¶ MH* ¶ Contains 7 songs. See 402 for a list of related imprints.

471 MASONIC SONG BOOK, | containing | a large collection | of the most approved | Masonic | songs, odes, anthems, &c. | embellished with | three appropriate engravings. | Published by M. Carey, | No. 121 Chesnut Street, Philadelphia. | T. S. Manning, printer. | 1814.

164, [4] p. [1:] title-page; [2:] copyright notice, Pa., 7 May 1814, Mathew Carey, proprietor; [3:] preface, dated Philadelphia, 8 May 1814; [4:] blank; [5]-164: songs; [165:] toasts and sentiments; [166]-[168:] index.

Barthelmess p. 28, Sabin 45529, Shaw 31089, Shaw 32027, Sonneck Copyright ¶ CSt, CtY, DSC* (2), IaCrM, MBFM (3), NN, PPPFM (lacks 1 plate), RPB (imperfect) ¶ Contains 113 Masonic songs (all indexed).

472 THE | MOCKING-BIRD: | a collection | of the | most admired
    songs. | Alexandria: | printed and published, by | John A. Stewart. |
    1814.
    175, v p. [1:] title-page; [2:] blank; [3]-175: songs; [i]-v: index.
    Sabin 49788, Shaw 32152 ¶ RPB* ¶ Contains 141 songs (all indexed).

473 THE | MOCKING-BIRD: | being a | choice collection | of the |
    most celebrated songs. | New-York: | printed and sold by Smith &
Forman, | at the Franklin Juvenile Bookstores, | 195 and 213 Green-
wich-Street. | 1814.
    140, [4] p. [1:] title-page; [2:] blank; [3]-140: songs; [141]-[144:]
index.
    Shaw 32153 ¶ DLC*, MWA ¶ Contains 124 songs (126 indexed). One
of 5 related imprints. For an outline of the relationships, see 457.

474 MOTHER GOOSE'S | MELODY, | or | sonnets for the | cradle. |
    Printed at Windsor, (Vt.) | by Jesse Cochran, | and sold wholesale
and retail at his | book-store. | 1814.
    31 p. [1:] blank; [2:] frontispiece; [3:] title-page; [4:] blank; 5-31:
text.
    McCorison 1641, Rosenbach 500, Shaw 32182, Welch 905.8 ¶ CtHi,
PP* ¶ Contains 29 juvenile songs. This edition is not related to those
of Isaiah Thomas listed in 38. *Later edition:* 494.

475 NATIONAL SONGSTER; | or, | a collection of the most admired
    | patriotic songs, | on the brilliant victories, | achieved | by the naval
and military heroes | of the United States of America, | over equal and
superior forces of the British. | From the best American authors. |
First Hagers-town edition. | Hagers-town: | printed by John Gruber
and Daniel May. | 1814.
    40 p. [1:] title-page; [2:] blank; [3]-40: songs.
    Filby B26, Shaw 31862 ¶ CSmH, CtY, DLC* (2), InU-Li, MdHi,
MWA, MWiW-C, NHi, NjP, PBL, PHi, PPRF, ViU; Oxford (Bodleian Library) ¶ Contains 24 songs.

Naval songster. Boston, Nathaniel Coverly, Jr., 1814.
    16 p.
    Shaw 32217 ¶ A ghost-title for 521, q.v., apparently based on a mis-
reading of the title-page of the CSmH copy.

476 THE | NAVAL SONGSTER, | containing | a collection of the
    best selected | American naval songs, | relating to the victories which
our | gallant seamen have so gloriously | atchieved [sic] during the |
present war. | Fredericktown, Md. | Printed by M. E. Bartgis. | 1814.

77, [2] p. [1:] title-page; [2:] dedication; [3]-77: songs; [78]-[79:] index; [79:] erratum.

Shaw 32218, Webb 412 ¶ DN*, MdHi ¶ Contains 38 songs (all indexed).

477 THE | NIGHTINGALE, | or | musical companion, | being | a collection of | entertaining songs. | New-York: | printed and sold by Smith & Forman, | at the Franklin Juvenile Bookstores, | 195 and 213 Greenwich-Street. | 1814.

72 p. [1:] title-page; [2:] blank; [3]-72: songs.

Bieber 233, Shaw 32357. Indexed in Devine ¶ CtY, DLC*, ICN, MB, MH, MWA, NBuG, NN, NcD, PHi, PPL, PU, RPB ¶ Contains 72 songs. One of 5 related imprints, of which this was undoubtedly the earliest issued. See 457 for an outline of the relationships.

478 OLD DAME MARGERY'S | HUSH-A-BYE: | embellished with fifteen elegant engravings on | copper-plates. | Philadelphia: | published by Johnson & Warner, | No. 147 Market-Street. | Ann Coles, printer. | 1814.

[16] p. [1:] title-page; [2:] blank; [8 plates, engraved;] [3]-[16:] text.

Rosenbach 503, Shaw 32399, Welch 959.2 ¶ CLU, DLC, MWA*, NHi, PP, PPL ¶ Contains 20 juvenile songs. The 15 plates called for on the title-page apparently are the single full-page plate and the 14 half-page plates included on the 8 inserted leaves. See 342 for a list of editions.

The sailor's companion, being a collection of the most favorite sea songs now in vogue. n.i. [1814?]

DLC* ¶ Reported by Neeser. This is an English songster.

479 THE | SKY LARK: | containing | a collection | of | new and approved | songs. | Hudson: | printed by Ashbel Stoddard, | No. 137— Warren-Street. | 1814.

103, [4] p. [1:] title-page; [2:] blank; [3]-103: songs; [104]-[107:] index.

Lowens U103, Shaw 32778. Indexed in Devine ¶ NHi (imperfect), RPB* (imperfect) ¶ Contains 76 songs (all indexed). The NHi copy lacks all after p. 98; the RPB copy lacks p. [107].

480 TO THE MEMORY OF | CAPTAIN LAWRENCE. | Naval ode. | Columbia. | General Wilkinson. | Baltimore Sep. 1814.

8 p. [1:] title-page; 2-8: songs.

Shaw 32943 ¶ DLC* ¶ Contains 4 songs, all named on the title-page.

1815

481 THE | AMERICAN | LADY'S POCKET BOOK | for | the year
      1815. | Containing | an almanac. | Ruled pages for memo- | randums
observations [sic] | and engagements; al- | so for accounts of | monies
received, paid | or lent, for every day | in the year. | Account of Pelew.
| List of verbs that double | the final consonant. | Selected poetry. | New
& celebrated songs. | A marketing table, and | several other useful |
tables. | To be continued annually. | Published by | A. Small, No. 37,
South Second St. Philadelphia. | (Successor to W. Y. Birch.) | Where
is published also, | The gentleman's annual pocket remembrancer.
      156 p. [1:] title-page; [2:] blank; 3: contents; [4]-139: text; [140]-
150: songs; [151]-156: tables.
      Drake 11035, Shaw 51356 ¶ PHi* (2) ¶ Contains 13 songs. See 120
for a list of editions.

482 THE | AMERICAN | SONG BOOK: | being | a new collection |of
      the | best patriotic, military, naval, amatory, | quizical [sic] and
sentimental | songs, | extant. | Printed | for the New-York and Boston |
book-sellers. | 1815.
      96 p. [1:] title-page; [2:] blank; [3]-93: songs; [94]-96: index.
      Brinley 6936, Shaw 33850. Indexed in Devine ¶ DLC*, MWA, RPB;
London (British Library) ¶ Contains 63 songs (all indexed).

483 THE | AMERICAN | SONGSTER'S COMPANION, | a new se-
      lection of | the most ap- | proved | songs. | Danville, (Vt.) | pub-
lished by Eaton & Baker. | 1815.
      84 p. [1:] title-page; [2:] blank; [3]-82: songs; 82-84: index.
      Gilman p. 14, McCorison 1700, Shaw 33851 ¶ VtHi* ¶ Contains 79
songs (all indexed).

484 BLACK EY'D SUSAN. | To which is added | the much admired
      songs of | Sainclaire's defeat, | and The | waterman. | Baltimore—
printed for the purchaser. | 1815.
      8 p. [1:] title-page; [2:] blank; [3]-8: songs.
      Shaw 34136 ¶ DLC* ¶ Contains 3 songs, all named on the title-
page. *Editions after 1820:* (a) 1822, Baltimore (MdBP); (b) 1825?,
Philadelphia: R. Swift (RPB).

485 BOSTON | MUSICAL MISCELLANY: | a selection of | songs, |
      sentimental, Anacreontic, humorous, | amatory, and national. | In
two volumes. | Volume I. | Boston: | printed and sold by J. T. Bucking-
ham, | No. 5, Marlborough-Street.—1815.
      216 p. [1:] title-page; [2:] blank; [3]-212: songs; [213]-216: index.
      Shaw 34174, Wolfe 994. Indexed in Devine ¶ DLC*, IaAS, MB,
MBAt, MH, MWA, RPB ¶ Contains 80 songs (79 indexed), all but

10 with musical notation. Essentially a reset edition of 383, q.v., with 5 songs omitted, 9 added, and 1 duplicated. See 486 for a related song-ster.

486 BOSTON | MUSICAL MISCELLANY: | a selection of | songs, | sentimental, Anacreontic, humorous, | amatory, and national. | In two volumes. | Volume II. | Boston: | printed and sold by J. T. Bucking-ham, | No. 5, Marlborough-Street.—1815.

216 p. [1:] title-page; [2:] blank; [3]-213: songs; [214]-216: index.

Shaw 34174, Wolfe 994. Indexed in Devine ¶ DLC*, IaAS, MB, MBAt, MH, MHi, MWA, RPB ¶ Contains 60 songs (all indexed), all but 5 with musical notation. See 383 and 485 for related editions.

487 THE | COLUMBIAN HARMONIST, | or | songster's repository; | being a | selection | of | the most approved | sentimental, patriotic, and other songs. | Albany: | printed and sold by G. J. Loomis & Co. | Corner of State and Lodge-Streets. | 1815.

180, [4] p. [1:] title-page; [2:] blank; [3]-180: songs; [181]-[184:] index.

Shaw 34406. Indexed in Devine ¶ CtY, RPB* ¶ Contains 148 songs (all indexed). Apparently related to the 5 imprints described in 457, q.v. This songster is identical with 493 except for title-page. What is essentially a revised and enlarged edition was issued by the same pub-lisher in 1822 under two titles, *The songster's museum* (MH, MWA) and *The minstrel* (RPB).

488 FEDERALISM DETECTED. | The first and second chapters of the | book of chronicles of North America. | A political sermon | on the | epistle of Paul to the Romans, chap. xiii. 3. | Two new songs, | the British and our account of the | battle of Orleans. | With other pieces both in prose and verse. | By John Guthry, Senior. | Philadelphia: | printed for the author. | 1815.

36 p. [1:] title-page; [2:] copyright notice, Pa., 17 Oct. 1815, John Guthry, Senior, author; [3]-8: preface, signed John Guthry, Senr., and dated Augusta county, 18 Sept. 1815; [9]-19: text; 20-36: songs.

Shaw 34835, Stoddard 107 ¶ NN, RPB* ¶ Contains 8 songs, ap-parently all by Guthry.

489 GENERAL | ARMSTRONG. | American | independence. | Royal | sport. | Sweet | William.

8 p. [1:] title-page; [2]-8: songs.

Shaw 34767, Weiss 246 ¶ NN* ¶ Contains 4 songs, all named on the title-page. Weiss dates this imprint 1815? and gives the place of publi-cation as New York on somewhat tenuous evidence. A later date, ca. 1820, would perhaps be a safer guess.

490 IRISH MELODIES, | by | Thomas Moore, Esq. | Philadelphia. | Published by M. Carey. | 1815.

[4], [9]-148 p. [1:] title-page; [2:] blank; [3]-[4:] index; [9]-148: songs.

Shaw 35313 ¶ MWA, NjP, PHi*, PPL ¶ Contains 72 songs by Moore (all indexed). Imprint on the PPL copy varies: Philadelphia. | Published by M. Carey. | 1815. | Printed at the Whitehall Office. This copy, otherwise identical with the other known copies, is apparently a later issue. The PHi copy includes the original cover-title, in which the imprint reads: Philadelphia | published by M. Carey, No. 121, Chesnut Street. | December 15, 1815. *Later editions:* 514, 515, 516, 543, 569, 591 (originally issued with 516 bound in). *Related editions:* 574, 616, 617.

491 JACHIN AND BOAZ: | or an | authentic key | to the door of | Free-Masrony [sic], ancient and modern. | Calculated, | not only for the instruction of every new made Mason, but al- | so, for the informa- tion of all who intend to be- | come Brethren. | Illustrated with | a beautiful frontispiece of the regalia, jewels and emblemat- | ical orna- ments belonging to Masonry; and an ac- | curate plan of the drawing on the | floor of a Lodge. | Interspersed with a variety of | notes and re- marks, | necessary to explain and render the whole clear to the meanest | capacity. | By a gentleman, | belonging to the Jerusalem Lodge; a fre- quent visitor at the | Queen's Arms, St. Paul's Church-Yard; the Horn, in Fleet- | Street; Crown and Anchor, Strand; and the Salutation, | Newgate Street. | Try me—prove me. | Poughkeepsie: | published by Paraclete Potter. | P. & S. Potter, printers. | 1815.

104 p. [1:] blank; [2:] frontispiece; [3:] title-page; [4:] blank; [5:] contents; [6:] advertisement; [7]-[8:] description of the frontispiece; [9]-11: preface; [12]-77: text; [78]-98: odes, anthems and songs; [99]- 104: toasts and sentiments.

Brinley 6733, Shaw 35831 ¶ Ct, DLC*, DSC, MBFM, MWA, NIC, PPPFM, PPL (imperfect) ¶ Contains 16 Masonic songs. As 112, q.v. See 73 for a list of editions.

492 [JAMES BIRD (and other poems). Philadelphia, 1815.]

No copy located ¶ Information from Wegelin 1304, who notes that the item contained 8 p.

493 THE | MOCKING-BIRD, | being a | choice collection | of the | most celebrated songs. | Albany: | printed and sold by G. J. Loomis & Co. | Corner of State and Lodge-Streets. | 1815.

180, [4] p. [1:] title-page; [2:] blank; [3]-180: songs; [181]-[184:] index.

Shaw 35295. Indexed in Devine ¶ MWA* ¶ Contains 148 songs (all indexed). Apparently related to the 5 imprints described in 457, q.v. This songster is identical with 487 except for the title-page. What is essentially a revised and enlarged edition was issued by the same publisher in 1822 under two titles: *The songster's museum* (MH, MWA) and *The minstrel* (RPB).

494 MOTHER GOOSE'S | MELODY, | or | sonnets for the | cradle. | Windsor, (Vt.) | printed by | Jesse Cochran, | and sold, wholesale and retail, at his | book-store. | 1815.
 31 p. [1:] blank; [2:] frontispiece; [3:] title-page; [4:] blank; [5]-31: songs.
 McCorison Addenda 1762A, Welch 905.9 ¶ MWA* ¶ Contains 29 juvenile songs as 474, q.v. The imprint on the cover differs from that on the title-page: Mother Goose's | melody. | Windsor, Vt. | Printed and sold by | Jesse Cochran.

495 THE | NAVAL SONGSTER: | being | a collection of naval victories, | and other excellent | songs. | Containing, | Patriotic song,— Sea and land victories, | William's return from Algiers, | The seven American sailors who were | massacreed [sic] in Dartmoor prison, | Truxton's victory, | Constitution and Guerriere, | The sailor's return, | The Wasp's frolic, | The Enterprize and Boxer, | Address to the crews of the fleet bound | to Algiers. | Printed by J. White, Charlestown, 1815.
 1 p.l., 16 p. [i:] blank; [ii:] frontispiece; [1:] title-page; [2:] blank; [3]-16: songs.
 Sabin 52085, Shaw 35397. Indexed in Devine ¶ MWA*, RPB ¶ Contains 9 songs, all named on the title-page.

496 THE | NIGHTINGALE, | or, | new collection | of | the most admired | American, English, Irish, Scotch, &c. | songs; | among which, are | a number of old ones, not to be found in common | song books. | Wilmington: | printed and sold by R. Porter. | 1815.
 107, [1] p. [1:] title-page; [2:] blank; [3]-107: songs; 107-[108:] index.
 Gibbons 309, Shaw 35498 ¶ DLC* ¶ Contains 96 songs (90 indexed).

497 PRETTY POEMS, | in easy language, | for the amusement of | little boys and girls. | By Tommy Lovechild. | Embellished with cuts. | Hartford: | Printed by Sheldon & Goodwin. | Stereotyped by J. F. & C. Starr.
 31 p. [1:] blank; [2:] frontispiece; [3:] title-page; [4:] an ABC; [5]-30: pretty poems, &c.; 31: verse.
 Welch 804.2, Welch 804.3 ¶ FTaSU, MWA*, NNC (variant), PP ¶ Contains 22 juvenile songs. The NNC copy varies—p. [31] is an advertisement for books. See 354 for a list of editions.

498 SAILOR'S RIGHTS; | or, | Yankee notions; | being a collection of | American patriotic, sentimental | and | comic | songs. | Among which are the following new songs, viz. | Bainbridge's Tid-re-I. | Laurence's [sic] victory. | America's rights on the ocean. | The soldier. | Dennis Durham's adventures. | Britania's [sic] lamentation. | Neptune's award—and | The rule of three. | New-York: | printed by John Hardcastle, No. 6, Cross Street | for Samuel Λ. Burtus. | 1815.

56 p. [1:] title-page; [2:] copyright notice, N.Y., 23 Apr. 1813, Hardcastle & Van Pelt, proprietors; [3]-56: songs.

Shaw 35835, Sonneck Copyright ¶ MWA* ¶ Contains 33 songs. Cover-title differs: Sailor's rights. | Published by S. A. Burtus, corner of Peck Slip, | and Water Street.

499 THE | SONGSTER'S COMPANION. | A | new selection | of the | most approved songs, | on various subjects, | at present extant. | To which is added, | an appendix, | containing several new and popular | songs, | on occasions produced by the late war | with Great Britain. | Brattleborough, Vt. | Printed for the book-sellers. | 1815.

312 p. [i:] title-page; [ii:] blank; [iii]-xii: index; [13]-312: songs.
Brinley 6943, Filby B29, McCorison 1783, Sabin 86950, Shaw 35980. Indexed in Devine ¶ CtY, DLC* (2), IU, MB (imperfect), MH (2), MWA, MdHi, MiU-C, NBuG, NN, NNUT, PU, RPB, VtBrt, VtHi, VtMiM, VtU; Oxford (Bodleian Library) ¶ Contains 260 songs (259 indexed).

500 THE | SONGSTER'S OLIO. | A | collection | of the | newest and most popular | patriotic, sentimental, comic, | and Masonic | songs. | Binghamton: | printed and published | by T. Robinson. | 1815.

152, [4] p. [1:] title-page; [2:] blank; [3:] preface, dated Binghamton, Sept. 1815; [4:] blank; [5]-152: songs; [153]-[156:] index; [156:] errata.

Shaw 35981 ¶ MWA* (imperfect) ¶ Contains 103 songs (all indexed). Pp. 7-8, 45-46 of the only copy extant are mutilated.

501 THE | THEATRICAL SONGSTER, | and | musical companion: | | containing | a selection of the most approved patri- | otic, comic, sentimental, and en- | tertaining songs. | Boston: | printed by Thomas Brown. | 1815.

216 p. [1:] title-page; [2:] copyright notice, Mass., 1 Aug. 1815, Thomas Brown, proprietor; [3]-47: patriotic songs; [48:] names of the patriotic songs; [49]-113: comic songs; [114]-115: heads of the comic songs; [116:] blank; [117]-203: miscellaneous songs; [204:] blank; [205]-208: heads of the miscellaneous songs; [209]-216: index.

Johnson p. 347, Sabin 95292, Shaw 36075, Sonneck Copyright ¶ LNHT, NBuG, NHi* ¶ Contains 171 songs (170 indexed).

502 THE | VOCAL COMPANION: | consisting of | songs, duets, glees, catches, canons, and canzonets, | selected from eminent European authors. | Part first. | Second edition. | Boston: | printed and sold by Joseph T. Buckingham. | 1815.

83, [1] p. [1:] title-page; [2:] blank; 3-83: songs; [84:] index.

Shaw 36454, Wolfe 9517 ¶ DLC*, MB, MH (imperfect), NN, RPB ¶ Contains 43 songs (42 indexed), all with musical notation. See 379 for an earlier edition. Usually issued with 432, q.v.

1816

503 THE | AMERICAN | LADY'S POCKET BOOK, | for | the year 1816. | Containing | an almanac. | Ruled pages for memo- | randums observations [sic] | and engagements; al- | so for accounts of mo- | nies received, paid or | lent, for every day in | the year. | Description of St. Paul's | Cathedral, London. | The whole duty of wo- | man. | Answers to last year's | enigmas. | New enigmas. | Selected poetry. | New songs. | A marketing table, and | several other useful | tables. | To be continued annually. | Published by | A. Small, No. 37, South Second St. Philadelphia. | (Successor to W. Y. Birch.) | Where is published also, | The gentleman's annual pocket remembrancer.

1 p.l., 156 p. [i:] blank; [ii:] frontispiece; [1:] title-page; [2:] blank; [3:] contents; [4:] common notes; [5]-141: text; 142-150: songs; [151]-156: tables.

Drake 110751, Shaw 51460 ¶ MH*, PHi ¶ Contains 9 songs. See 120 for a list of editions.

504 AMERICAN | PATRIOTIC AND COMIC | modern | song-book. | 'Hail to the heroes whose triumphs have brighten'd | 'The darkness which shrouded America's name, | 'Long shall their valor in battle that lighten'd, | 'Live in the brilliant escutcheons of fame.' | Newburyport, | printed and sold at W. & J. Gilman's book-store and circulating | library, No. 2, Middle-Street. | 1816.

53+ p. [1:] blank; [2:] frontispiece; [3:] title-page; [4:] illustration; [5]-53+: songs.

DLC (imperfect), MH (imperfect), MSaE* (imperfect) ¶ Contains at least 31 songs. The cover-title (in the DLC and MSaE copies, pasted to the recto of the frontispiece) differs from the title-page: American | patriotic & comic | modern | song-book. | Long may she ride our navy's pride. | And spur to resolution; | And seamen boast, and landsmen toast, | The frigate Constitution. | Newburyport, | published by W. & J. Gilman, | No. 2, Middle-Street. The DLC copy lacks pp. 3-8, all after p. 50, and the title-page is mutilated; the MH copy lacks pp. 51-52; the MSaE copy lacks pp. 51-52, and the verso of p. 53 is pasted to the back cover. As the songster is a 12mo and p. 53 is leaf E2, it is likely that it is incomplete.

505 THE | AMERICAN | PATRIOTIC SONG-BOOK, | a collection
of | political, descriptive, and humourous | songs, | of natural charac-
ter, | and | the production of American poets only. | To Hull, and such
heroes, a garland we raise, | Their valour in battle exultingly praise. |
Philadelphia: | printed and sold by John Bioren, No. 88, | Chesnut-
Street. | 1816.

88, [2] p. [1:] title-page; [2:] blank; [3]-88: songs; [89]-[90:] index.

Shaw 36733 ¶ DLC*, MWA ¶ Contains 53 songs (all indexed).
This is essentially the same in content as 436 without the music nota-
tion. The text of one song has been omitted; 3 others have been added.
See also 437 for a related edition.

506 THE | BLACK-BIRD: | consisting of | a complete collection of the
| most admired | modern songs. | New-York: | published by Evert
Duyckinck, | 102 Pearl-Street. | 1816. | J. C. Totten, printer.

140, [4] p. [1:] title-page; [2:] blank; [3]-140: songs; [141]-[144:]
index.

Shaw 37019 ¶ MWA* ¶ Contains 121 songs (all indexed). Very
similar in general content to 410, q.v. See 318 for a list of editions.

507 BRITISH | TAXATION. | The | Guinea | boy; | or, | black Yan-
kee. | And | The maid with elbows bare. | Printed and sold, at No.
212 Market Street, corner | Decatur Street.

8 p. [1:] title-page; 2-8: songs.

CSmH* ¶ Contains 3 songs, all named on title-page. Apparently
published in Baltimore by Samuel Jefferis, not before 1816. An edition
of 1811 contains only two songs.

508 THE FAVORITE SONG of | George Reily, | to which are added
| Patrick O'Neal. | Mary's dream. | And | Barbary Allen. | Balti-
more: | printed for the purchaser—1816.

8 p. [1:] title-page; [2]-8: songs.

Alagia 165, Shaw 37568 ¶ DLC* ¶ Contains 4 songs, all named on
the title-page. For an earlier edition, see 442.

509 THE | FOREST MINSTREL; | a | selection of songs, | adapted |
to the most favourite Scottish airs. | Few of them ever before pub-
lished. | By James Hogg, | the Ettrick shepherd, | and others. | Even the
rapt traveller would stay, | Forgetful of the closing day; | And noble
youths, the strain to hear, | Forsook the hunting of the deer; | And
Yarrow, as he flow'd along, | Bore burden to the minstrel's song. Scott.
| Philadelphia: | published by M. Carey, No. 121 Chesnut-Street: | and
for sale by | Wells & Lilly, Boston. | 1816.

[5]-244 p. [5:] half-title; [6:] colophon: Deare & Myer, printers,
New-Brunswick, New-Jersey; [7:] title-page; [8:] blank; [9:] dedication; [10:] blank; [11]-17: preface; [18:] blank; [19]-24: index; [25:]
half-title; [26:] blank; [27]-244: songs.

Shaw 37858 ¶ DLC (imperfect), MB, MWA*, NNMer, PPL ¶ Contains 83 songs (all indexed).

510 THE | FREEMASON'S MONITOR: | or | iltustrations [sic] of
Masonry. | In two parts. | By Thomas Smith Webb, | Past Grand
Master of the Grand Lodge of | Rhode Island, &c. | A new and improved edition. | Montpelier, Vt. | Published by Lucius Q. C. Bowles,
for sale | by him and by Cushing & Appleton, Salem, | Mass. (proprietors of the copy right.) | Walton & Goss, printers. 1816.

300 p. [i:] title-page; [ii:] copyright notice, Mass., 4 Nov. 1815,
Thomas Smith Webb, proprietor; [iii:] sanction, dated Providence, 7
July 5802; [iv:] erratum; [v]-vi: preface; [vii]-xii: contents; [13]-236:
Freemason's monitor, part 1; [237:] second title-page: The | Freemason's monitor; | or, | illustrations of Masonry: | in two parts. | By
Thomas Smith Webb, | Past Grand Master of the Grand Lodge of |
the State of Rhodeisland [sic], &c. | Part second. | Containing an account of the | ineffable degrees of Masonry, | and the history of | Freemasonry in America. | Montpelier, Vt. | Published by Lucius Q. C.
Bowles. | Walton & Goss, printers. | 1816; [238:] blank; [239]-[240:]
preface; [241]-291: Freemason's monitor, part second; [292:] blank;
[293]-300: Masonic songs.

McCorison 1885, Sabin 102238, Shaw 21983, Shaw 39749 ¶ CSmH
(imperfect), DLC*, DSC, IaCrM, MBFM, MH, MWA, NN, NNFM,
PMA, RHi, RPB, Vt, VtBFM, VtHi, VtMiM, VtMiS, VtU ¶ Contains 7 Masonic songs. Contents identical with 347, q.v. See 124 for a
list of editions.

511 THE | FREEMASON'S MONITOR; | or | illustrations of Masonry: | in two parts. | By Thomas Smith Webb, | Past Grand Master of the Grand Lodge of | Rhode Island, &c. | A new and improved
edition. | Salem: | published by Cushing and Appleton. | Flagg and
Gould, printers, Andover. | 1816.

322 p. [i:] title-page; [ii:] copyright notice, Mass., 4 Nov. 1815,
Thomas Smith Webb, proprietor; [iii:] sanction, dated Providence, 7
July 5802; [iv:] blank; [v]-vi: preface; [vii]-xii: contents; [13]-246:
Freemason's monitor, part first; [247]-[248:] blank; [249:] second
title-page: The | Freemason's monitor; | or | illustrations of Masonry: |
in two parts. | By Thomas Smith Webb, | Past Grand Master of the
Grand Lodge of | Rhode Island, &c. | Part second. | Containing | an account of the ineffable degrees of | Masonry; | and the | history of Freemasonry in America. | Salem: | published by Cushing and Appleton.
| Flagg and Gould, printers, Andover. | 1816; [250:] blank; [251]-252:
preface; [253]-313: Freemason's monitor, part second; [314:] blank;
[315]-322: Masonic songs.

Shaw 39750 ¶ C, CtY, DSC*, IaCrM, MB, MBFM, MWA, NNFM,

PPPFM (2), RHi ¶ Contains 7 Masonic songs. Contents identical with 347, q.v. See 124 for a list of editions.

512 THE | FREEMASON'S MONITOR; | or | illustrations of Masonry: | in two parts. | By Thomas Smith Webb, | Past Grand Master of the Grand Lodge of | Rhode Island, &c. | A new and improved edition. | Salem: | published by Cushing and Appleton. | Ezra Lincoln, printer, Boston. | 1816.

312 p. [i:] title-page; [ii:] copyright notice, Mass., 4 Nov. 1815, Thomas Smith Webb, proprietor; [iii:] sanction, dated Providence, 7 July 5802; [iv:] blank; [v]-vi: preface; [vii]-xii: contents; [13]-238: Freemason's monitor, part first; [239:] second title-page: The | Freemason's monitor; | or | illustrations of Masonry: | in two parts. | By Thomas Smith Webb, | Past Grand Master of the Grand Lodge of | Rhode Island, &c. | Part second. | Containing | an account of the ineffable degrees of | Masonry; | and the | history of Freemasonry in America. | Salem: | published by Cushing and Appleton. | Ezra Lincoln, printer, Boston. | 1816; [240:] blank; [241]-242: preface; [243]-303: Freemason's monitor, part second; [304:] blank; [305]-312: Masonic songs.

Barthelmess p. 30, Shaw 39751 ¶ DSC*, MBC, MBFM, NHi, NNFM, PPPFM, PU, RPB, ViU ¶ Contains 7 Masonic songs. Contents identical with 347, q.v. See 124 for a list of editions.

513 GOSPORT TRAEGDY [sic]; | shewing | how a young damsel was seduced by a ship-car- | penter, who led her into a lonesome wood, | and there destroyed her, and the infant | with which she was pregnant; how | her ghost haunted him when at | sea, and he died distracted. | To which is added, | Paul Jones, | and | Mary's dream. | Baltimore; | printed for the purchaser.

8 p. [1:] title-page; [2]-8: songs.

DLC* ¶ Contains 3 songs, all named on the title-page. See 253 for a list of editions.

514 IRISH MELODIES, | songs, | and | sacred songs. | By Thomas Moore, Esq. | Philadelphia: | published by Moses Thomas. | J. Maxwell, printer. | 1816.

2 p.l., 176 p. [i:] half-title: Irish melodies; | songs, | and | sacred songs; [ii:] blank; [iii:] title-page; [iv:] blank; [1]-[3:] index; [4:] blank; [5]-127: Irish melodies; [128:] blank; [129:] half-title: songs; [130:] blank; [131]-145: songs; [146:] blank; [147:] half-title: sacred songs; [148:] blank; [149]-176: sacred songs.

Shaw 38280 ¶ MWA* ¶ Contains 98 songs by Moore (all indexed). Identical in content through p. 127 with 490 (q.v. for a list of editions); 26 additional songs and sacred songs are found on subsequent pages.

515 IRISH MELODIES, | sacred melodies, | and | other songs. | By
   Thomas Moore, Esq. | Philadelphia: | published by Harrison Hall. |
   J. Bioren, printer. | 1816.

   [4], [9]-184 p. [1:] title-page; [2:] blank; [3]-[4:] index; [9]-148:
   Irish melodies; [149:] half-title; Gospel melodies, | and | other songs;
   [150:] blank; [151]-184: songs.

   Shaw 38279 ¶ CtW, PHi* ¶ Contains 91 songs by Moore (all indexed). Identical in content with 490 (q.v. for a list of editions)
   through p. 148; 19 additional songs are found on subsequent pages.

516 IRISH MELODIES: | by | Thomas Moore, Esq. | Washington, |
   published by W. Cooper. | 1816.

   1 p.l., 92, [2] p. [i:] title-page; [ii]-[2:] blank; [3]-92: songs; [93]-
   [94:] index.

   Shaw 38281 ¶ MWA* ¶ Contains 74 songs (all indexed). This imprint was also issued as an integral part of 594, q.v. See 490 for a list
   of editions. Two songs by poets other than Moore have been added
   on pp. 89-92.

517 THE | MASONIC MUSEUM; | or, | Free-Masons' companion. |
   A collection of | songs, | choruses, odes, &c. | adapted to the use of
   Chapters and Lodges, | compiled by Companion J. Hardcastle. | New-
   York: | printed by J. Hardcastle, | No. 6 Cross-Street. | And for sale
   by M'Dermot and Arden, City Ho- | tel; at St. John's Hall; Tammany
   Hall; Ma- | sonic Hall, 55 Nassau-Street; Kerr and Car- | lisle's, corner
   of Frankfort and Chatham Streets; | Jonas Humbert's, Ann-Street;
   and at Riley & | Adams' music store, Chatham-Street. | 5816.

   1 p.l., 8, [13]-76 p. [i:] blank; [ii:] frontispiece; [1:] title-page;
   [2:] blank; [3:] preface, signed John Hardcastle; [4]-6: advantages
   of Masonry; [7]-8: index; [13]-76: songs.

   Barthelmess p. 29, Shaw 37794, Wolfstieg 39964 ¶ DLC, DSC*,
   IaCrM, MBFM (2), MWA, NHi, NNFM, OCM, PPPFM, RPB ¶
   Contains 62 Masonic songs (61 indexed). The DSC copy cover-title
   differs in imprint: For sale by S. A. Burtus, corner of | Peck-Slip and
   Water-Street. | 5816. See 637 for a related imprint.

518 THE | MASONICK MINSTREL, | a selection of | Masonick, sen-
   timental, and humorous | songs, duets, glees, canons, rounds and
   canzonets | respectfully dedicated | to the | most ancient and honourable
   fraternity | of | Free and Accepted Masons. | "Orpheus' lute was strung
   with poet's sinews; | Whose golden touch could soften steel and stones,
   | Make tigers tame, and huge leviathans | Forsake unsounded deeps
   to dance on sands." | With | an appendix, | containing | a short historical
   account of Masonry: | and likewise, | a list of all the Lodges in the

United States. | Dedham: | printed by H. Mann and Co. for the author. | 1816.

2 p.l., 463, [1] p. [i:] half-title: Masonick minstrel; [ii]-[iii:] blank; [iv:] frontispiece; [i:] engraved title-page: A | selection | of | Masonic songs | arranged with choruses in parts | and | respectfully dedicated to the | Brethren | of the | most ancient & honourable fraternity | of | Free and Accepted Masons | Published for the author | by | Hermann Mann & Co. Dedham, (Mass.); [ii:] blank; [iii:] title-page; [iv:] copyright notice, R. I., 24 Oct. 1815, David Vinton, author, compiler, and proprietor; [v]-vi: preface; [vii:] advertisement and general acknowledgments; [viii:] directions for performing catches and canons; [9]-327: songs; [328:] illustration; [329:] additional title-page: Appendix | containing | extracts | from the most celebrated authors, | on | Masonry: | with | notes, | historical, critical, and elucidative. | "The grammar rules instruct the tongue and pen, | Rhetorick teaches eloquence to men; | By logick we are taught to reason well; | Musick has charms beyond our power to tell: | The use of numbers numberless we find; | Geometry gives measure to mankind; | The heav'nly system elevates the mind. | All those, and many secrets more, | The Masons taught in days of yore." | To which is subjoined, | a list of all the Lodges | in the | United States; [330:] blank; [331:] invocation to Masonry; [332]-334: poetry; [335]-338: introduction; [339]-420: appendix; 421-444: list of Lodges in the United States; [445:] toasts and sentiments; [446]-457: sententiae stellares; 458-[460:] songs; [461]-463: index; [464:] illustration.

Barthelmess pp. 28-29, Morris p. 183, Sabin 99835, Shaw 39693, Wolfe 9493, Wolfstieg 39966 ¶ CtY (imperfect), DLC (lacks half-title), DSC, ICHi (imperfect), ICN (lacks half-title), IaCrM, MB (lacks frontispiece), MBFM (3), MH, MSa, MWA, MiU-C, NHi (lacks frontispiece and engraved title-page), NIC, NNFM (lacks half-title and frontispiece), NRU, PPPFM (4 copies, 1 imperfect), PPL*, RPB (2); Berlin (Gross National-Mutterloge), Oxford (Bodleian Library) ¶ Contains 155 songs (150 indexed), all with musical notation or references to musical notation found in this songster. Additional plates are found facing pp. 169 and [329]. According to Morris, 12,000 copies were sold by subscription.

519 THE | MODERN SONGSTER; | consisting of | a collection of the most admired | American and English songs, | which have been sung with applause at the public | theatres. | Also, | some of the best and most favorite | Scotch, Irish, and Welsh songs, | including a variety of scarce old songs, not to be | found in any other collection. | Second Baltimore edition. | Baltimore, | printed by William Warner, | corner of South Gay and Market-Streets. | 1816.

211, [5] p. [1:] title-page; [2:] blank; [3]-211: songs; [212]-[216:] index.

Alagia 202, Sabin 49813, Shaw 38274 ¶ MWA*, MdBE, TxU; London (British Library) ¶ Contains 190 songs (189 indexed). See 302 for an earlier edition.

520 THE | MUSICAL MISCELLANY. | Being | a choice selection of favorite | patriotic, Yankee, Irish and Scotch | songs. | Why, soldier, why would we be melancholly [sic] boys? | Poughkeepsie: | printed by P. & S. Potter. | 1816.

100 p. [1:] title-page; [2:] blank; [3]-100: songs.

Shaw 38348 ¶ MWA, NBuG, NHi* ¶ Contains 67 songs. Identical in content with 426, q.v., but lacks index.

521 NAVAL SONGSTER. | Or | Columbian naval melody. | Being a choice collection of the | most approved | naval songs. | Boston: | printed by Nathaniel Coverly, Jun. | Price six cents.

1 p.l., [16] p. [i:] blank; [ii:] frontispiece; [1:] title-page; [2]-[16:] songs.

Shaw 38361 ¶ CSmH, MWA* ¶ Contains 11 songs. See 447 for a related songster.

522 THE | NIGHTINGALE, | or | the ladies [sic] | vocal companion. | "Sweet nightingale, no more complain. . . . | "No more, sweet bird, soft pity move." | Vergennes, Vt. | Published by Jepthah Shedd, | Walton & Goss, printers, | Montpelier, | 1816.

103, [5] p. [1:] title-page; [2:] blank; [3]-103: songs; [104:] blank; [105]-[108:] index.

McCorison 1860, Shaw 38472 ¶ RPB*, VtHi ¶ Contains 111 songs (all indexed). See 258 for a list of editions.

523 THE | PATRIOTIC | SONGSTER. | A collection of the most | approved patriotic, and | other songs. | Alexandria: | printed by Benjamin L. Bogan. | 1816.

152, [cliii]-clvi p. [1:] title-page; [2:] blank; [3]-152: songs; [cliii]-clvi: index; clvi: colophon: B. L. Bogan, printer.

RPB (imperfect), ViU* ¶ Contains 106 songs (all indexed). *Edition after 1820:* (a) 1826, Washington: John B. Bell (MWA).

524 THE POOR | BUT | HONEST SOLDIER. | To which is added, | the much admired songs | of | The American star. | Independence. | And | A sprig of shillelah. | Baltimore: | printed for the purchaser—1816.

8 p. [1:] title-page; [2]-8: songs.

Alagia 213, Shaw 38671 ¶ DLC* ¶ Contains 4 songs, all named on the title-page. See 449 for a list of other editions.

525 THE | SKY-LARK. | Or, | a new collection | of | choice, naval, pa-

triotic, and | sentimental | songs. | From late publications. | Hartford: | printed and published by B. & J. Russell, | State-Street. | 1816.
96 p. [1:] title-page; [2:] blank; [3]-96: songs.
Lowens U104, Shaw 38943 ¶ CtHi*, RPB (imperfect) ¶ Contains 53 songs.

526 SOME OF THE BEAUTIES of | Free-Masonry; | being | extracts from publications, | which have received the approbation of the | wise and virtuous of the fraternity: | with | introductory remarks, | designed to remove the various objections | made against the order. | By Joshua Bradley, A. M. | Member of Newport Royal Arch Chapter No. 2 —Kt. R. C. K. M. | —K. T.—and Grand Chaplain of Washington Encamp- | ment No. 2, of Newport, R. I. | Rutland, Vt. | Printed by Fay & Davison. | 1816.
vi, 318 p. [i:] title-page; [ii:] copyright notice, Vt., 17 Sept. 1816, Joshua Bradley, proprietor; [iii]-iv: preface; [v]-vi: contents; [i]-xviii: introduction; [19]-312: text; 313-318: songs.
Brinley 6705, McCorison 1827, Morris p. 184, Shaw 37076 ¶ CSmH, CtHT, DLC, DSC*, IaCrM, MBFM, MWA, MdBFM, NBLiHi, NN, NNFM, NjR, OClWHi, PPPFM, Vt, VtHi (imperfect), VtMiS, VtU ¶ Contains 5 Masonic songs. *Edition after 1820:* (a) 1821, Albany: G. J. Loomis & Co. (DSC, NN, NNFM).

527 THE | STAR SPANGLED BANNER: | being a collection of the best | naval, martial, patriotic songs, | &c. &c. &c. | chiefly written during, and in relation | to the late war. | Music!—Oh! how feint [sic], how weak, | Language fades before thy spell! | Why should feeling ever speak, | When thou can'st breathe her soul so well. | Moore. | Wilmington, Del. | Printed and sold by J. Wilson, No. 105, | Market Street. | 1816.
108 p. [1:] title-page; [2:] copyright notice, Del., 27 Feb. 1816, James Wilson, proprietor; [3]-108: songs; 108: index.
RPB* ¶ Contains 60 songs (59 indexed). *Later editions:* 528, 557, 558.

528 THE | STAR SPANGLED BANNER: | being a collection of the best | naval, martial, patriotic songs, | &c. &c. &c. | chiefly written during, and in relation | to the late war. | Music!—Oh! how feint [sic], how weak, | Language fades before thy spell! | Why should feeling ever speak, | When thou can'st breathe her soul so well. | Moore. | Wilmington, Del. | Printed and sold by J. Wilson, No. 105, | Market Street. | 1816.
143, [1] p. [1:] title-page; [2:] copyright notice, Del., 27 Feb. 1816, James Wilson, proprietor; [3]-143: songs; [144:] index.
Sabin 90503, Shaw 51631 ¶ DLC* ¶ Contains 91 songs (all indexed). See 527 for a list of editions.

529 THE | SYREN: | a collection of | the | most admired songs; | con-
taining many which have not before | been published. | Washington:
| published by W. Cooper. | 1816.

116, [4] p. [1:] title-page; [2:] blank; [3]-116: songs; [117]-
[120:] index.

Filby B31 ¶ MWA (imperfect), MdHi, NHi* ¶ Contains 116 songs
(all indexed). See 430 for a list of editions.

530 THE | TOWN AND COUNTRY | SONG BOOK; | a collection
of | new, favorite, and national | songs. | Baltimore: | printed and
sold by William Warner. | 1816.

105, [3] p. [1:] title-page; [2:] blank; [3]-105: songs; [106]-[108:]
index.

DLC* ¶ Contains 101 songs (all indexed). Not related to 311 despite
the identical title and pagination.

531 WILLIAM REILY'S | COURTSHIP, trial, answer, releasement,
and | marriage | with his | fair Coolen Bawn. | To which is added |
Paddy and no more. | Baltimore. | Printed for the purchaser.

8 p. [1:] title-page; [2]-8: songs.

DLC* ¶ Contains 5 songs. See 100 for a list of editions.

1817

532 THE | AEOLIAN HARP, | or | songster's cabinet; | being | a selec-
tion of the most popular | songs and recitations; | patriotic, senti-
mental, humorous, &c. | In two volumes. | Vol. I. | Printed and published
by | M. Swaim and J. Howe. | New-York. | 1817.

124, [4] p. [i:] title-page; [ii:] stereotyped by E. & J. White, and
Charles Starr; [iii]-iv: preface; [5]-96: songs; [97]-124: recitations;
[125]-[128:] index.

Shaw 39945 ¶ PP (imperfect), RPB* ¶ Contains 83 songs (all
indexed). *Later editions: 561, 632.*

533 THE | AEOLIAN HARP, | or | songster's cabinet; | being | a selec-
tion of the most popular | songs and recitations; | patriotic, senti-
mental, humorous, &c. | In two volumes. | Vol. II | Printed and published
by | M. Swaim and J. Howe. | New-York. | 1817.

124, [4] p. [1:] title-page; [2:] blank; [3]-98: songs; [99]-124;
recitations; [125]-[128:] index.

RPB* ¶ Contains 80 songs (all indexed). Very similar in character
to 532, but from its printing history, considerably more popular. After
1820, Vol. I is dropped; 634 and the post-1820 editions of this songster
omit the volume number entirely and reprint the contents of this collection. *Later editions: 562, 633, 634. Editions after 1820:* (a) n.d.,

Philadelphia: Charles Bell (MH, NHi); (b) 1829, Philadelphia: S. Hart & Son (MB, MWA); (c) 1830, Albany (PP).

534 THE | AMERICAN | LADY'S POCKET BOOK, | for | the year
    1817. | Containing | an almanac. | Ruled pages for memorandums, observations, and en- | gagements; also for accounts of monies received, | paid, or lent, for every day in the year. | Description of the Church of the Holy Sepulchre in | Jerusalem. | Dr. Gregory's legacy to his daughters. | Answers to last year's enigmas. | New enigmas and cha- rades. | Original and selected poetry. | New and celebrated songs. | A marketing and other useful tables. | To be continued annually. | Pub- lished by | A. Small, No. 112, Chesnut Street, Philadelphia. | [Two doors below the post office.] | Where is also published, | The gentleman's annual pocket remembrancer.
    1 p.l., 168 p. [i:] blank; [ii:] frontispiece; [1:] title-page; [2:] blank; [3:] contents; [4:] common notes; [5]-151: text; 152-162: songs; [163]-168: a new marketing table.
    Drake 11107, Lowens U105, Shaw 51548 ¶ ViU* ¶ Contains 15 songs. See 120 for a list of editions.

535 THE | AMERICAN STAR. | Being a | choice collection | of the
    most approved | patriotic & other songs. | Together | with many orig- inal ones, | never before published. | Second edition. | Richmond: | published by Peter Cottom, | and for sale at his bookstores in Rich- mond and Lynchburg, | and by M. Carey & Son, Philadelphia. | 1817.
    2 p.l., 215, [1] p. [i:] blank; [ii:] frontispiece; [iii:] additional engraved title-page: The American | star | being a | choice collection | of the most approved | patriotic and other songs; | together with many others never before published. | Second edition | Richmond | Pub. by Peter Cottom, at his law and | miscellaneous Book Store. | 1817; [iv:] blank; [1:] title-page; [2:] copyright notice, N. Y., 29 Aug. 1814, Peter Cottom, proprietor; at foot of page: Shepherd & Pollock, printers, Richmond, Va.; [3]-210: songs; [211]-215: index; [216:] advertisement for Peter Cottom.
    Filby B32, Langhorne 228, Sabin 1224, Shaw 39993, Swem 98 ¶ CtHT-W, DLC* (2), ICU (imperfect), IaU (imperfect), InU-Li, MB, MH (lacks frontispiece), MWA, NBuG, NN, NcD (imperfect), RPB, Vi (imperfect), ViU; London (British Library), Oxford (Bodleian Li- brary) ¶ Contains 168 songs (167 indexed). An enlarged and revised edition of 460, q.v.

536 THE | CABIN-BOY | and | forecastle sailor's | delight. | Being |
    Tim Magpie the Yankee's own | native notions. | Compiled by an American tar. | A collection of choice | songs, | recommended by ama- teurs of the highest com- | mendation, for the use of all care-killing |

singers. | New-York: | printed by John Hardcastle, and for sale by | most of the booksellers. | 1817.

34, [1] p. [1:] blank; [2:] frontispiece; [3:] title-page; [4:] blank; [5]-34: songs; [35:] index.

Shaw 40375 ¶ MWA, NHi* ¶ Contains 20 songs (all indexed). The cover-titles of the two extant copies differ considerably. The NHi copy reads: The | cabin-boy | and | forecastle sailor's delight. | A collection of choice | songs. | New-York.—Printed by J. Hardcastle, | for sale at the book-store of A. P. Brewer, No. | 27 Maiden-Lane. The MWA copy reads: The | cabin-boy | and forecastle sailor's | delight. | A collection of choice | songs. | New-York: | for sale by S. A. Burtus, | corner Peck-Slip & Water-St. | 1817.

537 CALCOTT'S MASONRY, | with | considerable additions | and | improvements. | Containing some original matter never | before printed. | Philadelphia: | published by Robert Desilver. | J. Maxwell, printer, | 1817.

5, [3], 208 p. [1:] title-page; [2:] copy-right secured according to law; [3]-5: contents; [6:] blank; [7:] half-title: Calcott's Masonry; [8:] blank; [1]-197: text; 197-208: songs.

Barthelmess p. 13, Shaw 40379 ¶ MBFM, MWA*, NN, NUtHi, PPPFM, PSt ¶ Contains 7 Masonic songs.

538 THE | DIAMOND SONGSTER: | containing | the most approved | humorous | Scottish, Irish, and national | songs. | Baltimore: | published by F. Lucas, Jun'r. | 1817.

1 p.l., 188, [4] p. [i:] engraved title-page: The | diamond | songster. | Vol. 1 | Baltimore | published by F. Lucas, Jr. | 1817; [ii:] blank; [1:] title-page; [2:] blank; [3]-188: songs; [189]-[192:] index.

MWA, NHi, PHi* ¶ Contains 131 songs (130 indexed). Essentially a combination of 414, 416, and 418, revised and enlarged. See 413 for a list of editions.

539 THE | DIAMOND SONGSTER: | containing | the most approved | sentimental | Scottish, Irish, and national | songs. | Baltimore: | published by F. Lucas, Jun'r. | 1817.

1 p.l., 186, [6] p. [i:] engraved title-page: The | diamond | songster. | Vol. 2. | Baltimore | published by F. Lucas Jr. | 1817; [ii:] blank; [1:] title-page; [2:] blank; [3]-186: songs; [187]-[192:] index.

MWA, PHi* ¶ Contains 194 songs (all indexed). Essentially a combination of 413, 415, and 417, revised and enlarged. See 413 for a list of editions.

540 THE | DIAMOND SONGSTER; | containing | the most approved, | sentimental and lively, | Scottish, Irish, and national |

songs. | Baltimore: | published by Fielding Lucas, Jun'r, 138 Market Street. | Pomeroy & Toy, print. | 1817.

1 p.l., 152, [4] p. [i:] engraved title-page: The | diamond | songster. | Baltimore. | Published by Fielding Lucas Jun'r | 1817; [ii:] blank; [1:] title-page; [2:] blank; [3]-152: songs; [153]-[156:] index.

Alagia 281, Filby B33, Shaw 40658 ¶ MdHi (lacks engraved title-page), NBuG, NIC, RPB* ¶ Contains 413 songs (406 indexed). Although the diamond type has been retained, allowing the printer to include an enormous number of songs, the format is normal rather than miniature. Essentially a combination of the six 1812 songsters of the same name (see 413 for a list), somewhat enlarged and revised.

Free-Masonry persecuted. Boston, 1817.
See 559.

541 THE | FREEMASONS' LIBRARY | and | general Ahiman Rezon; | containing | a delineation of the true principles | of | Freemasonry, | speculative and operative, religious and moral: | compiled from the writings of | the most approved authors, | with notes and occasional remarks. | By Samuel Cole, P. M. | of Concordia & Cassia Lodges, P. G. S. of the G. L. of Md. K. T. K. M. &c. | In principio erat sermo ille, et sermo ille erat apud Deum, eratque ille sermo Deus. | Evangelium secundum Joannem. | At first she will walk with him by crooked ways, and bring fear and dread upon him, and prove | him by her discipline, until she may trust his soul, and try him by her laws. Then will she return | the straight way unto him, and comfort him, and shew him her secrets.—Ecclesiasticus. | Baltimore: | printed and published by Benjamin Edes. 1817.

1 p.l., xii, 332, 93 p. [i:] blank; [ii:] frontispiece; [i:] title-page; [ii:] copyright notice, Md., 27 Oct. 1817, Samuel Cole and Benjamin Edes, proprietors; [iii:] sanction; [iv:] blank; [v]-vii: preface; [viii:] blank; [ix]-xii: index; [1]-332: The Freemason's library; [1]-93: appendix.

Alagia 286, Barthelmess p. 7, Brinley 6710, Morris p. 189, Shaw 40509, Shaw 40858, Wolfe 2680 ¶ CSmH, DLC (lacks frontispiece), DSC (lacks frontispiece), IaCrM, MWA*, MdBE, MdBFM, NIC, NN, NNFM, NjR, OCM, PHi, PP, PPPFM, PU ¶ Contains 9 Masonic songs, all with music, on pp. 214-217, 230-233, 254-256, [2nd pagination:] 83-93. An engraved plate faces p. 83 of the appendix. *Editions after 1820:* (a) 1822, Philadelphia: H. C. Carey (Spanish edition in 2 vols.); (b) 1826, Baltimore: Cushing and Jewett (DLC, DSC, MWA, PHi).

542 THE | HARP; | or, | selected melodies: | from | authors eminent for genius and taste. | Dedicated to the lovers of music and song. | "That strain—it had a dying fall; | O, it came o'er my ear like the

sweet south, | That breathes upon a bank of violets, | Stealing and giving odour." | Greenfield, Mass. | Printed and sold by Denio & Phelps. | 1817.

16 p. [1:] title-page; [2:] blank; [3]-16: songs.

Shaw 41001, Wolfe 3435 ¶ CSmH* ¶ Contains 16 songs, all with musical notation.

543 IRISH MELODIES, | sacred melodies, | and | other poems. | By Thomas Moore, Esq. | Salem, N. Y. | Published by J. P. Reynolds. | T. Hoskins' print. | 1817.

144 p. [1:] title-page; [2:] blank; [3]-90: Irish melodies; [91]-101: gospel melodies; [102:] blank; [103]-140: miscellaneous poems; [141]-144: index.

Shaw 41472 ¶ CSmH, MWA*, NNF, OU ¶ Contains 108 songs by Moore (all indexed). Identical in content with 490 (q.v. for list of editions) through p. 90; 36 additional songs are found on subsequent pages.

544 JACHIN AND BOAZ; | or, an | authentic key | to the door of | Free-Masonry, | both ancient and modern. | Calculated not only for the instruction of every new | made Mason; but also for the information of all who | intend to become Brethren. | By a gentleman of London. | Try me—prove me. | Printed in the year | 1817. | (Price 30 cents.)

58 p. [1:] title-page; [2:] contents; [3]-[4:] preface to the first edition; [5]-55: text; 55-58: odes, anthems, and songs.

Shaw 42025 ¶ DSC*, MBFM, MWA. ¶ Contains 7 Masonic songs. Norwich, Conn., is supplied in the DSC copy before the imprint, in a contemporary hand. See 73 for a list of editions.

Jachin and Boaz; or, an authentic key to the door of Free Masonry, both ancient and modern. Calculated not only for the instruction of every new made Mason; but also for the information of all who intend to become Brethren. Containing I. A circumstantial account of all the proceedings in making a Mason, with the several obligations of an Entered Apprentice, Fellow Craft, and Master; the prayers and also the sign, grip and pass word of each degree. II. The manner of opening a Lodge, and setting the Craft to work. III. The Entered Apprentice, Fellow Craft, and Master's lectures, verbatim, as delivered in all Lodges; with the song at the conclusion of each part. IV. The origin of Masonry; description of Solomon's temple; history of the murder of the Grand Master Hiram, by the three Fellow Crafts; their discovery and punishment; the burial of Hiram by King Solomon's order; with the five points of fellowship, &c. V. The ceremony of the installment of the Master of different Lodges on St. John's day; description of the regalia, &c. VI. Ceremony observed at the funeral of a Mason. VII. A safe and easy method proposed, by which a man may gain admittance into any Lodge, without passing through the form required, and thereby save a guinea or two in his pocket. Description of the frontispiece. Illustrated with a beautiful frontispiece of the regalia, jewels, and emblematical ornaments belonging to Masonry: and an accurate plan of the drawing on the floor of a Lodge. Interspersed with a variety of notes and remarks, sufficient to render the whole clear to the meanest capacity. London—printed. Boston: reprinted for the purchasers. 1817.

[iv], [9]-52 p.

Brinley 6734, Shaw 42026 ¶ DSC*, PPFM ¶ This edition contains no separate section of songs. See 73 for a complete list of editions.

545 THE | MERMAID, | or | nautical songster: | being | a selection of
    favorite | sea songs. | New-York: | published by A. & A. Tiebout, |
No. 238, Water-Street. | 1817.

    69, [2] p. [1:] blank; [2:] frontispiece; [3:] title-page; [4:] blank;
[5]-69: songs; [70]-[71:] index.

    Shaw 41410 ¶ MWA* ¶ Contains 47 songs (all indexed). See 75 for
a list of editions.

546 A | MESS OF MESSES, | or, | salmagundi outwitted, | for | the
    laughing philosophers; | consisting of | the most admired anecdotes,
    | and | song of songs. | Compiled by | Smellfungus and Mundungus,
    | descendants of the risible deities. | "Variety's the very spice of life."
    | Philadelphia: | published for the subscribers. | 1817.

    144 p. [i:] title-page; [ii:] blank; [iii]-iv: address to the laughing
philosophers; [v]-vi: contents; [7]-70; text; [71]-144: songs.

    Shaw 41416 ¶ CSmH* ¶ Contains 66 songs. Apparently related to
547 and 554.

547 A MESS | OF | SALMAGUNDI, | for | modern laughing philoso-
    phers: | consisting of | the most admired anecdotes, bon mots, | and
    modern approved | songs. | Compiled by | Smellfungus and Mundun-
    gus, | descendants of the risible deities. | "Variety's the very spice of
    life." | Philadelphia: | published for the subscribers. | 1817.

    1 p.l., 144 p. [i:] blank; [ii:] frontispiece; [i:] title-page; [ii:]
blank; [iii]-iv: address to the laughing philosophers; [5]-69: a mess
of salmagundi; [70:] blank; [71]-142: songs; [143]-144: index.

    Shaw 41417 ¶ MWA, NN*, RPB ¶ Contains 63 songs (62 indexed).
Apparently related to 546 and 554.

548 THE | NEW AMERICAN SONGSTER; | being a collection of
    naval, martial, patriotic songs, &c. &c. | chiefly written during the
    late war; | some of which | have never before appeared in print. |
    Music!—Oh! how feint [sic], how weak, | Language fades before thy

spell! | Why should feeling ever speak, | When thou can'st breathe her soul so well. | Moore. | Philadelphia: | printed by D. Dickinson. | 1817.

72 p. [i:] title-page; [ii:] blank; [iii]-[iv:] index; [v]-[viii:] unknown; [9]-72: songs.

Lowens U106, Shaw 41560 ¶ RPB* (imperfect) ¶ Contains 33 songs (all indexed). The only known copy lacks pp. [v]-[viii].

549 OLD DAME MARGERY'S HUSH-A-BYE, and hymns for infant minds. Adorned with cuts. Sidney's Press. New Haven. 1817.

31 p. [1:] blank; [2:] frontispiece; [3:] title-page; [4]-30: text; [31:] advertisement.

Welch 959.3 ¶ NNC-T (not seen) ¶ For a list of editions, see 342.

550 PERRY'S VICTORY. | "We have met the enemy and they are ours." | Hudson: | published by W. E. Norman.

8 p. [1:] title-page; [2:] blank; [3]-8: songs.

RPB* ¶ Contains 3 songs ¶ *Edition after 1820:* (a) 1825, n.p. (MH).

551 SONGS | FOR | THE NURSERY. | New-York: | published by Thomas B. Jansen, bookseller, | No. 11 Chatham-Street, opposite the City-Hall. | 1817.

36 p. [1:] title-page; [2:] copyright notice, S. Dist. of N. Y., 11 June 1817, Thomas B. Jansen, proprietor; [3]-36: songs.

Welch 1238.2 ¶ N* ¶ Contains 91 juvenile songs. See 428 for a list of editions.

552 SONGS | OF | LOVE AND LIBERTY. | By Thomas Kennedy. | "When the light of my song is o'er, | "Then take my harp to your ancient hall; | "Hang it up at that friendly door | "Where weary travellers love to call: | "Then if some bard, who roams forsaken, | "Revive its soft note in passing along, | "Oh! let one thought of its master waken | "Your warmest smile for the child of song." | Moore's Legacy. | Washington City: | printed by Daniel Rapine. | 1817.

98 p. [1:] title-page [2:] copyright notice, Md., 9 June 1817, Thomas Kennedy, author; [3]-96: songs; [97]-98: index.

Shaw 41184, Wegelin 1017 ¶ CSmH, ICU, MB, MWA*, NHi (imperfect), NN, RPB (2), ViU ¶ Contains 48 songs (all indexed) by Kennedy.

553 [SONGSTER, or ladies' vocal companion. Pittsburgh: Cramer & Spear, 1817 or earlier.]

Lowens U107 ¶ No copy located ¶ Information from a request for location by D. M. McMurtrie dated 28 May 1936 addressed to the National Union Catalog in the Library of Congress. Existence doubtful.

554 THE | SONGSTER'S MISCELLANY; | being a | choice selection | of the | most approved | English, Irish, Scotch, and American | songs. | "Frame your mind to mirth and merriment! | "It bars a thousand harms, and lengthens life." | Philadelphia: | published for the subscribers. | 1817.

72 p. [i:] title-page; [ii:] blank; [iii]-iv: index; [5]-72: songs.

Sabin 86954, Shaw 42166 ¶ DLC*, ICN, MWA, RPB ¶ Contains 63 songs (all indexed). Apparently related to 546 and 547.

555 THE | SONGSTER'S | NEW | POCKET COMPANION | embracing the most popular | new songs, | singing at the different theatres | in the | United States. | Embellished with six beautiful engravings. | "Begone dull care." | Boston. | Published by T. Swan, | engraved by M. Butler. | 1817.

1 p.l., 188, [6], 24 p. [i:] blank; [ii:] frontispiece; [1:] title-page; [2:] blank; [3]-188: songs; 188: colophon: Burrill and Tileston, printers, Haverhill; [189]-[193:] index; [194:] blank; [1]-24: Musical appendix to The songster's new pocket companion, engraved by S. Wood.

Shaw 42167, Wolfe 8452 ¶ CtY (lacks 1 plate), MHi (imperfect), RPB* ¶ Contains 162 songs (all indexed), 23 with tunes in an appendix. There are additional engraved plates facing pp. 7, 51, 89, and 128; apparently the title-page is included among the "six beautiful engravings." *Edition after 1820:* (a) 1821, Boston: T. Swan (CtHT-W, MWA).

556 THE | STAR. | A collection of | songs, | sentimental, humorous, and | patriotic. | Published by Butler & Lambdin, | Pittsburgh, | 1817. | From the press of | Butler & Lambdin.

170, [5] p. [1:] title-page; [2:] blank; [3:] half-title: Songs, | sentimental, humorous, & pathetic; [4:] blank; [5]-56: songs; [57:] half-title: Songs | comic & sentimental; [58:] blank; [59]-111: songs; [112:] blank; [113:] half-title: Patriotic | songs; [114:] blank; [115]-170: songs; [171]-[175:] index.

Lowens U108, Shaw 42207 ¶ CSt*, RPB (imperfect) ¶ Contains 104 songs (98 indexed). *Later edition:* 593.

557 THE | STAR SPANGLED BANNER: | being a collection of the best | naval, martial, patriotic songs, | &c. &c. &c. | chiefly written during, and in relation | to the late war. | Music!—Oh! how faint, how weak, | Language fades before thy spell! | Why should feeling ever speak, | When thou can'st breathe her soul so well. | Moore. | Second edition. | Wilmington, Del. | Printed and sold by J. Wilson, No. 105, | Market Street. | 1817.

108 p. [1:] title-page; [2:] copyright notice, Del., 27 Feb. 1816, James Wilson, proprietor; [3]-108: songs; 108: index.

DeWint, MWA*, MiU-C, PCC ¶ Contains 62 songs (59 indexed).

See 527 for a list of editions. Cover-title on the MWA copy reads: The | star spangled banner, | a collection of | songs, | chiefly relating to the late war. | Wilmington: | printed and sold by James Wilson. | 1817.

558 THE | STAR SPANGLED BANNER: | being a collection of the best | naval, martial, patriotic songs, | &c. &c. &c. | chiefly written during, and in relation | to the late war. | Music!—Oh! how faint, how weak, | Language fades before thy spell! | Why should feeling ever speak, | When thou can'st breathe her soul so well. | Moore. | Second edition. | Wilmington, Del. | Printed and sold by J. Wilson, No. 105, | Market Street. | 1817.

143, [1] p. [1:] title-page; [2:] copyright notice, Del., 27 Feb. 1816, James Wilson, proprietor; [3]-143: songs; [144:] index.

Filby B35, Loughran 41, Sabin 90503, Shaw 42209 ¶ DLC*, DeHi, DeWI, MdHi, NBuG, NHi, NIC, RPB; London (British Library) ¶ Contains 93 songs (92 indexed). See 527 for a list of editions.

559 [descriptive tag:] FREE-MASONRY PERSECUTED! | [title:] Unparalleled sufferings | of | John Coustos; | who nine times underwent the most cruel | tortures ever invented by man, and senten- | ced to the gallies [sic], four years, by command | of the inquisitors of Lisbon, in or- | der to extort from him the | secrets of Free Masonary [sic]. | To which is added, | a selection of | Masonic songs. | Boston: | printed for the purchasers. | February—1817.

59 p. [1:] title-page; [2:] blank; [3:] preface to a late New York edition; [4]-45: text; [46]-59: Masonic songs.

Lowens U109, Shaw 40578 ¶ DSC*, MBFM, NjR ¶ Contains 10 Masonic songs. See 136 for a list of editions.

560 [THE | VILLA]GE SONGSTER: | containing a selection of the | most approved | patriotic and comic | songs. | Haverhill: | printed by Burrill and Tileston, and sold at | their bookstore. | 1817.

72 p. [1:] title-page; [2:] blank; [3]-72: songs.

Lowens U110, Shaw 42791 ¶ MWA* (imperfect) ¶ Contains 52 songs. The only copy extant lacks pp. 23-26, and the title-page is mutilated. The title is reconstructed from the cover. Apparently derived from 555, q.v.

1818

561 THE | AEOLIAN HARP, | or | songster's cabinet; | being | a selection of the most popular | songs and recitations; | patriotic, sentimental, humorous, &c. | In two volumes. | Vol. I. | Stereotyped and published by | Charles Starr, | New-York. | 1818.

124, [4] p. [i:] title-page; [ii:] blank; [iii]-iv: preface; [5]-96: songs; [97]-124: recitations; [125]-[128:] index.

ICN*, MWA, NHi ¶ A later edition of 532, q.v. for a list of editions.

562 THE | AEOLIAN HARP, | or | songster's cabinet; | being | a selection of the most popular | songs and recitations; | patriotic, sentimental, humorous, &c. | In two volumes. | Vol. II. | Stereotyped and published by | Charles Starr, | New-York. | 1818.

124, [4] p. [1:] title-page; [2:] blank; [3]-98: songs; [99]-124: recitations; [125]-[128:] index.

ICN*, NHi (imperfect) ¶ A later edition of 533, q.v. for a list of editions.

563 THE | AMERICAN | LADY'S POCKET BOOK, | for | the year 1818. | Containing | an almanac.—Ruled pages for memorandums, observa- | tions, and engagements; also for accounts of monies re- | ceived, paid, or lent, for every day in the year.—De- | scription of Bonaparte's residence at Longwood.— | Account of the howling dervishes of Constantinople. | —Remarks on the habits of exaggeration, by Mrs. | A. Williams.—Remarks on behaviour in company, | by Lord Chesterfield.—Woman essential to social fe- | licity.—Natural history· of the wombach.—Description | of the great and wonderful cave in Warren County, | Kentucky.—Account of the empire, manners, cus- | toms, &c. of Morocco.—Selected poetry.—New coun- | try dances and waltzes.—Answers to last year's enig- | mas.—New enigmas, charades, &c.—New and cele- | brated songs.—A marketing and other useful tables. | To be continued annually. | Published by | A. Small, No. 112, Chesnut Street, Philadelphia. | [Two doors below the post office.] | Where is also published, | The gentleman's annual pocket remembrancer.

90+ p. [1:] title-page; [2:] blank; [3:] contents; [4]-90+: text.

Drake 11142, Shaw 51643 ¶ PHi* (imperfect) ¶ The only known copy lacks all after p. 90. See 120 for a list of editions. According to the table of contents, the almanac for 1818 contains at least 168 p.

564 THE | ANTIHIPNOTIC SONGSTER, | containing | original and select | songs. | Patriotic, sentimental, Anacreontic, | comic, & Masonic. | With | favorite airs, glees, and catches. | Philadelphia: | printed and published by T. Town and S. Merritt. | For sale by Robert Desilver, No. 110, Walnut Street, and at the | principal book stores in the city. | 1818.

1 p.l., 232, [8] p. [i:] blank; [ii:] frontispiece; [1:] title-page; [2:] copyright notice, Pa., 9 April 1818, Thomas Town, proprietor; [3]-232: songs; [233]-[240]: index.

Shaw 43089 ¶ DLC (lacks frontispiece), MWA, PPL*, RPB; Oxford (Bodleian Library) ¶ Contains 291 songs (287 indexed).

565 THE | BIRD OF BIRDS, | or a | musical medley; | being | a rich and diversified collection, | of | miscellaneous and patriotic | songs. | Printed and published | at | New-York. | 1818.

141, [3] p. [1:] title-page; [2:] blank; [3]-141: songs; [142]-[144:] index.

Shaw 43371, Wegelin 1247 ¶ MWA (imperfect), RPB* ¶ Contains 79 songs (all indexed).

566 THE | COLUMBIAN | SONGSTER: | a collection | of the most approved | patriotic and other | songs. | Pittsburgh, | printed by Eichbaum and Johnston, | and for sale at their bookstore, Second Street. | 1818.

[3]-179 p. [3:] title-page; [4:] blank; [5]-81: songs; [82:] blank; [83:] half-title: Songs, | comic and sentimental; [84:] blank; [85]-172: songs; [173]-179: index.

Shaw 43679 ¶ MWA*, PPiU ¶ Contains 136 songs (all indexed).

567 THE | FREEMASON'S MONITOR; | or | illustrations of Masonry: | in two parts. | By Thomas Smith Webb, | Past Grand Master of the Grand Lodge of | Rhode Island, &c. | A new and improved edition. | Salem: | published by Cushing and Appleton. | Thomas C. Cushing, printer. | 1818.

248, [4], 60 p. [i:] title-page; [ii:] copyright notice, Mass., 4 Nov. 1815, Thomas Smith Webb, proprietor; [iii:] sanction, dated Providence, 7 July 5802; [iv:] blank; [v]-vi: preface; [viii]-xii: contents; [13]-248: Freemason's monitor, part first; [1]-3: rules for the guidance of Christian Freemasons; [4:] blank; [i:] second title-page: The | Freemason's monitor; | or | illustrations of Masonry: | in two parts. | By Thomas Smith Webb, | Past Grand Master of the Grand Lodge of | Rhode Island, &c. | Part second. | Containing | an account of the ineffable degrees of | Masonry; | and the | history of Freemasonry in America. | Salem: | published by Cushing and Appleton. | Ezra Lincoln, printer, Boston. | 1818; [ii:] blank; [iii]-iv: preface; [5]-52: Freemason's monitor, part second; [53]-60: Masonic songs.

Barthelmess p. 30, Shaw 46737 ¶ DLC*, DSC, MB, MBFM, MH, MiU, NNFM, PPPFM ¶ Contains 7 Masonic songs. Contents identical with 347, q.v. See 124 for a list of editions.

568 THE | FREEMASON'S MONITOR; | or | illustrations of Masonry: | in two parts. | By Thomas Smith Webb, | Past Grand Master of the Grand Lodge of | Rhode Island, &c. | A new and improved edition. | Salem: | published by Cushing and Appleton. | Flagg and Gould, printers. | 1818.

312 p. [i:] title-page; [ii:] copyright notice, Mass., 4 Nov. 1815, Thomas Smith Webb, proprietor; [iii:] sanction, dated Providence,

7 July 5802; [iv:] blank; [v]-vi: preface; [vii]-xii: contents; [13]-248: Freemason's monitor, part first; [249:] rules for the guidance of Christian Freemasons; [250:] blank; [251:] second title-page: The | Freemason's monitor; | or | illustrations of Masonry: | in two parts. | By Thomas Smith Webb, | Past Grand Master of the Grand Lodge of Rhode | Island, etc. | Part second. | Containing | an account of the ineffable degrees of Masonry; | and the | history of Freemasonry in America. | Salem: | published by Cushing and Appleton. | Flagg & Gould, printers, Andover. | 1818; [252:] blank; [253]-256 [i.e., 254:] preface; [257]-304: Freemason's monitor, part second; [305]-312; Masonic songs.

Barthelmess p. 30, Shaw 46738 ¶ DSC*, MSaE, MWA, MWHi, NN, PPPFM (2), RPB, THi ¶ Contains 7 Masonic songs. Contents identical with 347, q.v. See 124 for a list of editions.

569 IRISH MELODIES, | songs, | and | sacred songs. | By | Thomas Moore, Esq. | New-York: | published by A. T. Goodrich & Co. | No. 124 Broadway, corner of Cedar-Street. | J. Seymour, printer. | 1818.
[3]-121 p. [3:] title-page; [4:] blank; [5]-[7:] index; [8:] blank; [9]-93: Irish melodies; [94]-104: songs; [105]-121: sacred songs.
Shaw 44891 ¶ CtHT-W, MWA*, MdBP ¶ Contains 99 songs by Moore (all indexed). Identical in content with 490 (q.v. for list of editions) through p. 93; 27 additional songs are found on subsequent pages.

570 JACHIN AND BOAZ: | or an | authentic key | to the door of | Free-Masonry, | ancient and modern, | calculated | not only for the instruction of every new made Mason, but | also, for the information of all who intend to be- | come Brethren. | Interspersed with a variety of | notes and remarks, | necessary to explain and render the whole clear to the | meanest capacity. | By a gentleman | belonging to the Jerusalem Lodge; a frequent visitor at the | Queen's Arms, St. Paul's Church-Yard; the Horn, in Fleet- | Street; Crown and Anchor, Strand; and the Salutation, | Newgate-Street. | Try me—prove me. | Wilmington: | printed and sold by R. Porter. | 1818.
108 p. [1:] title-page; [2:] blank; [3:] contents; [4:] advertisement; [5]-7: preface; [8]-74: text; [75]-102: odes, anthems, and songs; [103]-108: toasts and sentiments.
Loughran 57, Shaw 45604 ¶ DeWI, MdBL, MBFM, PPPFM* ¶ Contains 16 Masonic songs. As 112, q.v. See also 73 for a list of editions.

571 MAGAZINE OF WIT, | and | American harmonist. | Containing | a collection of the most admired | anecdotes, | and a variety of the best | songs, | chiefly composed in honour | of | the naval and military victories | gained during | the late war. | Embellished with a representa-

tion of Perry's victory. | Philadelphia: | published by M'Carty and Davis, | S. E. corner of Race and Ninth Streets. | 1818.

1 p.l., 144 p. [i:] blank; [ii:] frontispiece; [i:] title-page; [ii:] blank; [iii]-iv: address to the laughing philosophers; [5]-74: magazine of wit; [75]-142: songs; [143]-144: index.

Lowens Uiii, Shaw 44670 ¶ MWA (imperfect), RPB* (lacks frontispiece). Contains 70 songs (all indexed). Both known copies lack the plate mentioned on the title-page; this may be found in the 1821 edition. *Edition after 1820:* (a) 1821, Philadelphia: M'Carty & Davis (CtHT-W, DLC, MB, MWA, PHi, PP, PPL, RPB).

572 MASONIC CONSTITUTIONS, | or | illustrations of Masonry; | compiled by the direction | of the | Grand Lodge | of Kentucky, | and adopted by them for the regulation and govern- | ment of the subordinate Lodges under | their jurisdiction; | with an appendix, | containing remarks on the degrees of | Master Mark Masons, Super Excellent Master, and | Royal Arch Masons. | By James Moore and Cary L. Clarke, | members of the Grand Lodge of Kentucky. | Second edition, with amendments. | Lexington, K. | Printed by Worsley & Smith. | 1818.

218 p. [i:] title-page; [ii:] copyright notice, Ky., 30 Mar. 1808, James Moore and Cary L. Clarke, proprietors; [iii:] preface; [iv:] blank; [v]-xviii: introduction; [19]-182: text; [183]-208: odes, anthems, and songs; [209]-214: appendix; [215]-218: contents.

Morris pp. 197-198, Shaw 44086, Shaw 44885 ¶ CtY, DLC*, ICU, IaCrM, KyLoF, MBFM, MWA, NN, NdFM, TxU, WHi ¶ Contains 24 Masonic songs. See 349 for an earlier edition.

573 MASONICK MELODIES, | being | a choice selection | of the most | approved Masonick songs, | duets, | glees, | catches, | cannons [sic], | hymns, | odes, | dirges, and | choruses. | Appropriate to all Masonick occasions, | the whole | set to musick: | and respectfully dedicated to | the most ancient and honorable fraternity | of | Free and Accepted Masons. | By Br. Luke Eastman. | "Musick we have too— | Yet no loose strains excite unchaste desire, | No wanton sounds profane Urania's lyre— | There concord and decorum bear the sway, | And moral musick tunes the instructive lay— | For thee shall musick strike the harmonious lyre, | And while she charms the ear, morality inspire." | Boston—printed for the author by T. Rowe. | 1818.

204, [4] p. [i:] title-page; [ii:] copyright notice, Mass., 21 Jan. 1818, Luke Eastman, author; [iii:] preface and acknowledgments; [iv:] recommendations; [v]-vi: prologue; [vii:] explanation of the musical terms; [viii:] errata; [9]-204: songs; [205]-[206:] epilogue; [207]-[208:] index.

Barthelmess p. 29, Brinley 6723, Johnson p. 347, Shaw 43904, Wolfe

2646, Wolfstieg °39982 ¶ CtHT-W, DLC*, ICHi, IU, MB (2), MBAt, MBFM (2), MH, MWA, MdBFM, NHi, NN, NNFM, NNUT, OCM, OClWHi, PPPFM (2), RHi, RPB (2), WHi, WM; Oxford (Bodleian Library) ¶ Contains 88 Masonic songs (all indexed), all with musical notation or references to musical notation. *Edition after 1820:* (a) 1825, Boston: William Parker (DLC, MB, MBFM, MH, MHi, MWA, NHi, NNFM, PPPFM, RPB).

574 MELODIES, | songs, | and | sacred   songs. | By   Thomas   Moore, Esq. | Philadelphia: | published   by   M.   Carey,   &   Son, | No.   126, Chestnut Street. | 1818.

xi, [1], [19]-232 p. [i:] title-page; [ii:] at foot of page: Griggs & Co. printers; [iii]-vi: preface; [vii]-xi: index; [xii:] blank; [19]-211: Moore's melodies; [212:] blank; [213]-232: sacred songs.

Shaw 44894 ¶ MWA, PPL, PSt* ¶ Contains 165 songs (all indexed) by Moore. In effect, an expanded edition of 490, q.v. for a list of associated imprints. *Later editions:* 616, 617. *Editions after 1820:* (a) 1821, Philadelphia: Hickman and Hazzard (CtY); (b) 1821, New York: George Long (CtY, DLC, MH, NHi, NN, PPStJos); (c) 1822, Philadelphia: Hickman and Hazard [sic] (MWA); (d) 1822, New York: George Long (MWA); (e) 1825, Philadelphia: T. DeSilver (MH); (f) 1825, New York: G. Smith (CtY); (g) 1829, Exeter (MWA); (h) 1830, Philadelphia: T. DeSilver (CtY, PPPrHi); (i) 1836, Exeter: J. & B. Williams (MH, MWA); (j) 1838, Philadelphia: Thomas, Cowperthwait & Co. (MWA).

575 [THE MERRY FELLOW of Saturday-night, or weekly collection of all the anecdotes, jokes, comical sayings, witty remarks, laughable stories, bon-mots, repartees, epigrams, humorous adventures, nuts, salmagundies, puns, &c. &c. &c. Calculated to draw a nail, every Saturday-night, out of every good-fellow's coffin! Philadelphia: H. C. Lewis, 1818.]

Advertised 13 July 1818 in the *Ladies literary museum* as a "proposal for publishing, by subscription, a companion to the *Weekly song-book*." Probably not a songster.

576 THE | NEPTUNE: | or a | collection of the most entertaining | comic | and | sea songs. | Being a selection from the newest and most | favourite publications, and may prove | a merry, jovial and sprightly | companion for the sons | of hilarity and | mirth. | Boston: | printed for Nathaniel Coverly, | No. 16, Milk-Street. | 1818.

24 p. [1:] blank; [2:] frontispiece; [3:] title-page; [4]-24: songs.

Shaw 44969 ¶ MB* ¶ Contains 15 songs. See 326 for an earlier edition.

577 THE | NEW FREE-MASON'S | MONITOR; | or, | Masonic guide. | For the | direction of members of that | ancient and honourable fraternity, | as well as | for the information of those, who may be desirous | of becoming acquainted with its principles. | By James Hardie, A. M. | New-York: | printed and published by George Long, | No. 71 Pearl-Street. | 1818.

1 p.l., xv, [1], 360 p. [i:] blank; [ii:] frontispiece; [i:] title-page; [ii:] copyright notice, N. Y., 11 Dec. 1818, George Long, proprietor; [iii:] recommendation; [iv:] blank; [v]-ix: preface, dated New York, 9 Mar. 1818; [x:] blank; [xi]-xv: contents; [xvi:] blank; [1]-344: text; [345]-356: Masonic songs; [357]-360: Masonic toasts.

Barthelmess p. 30, Shaw 44259 ¶ CtY, DLC*, DSC, IaCrM, MBFM (lacks frontispiece), MWA, NHi, NIC, NNS, PPPFM (3) ¶ Contains 14 Masonic songs. *Later edition:* 618.

578 THE | NIGHTINGALE, | containing fourteen | beautiful songs. | Sweet nightingale! Queen of the spray, | Whose note is disturb'd by our song; | Ah! stretch not thy pinions away, | Alarm'd at the numerous throug [sic]; | But try the sweet warble again, | And challenge thy hearers so fine, | Though the muses attend on their train, | To make such a concert as thine. | Printed September 25th, 1818—for 6 cents.

16 p. [1:] title-page; [2:] illustrations; [3]-16: songs.

DLC* ¶ Contains 14 songs.

579 OLD DAME MARGERY'S | HUSH A BYE, | and | little hymns. | Adorned with cuts. | From Sidney's Press, | for John Babcock & Son. | 1818.

30, [1] p. [1:] blank; [2:] frontispiece; [3:] title-page; [4:] alphabet; 5-22: songs; 23-30: hymns; [31:] publisher's advertisement.

Welch 959.4 ¶ CtY*, PP ¶ Contains 20 juvenile songs and 6 "hymns for infant minds." See 342 for a complete list of editions.

580 THE | POEMS, ODES, SONGS, | and other | metrical effusions, | of Samuel Woodworth, | author of "The champions of freedom," &c. | New-York: Abraham Asten and Matthias Lopez, | 1818.

1 p.l., 288 p. [i:] blank; [ii:] frontispiece; [i:] title-page; [ii:] copyright notice, N. Y., 4 Oct. 1818, Matthias Lopez and Abraham Asten, proprietors; [iii]-xii: biographical sketch; [13]-89: poems; [90:] editorial note; 91-144: odes and songs; 145-183: occasional pieces; [184:] blank; [185]-284: miscellaneous poems; [285]-288: contents.

Shaw 46864, Wegelin 1220 ¶ CSmH, CtY, DLC*, MB, MH, MWA, MnU, NjR, PU, RPB ¶ Contains 23 odes and songs in the section so named, apparently all by Woodworth.

581 PRETTY POEMS, | in easy language, | for the amusement of |

little boys and girls. | By Tommy Lovechild. | Ornamented with cuts. | Hartford [Conn.]: | printed by Hale & Hosmer. | 1818.

30, [1] p. [1:] blank; [2:] frontispiece; [3:] title-page; [4:] an ABC; [5]-30: pretty poems, &c.; [31:] advertisement of printer's books.

Welch 804.4 ¶ MWA* ¶ Contains 22 juvenile songs. See 354 for a list of editions.

582 THE | SCOTTISH MINSTREL: | being a | complete collection | of Burns' songs, | together with his correspondence | with Mr. Thomson. | To which is added, | a new and complete glossary. | Phila-delphia: | published by Benjamin Warner, | No. 147, Market-Street. | Printed by Thomas H. Palmer. | 1818.

1 p.l., xxiv, 312 p. [i:] blank; [ii:] frontispiece; [i:] title-page; [ii:] blank; [iii]-xiv: contents; [xv]-xxiv: index; [1:] half-title: Correspon-dence | with | R. George Thomson; | including | poetry; [2:] blank: [3]-171: text; [172:] blank; [173:] note; [174:] blank; [175]-276: songs; [277:] half-title: A | new and complete | glossary | to the | Scottish words and phrases | in | Burns's poems; [278:] copyright notice for the glossary, Pa., 13 June 1818, Thomas H. Palmer, proprietor; [279]-312: glossary.

Shaw 43493 ¶ PPL*, MSaE, MWA ¶ Contains 110 songs by Burns (all indexed).

583 [caption-title:] SEVEN GOOD SONGS, viz. | 1 The star-spangled banner. | 2 The battle of the kegs. | 3 Jackson's victory. | 4 A hunting we will go. | 5 The soldier and his lady. | 6 Don't give up the ship. | 7 O this is no my ain lassie.

12 p. [1:] caption-title; [1]-12: songs; 12: colophon: Printed by Wm. Dickson, Lancaster, Pa. | February, 1818.

Shaw 45691 ¶ DLC*, RPB ¶ Contains 7 songs, all named in the caption-title.

584 A | SONG-BOOK | for little children. | Newburyport: | printed by W. & J. Gilman, | No. 2, Middle-Street. | 1818.

16 p. [1:] title-page; [2:] alphabet and advertisement for W. & J. Gilman; [3]-16: songs.

Shaw 45759, Welch 1235 ¶ MB*, MH, MWA (imperfect) ¶ Contains 8 juvenile songs. Cover-title differs: Song book. | Printed and sold | by W. & J. Gilman, | book-sellers, No. 2, Middle-Street, | Newburyport.

585 THE | SONG-SINGER'S AMUSING | COMPANION. | Being a | selection of the best philosophic, sen- | timental, national and moral songs: and also | a number of airy and amusing pieces. | Arranged | by Philo Musico, A. B. &c. &c. | Sweet enlivener of my hours. | Oft I've felt thy genial pow'rs; | Sentiment with music join'd, | Yields a pleasure most refin'd. | When from toil and labor free, | I refresh myself with

thee; | Banish'd hence be wrath and spite, | Songs and music, bring delight!! | Original. | Coppy-right [sic] secured. | Boston: | printed for Sterne and Mann, | No. 147, Market Street. | 1818.

28 p. [1:] title-page; [2]-28: songs; 28: colophon: end of the first number.

Shaw 45760 ¶ DLC*, ICN, MH, MWA, NN, NRU-Mus, RPB ¶ Contains 24 songs. Apparently no further numbers were issued; the identity of the compiler is unknown.

Songs, | comic and sentimental. [Pittsburgh, 1818.]
See 566.

586 SONGS | FOR | GENTLEMEN. | Old and new. | Patriotic, witty, lively; | nothing low or lewd. | New Haven. | Sidney's Press. | For J. Babcock & Son. | Sold also, by S. & W. R. Babcock, | Charleston, S. C. | 1818.

2 p.l., 124, [4] p. [i:] blank; [ii:] frontispiece; [iii:] title-page; [iv:] blank; [1]-124: songs; 124: colophon: from Sidney's Press; [125]-[128:] index.

Sabin 86909, Shaw 45761, Woodall 99 ¶ CtY, DLC*, RPB ¶ Contains 79 songs (all indexed). *Later edition: 642. Edition after 1820:* (a) 1825, New Haven: Sidney's Press (CtY, DLC, MWA).

587 SONGS | FOR THE | PARLOUR. | Modest, lively, merry. | New Haven. | Sidney's Press. | For J. Babcock & Son. | Sold also, by S. & W. R. Babcock, | Charleston, S. C. | 1818.

2 p.l., 123, [5] p. [i:] blank; [ii:] frontispiece; [iii:] title-page; [iv:] blank; [1]-123: songs; 123: colophon: from Sidney's Press; [124]-[128:] index.

Shaw 45762 ¶ RPB* ¶ Contains 103 songs (101 indexed).

588 SONGS, | NAVAL, PATRIOTIC, | and miscellaneous. | Printed and published | at New-York: | 1818.

36 p. [1:] title-page; 2-36: songs.
RPB* ¶ Contains 14 songs.

589 THE | SONGSTER'S MAGAZINE; | (published in numbers) | designed to contain | a | choice selection | of the most approved | patriotic, comic, sentimental, | amatory and naval | songs; | both ancient and modern. | No. I. | (third edition) | containing | thirty songs for a shilling, | with | two or three trifles gratis, | viz. | [a list of 34 songs in two columns | New-York: | published at the bookstore and circulating library, 249 Broadway, | corner of Murray-Street. | August 22, 1818.

1 p.l., 24 p. [i:] title-page; [ii:] copyright notice, N.Y., 20 Aug. 1818, David Carlisle, proprietor; 1-24: songs.

RPB* ¶ Contains 34 songs (all indexed). This was the first in a series of 12 24-page numbers of *The songster's magazine* to be published at intervals of roughly two months. In 1820, the 12 numbers were bound in two volumes containing six numbers each, with a new title-page, prefatory note, and index (cf. 647 and 648). The RPB set contains the first eight numbers bound in a single volume, with the individual tables of contents cut from what were apparently the wrappers in which each number was encased. No copies of a first or second edition of No. I are known; perhaps the word "edition" was being used as a synonym for "printing."

590 [THE SONGSTER'S MAGAZINE; (published in numbers) designed to contain a choice selection of the most approved patriotic, comic, sentimental, amatory and naval songs; both ancient and modern.] No. II. | (second edition) | containing | more than thirty songs for 12½ cents. | With | two or three trifles gratis, | viz. | [a list of 34 songs in two columns] | [New-York: published at the bookstore and circulating library, 249 Broadway, corner of Murray-Street. 1818.]

   1 p.l., 25-48 p. [i:] title-page; [ii:] copyright notice, N. Y., 20 Aug. 1818, David Carlisle, proprietor, and notice "to publishers" from E. Riley, No. 29 Chatham-Street, with a list of his copyrights; 25-48: songs.

   RPB* (imperfect) ¶ Contains 34 songs (all indexed). The only copy known lacks all of the title-page with the exception of the table of contents and the numeration, as indicated above. Cf. 589; see also 647. No copies of a first edition of No. II are known; perhaps the word "edition" was being used as a synonym for "printing." E. Riley's warning to other publishers is interesting enough to quote in its entirety: "In several publications of this city, Philadelphia, Baltimore, &c. &c. &c. songs, my property, (the copy-right regularly secured) have been published. All such publishers shall be proceeded against according to law, unless they discontinue their encroachments. To prevent mistakes, and that no publisher may plead ignorance, the subscriber has made arrangements with the publisher of the Songster's Magazine, that, in future, whenever a copy-right song of his is inserted in that work, it shall be stated as such under the title." A list of 9 titles on which he claims copyright is appended. After listing S. Woodworth's "Patriotic Diggers" as his property, Riley remarks: "A man of Baltimore published this song as his composition: how unlike a gentleman!"

591 [THE SONGSTER'S MAGAZINE; (published in numbers) designed to contain a choice selection of the most approved patriotic, comic, sentimental, amatory and naval songs; both ancient and modern.] N.º 3. | Containing | thirty-nine songs for 12 1-2 cents. | [a list of 39 songs in two columns] | [New-York: published and sold by J. B. Jansen, No. 15 Chatham-Street. Broderick & Ritter, printers. 1818.]

   1 p.l., 49-72 p. [i:] title-page; [ii:] copyright notice, N. Y., 20 Aug.

1818, David Carlisle, proprietor, and notice "to publishers" from E. Riley, No. 29 Chatham-Street, with a list of his copyrights; 49-72: songs.

RPB* (imperfect) ¶ Contains 39 songs (all indexed). The only copy known lacks all of the title-page with the exception of the table of contents and its numeration, as indicated above. Since a different typographical layout of the title-page is used, it can perhaps be assumed that it was with this number that J. B. Jansen and Broderick & Ritter took over the songster. Cf. 589 and 590; see also 647.

592 [THE SONGSTER'S WEEKLY COMPANION, or general remembrancer of all the most admired and favorite airs, melodies, marches, &c. Price 12 cts. a number. Philadelphia: H. C. Lewis, 1818.]

Advertised 3 Aug. 1818 in the *Lady's and gentleman's Weekly museum and Philadelphia reporter* as a proposal for publishing, by subscription, "a weekly collection of song-music." Probably never issued.

593 THE | STAR. | A | collection of | songs, | sentimental, humourous, | and | patriotic. | Pittsburgh: | published by Lambdin & Minis. | Butler and Lambdin, printers. | 1818.

174, [5] p. [1:] title-page; [2:] blank; [3:] half-title: Songs, | sentimental, humourous, and patriotic; [4:] blank; [5]-66: songs; [67:] half-title: Songs, | sentimental; [68:] blank; [69]-126: songs; [127:] half-title: Songs, | humourous; [128:] blank; [129]-174: songs; [175]-[179:] index.

Sabin 90485, Shaw 45791 ¶ MWA, NHi*, RPB ¶ Contains 118 songs (117 indexed). See 556 for an earlier edition.

The Suffolk garland; or, a collection of poems, songs, tales, ballads, sonnets, and elegies, legendary and romantic, historical and descriptive, relative to that county; and illustrative of its scenery, places, biography, manners, habits and customs. Ipswich: J. Raw, 1818.

404 p.

Shaw 45815 ¶ CU, DLC*, MH, MWA ¶ Not an American imprint. Shaw assumes Ipswich incorrectly to be in Massachusetts rather than in England.

594 THE | SYREN: | a collection of | the | most admired songs; | containing many which have not before been published. | To which is added, | a complete copy of the | Irish melodies, | by Thomas Moore. | Washington: | published by W. Cooper. | 1818.

116, [6], 92, [2] p. [1:] title-page; [2:] blank; [3]-116: songs; [117]-[120:] index; [121]-[122:] blank; [1:] second title-page: Irish melodies: by | Thomas Moore, Esq. | Washington, | published by W. Cooper. | 1816; [2:] blank; [3]-92: songs; [93]-[94:] index.

Shaw 45834 ¶ RPB* ¶ Contains 190 songs (all indexed). A combination of 516 and 529 with a new title-page. See 430 for a list of editions.

595 [UNIVERSAL SONG-BOOK; or, weekly collection of all the songs in the English language, (except the vulgar,) viz: American, English, Irish, and Scotch. No. I. Subscription price 6 cents. Philadelphia: H. C. Lewis, 1818.]
    18? p.
No copy located ¶ Advertised 23 May 1818 in the *Ladies' literary museum* as "just published." In all, 12 numbers of this songster (see 596, 597, 598, 599, 600, 601, 602, 603, 604, 605, and 606) were apparently brought out separately. With the 6th number, the alternate title became the regular title (see 600). After the 12 numbers were put together, some 18 songs were added, and the whole was advertised 9 Sept. 1818 in the *Lady's and gentleman's weekly museum, and Philadelphia reporter* under the title, *The weekly song book, Vol. I* as "this day . . . published." Vol. I appears to have been "bound in two books" (see 607). A second volume seems to have been begun serially, according to an advertisement in the 1 Jan. 1819 *Lady's & gentleman's weekly literary museum, and musical magazine* for "all the songs in the English language, except the immoral, viz. American, English, Irish, and Scotch . . . now publishing by subsbription [sic]." This second volume was probably entitled the *Theatrical weekly song-book* (see 630). But when it was combined with *The weekly song book,* Lewis preferred to call the two-volume set by still another name—*The new universal weekly song-book* (see 619), which he advertised as "for sale" in the 17 May 1819 *Literary & musical magazine.* Unfortunately, of all the songsters issued by Lewis in 1818 and 1819 (see also 575 and 592) only 596 has been located. According to a table of contents published on 10 Aug. 1818 in the *Lady's and gentleman's weekly museum, and Philadelphia reporter,* 595 contained 17 songs.

596 THE | UNIVERSAL SONG-BOOK; | (or, | weekly collection | of | all | the songs | in the | English language, | (except the vulgar,) | viz: | American, English, Irish, & Scotch;) | and | repository of originals. | Published in uniform parts, | by H. C. Lewis, | editor of the "Ladies' Literary Museum," | Part 2. | Philadelphia: | printed at 164 S. Eleventh Street. | Subscription price 6 cents. | 1818.
    [iv], [19]-34 p. [i:] blank; [ii:] frontispiece; [iii:] title-page; [iv:] prefatory remarks; [19]-34: songs.
    Shaw 46620 ¶ P* ¶ Contains 14 songs. Advertised 30 May 1818 in the *Ladies' literary museum* as "just published." See 595 for a sketch of the history of this songster.

597 [UNIVERSAL SONG BOOK; (or weekly collection of all the songs in the English language, [except the vulgar,]viz: American,

English, Irish, and Scotch;) and repository of originals. No. 3. Price 6 cents. Philadelphia: H. C. Lewis, 1818.]

No copy located ¶ Advertised 13 June 1818 in the *Ladies' literary museum* as "just published." Contained 15 songs, according to the table of contents in the 10 Aug. 1818 *Lady's and gentleman's weekly museum, and Philadelphia reporter.* See 595 for a sketch of the history of this songster.

598 [UNIVERSAL SONG BOOK; (or weekly collection of all the songs in the English language, [except the vulgar,] viz: American, English, Irish, and Scotch;) and repository of originals. No. 4. Price 6 cents. Philadelphia: H. C. Lewis, 1818.]

No copy located ¶ Advertised 24 June 1818 in the *Ladies' literary museum* as "also for sale." Contained 17 songs, according to the table of contents in the 10 Aug. 1818 *Lady's and gentleman's weekly museum, and Philadelphia reporter.* See 595 for a sketch of the history of this songster.

599 [UNIVERSAL SONG BOOK; (or weekly collection of all songs in the English language, [except the vulgar,] viz: American, English, Irish, and Scotch;) and repository of originals. No. 5. Price 6 cents. Philadelphia: H. C. Lewis, 1818.]

No copy located ¶ Advertised 24 June 1818 in the *Ladies' literary museum* as "just published." Contained 17 songs, according to the table of contents in the 10 Aug. 1818 *Lady's and gentleman's weekly museum, and Philadelphia reporter.* See 595 for a sketch of the history of this songster.

600 [THE WEEKLY SONG-BOOK, No. VI (or universal collection of all the songs in the English language, [except the immoral,] viz: American, English, Irish, and Scotch;) and repository of originals. Price 6 cents. Philadelphia: H. C. Lewis, 1818.]

No copy located ¶ Advertised 29 June 1818 in the *Ladies' literary museum* as "just published" on 27 June 1818. Note the inversion of the title. Contained 14 songs, according to the table of contents in the 10 Aug. 1818 *Lady's and gentleman's weekly museum, and Philadelphia reporter.* See 595 for a sketch of the history of this songster.

601 [THE WEEKLY SONG-BOOK, No. 7 (or universal collection of all the songs in the English language, [except the immoral,] viz: American, English, Irish, and Scotch;) and repository of originals. Price 6 cents. Philadelphia: H. C. Lewis, 1818.]

No copy located ¶ Advertised 6 July 1818 in the *Ladies' literary museum* as "just published." Contained 10 songs, as well as "toasts for the Fourth of July, etc.," according to the table of contents in the 10 Aug. 1818 *Lady's and gentleman's weekly museum, and Philadelphia reporter.* See 595 for a sketch of the history of this songster.

602 [THE WEEKLY SONG-BOOK, No. 8 (or universal collection
   of all the songs in the English language, [except the immoral,] viz:
American, English, Irish, and Scotch;) and repository of originals.
Price 6 cents. Philadelphia: H. C. Lewis, 1818.]

No copy located ¶ Advertised 13 July 1818 in the *Ladies literary
museum* as "just published." Contained 15 songs, according to the table
of contents in the 10 Aug. 1818 *Lady's and gentleman's weekly museum, and Philadelphia reporter*. See 595 for a sketch of the history
of this songster.

603 [THE WEEKLY SONG-BOOK, No. 9. Price 6¼ cents. Philadelphia: H. C. Lewis, 1818.]

No copy located ¶ Published before 27 July 1818, when No. 10 (604)
appeared. Contained 17 songs, according to the table of contents in
the 10 Aug. 1818 *Lady's and gentleman's weekly museum, and Philadelphia reporter*. See 595 for a sketch of the history of this songster.

604 [THE WEEKLY SONG-BOOK, No. 10. Price 6¼ cents. Philadelphia: H. C. Lewis, 1818.]

No copy located ¶ Advertised 27 July 1818 in the *Lady's and gentleman's weekly museum, and Philadelphia reporter* as "just published."
Contained 15 songs, according to the table of contents in the 10 Aug.
1818 issue of the same periodical. See 595 for a sketch of the history of
this songster.

605 [THE WEEKLY SONG-BOOK, No. 11. Price 6¼ cents. Philadelphia: H. C. Lewis, 1818.]

No copy located ¶ Advertised 3 Aug. 1818 in the *Lady's and gentleman's weekly museum, and Philadelphia reporter* as "just published."
Contained 16 songs, according to the table of contents in the 10 Aug.
1818 issue of the same periodical. See 595 for a sketch of the history of
this songster.

606 [THE WEEKLY SONG-BOOK, No. 12. Price 6¼ cents. Philadelphia: H. C. Lewis, 1818.]

No copy located ¶ Advertised 10 Aug. 1818 in the *Lady's and gentleman's weekly museum, and Philadelphia reporter* as "just published,"
and containing 15 songs. See 595 for a sketch of the history of this songster.

607 [THE WEEKLY SONG BOOK. Volume first. Price 87½ cents,
   neatly bound. Philadelphia: H. C. Lewis, 1818.]

No copy located ¶ Advertised 9 Sept. 1818 in the *Lady's and gentleman's weekly museum, and Philadelphia reporter* as "this day . . .
published" and "containing 200 fashionable and original songs," 18
songs more than the 12 numbers issued serially. The 30 Sept. 1818

issue of the same periodical adds the information that among the songs "are Philipps's and Incledons [sic]." According to the 18 Jan. 1819 *Lady's & gentleman's weekly literary museum, and musical magazine,* this volume appears to have been "bound in two books . . . for sale, price 87½ cts. each book." See 595 for a sketch of the history of this songster; see also 630 for a probable second volume, issued serially under a different title; see 619 for the two volumes combined, sold under still a third title.

608 THE | WHISTLE. | Or | a collection of songs; | sentimental and humorous | selected and composed | by S. Jenks. | Dedham: | H. & W. H. Mann, printers. | 1818.
    24 p. [1:] title-page; [2:] blank; [3:] advertisement; [4:] index; [5]-24: songs.
    Lowens* ¶ Contains 12 songs (all indexed).

609 [caption-title:] WILLIAM REILY'S | COURTSHIP, trial, and marriage.
    12 p. [1:] caption-title; [1]-12: songs.
    MdHi* ¶ Contains 4 songs. For a list of editions, see 100.

610 WREATHS | TO | THE CHIEFTAIN. | Hail to the chief. | The | American star. | The | death of Parker. | Shannon side. | Printed in the year, 1818.
    8 p. [1:] title-page; 2-8: songs.
    RPB* ¶ Contains 5 songs, all named on the title-page.

1819

611 THE | AMERICAN LADIES [sic] | POCKET BOOK | 1819 | [illustration] Walking dress | I. V. K. & Co. sc. | Published by | A. Small, Phila. | 1819.
    2 p.l., 180 p. [i:] blank; [ii:] frontispiece; [iii:] title-page; [iv:] blank; [1:] contents; [2:] blank; [3:] common notes; [4:] blank; [5]-161: text; 162-165: new country dances and waltzes, for 1818; 165-174: songs; 175-180: tables.
    Drake 11176, Shaw 51733 ¶ PHi*, RPB ¶ Contains 15 songs. See 120 for a list of editions.

612 AMERICAN | PATRIOTIC AND COMIC | MODERN SONGS, | commemorative of | naval victories, | during the late war. | We have met the enemy & they are ours. | New-York: | printed and published by John Low, No. 139 | Cherry-Street. | 1819. | Price 12½ cents single—one dollar per dozen.
    47 p. [1:] blank; [2:] frontispiece; [3:] title-page; [4:] illustration; [5]-47: songs.
    DLC* ¶ Contains 16 songs.

613 HARDCASTLE'S | ANNUAL | MASONIC REGISTER, | and |
pocket magazine, | for the year of | Masonry, | 5819. | Comprising | a
copious list of the Lodges, Chapters, Encamp- | ments, the Grand Con-
sistory, &c. | Together with | the names of the officers of all the different
grades of | the order of the ancient and honorable fraternity | of Free
and Accepted Masons, assembled in the | city of New-York. | Also, the
alphabetical, [sic] list of the Past Masters of | the different Lodges. |
New-York: | published by Bro. J. Hardcastle. | Southwick & Pelsue,
print. | 1818.

70 p. [1:] blank; [2:] advertisement for Franklin Office, Samuel
Maverick, engraver and copper-plate printer, No. 73 Liberty Strt, New
York; [3:] title-page; [4:] blank; [5]-61: text; [62:] blank; [63:] half-
title: Masonic odes | and | choruses; [64:] blank; [65]-70: songs.

Drake 6512, Shaw 48155 ¶ NHi* ¶ Contains 5 Masonic songs. An
1812 edition (Drake 6351) contains no songs. NHi reports that the
1824 edition mentioned below cannot be located at this time; imprint
and location are cited from Drake 6707. *Later edition:* 637. *Editions
after 1820:* (a) 1822, New York: J. Hardcastle (NHi); (b) 1823, New
York: J. Hardcastle (NHi, NNFM); (c) 1824, New York: J. Hardcastle (NHi).

614 THE | HARP; | or, | songster's companion: | being a choice selec-
tion of sentimen- | tal and entertaining songs. | Rochester: | printed
and sold by E. Peck & Co. | 1819.

50, [2] p. [1:] title-page; [2:] blank; [3]-50: songs; [51]-[52:] index.
Shaw 48168 ¶ NHi* ¶ Contains 43 songs (all indexed).

615 HORAE POETICAE; | or, the | transient murmurs of a solitary
lyre. | Consisting of | poems and songs, | in | English and Scotch. |
By John Burtt. | Enough for me, if, to some feeling breast, | My lines a
secret sympathy impart, | And as their pleasing influence flows confess'd,
| A sigh of soft reflection heave the heart. Gray. | Bridgeton, N. J. |
William Schultz, printer. | 1819.

183, [1] p. [i:] title-page; [ii:] copyright notice, N. J., 30 July 1819,
John Burtt, author; [iii]-vii: preface; [viii:] blank; [ix]-xi: contents;
[xii:] blank; [13]-73: poems; 74-113: songs; 114-158: miscellany; [159:]
blank; [160]-177: notes; [178]-183: glossary; [184:] errata.

Shaw 47474, Wegelin 894 ¶ CSmH, DLC, NN, NcA-S, PPL*,
RPB ¶ Contains 28 songs by Burtt (all indexed).

Masonic odes | and | choruses. [New York, 1819.]
See 613.

616 MELODIES, | SONGS, | sacred songs, | and | national airs. | Con-
taining several never before published | in America. | By Thomas

Moore, Esq. | New-York: | published by A. T. Goodrich & Co. | No. 124 Broadway, opposite the City Hotel. | J. Seymour, printer. | 1819.

1 p.l., xvi, [13]-238 p. [1:] half-title: Moore's poems; [ii:] blank; [i:] engraved title-page: Irish melodies | National airs | songs | and | sacred songs | by | Thomas Moore Esqr | New York | published by A. T. Goodrich & Co | No 124 Broad way; [ii:] blank; [iii:] title-page; [iv:] blank; [v]-ix: preface; [x:] blank; [xi]-xvi: index; [13]-205: Moore's melodies; [206:] blank; [207]-225: sacred songs; [226:] blank; [227]-238: national airs.

Shaw 48740 ¶ MWA*, PPL ¶ Contains 189 songs (all indexed) by Moore. See 574 for a list of editions, also 490 for a list of related imprints.

617 MELODIES, | SONGS, | sacred songs, | and | national airs. | Containing several never before published | in America. | By Thomas Moore, Esq. | New-York: | published by A. T. Goodrich & Co. | No. 124 Broadway, opposite the City Hotel. | J. Seymour, printer. | 1819.

xvi, [13]-256 p. [i:] title-page; [ii:] blank; [iii:] half-title; Moore's poems; [iv:] blank; [v]-ix: preface; [x:] blank; [xi]-xvi: index; [13]-205: Moore's melodies; [206:] blank; [207]-225: sacred songs; [226:] blank; [227]-238: national airs; [239]-256: Moore's Irish melodies.

MH*, MWA ¶ Contains 199 songs (189 indexed) by Moore. The index is that of 613. See 574 for a list of editions; see also 490 for a list of related imprints.

618 THE NEW | FREEMASON'S MONITOR; | or, | Masonic guide. | For the | direction of members of that | ancient and honourable fraternity | as well as | for the information of those, who may be desirous of | becoming acquainted with its principles. | By James Hardie, A. M. | Second edition. | Revised, enlarged, and corrected by the author. | New-York: | printed and published by George Long, | No. 71, Pearl-Street. | 1819.

1 p.l., 346, [1] p. [i:] blank; [ii:] frontispiece; [i:] title-page; [ii:] copyright notice, N. Y., 11 Dec. 1818, George Long, proprietor; [iii:] recommendation; [iv]-xii: preface to the second edition, dated New York, 11 Aug. 1819; [xiii]-xvi: contents; [17]-328: text; [329]-342: Masonic songs; [343]-346: Masonic toasts; [347:] list of the Lodges in the city of New York.

Barthelmess p. 30, Brinley 6728, Morris p. 210, Shaw 48157, Shaw 48847 ¶ DSC (lacks frontispiece), MB, MBFM (lacks frontispiece), MH, MWA, NHi*, NIC, NNFM, OCM, PPPFM (3) ¶ Contains 19 Masonic songs. For an earlier edition, see 577.

619 [THE NEW UNIVERSAL WEEKLY SONG-BOOK. First and second volumes. Philadelphia: H. C. Lewis, 1819.]

No copy located ¶ Advertised 17 May 1819 in the *Literary & musical magazine* as "for sale . . . price 75 cents per volume." According to this advertisement, the work contained "about five hundred fashionable and favorite songs." Apparently a combination of 607 and 630 issued under a different title. See 595 and 607 for a sketch of the history of the first volume of this songster; see also 630 for a sketch of the history of the second volume.

620 POEMS | AND | SONGS, | chiefly in the Scottish dialect. | By Robert Tannahill. | A notice respecting the | life and writings of the author, | is prefixed. | New-York: | published by John Cain. | Broderick & Ritter, printers, | No. 20 James-Street. | 1819.

228 p. [1:] title-page; [2:] blank; [3]-33: notice respecting the life and writings of Robert Tannahill; [34:] blank; [35:] half-title: Miscellaneous poetry; [36:] blank; [37]-130: miscellaneous poetry; [131:] half-title: Songs; [132:] blank; [133]-224: songs; [225]-228: table of contents.

Shaw 49552 ¶ NNC*, NjR ¶ Contains 57 songs, including 2 in the "miscellaneous poetry" section (all indexed) by Tannahill. *Later edition:* 640. *Edition after 1820:* (a) 1821, New York: Nathaniel Smith (MWA).

621 SONGS | FOR THE | NURSERY, | collected from the works | of the | most renowned poets, | and adapted to | favorite melodies. | Hudson: | printed by Ashbel Stoddard. | 1819.

33 p. [1:] title-page; [2:] blank; [3]-33: songs.

Shaw 49457, Welch 1238.3 ¶ MB* ¶ Contains 115 juvenile songs. See 428 for an earlier edition.

622 [THE SONGSTER'S MAGAZINE; (published in numbers) designed to contain a choice selection of the most approved patriotic, comic, sentimental, amatory and naval songs; both ancient and modern.] N°. 4. | Containing | thirty-six songs for 12 1-2 cents. | [a list of 38 songs in two columns] | [New-York: published and sold by J. B. Jansen, No. 15 Chatham-Street. Broderick & Ritter, printers. 1819.]

1 p.l., 73-96 p. [i:] title-page; [ii:] copyright notice, N. Y., 20 Aug. 1818, David Carlisle, proprietor, and notice "to publishers" from E. Riley, No. 20, Chatham-Street, with a list of his copyrights; 73-96: songs.

RPB* (imperfect) ¶ Contains 38 songs (all indexed). The only copy known lacks all of the title-page with the exception of the table of contents and its numeration, as indicated above. Cf. 589 and 590; see also 647.

623 [THE SONGSTER'S MAGAZINE; (published in numbers) designed to contain a choice selection of the most approved patriotic, comic, sentimental, amatory and naval songs; both ancient and modern.] N° 5. | Containing | thirty-six songs for 12 1-2 cents. | [a list of 37

songs in two columns] | [New-York: published and sold by J. B. Jansen, No. 15 Chatham-Street. Broderick & Ritter, printers. 1819.]

1 p.l., 97-120 p. [i:] title-page; [ii:] copyright notice, N. Y., 20 Aug. 1818, David Carlisle, proprietor, and notice "to publishers" from E. Riley, No. 29, Chatham-Street, with a list of his copyrights; 97-120: songs.

RPB* (imperfect) ¶ Contains 37 songs (all indexed). The only copy known lacks all of the title-page with the exception of the table of contents and its numeration, as indicated above. Cf. 589 and 590; see also 647.

624 [THE SONGSTER'S MAGAZINE; (published in numbers) designed to contain a choice selection of the most approved patriotic, comic, sentimental, amatory and naval songs; both ancient and modern.] | Nọ 6. | Containing | thirty-nine songs for 12 1-2 cents.] | [a list of 39 songs in two columns] | [New York: published and sold by J. B. Jansen, No. 15 Chatham-Street. Broderick & Ritter, printers. 1819.]

1 p.l., 121-144 p. [i:] title-page; [ii:] copyright notice, N. Y., 20 Aug. 1818, David Carlisle, proprietor, and notice "to publishers" from E. Riley, No. 29, Chatham-Street, with a list of his copyrights; 121-144: songs.

RPB* (imperfect) ¶ Contains 39 songs (all indexed). The only copy known lacks all of the title-page with the exception of the table of contents and its numeration, as indicated above. Cf. 589 and 590; see also 647.

625 [THE SONGSTER'S MAGAZINE; (published in numbers) designed to contain a choice selection of the most approved patriotic, comic, sentimental, amatory and naval songs; both ancient and modern.] | Nọ 7. | Containing | thirty-nine songs for 12 1-2 cents. | [a list of 40 songs in two columns] | [New-York: published and sold by J. B. Jansen, No. 15 Chatham-Street. Broderick & Ritter, printers. 1819.]

1 p.l., 24 p. [i:] title-page; [ii:] copyright notice, N. Y., 20 Aug. 1818, David Carlisle, proprietor, and notice "to publishers" from E. Riley, No. 29, Chatham-Street, with a list of his copyrights; 1-24: songs.

RPB* (imperfect) ¶ Contains 40 songs (all indexed). The only copy known lacks all of the title-page with the exception of the table of contents and its numeration, as indicated above. Cf. 589 and 590; see also 648.

626 [THE SONGSTER'S MAGAZINE; (published in numbers) designed to contain a choice selection of the most approved patriotic, comic, sentimental, amatory and naval songs; both ancient and modern.] | Nọ 8. | Containing | thirty-seven songs for 12 1-2 cents. | [a list of 38 songs in two columns] | New-York: | published and sold by J. B. Jansen, No. 15 Chatham-Street. | Broderick & Ritter, printers. 1819.

1 p.l., 25-48 p. [i:] title-page; [ii:] copyright notice, N. Y., 20 Aug. 1818, David Carlisle, proprietor, and notice "to publishers" from E. Riley, No. 29, Chatham-Street, with a list of his copyrights; 25-48: songs.

RPB* (imperfect) ¶ Contains 38 songs (all indexed). The only copy known lacks all of the title-page except for the bottom half, as indicated above. Cf. 589 and 590; see also 648.

627 [THE SONGSTER'S MAGAZINE; (published in numbers) designed to contain a choice selection of the most approved patriotic, comic, sentimental, amatory and naval songs; both ancient and modern. No 9. New-York: published and sold by J. B. Jansen, No. 15 Chatham-Street. Broderick & Ritter, printers. 1819.]
    1 p.l., 49-72 p.
No copy located ¶ Collation and pagination inferred from earlier numbers. Cf. 589 and 590; see also 648.

628 [THE SONGSTER'S MUSEUM. Intended to be the cheapest and most valuable collection of songs ever published in America. New York, 1819.]
    Lowens U113, Sonneck Copyright ¶ No copy located ¶ Copyright N. Y., 8 Feb. 1819, A[ngus] Umphraville, author. Existence doubtful.

629 THE | SONGSTER'S | POCKET COMPANION, | or | gentlemen and ladies' | vocal museum: | being a selection of the most elegant | and fashionable | modern songs. | New-Haven: | printed and published by | A. H. Maltby & Co. | No. 4, Glebe Building, Chapel-Street. | 1819.
    96 p. [1:] title-page; [2:] blank; [3]-96: songs.
    Sabin 86958, Shaw 49458, Woodall 160 ¶ DLC*, NN, RPB ¶ Contains 99 songs.

630 [THEATRICAL WEEKLY SONG-BOOK. Philadelphia: H. C. Lewis, 1819.]
No copy located ¶ Advertised 18 Jan. 1819 in the *Lady's & gentleman's weekly literary museum, and musical magazine* as "now publishing . . . each no. contains about 12 or 14 songs as sung at the Olympic and new theatre, this season, and one or two pages of favourite music—subscription price 25 cts. per month, or four nos. bound gratis every quarter, in pocket size volumes." This would appear to be a second volume of *The weekly song book* (607), since the same advertisement states that "the first volume of this work, bound in two books, is for sale, price 87½ cts. each book, which contains about 200 miscellaneous songs—but no music." Publication apparently began on 1 Jan. 1819, according to a notice in the periodical for that date which states that "all the songs in the English language, except the immoral,

viz. American, English, Irish, and Scotch, are now publishing by sub-sbription [sic]." The entire notice is worth quoting:

Plan.—The work to be published weekly, in uniform parts, or numbers; each part to contain at least 16 duodecimo pages, averaging from 14 to 17 songs a week.

New and popular songs always to receive the first attention.

Any subscriber requesting a favorite song, to be accommodated by its insertion as soon as possible.

Terms.—The work shall be handsomely printed, with new type, and on good paper.

A number shall contain at least 14 songs, and be done up in neat printed covers, and delivered every Saturday to subscribers at the following rates:

Per month, or 4 numbers, 25 cts. in advance,

Per quarter, or 13 numbers, 75 cents in advance.

The binding.—Every 3 or 6 months, the numbers are bound gratis for all subscribers who pay quarterly in advance.—All others can have their numbers bound for a very trifling expense, by applying to the publisher.

Agents entitled to one copy gratis, for every five subscribers obtained.

H. C. Lewis

No. 272 Market Street, or

No. 164 South Eleventh Street, Philadelphia

It would seem that the volume was completed, but together with 607, Lewis chose to give the set still a different name: *The new universal weekly song-book* (see 619). See 595 for a sketch of the earlier history of this songster.

631 THE TRUE | MASONIC CHART, | or | hieroglyphic monitor; | containing | all the emblems explained | in the degrees of | Entered Apprentice, Fellow-Craft, Master | Mason, Mark Master, Past Master, | Most Excellent Master, Royal | Arch, Royal Master, and | Select Master: | designed, and duly arranged, agreeably to the | lectures | by R. W. Jeremy L. Cross, G. L. | To which are added, | illustrations, charges, songs, &c. | New-Haven: | Flagg & Gray, printers. | Engravings by A. Doolittle. | 1819.

[xii] p., 40 engraved pl., [5]-172 p. [i:] title-page; [ii:] copyright notice, Conn., 24 Dec. 1819, Jeremy L. Cross, author; [iii:] dedication; [iv:] blank; [v]-[vii:] preface; [vii:] errata note; [viii:] blank; [ix]-[xii:] introduction; pl. [1], verso: recommendations; pl. [2], recto: additional title-page: The true | Masonic chart | or | hieroglyphic monitor | containing | all the emblems explained | in the degrees of | Entered Apprentice, Fellow Craft, Master Mason, | Mark Master, Past Master, Most Excellent Master, | Royal Arch, Royal Master and Select Master. | Designed and duly arranged | agreeable to the lectures | by | R. W.

Jeremy L. Cross, G. L. | To which are added | illustrations, charges, songs &c. | Engraved and printed for the author | by Comp. A. Doolittle New Haven, | 1819; pl. [3]-40: engravings; [5]-164: text; [165]-172: Masonic songs.

Barthelmess pp. 30-31, Brinley 6720, Shaw 47753, Woodall 130 ¶ CSmH, Ct, CtY, DSC*, IaCrM, MBFM, MH, MiD-B, NIC, NNFM, NdFM, OCM; London (British Library) ¶ Contains 7 Masonic songs. Shaw gives pagination incorrectly as 354 p. *Later edition:* 649. *Editions after 1820:* (a) 1824, 3rd ed., New Haven: the author; (DLC, DSC, MBFM, NNFM); (b) 1826, 4th ed., New Haven: the author (CtY, DSC, MB, MBFM, MHi, PHi); (c) 1845, 5th ed., New York: the author (DSC); (d) 1846, 6th ed., New York: the author (DLC, DSC, MB, MBFM, RPB); (e) 1850, 12th ed., New York: the author (DSC, MBFM); (f) 1851, 16th ed., New York: the author (DLC, DSC, MBFM, NN, PU); (g) 1854, 12th ed., New York: A. S. Barnes & Co. (DSC, MBFM, MH); (h) 1855, 12th ed., New York: A. S. Barnes & Co. (MBFM); (i) 1856, 12th ed., New York: A. S. Barnes & Co. (DSC, MBFM); (j) 1857, 12th ed., New York: A. S. Barnes & Co. (MBFM); (k) 1858, 12th ed., New York: A. S. Barnes & Co. (MBFM); (l) 1859, New York: S. A. Rollo & Co. (DSC, NN); (m) 1860, Philadelphia: Moss, Brother & Co. (DSC); (n) 1863, Philadelphia: Moss & Co. (DSC, NN).

1820

632 THE | AEOLIAN HARP, | or | songster's cabinet; | being | a selection of the most popular | songs and recitations; | patriotic, sentimental, humorous, &c. | In two volumes. | Vol. I. | Published by | R. & W. A. Bartow, | New-York, | 1820.

124, [4] p. [i:] title-page; [ii:] blank; [iii]-iv: preface; [5]-96: songs; [97]-124: recitations; [125]-[128:] index.

Shoemaker 41 ¶ PPL*, TxU ¶ Contains 83 songs (all indexed). A later edition of 532, q.v. for a list of editions.

633 THE | AEOLIAN HARP, | or | songster's cabinet; | being | a selection of the most popular | songs and recitations; | patriotic, sentimental, humorous, &c. | In two volumes. | Vol. II. | Published by | R. & W. A. Bartow, | New-York, | 1820.

124, [4] p. [1:] title-page; [2:] blank; [3]-98: songs; [99]-124: recitations; [125]-[128:] index.

Shoemaker 41 ¶ PPL*, TxU ¶ Contains 80 songs (all indexed). A later edition of 533, q.v. for a list of editions.

634 THE | AEOLIAN HARP, | or | songster's cabinet; | being | a selection of the most popular | songs and recitations; | patriotic, senti-

mental, humorous, &c. | Published by | R. & W. A. Bartow, | New-York. | 1820.

124, [4] p. [1:] title-page; [2:] blank; [3]-98: songs; [99]-124: recitations; [125]-[128:] index.

MWA* ¶ Contains 80 songs (all indexed). Identical to 633, except that the songster is no longer called "Vol. II." See 533 for a list of editions.

635 THE | AMERICAN LADIES | POCKET BOOK | 1820 | Published by | A. Small, Phila. | 1820.

2 p.l., 180 p. [i:] blank; [ii:] frontispiece; [iii:] title-page; [iv:] blank; [1:] contents; [2:] blank; [3:] common notes, &c.; [4:] blank; [5]-139: text; 139-146: songs; 147-172: text, continued; 173-174: new country dances and waltzes for 1820; [175]-180: tables.

Drake 11218, Shaw 46989 ¶ MWA*, NHi, RPB ¶ Contains 12 songs. See 120 for a list of editions.

636 THE | BLACKBIRD; | consisting of | a complete collection | of the most admired | modern songs. | New-York: | published by Christian Brown, | bookseller, bookbinder, and stationer, | No. 290 Water-Street. | Broderick & Ritter, printers, 20 James-St. | 1820.

140, [4] p. [1:] title-page; [2:] blank; [3]-140: songs; [141]-[144:] index.

Shoemaker 497 ¶ CtHT-W, DLC*, MH ¶ Contains 128 songs (all indexed). Identical in content to 410, but with the index set from new type and the text partly reset. See 318 for a list of editions.

637 HARDCASTLE'S | ANNUAL | MASONIC REGISTER, | and | pocket magazine. | For the year of | Masonry, | 5820, | comprising a copious list of the | Lodges, Chapters, Encampments, the | Grand Consistory, &c. | Together with | the names of the officers of all the different grades | of the order of the ancient and honourable | Free and Accepted Masons, assembled in | the city of New-York. | Also, a list of the Past Masters of the different | Lodges. | New-York: | published by Bro. J. Hardcastle. | D. McDuffee, printer, 1 Murray-St. | 1820.

[3]-48, [41]-110 p. [3:] title-page; [4:] blank; [5]-8: officers of the Grand Lodge; [9]-32: rectos, the almanac; versos, an article entitled "The State of Masonry"; [33]-48: text and list of Lodges; [41]-64: text; [65:] half-title: Refreshment! Pleasing & entertaining songs for Lodges and other places of moral amusement; [66:] enigmatic problems; [67]-76: songs; [77:] additional title-page: The | Masonic museum, | being a collection of | songs, | suitable to be sung in | Masonic Lodges | and other places of moral amusement. | Published by Brother J. Hardcastle. | 1820; 78-108: songs; [109]-110: index.

Drake 6550, Shoemaker 1510 ¶ NHi* ¶ Pp. 34-35 are misnumbered 33-34; p. 38 is misnumbered 40. Signature 6 (which should be numbered 49-56) is misnumbered [41]-48, repeating the numbering of Signature 5-2, and the remainder of the volume continues this erroneous numbering. The book therefore contains 118 pages even though the final page is numbered 110. Contains 40 songs (all indexed), 30 of which are in 517 and two of which are in German. See 613 for a complete list of editions.

The | Masonic museum, | being a collection of | songs, | suitable to be sung in | Masonic lodges | and other places of moral amusement. | Published by Brother J. Hardcastle. | 1820.
     See 637.

638 THE | MELODIST, | comprising | a selection | of the most favourite | English, Scotch, and Irish | songs, | arranged for the voice, flute, or violin. | By G. S. Thornton. | New-York: | published by George Singleton | at the office of the Ladies' Literary Cabinet, 194 Greenwich-Street. | Printed by Broderick and Ritter, | No. 2 Dey-Street. | 1820.
     vi, [3]-258 p. [i:] title page; [ii:] copyright notice, N. Y., 21 Feb. 1820, George Singleton, proprietor; [iii]-vi: index; [3]-258: songs; 258: at foot of page: End of Vol. I.
     Sonneck Copyright, Wolfe 9367 ¶ ICN*, PBL ¶ Contains 122 songs (all indexed), all with musical notation or reference to musical notation. See 639 for a related edition containing a second volume. *Editions after 1820:* (a) 1824, New York: W. & P. C. Smith (DLC, MWA, NN, PPL, RPB); (b) n.d., New York: Robert B. Simms & Co. (DLC).

639 THE | MELODIST, | comprising | a selection | of the most favourite | English, Scotch, and Irish | songs, | arranged for the voice, flute, or violin. | By G. S. Thornton. | New-York: | published by George Singleton | at the office of the Ladies' Literary Cabinet, 194 Greenwich-Street. | Printed by Broderick and Ritter, | No. 2 Dey-Street. | 1820.
     vi, [3]-258, 120 p. [i:] title-page; [ii:] copyright notice, N. Y., 21 Feb. 1820, George Singleton, proprietor; [iii]-vi: index; [3]-258: songs; 258: at foot of page: End of Vol. I; [1]-120: songs.
     Shoemaker 3435 ¶ DLC, MH, MWA*, N ¶ Contains 166 songs (122 indexed), all with musical notation or reference to musical notation. All known copies lack pp. 19-34 and 8 of the indexed songs found there; the second volume adds 51 songs. It is doubtful that this imprint appeared before 1821 at the earliest, but it is included here because of the 1820 date on the title-page of the first volume. Apparently Vol. II was issued in separate numbers. MWA has copies of Vol. II, 1 and 3, with a separate imprint for each:
          No. 1—Vol. II. | The melodist, . . . [as above] | By George Singleton. | New-York: | published by Samuel Huestis, | No. 284 1-2 Pearl-Street. | 1821.
          No. 3.—Vol. II. | Price 18 3-4 cents. | The melodist, . . . [as

above] | Conditions. | Each number shall contain twenty-four pages, eleven of which will make | a volume corresponding exactly with the first. | Persons residing out of the city must pay for the volume in advance, which | will be two dollars. | A title page and index will accompany the last number. | New-York: | published by Samuel Huestis, | No. 284 1–2 Pearl-Street. | Myers & Smith, printers. | 1821.

Apparently Vol. II was never completed. See 638 for an earlier edition and a list of post-1820 editions.

640 POEMS | AND | SONGS, | chiefly in the Scottish dialect. | By Robert Tannahill, | author of "Jessie of the Flower of Dumblane," and other celebrated lyrics. | To which is prefixed, | an account of his life and writings. | New-York: | published by Robert W. Mackie, | No. 5 Chatham-Row. | Broderick & Ritter, printers, 2 Dey-St. | 1820.

228 p. [1:] title-page; [2:] blank; [3]–33: notice respecting the life and writings of Robert Tannahill; [34:] blank; [35:] half-title: Miscellaneous poetry; [36:] blank; [37]–130: text; [131:] half-title: Songs; [132:] blank; [133]–224: songs; [225]–228: contents.

Shoemaker 3383 ¶ DLC*, MSa, MSaE, PHi, PP, PPiU, TNJ ¶ Contains 55 songs in the section so-named, 2 additional songs in the poetry section (all indexed). See 620 for a list of editions.

641 [THE POST-CHAISE COMPANION, or magazine of wit. By Carlo Convivio Socio, Jun'r. 1st ed. Philadelphia, before 1821.]

Lowens U113 ¶ No copy located ¶ Existence inferred from Edition (a) which contains 39 songs. Editions (b), (c), and (d) give as the author "Clio Convivius Socio, Fellow of the Academy of Humouristi," contain no songs, and bear the title: The post-chaise companion, *and* magazine of wit. *Editions after 1820:* (a) 1821, 2nd ed., Philadelphia (DLC); (b) 1828, 2nd ed. with corrections and additions, Baltimore (DLC) [contains no songs]; (c) 1830, 3rd ed., Baltimore (RPB) [contains no songs]; (d) 1831, 4th ed., Baltimore (MdHi) [contains no songs].

642 SONGS | FOR | GENTLEMEN, | patriotic, comic, and descriptive. | Sidney's Press. | Published by John Babcock & Son, New-Haven, | and S. & W. R. Babcock, Charleston. | 1820.

2 p.l., 156, [4] p. [i:] blank; [ii:] frontispiece; [iii:] title-page; [iv:] blank; 1–156: songs; [157]–[160:] index.

Shoemaker 3272 ¶ DLC (imperfect), MWA*, OC, RPB ¶ Contains 107 songs (all indexed). See 586 for an earlier edition.

643 SONGS | FOR | LADIES, | lively, pathetic, and sentimental. | Sidney's Press. | Published by John Babcock & Son, New-Haven, | and S. & W. R. Babcock, Charleston. | 1820.

2 p.l., 154, [6] p. [i:] blank; [ii:] frontispiece; [iii:] title-page; [iv:] blank; [1]-154; songs; [155]-[160:] index.

Shoemaker 3273 ¶ CtY, MH (imperfect), MWA* ¶ Contains 152 songs (all indexed). *Edition after 1820:* (a) 1825, New Haven: Sidney's Press (DLC, MWA, RPB).

644 [THE SONGSTER'S MAGAZINE; (published in numbers) designed to contain a choice selection of the most approved patriotic, comic, sentimental, amatory and naval songs; both ancient and modern. No. 10. New-York: published and sold by J. B. Jansen, No. 15 Chatham-Street. Broderick & Ritter, printers. 1820.]

1 p.l., 73-96 p.

No copy located ¶ Collation and pagination inferred from earlier numbers. Cf. 589 and 590; see also 648.

645 [THE SONGSTER'S MAGAZINE; (published in numbers) designed to contain a choice selection of the most approved patriotic, comic, sentimental, amatory and naval songs; both ancient and modern. No. 11. New-York: published and sold by J. B. Jansen, No. 15 Chatham-Street. Broderick & Ritter, printers. 1820.]

1 p.l., 97-120 p.

No copy located ¶ Collation and pagination inferred from earlier numbers. Cf. 589 and 590; see also 648.

646 [THE SONGSTER'S MAGAZINE; (published in numbers) designed to contain a choice selection of the most approved patriotic, comic, sentimental, amatory and naval songs; both ancient and modern. No. 12. New-York: published and sold by J. B. Jansen, No. 15 Chatham-Street. Broderick & Ritter, printers. 1820.]

1 p.l., 121-144 p.

No copy located ¶ Collation and pagination inferred from earlier numbers. Cf. 589 and 590; see also 648.

647 THE | SONGSTER'S MAGAZINE, | a choice selection | of the most approved | patriotic, comic, sentimental, | amatory and naval | songs, | both ancient and modern. | Vol. I. | New-York: | published and sold by J. B. Jansen, | No. 15 Chatham-Street. | 1820.

xii, 144 p. [i:] title-page; [ii:] prefatory note: The first twelve numbers of The songster's magazine, is [sic] now published, and for sale singly, or neatly bound in one or two volumes; forming a valuable pocket companion for the admirers of vocal music. This volume contains six numbers. At foot of page: Broderick & Ritter, printers, No. 20, James-Street; [iii]-vii: title index; [viii]-xii: first-line index; 1-144: songs.

Sabin 86951, Shoemaker 3274 ¶ DLC* (imperfect) ¶ Contains 218 songs (220 indexed). A gathering, with a new title-page and prefatory matter, of 589, 590, 591, 622, 623, and 624, issued serially in 1818-19. The only copy known lacks pp. 95-96.

648 THE | SONGSTER'S MAGAZINE, | a | choice selection | of the most approved | patriotic, comic, sentimental, | amatory, and naval | songs, | both ancient and modern. | Vol. II. | New-York: | published and sold by J. B. Jansen, | No. 15 Chatham-Street. | 1820.

xii, 144 p. [i:] title-page; [ii:] prefatory note: The first twelve numbers of The songster's magazine, is [sic] now published, and for sale singly, or neatly bound in one or two volumes; forming a valuable pocket companion for the admirers of vocal music. This volume contains six numbers. At foot of page: Broderick & Ritter, printers, No. 20, James-Street; [iii]-vii: title index; [viii]-xii: first-line index; 1-144: songs.

Sabin 86951, Shoemaker 3274 ¶ DLC* ¶ Contains 225 songs (226 indexed). A gathering, with a new title-page and prefatory matter, of 625, 626, 627, 644, 645, and 646, issued serially in 1819-20.

649 THE TRUE | MASONIC CHART, | or | hieroglyphic monitor; | containing | all the emblems explained | in the degrees of | Entered Apprentice, Fellow-Craft, Master | Mason, Mark Master, Past Master, | Most Excellent Master, Royal | Arch, Royal Master, and | Select Master: | designed, and duly arranged, agreeably to the | lectures | by | R. W. Jeremy L. Cross, G. L. | To which are added, | illustrations, charges, songs, &c. | Second edition. | New-Haven: | John C. Gray, printer. | Engravings by Companion A. Doolittle. | 1820.

2 p.l., 14, [2] p., 44 engraved pl., [13]-196 p. [i:] blank; [ii:] frontispiece; [iii:] title-page; [iv:] copyright notice, Conn., 24 Dec. 1819, Jeremy L. Cross, author; [1:] blank; [2:] illustration; [3:] dedication; [4:] blank; [5]-6: preface; [7]-9: introduction; [10]-14: recommendations; [15]-[16]: blank; pl. [1], verso: frontispiece; pl. [2], recto: additional title-page: The true | Masonic chart | or | hieroglyphic monitor | containing | all the emblems explained | in the degrees of | Entered Apprentice, Fellow Craft, Master Mason, | Mark Master, Past Master, Most Excellent Master, | Royal Arch, Royal Master and Select Master. | Designed and duly arranged | agreeable to the lectures | by | R. W. Jeremy L. Cross, G. L. | To which are added | illustrations, charges, songs &c. | Second edition. | Engraved and printed for the author | by Comp. A. Doolittle New Haven. | 1820; pl. 3-44: engravings by A. Doolittle; [13]-186: text; [187]-196: songs.

Barthelmess pp. 30-31, Shoemaker 916 ¶ CSmH, CtHi, CtW, DLC*, DSC (2), IaCrM, MBFM, MLy, MWA (2 copies, 1 imperfect), MWHi, MiD-B, MiU-C, NIC, NN, NNFM, NdFM, OCM, PPPFM (3), PPL, RPB, WMFM ¶ Contains 8 Masonic songs. See 631 for an earlier edition and a list of editions published after 1820.

GEOGRAPHICAL DIRECTORY
OF PRINTERS, PUBLISHERS, BOOKSELLERS,
ENGRAVERS, &c.

References are to entry numbers

CONNECTICUT

Hartford

1813	Hale & Hosmer, printers	451
1815	Sheldon & Goodwin, printers	
	J. F. & C. Starr, stereotypers	497
1816	B. & J. Russell, printers and publishers	525
1818	Hale & Hosmer, printers	581

Litchfield

1808	Hosmer & Goodwin, printers	354

Middletown

1790	M. H. Woodward, printer	56

New Haven

1786	Daniel Bowen, in Chapel Street, printer	
	Amos Doolittle, engraver	41
1798	George Bunce, printer	142
1802		226
1802		228
1812	Sidney's Press, printers	
	Increase Cooke & Co., Church-Street, publishers and booksellers	426
1812	Sidney's Press, printers	
	Increase Cooke & Co., Church-Street, publishers and booksellers	429
1817	Sidney's Press, printers	549
1818	Sidney's Press, printers	
	John Babcock and Son, publishers	579
1818	Sidney's Press, printers	
	J. Babcock & Son, publishers	586
1818	Sidney's Press, printers	
	J. Babcock & Son, publishers	587
1819	A. H. Maltby & Co., No. 4, Glebe Building, Chapel-Street, printers and publishers	629
1819	Flagg & Gray, printers	
	A. Doolittle, engraver and printer	631
1820	Sidney's Press, printers	
	John W. Babcock & Son, publishers	642
1820	Sidney's Press, printers	
	John W. Babcock & Son, publishers	643
1820	John C. Gray, printer	
	A. Doolittle, engraver	649

New London

1792 Samuel Green, printer	84
1797 [Charles Holt, printer and bookseller]	137
1800 James Springer, printer	192

Norwich

1798 J. Trumbull, a few rods west from the Court-House, printer, publisher, and bookseller	163

Suffield

1798	143
1800 Swann and Ely, printers	
A. Ely, engraver	203

Windham

1813 Samuel Webb, printer	445
1813 Samuel Webb, printer	453

DELAWARE

Wilmington

1797 [Peter Brynberg, printer]	119
1797 James Wilson, No. 5, High-Street, opposite the Upper Market-House, publisher and bookseller	
Bonsal and Niles, booksellers	132
1797 Bonsal and Niles, in Market-Street, printers and booksellers	
James Wilson, bookseller	133
1800 Bonsal and Niles, printers and booksellers	183
1804 Bonsal and Niles, printers and booksellers	270
1815 R. Porter, printer and bookseller	496
1816 J. Wilson, No. 105, Market Street, printer and bookseller	527
1816 J. Wilson, No. 105, Market Street, printer and bookseller	528
1817 J. Wilson, No. 105, Market Street, printer and bookseller	557
1817 J. Wilson, No. 105, Market Street, printer and bookseller	558
1818 R. Porter, printer and bookseller	570

DISTRICT OF COLUMBIA

Washington

1812 D. Rapine's book store, publisher	423a
1812 W. Cooper, printer and publisher	430
1816 W. Cooper, publisher	516
1816 W. Cooper, publisher	529
1817 Daniel Rapine, printer	552
1818 W. Cooper, publisher	594

KENTUCKY

Lexington
1808 Daniel Bradford, at the office of the Kentucky Gazette, on Main-
      Street, printer   349
1818 Worsley & Smith, printers   572

LOUISIANA

New Orleans
1809 Th. Lamberte, printer   359

MAINE

Augusta
1805 Peter Edes, printer   314
1811 Peter Edes, printer   394

Hallowell
1805 Ezekiel Goodale, publisher and bookseller   314
1811 Ezekiel Goodale, at the Hallowell Bookstore, sign of the Bible,
      publisher and bookseller   394

MARYLAND

Baltimore
1794 Keatinge's book-store, Market-Street, bookseller and publisher   83
1795 [Keatinge's book-store, bookseller and publisher]   90
1795 [Keatinge's book-store, bookseller and publisher]   95
1797 W. Pechin, printer
      George Keatinge's book-store, bookseller and publisher   126
1798 [Henry S. Keatinge, No. 148 Balt. Street, publisher]   140
1798 [Henry S. Keatinge, No. 148 Balt. Street, publisher]   151
1798 Henry S. Keatinge, publisher   156
1798 [Henry S. Keatinge, No. 148 Balt. Street, publisher]   159
1798 [S. Sower, 67, Market-Street, printer]
      [S. Sower's book-store, in Fayette-Street, bookseller]
      [Thomas, Andrews and Butler, booksellers]   161
1798 [H. S. Keatinge, publisher]   162
1798   166
1799 Warner & Hanna, No. 2, North Gay-Street, printers and booksellers   168
1799 Warner & Hanna, printers
      Thomas, Andrews, & Butler, publishers   169
1799 J. Rice, bookseller   170

1799	[Thomas Dobbin, printer and bookseller]	
	[Samuel Sower, Fayette-Street, bookseller]	181
1800	Bonsal & Niles, No. 173, Market-Street, booksellers	183
1800	Warner & Hanna, No. 2, North Gay-Street, printers and booksellers	185
1800	Bonsal & Niles, No. 173, Market-Street, printers and booksellers	190
1800	Warner & Hanna, corner of Market and South Gay Streets, printers	210
1801	Keatinge's book store, publisher	214
1801	George Fryer, printer	222
1802	G. Fryer, printer	229
1804	Sower & Cole, printers and booksellers	
	Samuel Butler, bookseller	267
1804	Bonsal & Niles, No. 192, Market-Street, booksellers	270
1804		280
1805	Cole and Hewes, printers	
	S. Butler, publisher	289
1805	G. Dobbin & Murphy, Market-Street, within one door of the bridge, printers	292
1805	Warner & Hanna, corner of South Gay & Market-Streets, printers	301
1805	Warner & Hanna, corner of South Gay & Market-Streets, printers	302
1805	Warner & Hanna, corner of South Gay & Market-Streets, printers	311
1806	[G. Dobbin & Murphy, publishers]	319
1807	[Fry & Rider, publishers]	340
1809	Coale & Thomas, publishers	
	Jean W. Butler, printer	360
1809	Warner & Hanna, printers and booksellers	361
1809	Warner & Hanna, printers and booksellers	363
1810	Geo. Dobbin and Murphy, 10 Baltimore-Street, printers	370
1812	William Warner, printer and bookseller	405
1812	William Warner, printer and bookseller	407
1812	William Warner, at the Bible and Heart office, printer and bookseller	411
1812	F. Lucas, Jun'r, publisher	
	B. W. Sower & Co., printers	413
1812	F. Lucas, Jun'r, publisher	
	B. W. Sower & Co., printers	414
1812	F. Lucas, Jun'r, publishers	
	B. W. Sower & Co., printers	415
1812	F. Lucas, Jun'r, publisher	
	B. W. Sower & Co., printers	416
1812	F. Lucas, Jun'r, publisher	
	B. W. Sower & Co., printers	417
1812	F. Lucas, Jun'r, publisher	
	B. W. Sower & Co., printers	418
1812	J. and T. Vance, publishers	
	J. Cole, publisher	
	G. Dobbin & Murphy, printers	419
1812	Warner & Hanna, printers and booksellers	
	John & Thomas Vance, booksellers	422
1812	F. Lucas, Jun., 136 Market-St., publisher	
	G. Dobbin & Murphy, printers	423
1813		442

1813		449
1814		480
1815		484
1816	[Samuel Jefferis,] No. 212 Market Street, corner Decatur Street printer and bookseller	507
1816		508
1816		513
1816	William Warner, corner of South Gay and Market-Streets, printer	519
1816		524
1816	William Warner, printer and bookseller	530
1816		531
1817	F. Lucas, Jun'r, publisher	538
1817	F. Lucas, Jun'r, publisher	539
1817	Fielding Lucas, Jun'r, 138 Market Street, publisher Pomeroy & Toy, printers	540
1817	Benjamin Edes, printer and publisher	541

Fredericktown
1814	M. E. Bartgis, printer	476

Hagerstown
1814	John Gruber and Daniel May, printers	475

MASSACHUSETTS

Andover
1816	Flagg & Gould, printers	511
1818	Flagg and Gould, printers	568

Boston
1750	[Fleet]	2
1768	W. M'Alpine, in Marlborough-Street, printer and bookseller	16
1768	[Mein & Fleeming]	17
1771	[John Boyle, in Marlborough-Street, printer]	21
1771	[William M'Alpine, in Marlborough-Street, printer and bookseller]	22
1772	William M'Alpine, in Marlborough-Street, printer and bookseller	23
1788	Isaiah Thomas and Co., booksellers	47
1793	Thomas & Andrews, Faust's Statue, No. 45, Newbury Street, printers	72
1794	N. Coverly, printer and bookseller	85
1794	J. Bumstead, printer E. Larkin, Cornhill, publisher	86
1795	William Spotswood, No. 55, Marlborough-Street, bookseller	89
1795	[E. Russell, near Liberty-Pole, printer and bookseller]	93
1795	[Samuel Hall, No. 53, Cornhill, printer and bookseller]	104
1795	J. White, near Charles-River Bridge, printer and bookseller W. T. Clap, in Fish-Street, bookseller	107
1796	J. White, near Charles' River Bridge, printer C. Cambridge, printer	111

1797	J. White, near Charles'-River Bridge, printer and bookseller	135
1798	Spotswood and Etheridge, printers and booksellers	149
1798	J. Bumstead, printer	
	E. Larkin, Cornhill, publisher	150
1798	J. White, near Charles-River Bridge, printer and bookseller	155
1798	[John W. Folsom, publisher]	157
1798	John W. Folsom, No. 30, Union-Street, printer and bookseller	158
1799	Nathaniel Coverly, printer and bookseller	173
1800	J. White, near Charles-River Bridge, printer	195
1800	S. Hall, Cornhill, printer	198
1801	J. White, near Charles-River Bridge, printer and bookseller	215
1801		220
1802	J. White, near Charles-River Bridge, printer	233
1802	John M. Dunham, printer	239
1803	Gilbert and Dean, No. 56, State-Street, printers	254
1803	Nathaniel Coverly, printer and bookseller	263
1804	E. Lincoln, printer	276
1805	Harrison & Hall, Mill Bridge, booksellers	295
1805	David Carlisle, Cambridge Street, printer	
	William Tileston Clap, No. 88, Fish-Street, publisher	313
1806	Thomas Fleet, in Cornhill, printer and bookseller	326
1807	Snelling and Simons, No. 5, Exchange Buildings, Devonshire Street, printers	335
1807	Russell & Cutler, publishers	
	Etheridge & Bliss, No. 12, Cornhill, booksellers	339
1807	Ephraim C. Beals, No. 10, State Street, publisher	343
1808	Joshua Cushing, No. 79, State Street, printer	347
1808	Thomas Fleet, No. 5, Cornhill, printer	352
1808	Wm. Blagrove, No. 61, Cornhill, publisher and bookseller	
	E. C. Beals, printer	353
1809	Russell and Cutler, Congress-Street, printers and booksellers	367
1810	J. White, near Charles' River Bridge, printer and bookseller	373
1810	Samuel Avery, No. 10 State-Street, printer	375
1810	Buckingham & Titcomb, Winter-Street, printers and booksellers	379
1811	J. T. Buckingham, printer	383
1811	J. Belcher, Congress-Street, printer and publisher	
	J. W. Burditt and Co., Court Street	403
1812	N. Coverly, Jun., Corner of Theatre Alley, printer	424
1812	N. Coverly, Jun., Corner of Theatre Alley, printer	425
1812	J. T. Buckingham, Winter-Street, printer and bookseller	432
1812	J. Belcher, printer and publisher	433
1813	Hans Lund, printer	439
1813	Charles Williams, No. 8, State-Street, publisher and bookseller	
	E. G. House, Court-Street, printer	443
1813	C. Williams, publisher	
	E. G. House, Court-Street, printer	444
1813	N. Coverly, Milk-Street, printer	447
1813	Thomas Wells, bookseller	450
1815	J. T. Buckingham, No. 5, Marlborough-Street, printer and bookseller	485

1815	J. T. Buckingham, No. 5, Marlborough-Street, printer and bookseller	486
1815	Thomas Brown, printer	501
1815	Joseph T. Buckingham, printer and bookseller	502
1816	Wells & Lilly, booksellers	509
1816	Ezra Lincoln, printer	512
1816	Nathaniel Coverly, Jun., printer	521
1817	T. Swan, publisher	
	M. Butler, engraver	
	S. Wood, engraver	555
1817		559
1818	Ezra Lincoln, printer	567
1818	Luke Eastman, publisher	
	T. Rowe, printer	573
1818	Nathaniel Coverly, No. 16, Milk-Street, publisher	576
1818	Sterne and Mann, No. 147, Market-Street, publishers	585

Brookfield

1795	Thomas and Waldo, printers	92
1798	E. Merriam & Co., printers and booksellers	147
1800	E. Merriam, printer and bookseller	189
1800	E. Merriam & Co., printers	208
1800		209

Charlestown

1811	J. White, Main-Street, printer and bookseller	393
1815	J. White, printer	495

Dedham

1800	H. Mann, printer	199
1805	Herman Mann, printer	286
1806		322
1806		323
1809	H. Mann, printer	362
1816	H. Mann & Co., printers	518
1818	H. & W. H. Mann, printers	608

Greenfield

1798	F. Barker, bookseller	139
1817	Denio & Phelps, printers and booksellers	542

Haverhill

1817	Burrill and Tileston, printers	555
1817	Burrill and Tileston, printers and booksellers	560

Newburyport

1805	Thomas & Whipple, booksellers	295
1811	Thomas & Whipple, publishers	403
1814	W. & J. Gilman, at their miscellaneous book-store, No. 2, Middle-Street, printers and booksellers	458

1815 W. & J. Gilman's book-store and circulating library, No. 2, Middle-
     Street, printers and booksellers   504
1818 W. & J. Gilman, No. 2, Middle-Street, printers and booksellers   584

Northampton

1798 Andrew Wright, printer
     Daniel Wright and Company, publishers and booksellers
     S. Butler, bookseller   139
1798   153
1800 Andrew Wright, printer   205
1802 Andrew Wright, printer
     Eliphalet Mason, publisher   227
1803 Andrew Wright, printer
     S. and E. Butler, publishers and booksellers   261

Salem

1805 Cushing & Appleton, booksellers   295
1808 Cushing & Appleton, at the sign of the Bible, publishers   347
1812 Cushing and Appleton, publishers
     Joshua Cushing, printer   420
1812 Cushing & Appleton, publishers   427
1813 Henry Whipple, publisher   444
1816 Cushing & Appleton, booksellers   510
1816 Cushing & Appleton, publishers   511
1816 Cushing & Appleton, publishers   512
1818 Cushing and Appleton, publishers
     Thomas C. Cushing, printer   567
1818 Cushing and Appleton, publishers   568

Worcester

1785 Isaiah Thomas, printer and bookseller   38
1786 Isaiah Thomas, printer and bookseller   40
1787 Isaiah Thomas, printer and bookseller   43
1788 Isaiah Thomas, printer and bookseller   47
1788 Isaiah Thomas, printer and bookseller   48
1792 Isaiah Thomas, printer   65
1794 Isaiah Thomas, printer and bookseller   87
1794 Isaiah Thomas, printer and bookseller   88
1795   98
1795 Isaiah Thomas, Jun., printer and bookseller   101
1797 Isaiah Thomas, Jun., printer, publisher and bookseller   130
1798 I. Thomas, Jun., bookseller   139
1798 Isaiah Thomas, printer   146
1798 G. Merriam, bookseller   147
1799 [Isaiah Thomas, Jun., printer]   174
1799 Isaiah Thomas, Jun., printer and bookseller   175
1799 Isaiah Thomas, Jun., printer and bookseller   179
1800   188
1800 Dan Merriam, bookseller   189
1805 I. Thomas, Jun., printer and bookseller   305

Wrentham
1799 Nathaniel Heaton, Jun., printer   171

NEW HAMPSHIRE

Amherst
1797 Samuel Preston, publisher   127

Exeter
1801 Henry Ranlet, publisher   218
1808 [Norris & Sawyer, publishers]   351

Portsmouth
1790 [John Melcher, printer]   52
1792 [John Melcher, printer and bookseller]   69
1798 J. Melcher, printer
      S. Larkin, at the Portsmouth Book-Store, publisher and bookseller   145
1798 J. Melcher, printer
      S. Larkin, publisher and bookseller   148
1799 Samuel Larkin, at the Portsmouth Bookstore, publisher and book-
      seller   178
1800 Charles Pierce, at the United States' Oracle-Office, printer and
      publisher   182
1804 W. & D. Treadwell, printers   273
1804 William and Daniel Treadwell, printers, publishers, booksellers,
      and stationers   279
1807 David Heaton, Main-Street, printer   334

NEW JERSEY

Bridgeton
1819 William Schultz, printer   615

Burlington
1795 I. Neale, printer   94

Newark
1797 John Woods, printer   121

New Brunswick
1816 Deare & Myer, printers   509

Trenton
1807 George Sherman, printer   337
1813 James J. Wilson, publisher   446

NEW YORK

Albany
1797 Spencer and Webb, Market-Street, publishers   124
1797 Charles R. & George Webster, in the White-House, corner of State
         and Pearl-Streets, printers   125
1798 [J. Fry, in State-Street, printer]   144
1802 John Barber, printer
         Daniel Steele, corner of Court and Hudson Streets, near the Court
         House, publisher, bookbinder, and stationer   236
1806 E. & E. Hosford, opposite the State Bank, printers and booksellers   327
1807 Packard & Conant, No. 41 State Street
         R. Packard, printer   341
1809 Benjamin D. Packard, No. 41 State Street, publisher
         R. Packard, printer   364
1811 B. D. Packard, publisher
         R. Packard, printer   386
1814 Packard & Van Benthuysen, printers   462
1815 G. J. Loomis & Co., corner of State and Lodge-Streets, printers and
         booksellers   487
1815 G. J. Loomis & Co., corner of State and Lodge-Streets, printers and
         booksellers   493

Binghamton
1815 T. Robinson, printer and publisher   500

Hudson
1804 Ashbel Stoddard, printer and bookseller   265
1805 Ashbel Stoddard, printer and bookseller   287
1809 H. Steel, publisher   358
1810   371
1814 Ashbel Stoddard, No. 137 Warren-Street, printer   479
1817 W. E. Norman, publisher   550
1819 Ashbel Stoddard, printer   621

Lansingburgh
1804 Francis Adancourt, printer, publisher, and bookseller
         Samuel Shaw, publisher   275

New York
1750 [James Parker, printer]   3
1760 James Rivington, bookseller   4
1761 [A. Thorne, next door to the Green-Dragon, near the Moravian
         Meeting-House, bookseller]   5
1761 [Hugh Gaine, printer]   6
1761 [James Rivington, publisher]   7
1762 [Hugh Gaine, printer]   9
1763 [James Rivington, publisher]   10
1764 [John Holt, at the Exchange, printer and bookseller]   11
1764 S. Brown, printer
         Garrat Noel, next door to the Merchant's Coffee-House, bookseller   12

1767 [Garrat Noel, bookseller]   15
1774 [Hodge and Shober, at the newest printing-office, in Maiden-Lane,
       near the head of the Fly-Market, publisher and bookseller]   25
1776 [William Bailey, in Beaver-Street, publisher and bookseller]   26
1779 [H. Gaine, publisher]   30
1779 James Rivington, printer   31
1780 [James Rivington, printer and bookseller]   32
1782 [Lewis and Horner, No. 17, Hanover-Square]   33
1785 S. Loudon, printer   36
1786 [Hugh Gaine, printer]   42
1788 Samuel Campbell, No. 44, Hanover-Square, publisher
       Thomas Allen, No. 16, Queen-Street, publisher   44
1788 John Reid, No. 17, Water-Street, printer, publisher, and bookseller   46
1789 Harrisson and Purdy, printers   51
1793 [Berry, Rogers & Berry, publishers]   73
1793 [John Harrisson, Yorick's Head, No. 3, Peck-Slip, printer and book-
       seller]   75
1793 John Harrisson, printer
       Berry & Rogers, booksellers
       John Reid, bookseller   78
1795 Samuel Campbell, No. 124 Pearl-Street, printer   102
1795 Samuel Loudon & Son, No. 82, Water-Street, printer   105
1796 Tiebout & O'Brien, printers
       Evert Duyckinck & Co., No. 110 Pearl-Street, booksellers and
       stationers   112
1796 John Harrisson, Yorick's Head, No. 3, Peck-Slip, printer and book-
       seller   114
1797 Greenleaf's Press, printers   122
1797 John Harrisson, No. 3 Peck-Slip, printer and bookseller   128
1797 Jacob S. Mott, printer
       Charles Smith, No. 51, Maiden-Lane, publisher   136
1798 [Benjamin Lopez, No. 97, Maiden-Lane, publisher, bookseller and
       stationer]   141
1798 John Harrisson, No. 3 Peck-Slip, printer and bookseller   152
1798 J. Harrisson, Yorick's Head, No. 3 Peck-Slip, printer and bookseller   154
1798 R. Wilson, 149, Pearl-Street, printer   160
1799 B. Gomez, Maiden Lane, publisher   176
1800 The Sporting-Club, publishers   186
1800   187
1800 Thomas B. Jansen & Co., No. 248 Pearl-Street, publishers   193
1800   196
1800 ——— No. 64, Maiden-Lane, bookseller   197
1800 Jacob Johnkin, Maiden Lane, publisher   200
1800 Isaac Collins, No. 189 Pearl-Street, printers   206
1801 David Longworth, at the Shakespeare Gallery, No. 11, Park, pub-
       lisher   212
1801 John Tiebout, No. 246 Water-Street, printer and bookseller   217
1802 John Tiebout, No. 246 Water-Street, publisher
       L. Nichols, printer   230
1802 Southwick and Crooker, No. 354, Water-Street, printers   231

1802	Evert Duyckinck, publisher	
	L. Nichols, printer	232
1802	Hugh M. Griffeth, No. 88, Water-Street, publisher	
	John Low, printer	235
1803	Samuel Campbell, No. 124, Pearl-Street, publisher	243
1803	Lazarus Beach, printer	
	John Tiebout, No. 246, Water-Street, publisher	246
1803	L. Nichols, No. 308 Broadway, printer	258
1805	John Tiebout, No. 238 Water-Street, printer	298
1805		304
1805	Southwick & Hardcastle, 2, Wall-Street, printers	312
1806	[Evert Duyckinck, publisher]	318
1806	Evert Duyckinck, No. 110 Pearl-Street, publisher	
	M'Farlane & Long, printers	325
1808	John Tiebout, publisher	348
1809	Christian Brown, No. 71, Water-Street, publisher	366
1810	Inskeep & Bradford, publishers	368
1811	Largin & Thompson, No. 189, Water-Street, printers	
	William Degrushe, publisher	388
1811	—— No. 38, and 64, Maiden-Lane, printers and booksellers	390
1811	Richard Scott, publisher and bookseller	391
1811	Christian Brown, 71 Water-Street, publisher	
	George Forman, printer	395
1811		396
1811	—— No. 38, and 64, Maiden-Lane, printers and booksellers	397
1811	Nathaniel Dearborn, No. 171, William St., publisher	
	W. Hopwood, engraver	399
1811	—— No. 64, & 38, Maiden-Lane printers and booksellers	400
1811	—— No. 38, and 64, Maiden-Lane, printers and booksellers	401
1812		406
1812	Evert Duyckinck, No. 102 Pearl-Street, publisher	
	G. Bunce, printer	410
1812		412
1812		421
1812		431
1812	D. Longworth, at the Dramatic Repository, Shakespeare-Gallery, publisher	434
1813	[Edward Gillespy, publisher]	440
1813	Edward Gillespy, No. 24 William-Street, nearly opposite the Post Office, printer and publisher	441
1814	Smith & Forman, at the Franklin Juvenile Bookstores, 195 and 213 Greenwich-Street, printers and booksellers	457
1814	Smith & Forman, at the Franklin Juvenile Bookstores, 195 and 213 Greenwich-Street, printers and booksellers	463
1814	Smith & Forman, at the Franklin Juvenile Bookstores, 195 and 213 Greenwich-Street, printers and booksellers	464
1814	E. Duyckinck, 102 Pearl-Street, publisher	
	Nicholas Van Riper, printer	468
1814	Smith & Forman, at the Franklin Juvenile Bookstores, 195 and 213 Greenwich-Street, printers and booksellers	473

1814 Smith & Forman, at the Franklin Juvenile Bookstores, 195 and 213
     Greenwich-Street, printers and booksellers   477
1815 John Hardcastle, No. 6, Cross Street, printer
     Samuel A. Burtus, corner of Peck Slip, and Water Street, publisher   498
1816 Evert Duyckinck, 102 Pearl-Street, publisher
     J. C. Totten, printer   506
1816 J. Hardcastle, No. 6 Cross-Street, printer
     M'Dermot and Arden, City Hotel, booksellers
     Kerr & Carlisle, corner of Frankfort and Chatham Streets, book-
        sellers
     Jonas Humbert, Ann-Street, bookseller
     Riley & Adams' Music Store, Chatham-Street, booksellers
     S. A. Burtus, Peck-Slip and Water-Street, bookseller   517
1817 M. Swaim and J. Howe, printers and publishers
     E. & J. White and Charles Starr, stereotypers   532
1817 M. Swaim and J. Howe, printers and publishers   533
1817 John Hardcastle, printer
     A. P. Brower, No. 27 Maiden-Lane, bookseller
     S. A. Burtus, corner Peck-Slip & Water-St., bookseller   536
1817 A. & A. Tiebout, No. 238, Water-Street, publishers   545
1817 Thomas B. Jansen, No. 11 Chatham-Street, opposite the City-Hall,
     publisher   551
1818 Charles Starr, publisher and stereotyper   561
1818 Charles Starr, publisher and stereotyper   562
1818   565
1818 A. T. Goodrich & Co., No. 124 Broadway, corner of Cedar-Street,
     publishers
     J. Seymour, printer   569
1818 George Long, No. 71 Pearl-Street, printer and publisher   577
1818 Abraham Asten and Matthias Lopez, publishers   580
1818   588
1818 Bookstore and Circulating Library, 249 Broadway, corner of Mur-
     ray-Street, publishers   589
1818 [Bookstore and Circulating Library, 249 Broadway, corner of Mur-
     ray-Street, publishers]   590
1818 [J. B. Jansen, No. 15 Chatham-Street, publisher and bookseller]
     [Broderick & Ritter, printers]   591
1819 John Low, No. 139 Cherry-Street, printer and publisher   612
1819 J. Hardcastle, publisher
     Southwick & Pelsue, printers
     Samuel Maverick, No. 73, Liberty Street, engraver and printer   613
1819 A. T. Goodrich & Co., No. 124 Broadway, opposite the City Hotel,
     publishers
     J. Seymour, printer   616
1819 A. T. Goodrich & Co., No. 124 Broadway, opposite the City Hotel,
     publishers
     J. Seymour, printer   617
1819 George Long, No. 71, Pearl-Street, printer and publisher   618
1819 John Cain, publisher
     Broderick & Ritter, No. 20 James-Street, printers   620

1819 [J. B. Jansen, No. 15 Chatham-Street, publisher and bookseller]
      [Broderick & Ritter, printers]   622
1819 [J. B. Jansen, No. 15 Chatham-Street, publisher and bookseller]
      [Broderick & Ritter, printers]   623
1819 [J. B. Jansen, No. 15 Chatham-Street, publisher and bookseller]
      [Broderick & Ritter, printers]   624
1819 [J. B. Jansen, No. 15 Chatham-Street, publisher and bookseller]
      [Broderick & Ritter, printers]   625
1819 [J. B. Jansen, No. 15 Chatham-Street, publisher and bookseller]
      [Broderick & Ritter, printers]   626
1819 [J. B. Jansen, No. 15 Chatham-Street, publisher and bookseller]
      [Broderick & Ritter, printers]   627
1819   628
1820 R. & W. A. Bartow, publishers   632
1820 R. & W. A. Bartow, publishers   633
1820 R. & W. A. Bartow, publishers   634
1820 Christian Brown, No. 290 Water-Street, publisher, bookseller, book-
      binder, and stationer
      Broderick & Ritter, 20 James-St., printers   636
1820 J. Hardcastle, publisher
      D. McDuffee, 1 Murray-St., printer   637
1820 George Singleton, at the office of the Ladies' Literary Cabinet, 194,
      Greenwich-Street, publisher
      Broderick and Ritter, No. 2 Dey-Street, printers   638
1820 George Singleton, at the office of the Ladies' Literary Cabinet, 194
      Greenwich-Street, publisher
      Broderick and Ritter, No. 2 Dey-Street, printers   639
1820 Robert W. Mackie, No. 5 Chatham Row, publisher
      Broderick & Ritter, 2 Dey-St., printers   640
1820 [J. B. Jansen, No. 15 Chatham-Street, publisher and bookseller]
      [Broderick & Ritter, printers]   644
1820 [J. B. Jansen, No. 15 Chatham-Street, publisher and bookseller]
      [Broderick & Ritter, printers]   645
1820 [J. B. Jansen, No. 15 Chatham-Street, publisher and bookseller]
      [Broderick & Ritter, printers]   646
1820 J. B. Jansen, No. 15 Chatham-Street, publisher and bookseller
      Broderick & Ritter, No. 20, James-Street, printers   647
1820 J. B. Jansen, No. 15 Chatham-Street, publisher and bookseller
      Broderick & Ritter, No. 20, James-Street, printers   648

Otsego
1810 H. & E. Phinney, Jun., printers and booksellers   372
1810 H. & E. Phinney, Jun., printers and booksellers   377

Poughkeepsie
1810   369
1810   376
1811 C. C. Adams, printer   391
1815 Paraclete Potter, publisher
      P. & S. Potter, printers   491
1816 P. & S. Potter, printers   520

Rochester
1819 E. Peck & Co., printers and booksellers   614

Sag Harbor
1811 Alden Spooner, publisher   398

Salem
1805 John M. Looker, printer
       William C. Foster, publisher   307
1817 J. P. Reynolds, publisher
       T. Hoskins, printer   543

Waterford
1797 James Lyon, printer and publisher   131

NORTH CAROLINA

Newbern
1805 John C. Sims and Edward G. Moss, publishers   285

PENNSYLVANIA

Carlisle
1806   330
1806   331
1812 Archibald Loudon, printer   428

Lancaster
1804 John Whiting, publisher   276
1812 Joseph Ehrenfried, printer   409
1818 Wm. Dickson, printer   583

Philadelphia
1734 Benjamin Franklin, printer   1
1760 James Rivington, bookseller   4
1762 [Andrew Steuart, printer]   8
1764 Andrew Steuart, in Second-Street, printer   13
1765 William Bradford, at the London Coffee-House, printer   14
1769 [William Woodhouse, in Front-Street near Chesnut-Street, book-
       seller, bookbinder, and stationer]   18
1769 Andrew Steuart, in Second-Street, printer and bookseller   20
1777 [Robert Bell, next door to St. Paul's Church in Third-Street,
       printer and bookseller]   27
1778 R. Bell, Third-Street, printer   28
1783 Hall and Sellers, printers   34
1783 [Bell's book store, near St. Paul's, Third-Street, booksellers]   35

1786 [W. Spotswood, Front-Street, between Market and Chesnut-Street, printer and bookseller]
1788 M. Carey, printer   39
Thomas Seddon, Market-Street, publisher   45
1789 [William Spotswood, Front-Street, between Market and Chesnut-Streets, printer]
[Spotswood and Clarke, in Market-Street, corner of Grant's Lane, booksellers] 49
1789 John M'Culloch, in Third-Street, near the Market, printer and bookseller 50
1790 W. Spotswood, Front-Street, publisher
T. Seddon, publisher
Rice & Co., publishers   53
1790 [Henry Taylor, printer]
[Robert Campbell, bookseller]   54
1790 W. Woodhouse, Front, near Market-Street, bookseller   55
1790 William Spotswood, printer   57
1791 William Spotswood, printer   58
1791 Henry Taylor, printer and bookseller   59
1791 [W. Woodhouse, at the Bible, No. 6, South Front-Street, printer and bookseller] 61
1791 [W. Woodhouse, at the Bible, No. 6, South Front-Street, printer, publisher, and bookseller] 62
1791 [Rice & Co., No. 50 Market-Street, publisher and bookseller]   63
1792 Stewart & Cochran, No. 34 South Second-Street, printers and booksellers   66
1792   68
1793 William Spotswood, printer   70
1793 William Spotswood, printer   71
1793 [H. Kammerer, printer and bookseller]   74
1793 [John M'Culloch, No. 1, North Third-Street, printer and bookseller]   76
1793 Enoch Story, No. 36, Fourth-Street nearly opposite the Indian Queen Tavern, printer and bookseller 77
1793 [William Spotswood, printer and bookseller]   79
1794 [Mathew Carey, printer]   80
1794 [Mathew Carey, bookseller and publisher]   82
1795 La Société Typographique, printers   91
1795 Neale and Kammerer, Jun., No. 24, North Third Street, publisher   94
1795 Neale & Kammerer, Jun., printers   97
1795   99
1795   103
1795   106
1796 Godfrey Deshong, printer
Richard Folwell, printer   108
1796 William Jones, printer   110
1796 Snowden & M'Corkle, printers
H. & P. Rice, No. 50 Market, and No. 16 South Second-Street, booksellers 113
1796 T. Stephens, publisher and bookseller   115

1796 [Richard Lee, publisher]   116
1796 Mathew Carey, No. 118, Market-Street, publisher   117
1796 Mathew Carey, No. 118, Market-Street, publisher   118
1797 J. Thompson, printer
     W. Y. Birch, No. 17 South Second Street, publisher   120
1797 R. Aitken, No. 22 Market-Street, printer
     Joseph Charless, publisher   123
1798 [William Y. Birch, No. 17, South Second Street, publisher]   138
1799 J. Gales, printer
     William Y. Birch, No. 17, South-Second-Street, betwixt Market
       and Chesnut-Streets, publisher   167
1799 J. Bioren, printer
     H. & P. Rice, publishers   170
1800 [William Y. Birch, publisher]   184
1800   201
1800 Mathew Carey, No. 118, High-Street, publisher   202
1800 Mathew Carey, No. 118, High-Street, publisher   207
1801 [William Y. Birch, publisher]   211
1801 Cochran & M'Laughlin, No. 108, Race-Street, printers   213
1801 John Bioren, No. 88, Chesnut-Street, printer
     John Rain, publisher   216
1801 Thomas and William Bradford, No. 8, South First Street, printers   219
1802 [William Y. Birch, publisher]   224
1802 John Morgan, publisher
     H. Maxwell, printer   225
1802   234
1803 John Bioren, printer
     William Young Birch, No. 17, South Second Street, publisher   240
1803 R. Carr, printer
     Samuel F. Bradford, publisher
     John Conrad and Co., publishers   241
1803 William Duane, No. 106, High-Street, printer   242
1803   249
1804   283
1805 John Bioren, printer
     William Young Birch, No. 37, South Second Street, publisher   288
1805 Bartholomew Graves, No. 40, N. Fourth-Street, printer   294
1805 B. Graves, No. 40, N. Fourth-Street, printer and publisher   306
1806 [John Bioren, printer]
     [William Y. Birch, publisher]   316
1806 B. Graves, No. 40, North Fourth-Street, printer and publisher   320
1807 John Bioren, printer
     William Y. Birch, No. 37, S. 2nd., publisher
     S. F. Bradford, No. 4, S. 3d. Street, publisher   333
1807 Jacob Johnson, No. 147 Market Street, publisher   342
1808 [John Bioren, printer]
     [William Y. Birch, publisher]   345
1808 Robert DeSilver, No. 110, Walnut-Street, publisher   350
1809 John Bioren, printer
     Wm. Y. Birch, No. 37, South Second St., publisher   356

1810 J. Bioren, printer
      W. Y. Birch, publisher
      Bradford & Inskeep, publishers   368
1811 [J. Bioren, printer]
      [William Y. Birch, publisher]   380
1811   384
1811 J. Edwards, No. 181, South Fifth Street, printer   389
1811   404
1812 W. Y. Birch, No. 37, South Second Street, publisher   408
1813 W. Y. Birch, No. 37, South Second Street, publisher   435
1813 W. M'Culloch, No. 306, Market Street, printer and bookseller   436
1813 W. M'Culloch, No. 306, Market Street, printer and bookseller   437
1813 J. Bioren, No. 88, Chesnut-Street, printer and publisher   438
1813 A. J. Blocquerst, No. 159 South Sixth Street, printer   452
1813 John Bioren, No. 88, Chesnut-Street, printer and bookseller   454
1813 Thomas Palmer, publisher
      Dennis Heartt, printer   455
1814 W. Y. Birch, No. 37, South Second Street, publisher   456
1814 Thomas Simpson, printer   465
1814   466
1814 Peter A. Grotjan, No. 58, Walnut Street, printer   467
1814 M. Carey, No. 121 Chesnut Street, publisher
      T. S. Manning, printer   471
1814 Johnson & Warner, No. 147 Market Street, publishers
      Ann Coles, printer   478
1815 A. Small (successor to W. Y. Birch) No. 37, South Second St.,
      publisher   481
1815 John Guthry, Senior, publisher   488
1815 M. Carey, publisher   490
1815   492
1816 A. Small (successor to W. Y. Birch), No. 37, South Second St.,
      publisher   503
1816 John Bioren, No. 88, Chesnut-Street, printer and bookseller   505
1816 M. Carey, No. 121 Chesnut-Street, publisher   509
1816 Moses Thomas, publisher
      J. Maxwell, printer   514
1816 Harrison Hall, publisher
      J. Bioren, printer   515
1817 A. Small, No. 112, Chesnut Street, publisher   534
1817 M. Carey & Son, booksellers   535
1817 Robert DeSilver, publisher
      J. Maxwell, printer   537
1817   546
1817   547
1817 D. Dickinson, printer   548
1817   554
1818 A. Small, No. 112, Chesnut Street, publisher   563
1818 T. Town and S. Merritt, printers and publishers
      Robert Desilver, No. 110, Walnut Street, bookseller   564
1818 M'Carty and Davis, S. E. corner of Race and Ninth Streets, pub-
      lishers   571

1818	M. Carey, & Son, No. 126, Chestnut Street, publishers	
	Griggs & Co., printers	574
1818	[H. C. Lewis, publisher]	575
1818	Benjamin Warner, No. 147, Market-Street, publisher	
	Thomas H. Palmer, printer	582
1818	[H. C. Lewis, publisher]	592
1818	[H. C. Lewis, publisher]	595
1818	H. C. Lewis, publisher	
	——— 164 S. Eleventh Street, printer	596
1818	[H. C. Lewis, publisher]	597
1818	[H. C. Lewis, publisher]	598
1818	[H. C. Lewis, publisher]	599
1818	[H. C. Lewis, publisher]	600
1818	[H. C. Lewis, publisher]	601
1818	[H. C. Lewis, publisher]	602
1818	[H. C. Lewis, publisher]	603
1818	[H. C. Lewis, publisher]	604
1818	[H. C. Lewis, publisher]	605
1818	[H. C. Lewis, publisher]	606
1818	[H. C. Lewis, publisher]	607
1819	A. Small, publisher	
	I. V. K. & Co., engravers	611
1819	[H. C. Lewis, publisher]	619
1819	[H. C. Lewis, publisher]	630
1820	A. Small, publisher	635
1820		641

Pittsburgh

1817	[Cramer & Spear]	553
1817	Butler & Lambdin, printers and publishers	556
1818	Eichbaum and Johnston, Second Street, printers and booksellers	566
1818	Lambdin & Minis, publishers	
	Butler and Lambdin, printers	593

Reading

1797	[Jungmann und Comp., printers]	129

Whitehall

1806	A. Loudon, printer	330
1806	A. Loudon, printer	331
1807	A. Dickinson, printer	342
1815		490

RHODE ISLAND

Providence

1779	John Carter, printer and bookseller	29
1791	B. Wheeler, publisher	64

1799 Nathaniel and Benjamin Heaton, printers
Joseph J. Todd, at the sign of the Bible and Anchor, publisher ... 172
1805 Henry Cushing, publisher
Thomas S. Webb, publisher ... 295
1808 Henry Cushing, at the Bible & Anchor, publisher ... 347

SOUTH CAROLINA

Charleston
1803 John J. Evans & Co., printers
Crow & Query, publishers ... 248
1807 J. J. Negrin, No. 106, Queen-Street, printer ... 336
1813 J. Hoff, 117, Broad-St., printer ... 448
1818 S. & W. R. Babcock, booksellers ... 586
1818 S. & W. R. Babcock, booksellers ... 587
1820 S. & W. R. Babcock, publishers ... 642
1820 S. & W. R. Babcock, publishers ... 643

VERMONT

Bennington
1795 Anthony Haswell, printer ... 96
1799 Anthony Haswell, printer ... 177
1800 Anthony Haswell, printer ... 191
1801 Anthony Haswell, printer ... 221
1802 Anthony Haswell, printer ... 237
1805 Haswell & Smead, printers ... 309
1806 Anthony Haswell, printer ... 321
1806 Anthony Haswell, printer ... 328
1809 Anthony Haswell, printer ... 365
1811 B. Smead, printer ... 387

Brattleboro
1815 ... 499

Danville
1815 Eaton & Baker, publishers ... 483

Fairhaven
1796 J. P. Spooner, publisher ... 109

Montpelier
1810 J. Parks, publisher ... 374
1811 Montpelier Book-Store, booksellers ... 381
1811 Montpelier Book-Store, booksellers ... 402

1816 Lucius Q. C. Bowles, publisher and bookseller
      Walton & Goss, printers   510
1816 Walton & Goss, printers   522

Putney
1798 C. Sturtevant, printer
      Justin Hinds, publisher   164

Rutland
1816 Fay & Davison, printers   526

Vergennes
1816 Jepthah Shedd, publisher   522

Windsor
1810 Farnsworth & Churchill, printers   374
1814 Jesse Cochran, printer and bookseller   470
1814 Jesse Cochran, printer and bookseller   474
1815 Jesse Cochran, printer and bookseller   494

VIRGINIA

Alexandria
1798 [Cottom and Stewart, printers]
      [Robert and John Gray, publishers]   165
1800 Cottom & Stewart, publishers, booksellers, and stationers   206
1801 Cottom & Stewart, printers
      Robert and John Gray, publishers, booksellers, and stationers   223
1804 Cottom & Stewart, printers and booksellers   272
1807 Cottom & Stewart, printers and booksellers   344
1814 John A. Stewart, printer and publisher   472
1816 Benjamin L. Bogan, printer   523

Fredericksburg
1804 Cottom & Stewart, booksellers   272
1807 Cottom & Stewart, booksellers   344

Lynchburg
1817 Peter Cottom, bookseller   535

Richmond
1791 John Dixon, printer   60
1814 Peter Cottom, at his law and miscellaneous bookstore, second door
      above the Eagle Tavern, publisher   460
1817 Peter Cottom, publisher and bookseller   535

Williamsburg
1772 [William Rind, printer]
      [Edward Cumins, at the new printing-office, bookseller]   24

NO PLACE

1769	19	1804	269	1808	346
1785	37	1804	271	1809	355
1792	67	1804	274	1809	357
1795	100	1804	277	1811	382
1797	134	1804	278	1811	385
1799	180	1804	281	1811	392
1800	194	1804	282	1814	459
1800	204	1804	284	1814	461
1802	238	1805	290	1814	469
1803	244	1805	291	1815	482
1803	245	1805	293	1815	489
1803	247	1805	296	1817	544
1803	250	1805	297	1818	578
1803	251	1805	299	1818	609
1803	252	1805	300	1818	610
1803	253	1805	303		
1803	255	1805	308		
1803	256	1805	310		
1803	257	1805	315		
1803	259	1806	317		
1803	260	1806	324		
1803	262	1806	329		
1803	264	1806	332		
1804	268	1807	338		

AN INDEX OF COMPILERS, AUTHORS, PROPRIETORS, AND EDITORS

References are to entry numbers

Adgate, Andrew
　See Aimwell, Absalom, *pseud.*
Aikin, John (compiler)
　Vocal poetry, 1811　403
Aimwell, Absalom, *pseud.* of
　Andrew Adgate (compiler)
　The Philadelphia songster, 1789　50
An American Tar (compiler)
　*The cabin-boy and forecastle
　sailor's delight,* 1817　536
Ashmore, Miss (compiler)
　The new song book, 1771　22
　*Miss Ashmore's choice collec-
　tion,* 1774　26
Asten, Abraham
　See Lopez, Matthias, and Abra-
　ham Asten
Belcher, Joshua (proprietor)
　*Paine: The works, in prose and
　verse,* 1812　433
Belknap, Daniel (compiler, author)
　The Middlesex songster, 1809　362
Bradley, Joshua (compiler, propri-
　etor)
　*Some of the beauties of Free-
　Masonry,* 1816　526
Bullard, Samuel (compiler)
　An almanack, 1806　286
Burtt, John (compiler, author)
　Horae poeticae, 1819　615
Brown, Thomas (proprietor)
　The theatrical songster, 1815　501
Calcott, Wellins (author)
　A candid disquisition, 1772　23
Carey, Mathew (proprietor)
　Masonic song book, 1814　471
Carlisle, David (proprietor)
　The songster's magazine,
　　No. 1, 1818　589
　　No. 2, 1818　590
　　No. 3, 1818　591
　　No. 4, 1819　622
　　No. 5, 1819　623
　　No. 6, 1819　624
　　No. 7, 1819　625
　　No. 8, 1819　626
Carlo Convivio Socio, Jun'r, *pseud.*
　(compiler)

　The post-chaise companion,
　1820　641
Carson, Jemmy (compiler)
　Jemmy Carson's collection,
　1762　8
Citizen of Boston, A [George Rich-
　ards] (author)
　*The declaration of indepen-
　dence,* 1793　72
Clarke, Cary L.
　See Moore, James, and Cary L.
　Clarke
Cole, John (compiler, editor, pro-
　prietor)
　The minstrel, 1812　423
Cole, Samuel (compiler)
　*The Freemason's library and
　general Ahiman Rezon,* 1817　541
Cole, Samuel, and Benjamin Edes
　(proprietors)
　*The Freemason's library and
　general Ahiman Rezon,* 1817　541
Cottom, Peter (proprietor)
　The American star, 1814　460
　The American star, 1817　535
Cross, Jeremy L. (compiler, author)
　The true Masonic chart, 1819　631
　The true Masonic chart, 1820　649
Cutler
　See Russell & Cutler
Daudet, Alexis (compiler)
　Le chansonnier des graces, 1809　359
Degrushe, William (compiler)
　The humourist, 1811　388
Dermott, Lau. (compiler)
　The true Ahiman Rezon, 1805　312
Dunlap, William (compiler)
　Yankee chronology, 1812　434
Eastman, Luke (compiler, author)
　Masonick melodies, 1818　573
E[bsworth], D[aniel] (compiler)
　The Republican harmonist,
　1801　220
E[bsworth], D[aniel] (compiler,
　proprietor)
　The Republican harmonist,
　1800　201

Edes, Benjamin
See Cole, Samuel, and Benjamin Edes
Ellis, R. (compiler)
A choice collection of songs, 1814 — 462
Finch, Margaret (queen of the gipsies) (compiler)
The universal fortune-teller, 1811 — 402
The little gipsy-girl, 1814 — 469
The little gipsy girl, 1814 — 470
Foster, William C. (author)
Poetry on different subjects, 1805 — 307
A gentleman belonging to the Jerusalem Lodge (compiler)
Jachin and Boaz, 1796 — 112
Jachin and Boaz, 1796 — 113
Jachin and Boaz, 1797 — 125
Jachin and Boaz, 1802 — 232
Jachin and Boaz, 1808 — 348
Jachin and Boaz, 1811 — 391
Jachin and Boaz, 1814 — 468
Jachin and Boaz, 1815 — 491
Jachin and Boaz, 1818 — 570
A gentleman of London (compiler)
Jachin and Boaz, 1811 — 392
Jachin and Boaz, 1817 — 544
Gillespy, Edward (compiler, proprietor)
The Columbian naval songster, 1813 — 440
The Columbian naval songster, 1813 — 441
Guthry, John, Senior (compiler, author)
Federalism detected, 1815 — 488
Un habitant d'Hayti (compiler)
Idylles et chansons, 1811 — 389
Hardcastle, John (compiler)
The Masonick minstrel, 1816 — 518
Hardcastle's annual Masonic register, 1819 — 613
Hardcastle's annual Masonic register, 1820 — 637
Hardcastle & Van Pelt (proprietors)
Sailor's rights, 1815 — 498
Hardie, James (compiler)
The new Free-Mason's monitor, 1818 — 577
The new Free-Mason's monitor, 1819 — 618
Harris, Thaddeus Mason (compiler)
The constitutions of the ancient and honourable fraternity, 1798 — 146

Haswell, Anthony (compiler)
An oration, 1799 — 177
An oration, 1802 — 237
Hogg, James (compiler)
The forest minstrel, 1816 — 509
Holland, Edwin C. (compiler)
Odes, naval songs, 1813 — 448
Hoskins, Francis (author)
The beauties and super-excellency of Free Masonry, 1801 — 213
Hutchinson, Wm. (author)
The spirit of Masonry, 1800 — 206
Jenks, Stephen (compiler)
The jovial songster, No. 1, 1806 — 322
The whistle, 1818 — 608
Jenks, Stephen (compiler, author)
The jovial songster, No. II 1806 — 323
Jungmann, Gottlob (proprietor)
Eine schöne Sammlung, 1797 — 129
Keatinge, G[eorge] (compiler)
The Maryland Ahiman Rezon, 1797 — 126
Kennedy, Thomas (author)
Songs of love and liberty, 1817 — 552
Langdon, Chauncey
See Philo Musico, pseud.
Larkin, Samuel (compiler)
The Columbian songster and Freemason's pocket companion, 1798 — 145
The Free-Mason's pocket companion, 1798 — 148
Nightingale, 1804 — 279
Lathrop, John, Jr. (compiler)
The gentleman's pocket register, 1813 — 443
The gentleman's pocket register, 1813 — 444
Lee, Richard (author)
Songs from the rock, 1796 — 116
Long, George (proprietor)
The new Free-Mason's monitor, 1818 — 577
The new Free-Mason's monitor, 1819 — 618
Longworth, D. (proprietor)
Yankee chronology, 1812 — 434
Lopez, Matthias, and Abraham Asten (proprietors)
The poems, odes, songs, 1818 — 580
Lovechild, Nurse (compiler)
Tommy Thumb's song book, 1788 — 48
Tommy Thumb's song book, 1794 — 88

Tom Thumb's song book, 1795 104
Lovechild, Tommy (compiler)
   Pretty poems, songs, 1808 354
   Pretty poems, songs, 1813 451
Lyon, James (compiler)
   Songs, oratorio [sic], *odes,* 1797 131
Mason, Eliphalet (compiler)
   The complete pocket song book, 1802 227
Moore, Edward (author)
   Fables for the female sex, 1800 191
Moore, James, and Cary L. Clarke (compilers, proprietors)
   Masonic constitutions, 1808 349
   Masonic constitutions, 1818 572
Moore, Thomas (compiler, author)
   Irish melodies, 1815 490
   Irish melodies, 1816 514
   Irish melodies, 1816 515
   Irish melodies, 1816 516
   Irish melodies, 1817 543
   Irish melodies, 1818 569
   Melodies, songs, and sacred songs, 1818 574
   The syren, 1818 594
   Melodies, songs, and sacred songs, 1819 616
   Melodies, songs, and sacred songs, 1819 617
O'Neil, Dennis (compiler)
   The harp of Erin, 1812 422
Paine, Robert Treat, Jun. (compiler, author)
   The works, in prose and verse, 1812 433
Palmer, Thomas (proprietor)
   The victories of Hall, 1813 455
Palmer, Thomas H. (proprietor)
   The new Free-Mason's monitor, 1818 577
Phillips, John (compiler, proprietor)
   The Free-Mason's companion, 1805 294
Philo Musico, *pseud.* of Chauncey Langdon (compiler)
   The select songster, 1786 41
Pownall, Mrs. Mary A. (author)
   Mrs. Pownall's address, 1793 77
Preston, William (compiler)
   Illustrations of Masonry, 1804 272
   Illustrations of Masonry, 1804 273
Rain, John (compiler)
   Masonic almanac, 1801 216
Read, John K. (compiler)
   The new Ahiman Rezon, 1791 60

Richards, George (author)
   The accepted of the multitude, 1800 182
   See also *Citizen of Boston, A*
Royal Arch Mason, A [Thomas Smith Webb] (compiler)
   The Freemason's monitor, 1797 124
Russell & Cutler (proprietors)
   The lady's cabinet, 1807 339
Singleton, George (proprietor)
   The melodist, 1820 638
   The melodist, 1820 639
Smellfungus and Mundungus, pseuds. (compilers)
   A mess of messes, 1817 546
   A mess of salmagundi, 1817 547
Smith, William (author)
   Ahiman Rezon, 1783 34
Socio, Carlo Convivio, Jun'r
   See Carlo Convivio Socio, Jun'r
Spencer and Webb (proprietors)
   The Freemason's monitor, 1797 124
   The Freemason's monitor, 1802 231
Spicer, [Ishmail] (compiler)
   Spicer's pocket companion, 1800 205
Stevens, George Alexander (author)
   Songs, comic, satyrical, 1777 27
   Songs, comic, satyrical, 1778 28
   Songs, comic and satirical, 1802 238
   Mirth and song, 1804 276
Stewart, William M. (compiler)
   The young Mason's monitor, 1789 51
   The young Mason's monitor, 1792 69
Swan, T[imothy] (compiler)
   The songster's assistant, 1800 203
Tannahill, Robert (compiler)
   Poems and songs, 1819 620
   Poems and songs, 1820 640
Thomson, R. (compiler)
   A tribute to the swinish multitude, 1795 105
   Tom Paine's jests, 1796 117
Thornton, G. S. (compiler)
   The melodist, 1820 638
   The melodist, 1820 639
Town, Thomas (proprietor)
   The antihipnotic songster, 1818 564
Umphraville, Angus (author)
   The songster's museum, 1819 628
Van Pelt
   See Hardcastle & Van Pelt
Vinton, David (compiler, author, editor, proprietor)
   The Masonick minstrel, 1816 518

Watts, Isaac (author)
    Songs, divine and moral, 1813   453
Webb, Thomas Smith (compiler)
    The Freemason's monitor, 1802 231
Webb, Thomas Smith (compiler,
    proprietor)
    The Freemason's monitor, 1805 295
    The Freemason's monitor, 1808 347
    The Freemason's monitor, 1812 420
    The Freemason's monitor, 1816 510
    The Freemason's monitor, 1816 511
    The Freemason's monitor, 1816 512
    The Freemason's monitor, 1818 567
    The Freemason's monitor, 1818 568

    See also Royal Arch Mason, A
    See also Spencer & Webb
Well-fed   Domine   Double-Chin,
    pseud. (compiler)
    The feast of merriment, 1795   94
Wheeler, B. (compiler)
    The young Mason's monitor,
      1791   64
Wild, Thomas (compiler)
    The budget of mirth, 1807   335
Wilson, James J. (compiler)
    A national song-book, 1813   446
Woodworth, Samuel (compiler)
    The poems, odes, songs, 1818   580

A Table
Correlating Years and Item Numbers

Numbers	Year	Numbers	Year	Numbers	Year
1	1734	34-35	1783	240-264	1803
2-3	1750	36-38	1785	265-284	1804
4	1760	39-42	1786	285-315	1805
5-7	1761	43	1787	316-332	1806
8-9	1762	44-48	1788	333-344	1807
10	1763	49-51	1789	345-354	1808
11-13	1764	52-57	1790	355-367	1809
14	1765	58-64	1791	368-379	1810
15	1767	65-69	1792	380-404	1811
16-17	1768	70-79	1793	405-434	1812
18-20	1769	80-88	1794	435-455	1813
21-22	1771	89-107	1795	456-480	1814
23-24	1772	108-118	1796	481-502	1815
25-26	1774	119-137	1797	503-531	1816
27	1777	138-166	1798	532-560	1817
28	1778	167-181	1799	561-610	1818
29-31	1779	182-210	1800	611-631	1819
32	1780	211-223	1801	632-649	1820
33	1782	224-239	1802		

TITLE INDEX

Titles in italics refer to actual titles; titles in Roman refer to subtitles.
References are to entry numbers or to year of supposed publication.

The accepted of the multitude, 182
An account of the unparalleled sufferings of John Coustos, 163
The adventures of Robert Earl of Huntington, commonly called Robin Hood, 405
The Aeolian harp, or songster's cabinet, 634
The Aeolian harp, or songster's cabinet, vol. i, 532, 561, 632
The Aeolian harp, or songster's cabinet, vol. ii, 533, 562, 633
Ahiman Rezon, 34
The Ahiman Rezon and Masonic ritual, 285
Alexandria songster, 355
All's well, 406
An almanac; for the year of our Lord, 1806, 286
The American academy of compliments; or, the complete American secretary, 80, 108, 119, 265, 287, 407
The American cock robin: or, a choice collection of English songs, 11
The American jest book, 183
The American ladies pocket book, 120, 138, 167, 184, 211, 224, 225, 240, 266, 288, 316, 333, 345, 356, 368, 380, 408, 435, 456, 481, 503, 534, 563, 611, 635
The American ladies' pocket-book: or, an useful register of business and amusement, 241
The American medley, of wit and entertainment; or, a selection of humourous, witty, singular, wonderful, droll, and interesting narraitves [sic]*, stories, anecdotes, &c.,* 357
The American mock bird, 4
The American mock-bird; or, cabinet of Anacreon, 212
The American mock-bird, or songster's delight, 12
The American muse: or, songster's companion, 457
The American musical miscellany, 139
American patriotic and comic modern song-book, 504
American patriotic and comic modern songs, 458, 612

The American patriotic song-book, 436, 437, 505
The American republican harmonist; or, a collection of songs and odes, 242
American robin, 25
American sky lark. See *The union song book; or American sky lark*
The American song book, 482
American songs, 109
The American songster, 44, 52, 89, 243, 334, 459
The American songster; or, federal museum of melody & wit, 168, 185
The American songster, or gentleman's vocal companion, 438
The American songster's companion, 483
The American star, 460, 535
The American syren. See *The storer, or the American syren.* See also The storm, or the American syren
The American vocal companion, 358
The amorous songster, 186
Amusement, or a new collection of pleasing songs, humorous jests, and the most approved country dances, 381
Amusing companion. See *The theatrical songster: or amusing companion*
The ancient and modern music of Ireland. See under 1810
The antichristian and antisocial conspiracy, 409
The antihipnotic songster, 564
The apollo, 49, 58, 70, 71
An authentic key to the door of Free-Masonry. See *Jachin and Boaz: or an authentic key to the door of Free-Masonry*
The bachelor decoyed, or the successful virgin, 369
The Baltimore musical miscellany, or Columbian songster, vol. I, 267
The Baltimore musical miscellany, or Columbian songster, vol. II, 289
The Baltimore songster, 91, 169; see also under 1794
The Baltimore songster; or festive companion, 140
The bare fac'd lies. See *The lying ballad, or the bare fac'd lies*

The battle of Flodden, 244
The battle of the Boyne, 290
The battle of the kegs, 245; see also
  under 1807
*The beauties and super-excellency of
  Free Masonry attempted,* 213
The beggar girl, 317
The bird of birds, or a musical medley,
  565
The birth-day of freedom, 461
The black-bird, 141, 410, 506
The blackbird, 318, 636; see also 325
Black bird songbook, 18
Black ey'd Susan, 484
The blithesome bridal, 268
The bold mariners, 382
The Boston musical miscellany, 383
The Boston musical miscellany, vol. i,
  485
The Boston musical miscellany, vol. ii,
  486
The Bristol bridegroom, 81
British harmony. See *Victory; or British
  harmony*
British taxation, 507; see also under 1811
Bryan & Pyreene, 269
*Buck's delight; or a pill to purge mel-
  ancholy,* 187
The buck's pocket companion, 270
*The buck's pocket companion; or, merry
  fellow,* 142, 246
The budget of mirth, 335
*The cabin-boy and forecastle sailor's de-
  light,* 536
Cabinet of Anacreon. See *The American
  mock-bird; or, cabinet of Anacreon*
Callcott's Masonry, 537
A candid disquisition, 23
*Captain Barney's victory over General
  Monk,* 291
*Captain Glen's unhappy voyage to New-
  Barbary,* 247
The Carolina harmonist, 248
Catskin's garland. *See* The wandering
  young gentlewoman: or Catskin's gar-
  land
Le chansonnier des graces, 359
Le chansonnier républicain, 91
The charmer, 53
Charms of melody, 82. See also *The
  nightingale; or charms of melody*
*The charms of melody: or, a choice col-
  lection of the most approved songs,
  catches, duets, &c.,* 45
The cheerful songster's companion. See
  *Social harmony; or, the cheerful song-
  ster's companion*

The child's plaything. See *The new
  holyday present; or, the child's play-
  thing*
A choice collection of above one hun-
  dred and twenty. . . . See 98
A choice collection of admired songs,
  292
A choice collection of approved songs,
  See 357
A choice collection of English songs.
  See *The American cock robin: or a
  choice collection of English songs*
A choice collection of Free Masons
  songs. See under 1779
A choice collection of Masonic songs.
  See under 1798
A choice collection of Masons songs, 29
A choice collection of popular songs, 346
A choice collection of songs, 226
*A choice of collection of songs, duetts
  and catches,* 462
*A choice collection of songs (neatly
  bound),* 143
A choice collection of the most approved
  songs, catches, duets, &c. See *The
  charms of melody: or, a choice col-
  lection of the most approved songs,
  catches, duets, &c.*
Choice songs, sentimental, lively, jovial,
  and amorous. See *New musical banquet; or, choice songs, sentimental,
  lively, jovial, and amorous*
Clio and Euterpe, 10
*Collection des différens discours et pièces
  de poésie,* 360
A collection of elegant songs. See *The
  select songster or a collection of elegant songs*
*A collection of essays, of a variety of
  subjects,* 121
Collection of fashionable songs. See
  Humming bird, or collection of fashionable songs
A collection of Masonic songs. See under 312; see also under 1805
A collection of poems, songs, tales,
  ballads. See *The Suffolk garland; or,
  a collection of poems, songs, tales,
  ballads*
A collection of songs and odes. See *The
  American republican harmonist; or, a
  collection of songs and odes*
A collection of songs, designed for entertainment. See under 1786
*A collection of songs, selected from the
  latest publications,* 384

A collection of songs, selected from the works of Mr. Dibdin, 170

A collection of songs; sentimental and humorous. See *The whistle, or a collection of songs; sentimental and humorous*

A collection of the most admired patriotic songs. See *National songster; or, a collection of the most admired patriotic songs*

A collection of the most entertaining comic and sea songs. See *The neptune: or a collection of the most entertaining comic and sea songs*

A collection of the newest and choicest songs. See under 98

A collection of the newest cotillions and country dances, 188

The Columbian harmonist, 465

The Columbian harmonist, or songster's repository, 463, 464, 487

The Columbian naval melody, 430; see also *Naval songster, or Columbian naval melody*

The Columbian naval songster, 440, 441

The Columbian songster, 92, 93, 171, 411, 466, 566. See also *The Baltimore musical miscellany, or Columbian songster, vols.* I and II; *The echo: or Columbian songster*

The Columbian songster and Freemason's pocket companion, 145

The Columbian songster, or jovial companion, 122

Comic songs, 467

The comic songster, 370

The comic songster for 1809. See under 370

The comic songster, or a pill for care, 319

The companion, 172

The complete American secretary. See *The American academy of compliments; or, the complete American secretary*

Complete Irish jester, and wits vademecum. See *The jolly Hibernian in full glee; or, complete Irish jester, and wits vade-mecum*

The complete modern songster, or vocal pocket companion, 320

The complete pocket song book, 227

Complete secretary. See *A new academy of compliments: or, complete secretary*

A complete vocal pocket companion. See *The Philadelphia songster; or a complete vocal pocket companion*

Concert songs, on the secret of happiness, 228

The constitutions of the ancient and honourable fraternity of Free and Accepted Masons, 65, 146

The constitutions of the Free-Masons, 1, 2

The cruel lover. See *Rosanna, or the cruel lover*

Cupid's miscellany, 249

Cupid's miscellany, &c. See under 438

Cure for dulness [sic]. See *The warbling songster, or cure for dulness* [sic]

A cure for the spleen. See *The medley; or, a cure for the spleen*

Death of Gen. Wolfe, 412

The death of Wolfe, 250

The declaration of independence, 72

Delights of harmony. See *The nightingale of liberty: or delights of harmony*

The democratic songster, 83, 214; see also under 1794

The diamond songster, 413, 414, 415, 416, 417, 418, 538, 539, 540

Dibdin's museum, 123

A discourse delivered at the dedication of the new Congregational meetinghouse in Bennington, 321

The disobedient son, and cruel husband. See under 1796

The eagle and harp, 419

The echo: or Columbian songster, 189

The echo: or, federal songster, 147

Elements of Free-Masonry delineated. See *The Free-Mason's pocket companion, or elements of Free-Masonry delineated*

The enchanting humming-bird, 59

Essais de poësie créole. See Idylles ou essais de poësie créole

Evenings [sic] amusement. The jovial companion. See under 215

The execution of Jamie O'Brian. See *The Kilmainham minute, or the execution of Jamie O'Brian*

The exile of Erin, 251

Fables for the female sex, 191

The fair thief, 293

The fair warbler, and ladies' vocal remembrancer, 229

The famous Tommy Thumb's little story-book, 16, 17, 21

Fashionable songs for the year 1798. See under 172

Favorite companion. See *The linnet; or favorite companion*

The favorite song of George Reily, 442, 508

Feast of merriment, 94

Federal museum of melody & wit. See *The American songster; or Federal museum of melody & wit*

The Federal songster, 192; see also *The echo: or, Federal songster*

Federalism detected, 488

The festival of mirth, and American tar's delight, 193

Festive companion. See *The Baltimore songster; or festive companion.* See also *The pleasing songster; or festive companion*

The forest minstrel, 509

Four excellent new songs, 46

Four new songs, 110

Fourth of July pocket companion. See *The patriotic vocalist, or fourth of July pocket companion*

Fratrimonium excelsum. See under 1782

Free trade and sailors' rights. See under 455

Free-Masonry. Unparalleled sufferings of John Coustos. See under 136 and 263

Free-Masonry persecuted. See under 559

The Free-Mason's companion, 230

Free-Masons' companion. See *The Masonic museum; or Free-Masons' companion*

The Free Mason's companion, or pocket preceptor, 294

The Freemasons' library and general Ahiman Rezon, 541

The Freemason's monitor; or, illustrations of Masonry, 124, 231, 295, 347, 420, 510, 511, 512, 567, 568

The Free Masons pocket book, 33

The Free-Mason's pocket companion, 148

The Free-Mason's pocket companion, or elements of Free-Masonry delineated, 36, 84; see also under 1794

The Free-Mason's vocal assistant, 336

General Armstrong, 489

General regulations for the government of the grand lodge of New-Jersey, 337

General remembrancer. See *The songster's weekly companion, or general remembrancer*

The gentleman's pocket register, and Free-Mason's annual anthology, 443, 444

Gentleman's vocal companion. See *The American songster, or gentleman's vocal companion*

Gentlemen and ladies' complete songster. See *The sky lark; or gentlemen and ladies' complete songster*

Gentlemen & ladies' vocal magazine. See *The sky-lark, or gentlemen & ladies' vocal magazine*

Gentlemen and ladies' vocal museum. See *The songster's pocket companion, or gentlemen and ladies' vocal museum*

Gesänge für Freimaurer. See under 1792

The girl I left behind me, 252, 385

The gold-finch, 386

The Gosport tragedy, 253, 513. See also Ship-carpenter or, the Gosport tragedy

The Gosport tragedy, or the perjured ship carpenter, 421; see also under 1798

Green upon the cape. See under 1796

The happy shepherd, 271

Hardcastle's annual Masonic register, 613, 637; see also under 1812

The harp, 387

The harp of Erin, or the Hibernian melody, 422

The harp; or, selected melodies, 542

The harp; or, songster's companion, 614

The harper, 296

The Hibernian melody. See *The harp of Erin, or the Hibernian melody*

Hieroglyphic monitor. See *The true Masonic chart, or hieroglyphic monitor*

The history of a little boy found under a haycock, 111

The history of a little child, found under a haycock, 85

The history of birds and beasts. See *Jackey Dandy's delight, or the history of birds and beasts*

The history of Robin Hood. See under 1812

Horae poeticae; or, the transient murmurs of a solitary lyre, 615

Horrid tortures; or, the unparalleled sufferings of John Coustos, 164, 208

Humming bird, or collection of fashionable songs. See under 1791

The humming bird, 361; see also 59 and 363

The humming bird; or, new American songster, 149

The humourist, 388

Hunting songs. See under 283 and 298

Huzza for the constitution. See *Yankee chronology; or, huzza for the constitution*

Idylles et chansons, 389

Idylles ou Essais de poësie créole. See under 1804

Illustrations of Masonry, 272, 273. See also *The Freemason's monitor; or, illustrations of Masonry;* and *Masonic constitutions, or illustrations of Masonry*

Irish melodies, 490, 514, 515, 516, 543, 569; see also 594

The Irish pedler, 390

Jachin and Boaz; or, an authentic key to the door of Free-Masonry, 73, 86, 112, 113, 125, 150, 232, 254, 348, 391, 392, 468, 491, 544, 570; see also 409; see also under 1799, 1801, 1808, and 1817

Jackey Dandy's delight, or the history of birds and beasts, 173

Jamie Reily and Cooleen Bawn, 297

Jamie Reily's courtship to Cooleen Bawn, 371

Jemmy Carson's collection, 8

The jolly fisherman, 194

The jolly Hibernian in full glee; or, complete Irish jester, and wits' vade-mecum, 54

The jovial companion, 215. See also *The winter evenings amusement, or jovial companion;* and *The Columbian songster, or jovial companion*

Jovial sailors' delight. See *The merry songster; or, jovial sailors' delight*

The jovial songster, 74, 95, 151, 152, 195, 233, 298, 393

The jovial songster, no. I, 322

The jovial songster, no. II, 323

Katharine Ogie, 299

The Kilmainham minute, or the execution of Jamie O'Brian, 338

King Crispin's garland, or, the praise of the grand procession of the shoemakers in Falkirk, October 25th, 1796, 300

The ladies new memorandum-book for 1794. See under 1794

Ladies songster. See *The vocal muse; or ladies songster*

Ladies' vocal companion. See *The nightingale: or ladies' vocal companion*

The ladies vocal companion. See *The nightingale, or the ladies vocal companion*

Ladies' vocal companion. See *Songster, or ladies' vocal companion*

Lady Washington's enquiry, 324

Lady Washington's lamentation, 255

The lady's cabinet of polite literature, vol. I, 339

The lark, 153

Liberty songs, 37

The life and death of Robin Hood, 66, 196

The linnet, 372

The linnet; or favorite companion, 325

The little gipsy-girl, or universal fortune-teller, 469, 470

A little pretty pocket-book, 9, 39, 43

Little robin red breast, 40, 174; see also under 1787

The little scholar's pretty pocket companion, or youth's first step on the ladder of learning, 96

The lover's secretary. See *A new academy of compliments: or, the lover's secretary*

Loyal and humorous songs, 30

The lute. See under 339

The lying ballad, or the bare fac'd lies, 274

The magazine of wit. See *The postchaise companion, or magazine of wit*

Magazine of wit, and American harmonist, 571

Mad Mary, 256

The maid with elbows bare, 257

The Maryland Ahiman Rezon, 126

Mary's dream, 197

Masonic. Songs, oratorio [sic], odes, anthems, prologues, epilogues, and toasts. See under 131

The Masonic almanac, and pocket companion, 216

Masonic constitutions, or illustrations of Masonry, 349, 572

Masonic guide. See *The new Free-Mason's monitor: or, Masonic guide*

Masonic melodies. See *Masonick melodies*

The Masonic minstrel. See *The Masonick minstrel*

The Masonic museum. See under 637

The Masonic museum: or Free-Masons' companion, 517

Masonic odes and choruses. See under 613

Masonic song book, 471

Masonic songs. See under 230, 298, and 475

Masonick melodies, 573

The Masonick minstrel, 518

The Mason's pocket companion. See under 217

The masque, a new song book, 15

The medley; or, a cure for the spleen, 234

The medley; or, new Philadelphia songster, 97

Melodies, songs, and sacred songs, 574, 616, 617

The melodist, 638, 639

The mermaid, or nautical songster, 75, 114, 154, 545

The merry companion, 155

Merry fellow. See *The buck's pocket companion; or, merry fellow*

The merry fellow of Saturday-night, or weekly collection of all the anecdotes, jokes, 575

The merry medly [sic], *or, pocket companion,* 275

The merry songster; or, jovial sailors' delight, 373

A mess of messes, or, salmagundi outwitted, 546

A mess of salmagundi, 547

The Middlesex songster, 362

The military songster, and soldier's camp companion, 340

The minstrel, 423; see also under 1811

Mirth and music; or, a collection of the newest and choicest songs. See under 98

Mirth and song, 276

Miss Ashmore's choice collection of songs, 26

Mock-bird, 301

The mock bird; or new American songster, 5

The mocking-bird, 76, 472, 473, 493

Modern Apollo, 423a

The modern songster, 519

The modern songster; or, universal banquet of vocal music, 302

Molly Mog, 303

Monstrous good songs for 1792, 67

The Morris-town ghost delineated, and patriotic revolutionary songs. See under 1797

Mother Goose's melody: or sonnets for the cradle, 38, 87, 175, 198, 277, 424, 445, 474, 494

The mother's gift, or Nurse Truelove's lullaby, 425

The mountains high, 278

Mrs. Pownall's address, 77

Muse of Masonry, 217

Musical bouquet. See *The syren or musical bouquet*

Musical companion. See *The nightingale, or musical companion*

A musical medley. See *The bird of birds, or a musical medley*

The musical miscellany, 426, 520

The musical repertory, 394

The musical siren, 304

A national song-book, 446

The national songster, 350

National songster; or, a collection of the most admired patriotic songs, 475

Nautical songster. See *The mermaid, or nautical songster*

Nautical songster or seamans [sic] *companion,* 156

Naval songster. See under 1814

The naval songster, 476, 495

Naval songster, or Columbian naval melody, 521

The naval songster, or the sailor's pocket companion, 447

The neptune: or a collection of the most entertaining comic and sea songs, 326, 576

The New A B C, 305

A new academy of compliments: or, complete secretary, 176, 235

A new academy of compliments: or, the lover's secretary, 98

The new Ahiman Rezon, 60

The new American mock-bird, 6

New American songster. See *The humming bird; or, new American songster.* See also *The mock bird; or new American songster*

The new American songster, 548

A new and select collection of the best English, Scots and Irish songs, catches, duets, and cantatas, 32

A new collection of choice, naval, patriotic, and sentimental songs. See *The sky-lark, or, a new collection of choice, naval, patriotic, and sentimental songs*

A new collection of fashionable modern songs. See *The vocal medley; or, a new collection of fashionable modern songs*

A new collection of pleasing songs, humorous jests, and the most approved country dances. See *Amusement, or a new collection of pleasing songs, humorous jests, and the most approved country dances*

New collection of the most admired American, English, Irish, Scotch, &c. songs. See *The nightingale, or, new collection of the most admired American, English, Irish, Scotch, &c. songs*

The new entertaining Philadelphia jest-

book, and chearful [sic] witty companion, 55, 61
New federal songster, 157
The new Free-Mason's monitor; or, Masonic guide, 577, 618
The new holyday present; or, the child's plaything, 158, 218, 351
New joke upon joke, 363
The new ladies memorandum-book, for the year M.DCC.XCIV. See under 1794
New musical banquet; or, choice songs, sentimental, lively, jovial, and amorous, 374
New Philadelphia songster. See The medley; or, new Philadelphia songster
The new song book being Miss Ashmore's favorite collection of songs, 22
The new universal weekly song-book, 619
The new whim of the night, or, the vocal encyclopaedia, 352
The New-York remembrancer, or the songster's magazine, 236
The New-York songster, 395
Newest fashion. The jovial songster. See under 195 and 233
Nightingale, 279
The nightingale, 127, 327, 396, 578; see also under 1791
The nightingale of liberty: or delights of harmony, 128
The nightingale; or charms of melody, 159
The nightingale: or ladies' vocal companion, 258, 341, 364
The nightingale, or musical companion, 477
The nightingale, or, new collection of the most admired American, English, Irish, Scotch, &c. songs, 496
The nightingale; or, polite amatory songster, 353
The nightingale; or rural songster, 199
The nightingale; or, songster's companion, 62
The nightingale, or the ladies vocal companion, 522
Nurse Truelove's lullaby. See The mother's gift, or Nurse Truelove's lullaby
Old dame Margery's hush-a-bye, 342, 478
Old dame Margery's hush-a-bye, and hymns for infant minds, 549
Old dame Margery's hush-a-bye, and little hymns, 579

An oration delivered at Bennington, 177
An oration delivered at Shaftsbury, 237
Original odes, designed to be sung at the dedication of the meeting-house in Bennington, 328
Paddy's resource, 115, 160
Pastoral songs. Philadelphia, 1793. See under 77
Pastorals, and beautiful sentimental songs. See under 191
Patrick O'Neal, 259
Patriotic medley, 200, 280
Patriotic songs. See under 121
The patriotic songster, 523
The patriotic songster for July 4th, 1798, 161
The patriotic vocalist, or Fourth of July pocket companion, 427
The patriotick and amatory songster, 375
The perjured ship carpenter. See The Gosport tragedy, or the perjured ship carpenter
Perry's victory, 550
Philadelphia jest book, and cheerful witty companion. See under 1790
The Philadelphia songster. Part 1, 50
The Philadelphia songster; or a complete vocal pocket companion, 306
A pill for care. See The comic songster, or a pill for care
A pill to purge melancholy. See Buck's delight; or a pill to purge melancholy
The pleasing songster; or festive companion, 99
Pocket companion. See The merry medly [sic], or, pocket companion
Pocket preceptor. See The Free Mason's companion, or pocket preceptor
Poems and songs, chiefly in the Scottish dialect, 620, 640
The poems, odes, songs, and other metrical effusions of Samuel Woodworth, 600
A poetical description of song birds, 47
Poetry on different subjects, 307
Polite amatory songster. See The nightingale; or, polite amatory songster
The poor but honest soldier, 449, 524
Popular songs, and ballads, patriotic, sentimental, and miscellaneous, 450
The post-chaise companion, or magazine of wit, 641
The praise of the grand procession of the shoe-makers in Falkirk, October 25th, 1796. See King Crispin's garland, or, the praise of the grand procession

of the shoe-makers in Falkirk, October 25th, 1796
The prentice boy, 308
Pretty poems, 354, 451, 497, 581
Push the grog about, 397
The rambling boy, 329
Recueil de cantiques, 219, 452
Reily's courtship to Cooleen Bawn, 100
Repository of wit and ionocent [sic] amusement. See The youthful jester, or repository of wit and ionocent [sic] amusement
The republican harmonist, 201, 220
Republican songs, 365
The republican songster, 281, 398
Robin Hood's garland. See under 66
Rosanna, or the cruel lover, 376
Rural songster. See The nightingale; or rural songster
The sailor's companion. See under 1814
The sailor's medley, 202
The sailor's pocket companion. See The naval songster, or the sailor's pocket companion
Sailor's rights; or, Yankee notions, 498
Sally and Thomas, 260
Salmagundi outwitted. See A mess of messes, or salmagundi outwitted
Eine schöne Sammlung der neuesten Lieder zum gesellschaftlichen Vergnügen, 129
The Scottish minstrel, 582
Seamans [sic] companion. See Nautical songster or seamans [sic] companion
Sechs neue politische Lieder, 19
Select anthems and songs. See under 1798
A select collection of English songs. See Vocal poetry, or a select collection of English songs
The select songster or a collection of elegant songs, 41
Selected melodies. See The harp; or, selected melodies
A selection of humourous, witty, singular, wonderful, droll, and interesting narraitives [sic], stories, anecdotes, &c. See The American medley, of wit and entertainment; or, a selection of humourous, witty, singular, wonderful, droll, and interesting narraitives [sic], stories, anecdotes, &c.
A selection of one hundred and forty of the most favourite English, Scotch, Irish, and American songs, 330, 331
The sentimental songster, 309
Seven good songs, 583

The Sheffield 'prentice, 282
Ship-carpenter or, the Gosport tragedy. See under 1805. See also The Gosport tragedy
The sky lark, 479
The sky-lark. Or, a new collection of choice, naval, patriotic, and sentimental songs, 525
The sky lark: or gentlemen and ladies' complete songster, 101, 130
The sky-lark, or gentlemen & ladies' vocal magazine, 377
The social companion and songster's pocket book, 178
Social harmony; or, the cheerful songster's companion, 102
Some of the beauties of Free-Masonry, 526
A song book. See under 1798
A song-book for little children, 584
A song book which contains all the new songs, 7
The song-singer's amusing companion, 585
Songs and lullabies of the good old nurses, 179
Songs, comic and satirical, 238
Songs, comic and sentimental. See under 566
Songs, comic, satyrical, and sentimental, 27, 28
Songs, divine and moral, 453
Songs for gentlemen, 586, 642
Songs for ladies, 643
Songs, for the amusement of children, 56
Songs for the nursery, 428, 551, 621
Songs for the parlor, 587
Songs, for the 16th of August, 1801, 221
Songs from the rock, 116
Songs, naval and military, 31
Songs, naval, patriotic, and miscellaneous, 588
The songs of Robin Hood, 3
Songs of love and liberty, 552
Songs, oratorio [sic], odes, anthems, prologues, epilogues, and toasts, 131
Songs. The battle of the Nile, 366
Songs, written for the celebration of the 16th of August, 1810, 378
Songster, or ladies' vocal companion, 553
The songster's assistant, 203
Songster's cabinet. See The Aeolian harp, or songster's cabinet, vols. I & II
The songster's companion, 499
Songster's companion. See The American muse: or, songster's companion.

See also *The harp; or, songster's companion.* See also *The nightingale; or, songster's companion.* See also *Variety; or, the songster's companion*

Songster's delight. See *The American mock-bird, or songster's delight*

The songster's magazine, 103; see also under 1803; see also *The New-York remembrancer, or the songster's magazine*

The songster's magazine, vol. i, 647

The songster's magazine, vol. ii, 648

The songster's miscellany, 554

The songster's museum, 628

The songster's museum; or, a trip to Elysium, 261

The songster's museum, or, gentlemen and ladies' vocal companion, 429

The songster's new pocket companion, 555

The songster's olio, 500

The songster's pocket companion. See under 286

The songster's pocket companion, or gentlemen and ladies' vocal museum, 629

Songster's repository. See *The Columbian harmonist, or songster's repository*

The songsters [sic] *repository,* 399

The songster's weekly companion, or general remembrancer, 592

Sonnets for the cradle. See *Mother Goose's melody: or sonnets for the cradle*

Spain, 367

Spanking Jack, 180, 262

The spendthrift clapt into limbo, 204

Spicer's pocket companion; or, the young Mason's monitor, 205

The spirit of Masonry, 206

The star, 556, 593

The star spangled banner, 527, 528, 557, 558

The Storer, or the American syren, 24

The storm, or the American syren. See under 1773

The successful virgin. See *The bachelor decoyed, or the successful virgin*

The Suffolk garland; or, a collection of poems, songs, tales, ballads. See under 1818

The syren, 207, 430, 529, 594

The syren or musical bouquet, 78

The syren, or vocal enchantress, 132, 133

T. Thumb's song book, 42

The tea-drinking wife, 134

The temple of harmony, and songster's pocket companion, 162, 222

The theatrical songster, and musical companion, 501

The theatrical songster: or amusing companion, 135

Theatrical weekly song-book, 630

Tid re i, 400

To a woodman's hut, 431

To the memory of Captain Lawrence, 480

Tom Bowling, 332

Tom Paine's jests, 117; see also under 1794

Tom Thumb's song book, 104

Tom Tuff, 310

Tommy Thumb's song book, 48, 88

The town & country song-book, 311, 454

The town and country song book, 530

Town and country songster. See *The vocal enchantress, or town and country songster*

The transient murmurs of a solitary lyre. See *Horae poeticae, or, the transient murmurs of a solitary lyre*

Tribut de reconnaissance. See under 360

A tribute to the swinish multitude, 105; see also under 1794; see also under 117

A trip to Elysium. See *The songster's museum; or, a trip to Elysium*

The true Ahiman Rezon, 312

The true American, 401

The true Masonic chart, or hieroglyphic monitor, 631, 649

The union song book; or American sky lark, 313

Universal banquet of vocal music. See *The modern songster; or, universal banquet of vocal music*

Universal collection of all the songs in the English language. See *The weekly song-book, no.* vi, 7, 8 (*or universal collection of all the songs in the English language*)

Universal fortune-teller. See *The little gipsy-girl, or universal fortune-teller*

The universal fortune-teller, and complete dream dictionary, 402

Universal song-book; or, weekly collection of all the songs in the English language, 595, 596, 597, 598, 599

Unparalleled sufferings of John Coustos, 136, 137, 263, 559

An useful register of business and amusement. See *The American ladies' pocket-book: or an useful register of business and amusement*

Variety; or, the songster's companion, 283

Vauxhall songs for 1793. See under The new ladies memorandum-book, for the year M.DCC.XCIV

The victories of Hull, Jones, Decatur, Bainbridge, 455

Victory; or British harmony, 343

The village songster, 560

The Virginia nightingale, 344

The vocal charmer. See under 1793

The vocal companion, 118, 379, 502; see also under 234

The vocal companion, and Masonic register, 239

The vocal companion, part second, 432

Vocal enchantress. See *The syren, or vocal enchantress*

The vocal enchantress, or town and country songster, 63

The vocal encyclopaedia. See *The new whim of the night, or, the vocal encyclopaedia*

The vocal magazine of new songs, 35

The vocal medley: or, a new collection of fashionable modern songs, 165, 223

The vocal muse; or ladies songster, 68; see also under 1812

Vocal pocket companion. See *The complete modern songster, or vocal pocket companion*

Vocal poetry, or a select collection of English songs, 404

Vocal remembrancer. See *The volunteer songster, or vocal remembrancer*

The vocal remembrancer, 57, 79

The vocal syren. See under 283

The volunteer songster, or vocal remembrancer, 181

La vraie Maçonnerie d'adoption. See under 1783

The wandering young gentlewoman: or Catskin's garland. See under 1764

The wandering shepherdess, 284

Warbler, 314

The warbling songster, or cure for dulness [sic], 106

Washington garland, 404

Weekly collection of all the anecdotes, jokes. See *The merry fellow of Saturday-night, or weekly collection of all the anecdotes, jokes*

Weekly collection of all the songs in the English language. See *Universal songbook; or, weekly collection of all the songs in the English language*

The weekly song-book, no. vi, 7, 8 (or universal collection of all the songs in the English language), 600, 601, 602

The weekly song-book, nos. 9-12, 603, 604, 605, 606

The weekly song book. Volume first, 607

The whim of the day. *The merry companion*. See under 155

The whistle, or a collection of songs; sentimental and humorous, 608

William & Margaret, 264

William Crotty, 20

William Reily's courtship, trial, answer, releasement, and marriage with his fair Cooleen Bawn, 531

William Reily's courtship, trial, and marriage, 609

William Riley's courtship to Collian Band, 209

The winter evenings [sic] amusement, or, jovial companion, 107

The wood-lark, 14

The works, in verse and prose, of the late Robert Treat Paine, Jun., Esq., 433

Wreaths to the chieftain, 610

Yankee chronology; or, Huzza for the constitution, 434

Yankee notions. See *Sailor's rights; or, Yankee notions*

The Yorkshire tragedy, 315

The young Mason's monitor, 64, 69; see also *Spicer's Pocket companion; or, the young Mason's monitor*

The young Mason's monitor, and vocal companion, 51

The youthful jester, or repository of wit and ionocent [sic] amusement, 210; see also under 1806

Youth's first step on the ladder of learning. See *The little scholar's pretty pocket companion, or youth's first step on the ladder of learning*